I DIED A MILLION TIMES

I DIED A MILLION TIMES

GANGSTER NOIR IN MIDCENTURY AMERICA

ROBERT MIKLITSCH

UNIVERSITY OF
ILLINOIS PRESS
Urbana, Chicago, and Springfield

Library of Congress Cataloging-in-Publication Data
Names: Miklitsch, Robert, 1953- author.
Title: I died a million times : gangster noir in midcentury
    America / Robert Miklitsch.
Description: Urbana : University of Illinois Press, 2021. |
    Includes bibliographical references and index.
Identifiers: LCCN 2020023673 (print) | LCCN 2020023674
    (ebook) | ISBN 9780252043611 (ISBN) | ISBN
    9780252085543 (paperback) | ISBN 9780252052491
    (ebook)
Subjects: LCSH: Gangster films—United States—History
    and criticism. | Film noir—United States—History and
    criticism. | Motion pictures—Social aspects—United
    States—History—20th century.
Classification: LCC PN1995.9.G3 M54 2021 (print) | LCC
    pn1995.9.g3 (ebook) | DDC 791.43/655—dc23
LC record available at https://lccn.loc.gov/2020023673
LC ebook record available at https://lccn.loc.gov/
    2020023674

For Robert W. Miklitsch Sr. (1926–2020)

Pater noster, qui es in caelis . . .

The criminal is the creative artist; the detective only the critic.

—Valentin, in C. K. Chesterton's "The Blue Cross"

CONTENTS

ACKNOWLEDGMENTS

First and foremost, I want to thank my editor at the University of Illinois Press, Danny Nasset, for his steadfast belief in and appreciation of my work.

This book would not read nor look as it does without the expertise and dedication of the staff at Illinois. A heartfelt thanks, then, to Kevin Cunningham for the catalog copy, Jennie Fisher for the cover design, Tad Ringo for managing the project, and Roberta Sparenberg for sales and marketing. I owe a special debt to Jill R. Hughes for scrupulously copyediting the manuscript and catching all sorts of "gremlins."

The English department at Ohio University has been an unusually collegial place to work, especially for someone whose interests have, over time, gravitated more and more to popular culture and moving-image studies. Linda Rice has been a wonderfully supportive chair, and I am particularly indebted to the students in my "Kiss Me Deadly" class, who continue to engage and enlighten me. I also want to acknowledge the Research and Sponsored Programs at Ohio University for providing me with funds to purchase illustrations for this book and Barb Grueser, Connie Pollard, and Nancy Vandeman for assisting me so ably and graciously with respect to matters both large and small. Thank you as well to Daryl Malarry Davidson, fellow cinephile, for graciously offering to proofread the manuscript, and the trio—Andrea Christensen, Nina Jung, and Esther Lynard—for helping me to translate the Danish illustrated film programs.

ACKNOWLEDGMENTS

Thank you to Alain Silver and James Ursini for including an earlier version of chapter 4 in *Film Noir Prototypes: Origins of the Movement* and to Homer Pettey for including part of chapter 5 in the collection *Cold War Film Genres*.

Closer to home, I want to single out my family—my father, Robert Sr., my brother Dave, and my sisters Cathy, Teresa, Mary Fran, and Rosemary—for *being there* and for being such wonderful siblings.

Last and anything but least, I can't imagine having written this book without Jessica Jayne Burchard, without whose light, which shines bright like a diamond—a diamond ring (one white and two pink)—I would be totally lost like a '50s detective alone in the dark city at night.

DIRECT ADDRESS: TO THE READER

The fact that I know how to steal admirably for
earthly profit is unimportant; what I have sought
most of all has been to be the consciousness of the
theft whose poem I am writing.

—Jean Genet, *The Thief's Journal*

Reading a book is like re-writing it for yourself.

—Angela Carter

Since this book is a hybrid of sorts, addressed to both scholars and aficionados of
the crime film, I want to be clear at the outset about my aim, which I hope—to
sample Elvis Costello—is truer than not.

One of the working theses of *I Died a Million Times* is that individual films
should not be subordinated to an overarching argument or theoretical approach.
My considered sense is that any film exceeds whatever frame one employs to read
it and that this excess or exorbitance is integral to its identity. Because the devil
for me is in the details, my aim has been to respect the diegetic specificity, even
otherness, of a given "motion picture." In a world that appears to be moving faster
and faster, "close" or "slow" reading, it seems to me, is a real good.

On a related note, while the structure of each section is chronological, the
narrative approach of each chapter is also informed, like the above imperative,
by the book's dual address. My sense here is that although some readers will be
familiar with some of the films I discuss here—say, for example, *Touch of Evil*
(1958)—most readers will be unfamiliar with many, if not most, of them. I have
therefore reverted to what I think of as a certain novelistic slant. In fact, in those
instances where I adopt a narrative voice, I've become acutely aware—in the
process of writing—of the force of narration and have consequently endeavored

to shape or sculpt my analysis in order to exploit this impetus. In this sense, the book's style is self-consciously performative.

All of this said, *I Died a Million Times* is not without, to introduce a cinematic conceit, a wider angle. In the preface, I delineate one topic that informs the book: the vexed dialectic between the individual and the collective in the 1950s crime film. Another leitmotif is the notion of "gangster noir." While for many critics never the twain shall meet, the relation between the gangster picture and film noir in the 1950s is, I believe, more entangled than not. If the gangster picture, notwithstanding an anomaly like *Dillinger* (1945) or *The Gangster* (1947), submerges like a submarine in the 1940s, with the increasing cognizance of organized crime in the 1950s it begins to rematerialize in generic noir types such as corrupt cops, "big combos," and heist gangs.

Finally, as with my previous book *The Red and the Black*, *I Died a Million Times* may be construed as an argument about the 1950s or, at least, how "the Fifties" have been remediated. The syndicates, rogue cops, and "big capers" that populate the '50 crime film suggest that the mid-century America understood as the "happy days" of the republic is a fiction. While one of the very real pitfalls of retrospective wisdom is the belief that earlier periods were somehow less contentious and more innocent than the present one, the abiding interest of works of art—in this case, '50s gangster noirs—is the way they articulate the antinomies and contradictions of a particular era, a structure of feeling that's as complex as it is high-contrast.

PREFACE

GANGSTER/NOIR

> While it is possible to define individual gangster
> films and thrillers, the limits of each form are fluid.
>
> —Colin McArthur, *Underworld U.S.A.*

It's a truism that with the release of Raoul Walsh's *High Sierra* in 1941, the classic gangster picture begins to recede like a mirage in the rear window of the speeding sedan that was the 1940s on the brink of the Second World War.[1] Orson Welles's *Citizen Kane* (1941), the *ur* film noir, and John Huston's *Maltese Falcon* (1941), in which "Bogart," having been picked off by a sniper at the end of *High Sierra*, is reborn as private eye Philip Marlowe, are the monumental road signs that mark the commencement of classic film noir. As opposed to the 1940s, the status of film noir and the gangster movie in the 1950s, due in no small part to the emergence of television, has historically presented a muddier picture, as if the issue were a function of bad reception and the clarity of celluloid film had been replaced by the flickering, picture-tube pixels of TV.

Hence my recourse in this preface to the locution "gangster/noir" where the virgule (/) denotes both conflation and differentiation. With respect to the former confluence, Fran Mason has succinctly noted that it's "difficult to sustain consistency in the iconography, narrative structure and cultural thematics of gangster *noir* . . . because it partakes of the same flexibility and diversity that the gangster genre displays."[2] It's important to make two qualifications here. First, although Mason in the above passage also states that "gangster noir is part of film *noir*" (this is the clause that's been elided),[3] in the 1950s neither genre is dominant. In other words, whereas the word "gangster" in the locution "gangster noir" is an adjective, in "gangster/noir" both genres are, as it were, nouns, and transactional ones at that. Second, Mason's observation about the diversity and flexibility of the gangster genre is equally true of film noir, which critics have invoked as a meta-genre to illustrate the undecidable limits of the law of the genre.[4]

As for the issue of differentiation, one can posit some global differences between the 1940s and the 1950s. The most obvious difference is war. While the United States in the 1940s was consumed with the Second World War—with, that is, the Western, fascist and Pacific, imperial theaters—the American mentalité in the 1950s was preoccupied with the Cold War, which erupted in 1949 with the Soviet detonation of an atomic device. This postwar moment, which is reflected in various '50s nuclear noirs such as *The Thief* (1952), *The Atomic City* (1952), *Split Second* (1953), *World for Ransom* (1954), *Shack Out on 101* (1955), and *City of Fear* (1959), is bookended by *D.O.A.* (1950) at the beginning of the decade and *Odds against Tomorrow* (1959) at the end.[5]

Another difference between the 1940s and the 1950s is the Big Other understood as the nation's real and fantasmatic "public enemies." While the Soviet Union and China, not to mention Korea, were the main foreign objects of American aggression in the 1950s, one could argue that, post–World War II, the enemy had become internalized and therefore domestic, if not domesticated.[6] I'm referring here to the "red menace," a moment that's registered in such films as *The Woman on Pier 13* (1950), *The Whip Hand* (1951), *I Was a Communist for the F.B.I.* (1951), and *Walk East on Beacon!* (1952) as well as, more complexly, *Pickup on South Street* (1953) and *Kiss Me Deadly* (1955).[7] In "Gang Busters: The Kefauver Crime Commission and the Syndicate Films of the 1950s," Ronald Wilson comments on the role of the atomic bomb and the "red scare" in the Age of Anxiety: "The Cold War produced a culture in which anxieties about communism and the atomic bomb centered on the internal infiltration of 'normal' life by alien 'others.'"[8] In other words, in the 1950s the other becomes a reversible figure in which the gangster is a commie, and vice versa, and both figures are troped in turn as aliens from outer space.

Yet another—in this case, medium-specific—difference between the 1940s and the 1950s with respect to gangster/noir is style. While it's difficult, as Mason has noted, to make stylistic distinctions between film noir and the gangster picture in the 1950s, with the exception of the subgeneric cycle of retro gangster biopics such as *Baby Face Nelson* (1957), *Machine Gun Kelly* (1958), *The Bonnie Parker Story* (1958), and *Al Capone* (1959),[9] one difference between the 1940s and 1950s crime film is that while gangster noirs are just as dark, thematically speaking, as '40s film noirs, they are literally lighter. What Jack Shadoian says about what he calls the "late fifties gangster crime film" can be applied to '50s gangster/noir as a whole:

> Late fifties gangster crime films have . . . less dramatic use of black and white, flatter visuals, and a cooler, brighter, more neutral look—a prelude, perhaps, to the moral neutrality automatic to the loss of drama in the more even dis-

tribution of light and emphasis in the color film but also in keeping with a sinister assumption about the invisibility of crime and its efficient fusion into the mainstream of modern life.[10]

This is an astute observation about '50s gangster/noir, though there's a missing link, and this link is television. If gangsters were relatively invisible, like Communists, in the 1950s, the searchlight that the Kefauver Crime Committee shone on the underworld's shadow government also made them hyper-visible: just as the bombing of Hiroshima and Nagasaki produced sci-fi monsters, so too the broadcast coverage of the congressional committee hearings on organized crime begat its own monstrous figure, the octopus, a figure first introduced by Harry Anslinger, popularized by Estes Kefauver, and immortalized in a *Time* cover.[11]

The syndicate picture is, however, only one of three subgenres, together with the rogue cop and heist film, that emerged and flourished in the 1950s. All three can be interpreted, as I do in the body of this book, in terms of genre and history, production and cultural politics, but one symptomatic leitmotif is the way they dramatize the relation between the individual criminal versus the system or organization in the postwar era. More specifically, in the mid-century crime film, the individual criminal is more invested in the "national structures of the gang" than the classic gangster who dominated the media landscape of the 1930s.[12]

The *proto*-prototypical syndicate picture is Abraham Polonsky's *Force of Evil* (1949), which was released in the aftermath of the first round of hearings of the House Committee on Un-American Activities (HUAC). (Polonsky would eventually be blacklisted, and during the second round of hearings, John Garfield, who played the protagonist Joe Morse in *Force of Evil*, would appear as a "friendly witness," to his later immense regret.) Still, in terms of the logic of the syndicate picture, *Force of Evil* is seminal less because of its left, progressive bona fides than its rack focus on criminal enterprise as a racket where crime "is organized and legitimate, creating jobs for large *numbers* of workers who are either oblivious to what they are involved in or prefer not to think twice about."[13] The word "numbers" is especially apposite since the racket in *Force of Evil* is, precisely, numbers in which the individual citizen and criminal are subject to the "tyranny of a deterministic logic," a combination that is distinctly at odds with the American myth of individualism and entrepreneurialism.[14]

While Joe Morse's occupation as a legitimate lawyer for the organization in *Force of Evil* foregrounds the force of the syndicate law in gangster/noir, two films that represent not only an internal critique of this law but also the positive and negative poles of the subgenre are Joseph Newman's *711 Ocean Drive* (1950) and Phil Karlson's *The Brothers Rico* (1957). In *The Brothers Rico* Eddie Rico (Richard Conte) is a legitimate businessman who, like Joe Morse in *Force of Evil*, cannot extricate himself from the tentacles of the syndicate. Even more so than in

Force of Evil, though, Karlson's film ratchets up the tension between the claims of the family and those of the Family. *The Brothers Rico* is not, in fact, without a certain ethnic resonance, as if Italian American Eddie Rico were the self-reliant, individualistic-minded gangster of the 1930s—think Rico Bandello (Edward G. Robinson) in *Little Caesar* (1931)—rebelling against the deracinating forces of the '50s syndicate. (The name of the syndicate boss in *The Brothers Rico* is Sid Kubik [Larry Gates].) The difference between Karlson's film and *711 Ocean Drive* is that whereas Eddie Rico cuts off the head of the octopus and, unlike his two brothers, escapes with his life, at the end of Newman's film Mal Granger (Edmond O'Brien) dies in a hail of bullets like a '30s gangster while the head of the Eastern syndicate, Carl Stephans (Otto Kruger), is still alive and prospering, having earlier flown off to see his children in Ohio.

Despite the emphasis on the utter ubiquity of the underworld in the above syndicate pictures, one of the ironies of the subgenre is a certain "surplus of the law" in the chimerical shape of the organization and, as illustrated by the racket in *Force of Evil*, its mirror opposite, monopoly capitalism.[15] From the latter socioeconomic perspective, the rogue cop film—or at least one variation of it—constitutes a dialectical response to the totalitarian disposition of the syndicate picture. Hence the force of Fritz Lang's *The Big Heat* (1953), which can be said to represent a negative critique of the genre. As opposed to the prototypical rogue cop film, Otto Preminger's *Where the Sidewalk Ends* (1950), which locates the problem represented by the syndicate in the protagonist's unresolved relationship to his dead father, in *The Big Heat*, as in *The Brothers Rico*, the family and everything it represents—the '50s suburban American dream—is under siege and the rogue cop, Dave Bannion (Glenn Ford), is pitted against the ersatz family fronted by mobster Mike Lagana (Alexander Scourby). At the same time, unlike *The Brothers Rico*, which concludes on an auspicious note with the Ricos starting a new family, *The Big Heat* ends on an ambiguous one, since Bannion's reconciliation with the dying moll Debby Marsh (Gloria Grahame) cannot redeem the death of his wife, Katie (Jocelyn Brando), the violence of which highlights the constitutive, if problematic, role of women in gangster/noir.

If the violent, mob-related murder of three women, including two "B-girls," in *The Big Heat* can be interpreted as a critique of gangster/noir, the qualified happy ending of *Where the Sidewalk Ends* is predicated in part on the fact that model Morgan Taylor (Gene Tierney) helps Mark Dixon (Dana Andrews) work through his animus against his dead father. *Where the Sidewalk Ends* is a prototypical rogue cop film, however, not because Dixon collars mobster Tommy Scalise (Gary Merrill) but because his accidental killing of a Scalise associate transforms the detective into just the sort of "nickel rat" he detests with a vengeance.

Preminger's film nevertheless offers up, like *The Brothers Rico*, an affirmative critique of the rogue cop since in the concluding scene (and thanks to Morgan),

Dixon confesses to his crime and thereby submits to the letter of the law. Women are also integral to those non-syndicate rogue cop pictures such as, par excellence, *The Prowler* (1951), where a beat cop abandons the law in the pursuit of sex and money. In these films the law of capital returns with the force of the repressed, and the bad cop becomes an especially perverted instance of possessive individualism. As in *711 Ocean Drive*, it's as if the classic gangster figure returns like a revenant, albeit as a working-class cop who's intent on realizing the American Dream—in Joseph Losey's words, "100,000 bucks, a Cadillac, and a blonde"[16]—at any price.

If it's fair to say that the syndicate picture privileges the system and the rogue cop film favors the individual, the '50s heist movie represents something of a synthesis. On one hand, the "big caper" picture *re*posits the gang not in the alienated form of the syndicate but in the form of the family, a tightly knit team or crew that is reminiscent of the army unit in the "mission-that-could-shorten-the-war combat film."[17] The classic as opposed to the proto-heist picture is, in this sense, an emphatically *post*war phenomenon in which the subgenre is a variation of the combat film in which "men worked together toward a goal . . . that stressed teamwork."[18]

The family in the caper picture may not be a genuine gemeinschaft (Jonathan Munby argues that the gang in *The Asphalt Jungle* [1950] is a "false community" or "melting pot"), but the sympathetic presentation of the crew in Huston's film is one of the semantic elements, together with the ethos of professionalism, that distinguishes the classic heist picture from its '40s predecessors.[19] In *The Asphalt Jungle* this sympathetic perspective is encapsulated by the character of Alonzo Emmerich (Louis Calhern), who famously remarks that "crime is only a left-handed form of human endeavor." The notion of *left*-handed endeavor is salient because despite the fact that "many leftist filmmakers were treated as outlaws" after 1947, they nonetheless proceeded to "make some of their best pictures from the point of view of criminals."[20]

On the other hand, the gang in the classic heist film is, at base, a paradoxical subject position,[21] split between the individual criminal's desire and a crew that demands the subsumption of that same desire in the interests of the greater good. Consequently, fragmentation in the form of individual desire reasserts itself "as soon as the heist is over," though it may well be more accurate to say that the law of desire understood as fate is inscribed in the very idea of a "big score,"[22] a fatality endorsed, if not mandated, by the Production Code Administration (which insisted, against the syntactic thrust of the classic heist picture, that crimes should not be depicted in detail).

The Asphalt Jungle is a paradigmatic example of this fatal libidinal economy. While the brains of the heist, Erwin "Doc" Riedenschneider (Sam Jaffe), as well as muscle Dix Handley (Sterling Hayden), "boxman" Louis Ciavelli (Anthony Caruso), and driver Gus Minissi (James Whitmore) come together as a team, the financier of the heist, Emmerich, not only shifts the financial burden of the job back onto bookie Cobby (Marc Lawrence) but plans to double-cross the crew. Emmerich's professional-managerial status (he's a lawyer) and his motivation—his lush life and his mistress, Angela Phinlay (Marilyn Monroe), have completely bankrupted him—comment on the abject corruption of the "haves." In the end, the film's sympathies therefore lie not with Emmerich, who commits suicide, or Cobby, who becomes a snitch, nor, for that matter, with the police, who are either corrupt like Lieutenant Ditrich (Barry Kelley) or hypocritical like Police Commissioner Hardy (John McIntire), but with the "have-nots": Louis, who is initially pictured with his wife and baby son; Gus, who remains loyal to Dix and Louis; and Doc, who, despite his patrician manner, forges a genuine bond with the "hooligan" Dix. Indeed, the dream that animates *The Asphalt Jungle* is embodied by Dix, whose desire to hit it big is motivated not by a wish to live like a big shot or to chase señoritas in Mexico but to buy back the farm that his family lost in the Depression, a heart's desire that connects Huston's caper movie with the historical origins of the classic gangster picture.

With its racetrack setting and Sterling Hayden as mastermind Johnny Clay, Stanley Kubrick's *The Killing* (1956) owes an obvious debt to *The Asphalt Jungle*; it also reaccentuates, in the body of the femme fatale, the "noir" in gangster/noir. More importantly perhaps, it advances a radical demystification of the "Rooseveltian vision" of Huston's film.[23] In Kubrick's heist picture, the individual is all: Johnny's desire is motivated by the idea, born of hard time in the "big house," of making a big killing, and the gang is not a microcosm of the masses but, as in Quentin Tarantino's *Reservoir Dogs* (1992), a film crew. It would not be until the end of the decade with the raced heist picture *Odds against Tomorrow* that gangster/noir would plumb the political unconscious of *The Phenix City Story* (1955), an explosive syndicate film that advances a portrait of the individual citizen and the polis that evokes the past—in Karlson's film, the last days of Pompeii—even as it looks forward to the new social movements of the 1960s.

The dialectic between the individual and collective in gangster noir continues in the post-'50s period. The individualist emphasis is most obvious in the syndicate and rogue cop film, achieving something of a classical synthesis in Samuel Fuller's *Underworld, U.S.A.* (1961) and, courtesy of Robert Mitchum's bravura performance as Max Cady, a baroque climax in J. Lee Thompson's *Cape Fear* (1961). While the postclassic heist movie can be categorized in terms of its "cosmopolitan," "Las Vegas," and "civil rights" variants, Lewis Milestone's *Ocean's 11* (1960) exhibits these various subgenres and proffers a postmodern gloss on the oppositional collective implicit in *The Phenix City Story* and *Odds against Tomorrow*.

INTRODUCTION

FROM THE SYNDICATE TO THE CLASSIC HEIST PICTURE

ORGANIZED CRIME AS "BIG COMBO": THE OCTOPUS

It was an organization that stretched out its tentacles all over the world with the tips reaching into the highest places possible. . . .

While I waited for [Lily] I turned out the light and stood in front of the window watching the city. The monster squirmed, its bright-colored lights marking the threshing of its limbs, a sprawling octopus whose mouth was hidden under a horribly carved beak.

—Mickey Spillane, *Kiss Me Deadly*

On January 5, 1950, Estes Kefauver introduced a Senate resolution calling for an investigation of organized crime—in particular, interstate gambling—in the United States. On May 10, 1950, the freshman senator from Tennessee became chairman of the Special Committee to Investigate Organized Crime in Interstate Commerce, and the "crime committee was in business."[1] Jack Anderson and Fred Blumenthal's brisk, reportorial description in "Birth of a Crime Buster" is apt because, as they remark in the following chapter, "The Limelight," "By the time the probe was completed America knew that organized crime had become Big Business."[2] According to Kefauver, the annual revenues of organized crime circa 1950 were estimated to be "$17 to 25 billion, almost as large as the annual appropriation for defense."[3] The reference to the US government is also apt because the precedent for the crime committee was the House Judiciary subcommittee that Kefauver had chaired in 1945 as a congressman and that had discovered "links between the underworld and the judiciary."[4]

The crime committee set itself three tasks: (1) "to determine whether organized crime utilizes the facilities of interstate commerce ... to promote any transactions" that violated either state or federal law; (2) to investigate the "manner and extent of such criminal operations ... with the identification of the persons, firms, or corporations involved"; and (3) to determine "whether such interstate criminal operations were developing corrupting influences in violation of Federal law or the laws of any state."[5] Though the hearings were initially held behind closed doors, the committee "gained more and more publicity and stirred more and more interest" as it opened its doors to the public and moved from city to city—from Miami to Kansas City, Chicago to Los Angeles, New Orleans to San Francisco.[6]

Still, the Kefauver Committee would not be remembered today to the extent that it is were it not for television. Originally, television coverage of the committee's activities was typically confined, as in previous congressional hearings, "to short takes for use on regularly scheduled news programs."[7] In January 1951, however, a local television station in New Orleans began to televise the proceedings. The climax of the investigation was the coverage of the New York City hearings in March 1951, which was carried by the national networks. These hearings represented a watershed moment in the history of American broadcasting: "The twelve months preceding the Kefauver Committee's hearings in New York City had seen the percentage of homes in the New York metropolitan area with TV sets rise sharply, from 29 to 51 per cent. . . . It was estimated that an average of 86.2 per cent of those viewing television watched the hearings."[8] Overnight, Americans "became glued to their television screens to hear talk of 'bagmen' and 'ice' and 'the fix.'"[9] They watched spellbound as Kefauver, he of the "Southern drawl" and "jack-o'-lantern smile,"[10] interrogated such characters as "The Camel," "The Enforcer," and "Jimmy Blue Eyes."

The undisputed star of the investigation was Frank Costello, at the time the "most influential underworld leader in America," who "appeared before the committee impeccably and conservatively dressed, looking like an absorbed and worried business executive, his name embroidered in red on his white breast-pocket handkerchief."[11] Costello, a former bootlegger, slot machine operator, and gambling casino partner, was an investor in legitimate interests such as Texas oil and Wall Street real estate, not to mention, to the immense amusement of the press, the manufacture of punchboard Kewpie dolls and chocolate-covered ice-cream cakes. When what *Time* called the "man in the cathode mask" complained about being televised, the committee ordered the cameras to refrain from showing his face, and as in a classic Hollywood close-up, only his nervously twitching hands—or as the pundits put it, his "hand ballet"—were visible on screen.[12]

As if typecast, "Costello and other underworld figures reacted so predictably to the committee's questions that it was almost as if they had learned their lines by watching old gangster movies of the 1930s."[13] But outside the courtroom, on the streets, these newfangled gangsters did not act anything like their old-fashioned predecessors. While the "willingness to bomb and kill without scruple remains an indispensable business accessory of the mobs," Kefauver wrote in *Crime in America* (1951), a *New York Times* best seller ghostwritten by Sidney Shalett that was serialized in over a hundred newspapers, "brain has supplanted muscle as the dominant factor in mob leadership."[14] The "new aristocrats of the criminal world" such as Costello couldn't have been more different than the Al Capones, Dutch Schultzes, and "Big Bill" Dwyers of the earlier, more violent era of hijacking and rum-running.[15] For example, in 1946, "Costello became so distraught and sleepless" over the rumors swirling around him that he saw a Park Avenue psychiatrist, who suggested that he meet more "nice people."[16] In the United States of America in the early 1950s, though, it was becoming increasingly difficult to tell the difference between the nice and not-so-nice people—between, that is to say, Madison Avenue "mad men" and executive-level mobsters.

THE SYNDICATE PICTURE: BRIGHT CITY CONFIDENTIAL

In *Underworld U.S.A.* Colin McArthur submits that the "gangster film that forms the watershed between the Forties and Fifties is *Murder, Inc.*"[17] (The working American and eventual British title for *The Enforcer* was *Murder, Inc.*, not to be confused with the 1960 Twentieth Century Fox film of the same title.) In *Murder, Inc.: The Story of the "Syndicate"* (1951), which appeared the same year as *The Enforcer*, Burton B. Turkus and Sid Feder reported that "early in 1940 . . . the District Attorney's office in Brooklyn ran head-on into an unbelievable industry. This organization was doing business in assassination and general crime across the entire nation, along the same corporate lines as a chain of grocery stores."[18] Turkus and Feder's exposé was published in the immediate wake of the Kefauver Crime Committee hearings and roundly criticized the Tennessee senator for not emphasizing the national, integrated character of the syndicate: "The Committee report . . . pins the classification of 'syndicate' on almost any local mob at all, loosely as Hollywood bestows 'glamor.'"[19] The reality, according to the authors, was that the "single national syndicate is bound by a government of its own, just as tightly as General Motors."[20]

The Enforcer was released on February 21, 1951, and played in New York City during the Kefauver hearings on a double bill with *Operation X* (1951) at the Beacon and Yorktown theaters. Although Turkus and Feder's book appeared after principal photography had been completed on *The Enforcer*, the picture can profitably be read as a *film à clef* about the earlier, Turkus-led investigation that occurred on the heels of Abe "Kid Twist" Reles's revelations about Murder, Inc. The central narrator of *The Enforcer* is Joseph Rico (Ted de Corsia), who's based on Reles and who's a lieutenant for Albert Mendoza (Everett Sloane), who, as we learn from Rico in the film's final flashback, invented a corporation whose sole and singular service is "murder for hire."[21] (Rico is based, in turn, on Louis "Lepke" Buchalter, who operated Murder, Inc. with the able assistance of Albert "High Lord Executioner" Anastasia.[22]) The crusading prosecutor, modeled on special investigator Thomas E. Dewey and Assistant District Attorney Turkus, is DA Martin Ferguson (Humphrey Bogart), who eventually manages to assemble the pieces of a graphically violent picture-puzzle that is reflected in the film's intricate "Chinese-box structure."[23]

Unlike *The Enforcer*, which is set in New York City and is stylistically dark, so much so that it appears to belong to the previous, expressionist period of film noir, *711 Ocean Drive* is a paradigmatic West Coast gangster noir. Like other LA noirs from *Double Indemnity* (1944) to *The Crimson Kimono* (1959), *711 Ocean Drive* exploits—to change up Mike Davis—the sunshine *and* noir of the "city of quartz,"[24] reveling in the golden light for which Southern California is famous. (The film was shot by Austrian expatriate Franz "Frank" Planer, who had photographed *Criss Cross* [1949] the previous year.)

The Malibu location of the title—711 Ocean Drive—is illustrative. While film noir, according to Davis, shifted after James M. Cain and Raymond Chandler from the "bungalows and suburbs to the epic dereliction of Downtown's Bunker Hill,"[25] *711 Ocean Drive* constitutes a countermovement signaled by pictures such as *White Heat* (1949) and *Thieves' Highway* (1949) away from the heart of the metropolis to, in Joseph F. Newman's film, Malibu, Palm Springs, and beyond—that is to say, Las Vegas. Thus, if Mal Granger's execution of Larry Mason (Donald Porter) in *711 Ocean Drive* recalls the gangland slaying of the man who first imagined Las Vegas, Bugsy Siegel, the location of Granger's own bullet-riddled death at Boulder Dam documents not only the increasing recourse to location shooting in '50s noir but also the ex-urbanization of American culture in the same period, a centrifugal line of flight occasioned by, among other things, cars and commuter trains, freeways and the interstate highway system.

The Brothers Rico, appearing as it does in 1957, effects a "stylistic and thematic consolidation of the dominant trend in film noir in the 1950s."[26] Stylistically speaking, *The Brothers Rico* mirrors the emerging impact of television on the classic noir series registered most dramatically in Jack Arnold's 3-D noir, *The Glass Web* (1953).[27] However, if the camera setups in Karlson's film appear more functional than not relative to '40s classic noir, Geoff Mayer's claim that *The Brothers Rico* "differs little from the average late 1950s television series" minimizes the film's painstaking mise-en-scène and innovative use of high-key, day-for-day lighting.[28] In fact, Bernard Guffey's cinematography is inseparable from the film's conceit: that organized crime is indistinguishable from corporate America personified in the film by Sid Kubik, a mobster who rules his criminal empire from a regal suite in the Excelsior Hotel in Miami.

The South Floridian setting of *The Brothers Rico* is central to its sun-drenched, coruscating vision of late '50s America. Unlike *The Enforcer* and *The Captive City* (1952), which are set in the East and Midwest, respectively, Karlson's film is set in the South, the West, and the Southwest (Florida, California, and Arizona, respectively). The last Sunbelt locations may seem antithetical to the inky-black look of classic noir, but, as Jack Shadoian writes, "Karlson records the American landscape with a diabolical equanimity . . . that makes [it] more sinister than any diagonalized dark alley."[29] The reason is as simple as it is profound: crime is not just here or there—say, New York or Miami, Phoenix or Los Angeles—it's everywhere. Hence Karlson's unwavering gaze, "which is as clear and unmistakable as daylight."[30]

The Brothers Rico is, as I argue in chapter 3, an extraordinary film, but it's only one in a series of '50s crime pictures whose focus, whether deep or shallow, is on organized crime in the octopus-like guise of the syndicate. In his entry on *The Captive City* in *Film Noir*, Robert Porfirio writes that the "exposé film represents one of a handful of film genres, such as the police documentary, . . . that grew out of the film noir tradition as it fragmented . . . in the 1950s."[31] The documentary-like slant of *The Captive City* is manifest in the reel-to-reel tape recording—"a sort of verbal and visual affidavit"[32]—that protagonist Jim Austin (John Forsythe) makes in a police station before he's escorted to Washington, DC, to testify before the Kefauver Crime Committee about organized crime in Kennington, a Midwestern city where he's the editor of the local newspaper.

While the film's flashback structure, which also informs *The Enforcer* and *711 Ocean Drive*, is complemented by Lee Garmes's deep-focus, high-contrast cinematography, the investigative angle, as in *Citizen Kane* (which *The Captive City* explicitly references), is transferred from the private detective to the intrepid reporter. In this, *The Captive City* can be interpreted as part of a national trend in which the "initiative in the campaign against organized crime had clearly passed from the crime-committee movement to the press."[33] (Witness, for instance, the series of "confidential" books authored by Lee Mortimer and Jack Lait: *New York Confidential* [1948], *Chicago Confidential* [1950], and *Washington Confidential* [1951].) At the very same time, in its "resistance to an exploitational logic," *The Captive City* may well be the "most earnestly reformist and respectable of those films with direct links to the Kefauver Committee."[34]

This reformist, anti-exploitational agenda notwithstanding, *The Captive City* anticipates a cycle of rather less earnest and respectable exposés that emerged in the middle to late 1950s in the aftermath of the Kefauver hearings, such as *The Miami Story* (1954), *Chicago Syndicate* (1955), *New Orleans Uncensored* (1955), *New York Confidential* (1955), *The Houston Story* (1956), *Miami Exposé* (1956), *Chicago Confidential* (1957), *Portland Exposé* (1957), and *New Orleans after Dark* (1958). A representative, national sample of this series—*Miami Exposé*, *Chicago Syndicate*, and *Portland Exposé*—reflects something of the flavor of these sometimes flamboyantly B pictures. (Both *Chicago Syndicate* and *Miami Exposé* were produced by "discount," "get it done" mogul Sam Katzman and directed by the redoubtable Fred Sears.) Each of these three films demonstrates a specific subgenre of the syndicate film: the "undercover man," "female witness," and "one man against the mob" picture, respectively. Moreover, all three pictures exhibit the sort of location photography and stentorian, voice-over narration popularized by classic semi-documentary noirs such as *The Naked City* (1945).

For instance, *Miami Exposé* was not only photographed in Miami and the Florida Everglades, but it also capitalizes on the link between the mob and Havana, Cuba. As with a number of other syndicate films such as *711 Ocean Drive*, *Miami Exposé* commences with a prologue—in this case, by then Miami mayor Randy Christmas: "The film you are about to see is a stunning exposé based on fact. It concerns a vicious attempt by organized crime to take over the entire state of Florida." The mayor's second-person address—"it could happen in *your* state"—is succeeded by the voice-over narration that initiates the body of the film: "You're in a transport plane flying over the state of Florida. You are too high to see what has happened to Florida, to see that it has become the fastest-growing state in the nation, that its population is more than five million during tourist season. Perhaps you don't care about statistics." Suddenly the plane explodes, killing all forty-one people on board, including the intended victim, Georgie Evans, a hood who has been singled out by a rival syndicate. The film's narrator, though, is not about to let "you," the escape-minded tourist-viewer, off the hook: "Yes, you should have thought about those statistics; they might have saved your life." This address, which appears right before the credits, is uniquely perverse in its simultaneous desire to chastise *and* titillate the viewer. (One can only imagine what it would be like to watch the film today while flying to Miami for, as the narrator puts it, "fun, romance, adventure, and excitement.")

Portland Exposé takes a slightly different, albeit equally in-your-face tack.[35] True to the exploitational rhetoric of the exposé, it parades a story line about narcotics and prostitution even as it broaches a subplot about a pedophilic hood (Frank Gorshin) who tries to rape the daughter of tavern-owning, anti-pinball protagonist George Madison (Edward Binns). When mobster Philip Jackman

"Gun-Goons and Blackmail Babes": pressbook for *Miami Exposé* (1956), "the inside story of the mob's battle … to turn America's lush vacation paradise into a bullet-flaming hell!"

(Russ Conway) discovers that George is wearing a wire—labor leader Alfred Grey (Francis De Sales) and reporters Speed Bromley (Kort Falkenberg) and Ted Carl (Joe Flynn) are investigating the pinball racket—Jackman's thugs abduct George's daughter and hustle her to a warehouse where they've already beaten her father and where they threaten to throw acid in her face while George, bound and bloodied, helplessly watches. George's surname, Madison, and the concluding shot of the state capitol proffer a positive spin on the preceding, otherwise "pity and terror"–inducing events.

Still, the paradigmatic '50s exposé is, as I've already intimated, *The Phenix City Story*. Phil Karlson's film, which is set in Phenix City, Alabama, "The Wickedest City in America," possesses voice-over narration and location photography like the above exposés, but it emits a verité vibe that's unmatched in the '50s crime canon. Though Shadoian describes *The Phenix City Story* as a "generic dramatization of the actual events leading up to [Albert L.] Patterson's murder"—Patterson was the Democratic candidate for attorney general of Alabama before his untimely death at the hands of the Phenix City syndicate[36]—Shadoian's use of the word "generic" is not pejorative but literal. Which is to say that the events of *The Phenix City Story* are anything but generic. What separates Karlson's film from every other "city confidential," not to mention syndicate picture, is its deep racial-political subtext, which in the martyred figure of "Pat" Patterson evokes the pacifist civil rights movement spearheaded by Martin Luther King Jr. Accordingly, if a "significant and important group of anti-communist films of [the 1950s] collectively make up a kind of 'national confidential'," *The Phenix City Story* exposes the raced political unconscious of the syndicate picture even as it foregrounds its status as both a local *and* national confidential.[37]

THE SYNDICATE/ROGUE COP FILM: *THE RACKET*

In "Urban Confidential" Will Straw, writing about the rogue cop, comments that the "tensions between different orders of authority"—political, professional, bureaucratic—"are what mark the difference of the police film from the private-eye tradition, and their emergence as fictional themes in the 1950s is inseparable from the preoccupation with the institutions of law enforcement which the Kefauver hearings helped to nourish."[38] Straw's characterization of the urban policeman as an "often tragic figure" with "dramatic complexity" is an important corrective to the simple, stereotypical conception of law enforcement that has dominated the critical literature on the postwar crime film.[39]

In fact, inasmuch as the rogue cop film emerges as a subgenre in response to gangster noir as it mutates into the syndicate picture, it can best be understood by considering a transitional feature, *The Racket* (1951). Howard Hughes had produced and Lewis Milestone had directed the silent 1928 version of the Bartlett Cormack Broadway play. By contrast, the screenplay for the 1951 version was scripted by various hands, including Samuel Fuller and W. R. Burnett, and Nicholas Ray, among other Fox personnel, shot punch-up scenes after John Cromwell had completed principal photography.[40]

At the beginning of *The Racket*, set in a boardroom where a crime committee is meeting to discuss the "big syndicate, national in scope, [that] has already moved into the city and is starting to operate," we learn that local boss Nick Scanlon (Robert Ryan) is part of a new, "vast monopoly" that's run by the "Old Man," who is "very powerful but unknown." The ascendance of the syndicate in the form of the faceless figure of the Old Man suggests that gangsters like Nick are redundant or, more to the point, counterproductive. In an era of increasing incorporation and centralization, brains are in and brawn is out. As R. G. Connolly (Don Porter), the bland face of the syndicate, tells Nick, who's impatient to do something about the fact that Assistant State Attorney Roy Higgins (Howland Chamberlain) has "spilled to the Crime Commission," "physical violence is outmoded."

Yet even as Connolly and Scanlon are arguing about the appropriate response, Nick has already ordered a hit on Higgins. Nick is pleased as punch (there's a high-angle shot from the window of Conway's office of Higgins facedown on the pavement), but when patrolman Bob Johnson (William Talman) later recognizes the killer at a stoplight, it's apparent that Scanlon's impulsive act of violence has set in motion a series of events that will end with his own execution. In just this sense, Nick—"alone, alienated, and doomed"[41]—is a tragic figure.

If Nick Scanlon can be said to be a mobster set against both the mob and law enforcement, Captain Thomas McQuigg (Robert Mitchum) is at once a foil and a double. On one hand, his "old-style police integrity" and sense of "civic duty" portray him, like Scanlon, as an anachronism in an age of conformity and corporatism.[42] On the other hand, his antagonism against Nick incites him to flout the law and thereby other himself. The fact that at the end of the film, both the "face" and "front" of the syndicate, Connolly and the Acme Real Estate Company, remain firmly in place, as does the absent prime mover, the Old Man, sends a distinctly mixed message to the audience. Even as it intimates that the real law is the law of the syndicate,[43] it brutally delimits the effectivity of the rogue cop, whose lunatic actions are no match, it's clear, for what the pre-mortem Nick contemptuously refers to as the "fancy," coroner-free methods of the syndicate.

THE ROGUE COP FILM: *DRAGNET* VS. "BLOODY CHRISTMAS"

The Racket remains a representative transitional instance of the rogue cop film, but the subgenre cannot be reduced, thematically speaking, either to vigilante violence or governmental corruption. Consider, for instance, one of the seminal rogue cop films, *Where the Sidewalk Ends*, which is the subject of chapter 4. In Otto Preminger's picture, Mark Dixon's (Dana Andrews) encounter with criminal suspects is marked by physical violence and grim self-righteousness, although not unlike Jim McLeod (Kirk Douglas) in *Detective Story* (1951), his crusading behavior derives less from some misguided notion of idealism than from the fact that his father was a mobster. If other policemen such as Ed Cullen in *The Man Who Cheated Himself* (1951), Chris Carmody in *Rogue Cop* (1954), and Paul Sheridan in *Pushover* (1954) are driven by sex—or, in the case of Webb Garwood in *The Prowler*, Barney Nolan in *Shield for Murder* (1954), and Cal Bruner in *Private Hell 36* (1954), sex *and* money[44]—still others, like Jim Wilson (Robert Ryan) in *On Dangerous Ground* (1951), suffer from the occupational hazards of the life, burnout verging on unbalance.

Inasmuch as the rogue cop film has been conflated with the alleged demise of film noir and the resurrection of the G-man in the 1950s, it's worth revisiting, however briefly, the origins of the "crooked cop" subgenre. Part of the received wisdom and grand narrative about classic noir is that, as Pierre Kast wrote in 1953 in *Positif*, the "noir detective film" had "suffered a historical liquidation." (Kast's corpus delicti is William Wyler's rogue cop picture *Detective Story*.)[45] This point of view was canonized by Raymond Borde and Étienne Chaumeton in *A Panorama of American Film Noir, 1941–1953* (1955), where they assert that "from 1949 on, the career of the noir genre, properly so-called, comes to an end."[46] From this terminal perspective, the 1950s was, for Borde and Chaumeton, a "period of decadence and transformation" that saw the "effacement of the private detective in favor of the police force."[47]

In *Film Noir, American Workers, and Postwar Hollywood*, Dennis Broe, invoking Borde and Chaumeton, identifies the period of 1950 to 1955 as the "criminal cop moment of the *McCarthyite* crime film" and traces this semi-documentary, politically regressive declension to HUAC and the FBI.[48] If the paradigmatic semi-documentary police procedural is, for Broe, Jules Dassin's *The Naked City*, Broe's claim abut Dassin's film is reminiscent of *A Panorama of American Film Noir*, where, in "Toward a Definition of Film Noir" (and in light of *The Naked City*), the authors write, "An edifying film, the American police documentary is a documentary to the glory of the police."[49]

This said, both Borde and Chaumeton's as well as Broe's categorical judgment about *The Naked City* does not do nearly enough justice, poetic or otherwise, to the political and industrial conditions of possibility of Dassin's film.[50] As Will Straw has shrewdly observed with respect to *The Naked City* and *Call Northside 777* (1948), the "institutional frame was one from which characters departed": "as narratives got under way and characters followed their investigative paths, the richness and diversity of these 'social textures' was always at odds with the solemn flatness of the institutional point of view."[51]

Moreover, even if, as Borde and Chaumeton contend about *The Naked City*, the "murderers, heavies, and their accomplices traverse the screen solely in order to be tailed, spied on, interrogated, hunted down, or killed,"[52] a film like *T-Men* (1948), despite Broe's invocation of it as an example of the HUAC-influenced police procedural, is not just about "surveillance, investigation, order, control."[53] Rather, the corruption in *T-Men*, "the way in which it enables the individual officer to set himself above the law," "stands in sharp contrast to the glorified validation of the police in *The Naked City*" and thereby anticipates the "concerns of the early 1950s cycle of rogue-cop thrillers."[54] *T-Men* is, to be sure, an unusually complex text. As Broe himself comments in passing about Anthony Mann's picture (and in an uncanny echo of Straw's reading of *The Naked City*), *T-Men*'s "expressionist technique often seem[s] at war with its police procedural veneer."[55]

The same might be said about the concluding sequence of *He Walked by Night* (1948), which was also directed by Mann and which, according to Broe, "refocalizes a police procedural around the fugitive's desperate plight."[56] More generally, *He Walked by Night* demonstrates the "differences between the representational modes of the so-called 'film noir' and the 'semi-documentary'," not least if one takes into account Jack Webb's role in the film and his extra-diegetic career as the "auteur" of *Dragnet*. In other words, if *He Walked by Night* foreshadows *Where the Sidewalk Ends*, in which the rogue cop becomes a metaphorical fugitive, it also antedates the fetishization of technology and, by extension, law enforcement in *Dragnet*. In this sense, a police procedural or semi-documentary picture such as *He Walked by Night* can be said to lead straight to *Dragnet*, "a no-holds-barred celebration of the Los Angeles Police Department."[57]

Webb's Hollywood career reflects, in fact, the transition from private detective to policeman in the 1950s crime film. In 1946, when the French were "inventing" film noir, Webb and his writing partner, Richard Breen, created the radio drama *Pat Novak for Hire* (KGO Radio, 1946–1947/ABC Radio, 1949). Webb voiced the cynical, world-weary PI Pat Novak, and in 1948 a Hollywood casting director, having caught one of Webb's "private-eye plays," offered him a small part as a lab technician in *He Walked by Night*.[58] The rest is, as it were, history. What the latter bromide obscures is that *Pat Novak for Hire* "presented policemen in an almost uniformly bad light."[59] The conversion occurred when Webb befriended Det. Sgt. Marty Wynn, a technical advisor from the LAPD on *He Walked by Night*—shades of Jack Vincennes (Kevin Spacey) in *L.A. Confidential* (1997)—and then when Wynn and his partner, Vance Brasher, introduced Webb to LAPD captain Jack Donahue, who agreed to provide case files so that Webb could work up a pilot episode for TV.

TV Auteur: Harry Morgan and Jack Webb (behind camera) on the set of *Dragnet*.

Although Webb's collaboration with the LAPD is reminiscent of Louis de Rochemont's reciprocity with the FBI on *House on 92nd Street* (1945), J. Edgar Hoover subsequently became enraged at NBC, which was airing *Dragnet*, when Webb, the studio, and the LAPD refused to conclude each program, as the director wanted, with a tribute to a graduate of the FBI's National Academy. There's an additional irony: When Webb was pitching *Dragnet* as a television series and in order to curry favor with LAPD chief William H. Parker, he agreed that the police department would be allowed to vet every single script. The result was that Parker effectively became a senior producer on the series. The program's aim: "Total commitment to the highest ideals of the police profession."[60] Translation: "Police officers never lied, stole, cheated, had sex, slugged a lowlife, tricked a witness, or acted in any way other than as neutered Eagle Scouts."[61]

Dragnet premiered on NBC on January 3, 1952, and was an immediate sensation. However, when the "Bloody Christmas" scandal broke that March—on Christmas Eve 1951 LAPD police officers at Central Division and, later, Lincoln Heights brutalized seven young men, five of whom were Latinos—it inadvertently recalled *Pat Novak for Hire*, almost every episode of which featured a "dumb, brutal police officer who hinders, threatens, and sometimes beats up [the PI] as he attempts to solve the case."[62] It also raised a troubling question: "Which was the true face of the LAPD, the carefully controlled professionalism of Joe Friday, or the brutal realities of the Lincoln Heights jail on a drunken Christmas night?"[63]

"GANGSTER WITH A BADGE": *ON DANGEROUS GROUND*

On Dangerous Ground was released in the brief span of time between the breaking news about the "Bloody Christmas" scandal and *Dragnet's* premiere on television. Jim Wilson, the troubled protagonist of the film, is no Joe Friday.

Indeed, the first, metropolitan part of Nicholas Ray's film may well be the purest expression of the rogue cop sensibility because, unlike Dixon in *Where the Sidewalk Ends*, Jim McLeod in *Detective Story*, or Hank Quinlan in *Touch of Evil*, there's no psychological backstory to explain Wilson's brutalist perspective on the world. The second part of *On Dangerous Ground*, which mobilizes the codes of romance and melodrama, inverts the first, urban part of the film. Just as the photography changes, relatively speaking, from black to white, the terrain shifts—via the "use of dreamlike dissolves"[64]—from the city to the country. At the same time, Ray's film deconstructs these visual and geographical oppositions: it's not simply that there's "blood on the snow"[65]—a young girl has been killed—but that her father, Walter Brent (Ward Bond), is a virtual mirror image of Wilson. Brent's tirade constitutes an ironic act of misrecognition. The positive aspect of Jim's face-to-face encounter with his double is that it precipitates a change of heart, one that deepens when he meets a blind woman, Mary Malden (Ida Lupino), who entrusts him with the fate of her brother Danny (Sumner Williams).

If Brent is Wilson's "rural alter ego,"[66] Danny signifies the repressed sexual aspect of the detective's psyche. (Jim's earlier encounter in the city with Myrna Bowers [Cleo Moore] is suffused with sexual violence, while the film implies that Danny molested the dead girl.) Mary is not dumb—she knows that her brother's guilty—but she wants to see him live to be institutionalized. Brent, though, chases Danny out of his hiding place, across the barren landscape, and finally up into the mountains, like Roy Earle at the end of *High Sierra*, where he falls to his death. Jim is driving back to the city when the past returns in the form of Mary's voice: "Sometimes people who are never alone are the loneliest." Dissolve to Mary's house, where, in the storybook ending, Jim and Mary kiss.

Both Ray and the film's screenwriter, A. I. Bezzerides, wanted a different, less miraculous ending. Bezzerides later insisted, "The cop must go back to the city, the city filled with violence. And the cop knows that violence is in him, it's going to be a struggle."[67] This ambiguous ending is consonant with Bezzerides's original vision of the climactic scene of the second part of *On Dangerous Ground*, in which Danny's fall is caused not by the father, Brent, but the cop, Wilson, who, when he confronts the kid at the edge of the cliff, says, "'Look, I'm not going to hurt you. I have to arrest you, but don't be afraid.' But the kid is afraid of the policeman's power."[68]

Bezzerides's interpretation of the relation between the cop and the kid in *On Dangerous Ground* subtly reiterates what Orson Welles, commenting on *Touch of Evil*, calls the "abuse of police power."[69] *Touch of Evil* is especially pertinent in this context because, despite the fact that it's dominated by Welles's performance as corrupt police captain Hank Quinlan, it's not customarily thought of as a rogue cop picture. Just as, say, Hitchcock's *Vertigo* (1958) has transcended its generic status as a private-detective film, so too *Touch of Evil*, thanks to its extraordinary formal ingenuity and expressionist rhetoric, has long since transcended its origins in Whit Masterson's pulp fiction, *Badge of Evil* (1956).[70] Welles's picture nevertheless remains a product of a particular cultural-historical moment in which it represents not only the "end of the line" of gangster noir—"a temporary epigraph to a dissenting cinematic tradition first nurtured by the early 1930s gangster picture"—but also the "passing of two distinctive crime types": "the femme fatale," Tanya (Marlene Dietrich), and the "morally ambivalent rogue cop," Hank Quinlan.[71]

THE HEIST PICTURE: "NASTY, UGLY PEOPLE DOING UGLY, NASTY THINGS"

To understand the history of the heist picture, it's necessary to understand something of the classic phase of the gangster film and the economic crisis out of which it first emerged: "During the great Depression, many banks foreclosed on their customers' homes, or when the banks went under—as nine thousand of them (a full third) did between 1929 and 1939—swallowed their depositors' savings."[72] In this climate of widespread disenchantment with financial institutions, gangster films such as, most famously, *The Public Enemy* (1931), *Little Caesar*, and *Scarface* (1932) flourished like so many weeds. Moreover, when, with the ratification of the Twenty-First Amendment, Prohibition was repealed on December 5, 1933, a crime wave—"perhaps the greatest . . . in American history"[73]—swept the nation.

However, if 1934 was "The Year of the Gangster," it was also the beginning of the end of the aforementioned, gangster-fueled crime wave both on and off the screen. On May 18, 1934, Franklin D. Roosevelt signed the Federal Bank Robbery Act into law, and in June he signed a number of acts that empowered the Division of Investigation (which eventually, together with the Bureau of Investigation, became the FBI). Before the year was out, a number of public enemies had met their maker: John Dillinger, betrayed by the "woman in red," was shot and killed outside the Biograph Theater in Chicago on July 22, 1934 ("Handsome Johnny" had just seen *Manhattan Melodrama* [1934]); Pretty Boy Floyd was shot and killed outside East Liverpool, Ohio, on October 22; and Baby Face Nelson was shot and killed outside Barrington, Illinois, on November 27.

In 1935, in the aftermath of Dillinger's spectacular death, Will Hays, the head of the Motion Picture Producers and Distributors of America, declared a moratorium on the production of gangster films. Suddenly, Public Enemy Number One became *Public Hero Number One* (1935). Offscreen, the Federal Bank Robbery Act, in addition to five other federal anticrime laws enacted in 1934, had an immediate and profound impact on the commission of bank robberies. For example, according to *A History of Heists*, only twelve bank robberies were recorded from May 18 until the end of 1934—by comparison, in 1933 banks were being robbed almost twice a day—and in 1944, the annus mirabilis of American film noir, only seventeen were recorded, "the lowest number . . . for a full fiscal year."[74]

Two observations are, I think, noteworthy here. First, by 1951 the number of bank robberies had risen to 103. Second, as informative as *A History of Heists* is, it does not mention the Brooklyn armored car robbery, which, as I discuss in chapter 8, occurred on August 21, 1934, not only represented the "nation's biggest cash heist at the time" but also provided the raw source material for Richard Fleischer's *Armored Car Robbery* (1950), an RKO B picture that was released the very same day as the acknowledged prototypical heist film, John Huston's *The Asphalt Jungle*.[75]

The fact that *Armored Car Robbery* was based on the 1934 armored car robbery is not, however, without irony as the Great Brink's Robbery in Boston occurred at the very beginning of the 1950s—on January 17, 1950. The Boston armored car robbery is, like the Brooklyn one, consequential with respect to the history of the American heist film given that there's a certain consonance between 1934 and 1950 as well as between the classic and neo-gangster picture. For one thing, these dates mark periods of "severe economic crisis" in the history of the motion picture industry.[76] Moreover, the heist picture could not, and did not, crystallize as a genre until 1950, because the Production Code expressly forbid filmmakers from showing the preparation and commission of heists: "Methods of crime shall not be explicitly presented or detailed in a manner to . . . inspire imitation."[77] But with the success of film noir, which demonstrated the changing tastes and sensibilities of the audience in the postwar years, and the 1948 "divorcement" decree, which increased competition between studios, Hollywood was desperately looking for ways to lure moviegoers away from their new, TV-enthroned homes.

One strategy on the part of the motion picture industry was technological innovation in the form of 3-D, color, widescreen, and stereo. Another strategy, precipitated by the media controversy surrounding *The Bicycle Thief* (1949), was to "challenge the Code": "If fans of gangsters and crime films required something new to get 'em off their duffs and into theatres, then, by God, [the studios would] give it to them, the Code be damned."[78] Yet another strategy was to continue to produce B movies. In other words, one precondition for the birth of the heist film (and despite the conventional wisdom about the death of the B movie in the wake of the Paramount Decree) was the afterlife of the low-budget feature film.[79] If *Armored Car Robbery* demonstrates the vitality of B movies before the majors decided to cease production of them in 1951, *Plunder Road* (1957), produced by Regal Films in conjunction with Warner Bros., testifies to the rise of independent production and the sort of niche markets favored by younger viewers hungry for more daring fare than had previously been available.[80]

Compared to *Armored Car Robbery* and *Plunder Road*, *The Asphalt Jungle*, "an independent John Huston production distributed through M-G-M," was a bona fide A production. (The budget for *The Asphalt Jungle* was $1.232 million compared to, for example, $1.215 million for *Father of the Bride* [1950].) Though it might seem odd that the "Tiffany" studio distributed *The Asphalt Jungle*, the fact that Dore Schary, who had overseen such controversial "social problem" pictures at RKO such as *Crossfire* (1947), speaks to the way in which Metro, despite its reputation for big stars and high production values, "could not ignore the public appetite for crime thrillers."[81] The B crime movies produced at MGM during Schary's tenure (1948–1956)—*Border Incident* (1949), *Scene of the Crime* (1949), *Mystery Street* (1950), *The Strip* (1951), *Cause for Alarm!* (1951), and *Rogue Cop*—exemplify how the majors, in concert with smaller studios and independent producers, were "prepared to risk the wrath of censors" in order to make crime movies.[82]

In fact, when the script for *The Asphalt Jungle* was submitted to the Production Code Administration, the PCA worried that "Huston planned to show a robbery in detail," which, of course, was one of the code's "thou shalt not" commandments. The completed film retained the heist sequence, yet *The Asphalt Jungle* was approved because, according to the reviewer, "justice triumphs through efforts of the law."[83] While it's true that all of the members of the heist gang in Huston's film end up either dead or in jail, such a conclusion singularly fails to take into account the complex play of identification that occurs across the duration of *The Asphalt Jungle*, which creates not only "sympathy for the criminal but for the way he does his job."[84]

"Hunted by the Radio-Police": Danish program for "terrific" double bill of *Armored Car Robbery* (*Jaget af Radio-Politiet*) and *The Narrow Margin* (*Mord I Tog 63*).

The "two-part semantic shift" in the genre effected by *The Asphalt Jungle*—"its sympathetic treatment of the criminal gang . . . and the correlated audience response to their professionalism"[85]—is crucial to the evolution of the heist picture. The importance of the first part of this semantic shift can be seen if one compares *The Asphalt Jungle* to *Armored Car Robbery*. In the latter picture, which was made at RKO, the "house of noir," none of the gang members in Fleischer's film is even remotely sympathetic. The audience is instead encouraged to identify with the investigating detective, whose original partner has been killed by the heist gang. Since the police-procedural elements of *Armored Car Robbery* trump the heist ones, the PCA reviewer's judgment about Huston's heist picture appears, in retrospect, to apply more to Fleischer's film than to *The Asphalt Jungle*.

It's no surprise, then, given the conservative, even reactionary character of MGM circa 1950, that Louis Mayer, having screened *The Asphalt Jungle*, opined that it was "full of nasty, ugly people doing ugly, nasty things. I won't walk across the room to see a thing like that."[86] Mayer was no doubt put off by the film's sympathetic invocation of the Great Depression, which itself had not a little to do with a "specific community that could no longer maintain the Depression-era faith [in] America."[87] This disenchantment is reflected in that subversive corpus of films associated with *film gris* and with Huston's own career at this particular moment in time. (Huston was a member of the anti-HUAC Hollywood Committee for the First Amendment and in 1949 had just made *We Were Strangers*, which had caused rabid anti-Communist Hedda Hopper to see red.) It's also a core component of W. R. Burnett's novels from *Little Caesar* (1929) to *The Asphalt Jungle* (1949). The vanishing mediator here is Roy Earle in *High Sierra*, "a figure modelled on one of America's most celebrated gangsters," John Dillinger, who "operated in the landscape of the Midwest"—in other words, at the same time as the Dust Bowl, farm closures, and bank failures.

THE PROTO-HEIST FILM: *HIGH SIERRA* AND BEYOND

If Raoul Walsh's *High Sierra* signifies the beginning of the end of the classic gangster picture in the form of the so-called death of the big shot—see, for example, *The Big Shot* (1942)—it's also a precedent for the classic heist film, since W. R. Burnett went on to write the source material for *The Asphalt Jungle*. In addition to referencing the Western (Walsh remade *High Sierra* as *Colorado Territory* in 1949), *High Sierra* presages, via Humphrey Bogart's charismatic turn as Roy "Mad Dog" Earle, the first expressionist phase of classic noir.

While *High Sierra* is *the* proto-heist picture, Robert Siodmak's *The Killers* (1946), produced, like Walsh's film, by Mark Hellinger and co-scripted by John Huston, represents one trajectory of the "big caper" movie. "The gangster's criminal activity in *High Sierra* and *The Killers*," as Shadoian remarks, "takes the form of a caper—a crime not against a person but an institution."[88] The same formula obtains in Siodmak's *Criss Cross*. Not unlike Walsh's proto-heist picture, Siodmak's films feature stand-alone planning scenes—the gang clustered around a table, "tensely breaking a caper into its individual assignments"—as well as (and this is what distinguishes *The Killers* and *Criss Cross* from *High Sierra*) highly stylized robbery sequences that verge on musical-like spectacle.[89] Before Siodmak, a robbery may have existed as a "semantic feature" or "narrative element" of a crime film, but its "amplified role" in *The Killers* and *Criss Cross* constitutes a dramatic transformation of the very syntax or grammar of the gangster film.[90]

In other words, the difference between Siodmak's double-cross heist films and a "slow-fuse" caper picture like *The Asphalt Jungle* is that crime, for Siodmak, is a *crime passionnel*.[91] Hence Shadoian's capsule description of the '40s heist film: "a motley crew united by a specific task, the concern with expertise and precise execution, the lone woman ... amid the atmosphere charged with male ego."[92] If the initial components here ("motley crew," "expertise," etc.) are part of the lexicon of the classic heist film, the "lone woman" and "male ego" are peculiar to Siodmak's weltanschauung. This fatal romanticism is accented in *The Killers* and *Criss Cross* by a distancing device in which, as in *High Sierra*, a "participant relates a story of a failed caper on the eve of one coming up,"[93] a device that, not unlike the fateful, high-angle perspective on the robberies in Siodmak's films, obviates the suspense and audience engagement associated with the classic heist picture.

More specifically, *Criss Cross* can be said to effect a transition in the proto-heist picture from *High Sierra* to Walsh's *White Heat*. In Siodmak's masterful film, Steve Thompson's (Burt Lancaster) occupation as a security guard at Horten's Armored Car Company means that he's the "inside man" on the job, a generic twist that's tweaked in *White Heat*, in which the use of a fuel tanker as a Trojan horse is a "classical archetype for the inside-man heist."[94] That Treasury Agent Vic Pardo, aka Hank Fallon (Edmond O'Brien), is a member of Cody Jarrett's (James Cagney) gang provides yet another turn of the generic screw, since he's at once inside and outside—that is to say, undercover.

The object of Jarrett's ruse—the company payroll at a chemical plant—is, however, less significant for the caper movie than the way *White Heat* harkens back to the past even as it looks forward to the future of the heist picture. With respect to the former orientation, the death of the big shot enacted in *White Heat* recalls the rise and fall—or, more properly, "fall and rise"—of Roy Earle in *High Sierra*.[95] With respect to the future of the heist movie, just as the opening train robbery in *White Heat* prefigures the Treasury train robbery that propels the locomotive plot of *Plunder Road*, so the incendiary conclusion of Walsh's film, in which Jarrett blows himself up even as he's proclaiming his rise to the top—"Made it, Ma! Top o' the world!"—foreshadows the "nuclear" explosion that concludes *Odds against Tomorrow*, which apocalyptic conflagration tenders, true to the 1950s, a fitting climax to both the heist picture and gangster noir.

PART ONE

THE SYNDICATE PICTURE

1

THE COMBINATION

The Syndicate's tentacles reached everywhere. . . .
However, murder . . . was not the *big* business. The
rackets were. The assassinations were ordered,
contracted, and performed solely to sustain those
rackets.

Fantastic? It can't happen in your town. It did!

—Burton B. Turkus and Sid Feder, *Murder Inc.:
The Story of "The Syndicate"*

711 OCEAN DRIVE: CALIFORNIA DREAMING

In an attempt to determine whether a national crime syndicate in fact existed, the first "menace" that the Kefauver Committee decided to tackle was the racing news wire service, which was the "skeleton of organized crime in America."[1] In the wake of Prohibition, after organized crime had switched from bootlegging to other sources of revenue, the "principal facet" of the new rackets was illicit bookmaking on horse racing, "in which bookies were supplied directly or indirectly with racing information by the monopolistic Continental Press Service, an organization that leased 23,000 miles of telegraph circuits from Western Union and grossed more than 2 million, by its own estimate, in 1949."[2]

The California Crime Commission established that "up-to-the-minute reports on track conditions, shifts of jockeys, and changes in odds promoted more fervent play and a more rapid turnover of money by the bigger bookmakers, which in turn ensured larger profits."[3] And where large profits were being made, the organization was not far behind. A tool, according to Kefauver, of the "Chicago-Capone Syndicate," the wire service would relay its "news hot to the bookies by getting concessions at race tracks or even by such exotic methods as spying with high-powered binoculars and using semaphore signals."[4] The operation was so efficient and remunerative that Kefauver referred to the racing news wire service as "Public Enemy Number One."[5]

Directed by Joseph Newman, *711 Ocean Drive* (1950) is in many ways a fictional account of what Lt. Pete Wright (Howard St. John) of the LAPD "gangster squad" calls the "National Wire Service, Inc.," a syndicate whose revenues exceed, as he observes in voice-over, the "combined earnings of the twenty-five largest corporations." Given the reference to the National Wire Service, *711 Ocean Drive* bears, not surprisingly, an intimate relation to the Kefauver hearings on organized crime. In fact, Vice President Alben Barkley had appointed Alexander Wiley, the Republican senator from Wisconsin, to the crime committee, and Wiley was originally supposed to appear onscreen to endorse the film. Although this endorsement was eventually cut, a written prologue still precedes the title credits:

> Because of the disclosures made in this film, powerful underworld interests tried to halt production with threats of violence and reprisal. It was only through the armed protection provided by members of the Police Department in the locales where the picture was filmed that this story was able to reach the screen.

Frank Seltzer, the film's producer, reported to a special Senate Crime Investigating Committee that Las Vegas gamblers pressured the film crew to halt production at a number of locations, including Las Vegas, Palm Springs, and Boulder Dam, because they were unhappy with the picture's portrait of "past-posting."[6]

As the above prologue indicates, *711 Ocean Drive* is informed by the semi-documentary movement that was a major influence on postwar classic noir. This semi-documentary angle is epitomized by the fact that the film concludes with an admonitory epilogue that complements both the prologue and Lieutenant Wright's intermittent voice-over narration. At the same time, if the "voice-over commentary by an establishment figure" (i.e., police officer) is indicative of the film's "links to the semi-documentary subgenre," the "swaggering central turn" by the film's star, Edmond O'Brien, arguably undercuts this exhortative message.[7]

O'Brien's character in *711 Ocean Drive*, Mal Granger, is reminiscent of his character in *White Heat*, Hank Fallon, in that both men are "masters of technology."[8] The difference is that Mal is a criminal, like Fallon's undercover alter ego, Vic Pardo, in *White Heat*. While O'Brien's performance in *711 Ocean Drive* recalls his frenetic turn as Frank Bigelow in *D.O.A.*, which had appeared three months earlier, it also anticipates *Shield for Murder*, where O'Brien plays Barney Nolan, a "bad cop" who has been corrupted by his obsession with striking it rich.

Lieutenant Wright references this compulsion both in the initial sequence of *711 Ocean Drive* and in his subsequent voice-over narration. In the former, while conversing with a junior officer in a patrol car on the way to the airport for a flight to Las Vegas, where they hope to apprehend Granger, Wright speculates that Mal's problem may have been "too much ambition"; in the latter, Wright concludes that Granger "wasn't a criminal. He was just a guy working for the telephone company."

When the film cuts to Mal on the job, it's obvious that he's smart—he jokes about "inventing the telephone"—as well as bighearted because he insists on lending money to a coworker whose daughter is sick. Sentiment aside, the scene is significant because the mise-en-scène—the background is cluttered with electronic equipment—suggests that Mal is ensnared by the very same thing that's the source of his genius. Mal, in fact, has been supplementing his meager wages by playing the ponies—and not the even money, as his bookie, Chippie Evans (Sammy White), reminds him, but the long shots: "box cars or nothing." Chippie therefore encourages Mal to "lay off the races" and, instead, use his know-how about telephones and electronics: "Dames, clothes, automobiles. You can have anything you want, kid, if you know the right guy."

Vince Walters (Barry Kelley), the owner of the Tri-State Press Wire Service, is the right guy, and after Chippie phones in another long shot for Mal, he takes him to meet "Mister Big." At the Liberty Finance Company (a front, according to Wright, for "one of California's largest bookmaking operations"), Mal and Chippie breeze past the legitimate part of the business—a sign reads "CREDIT IS YOUR GREATEST ASSET"—to the rear of the store. Chippie presses a buzzer and they go through a door and down to where the real action is. For the first time in the film, with the exception of the credit sequence, the lighting is distinctly low-key, and chiaroscuro shadows tattoo the wall. The descent is literal and metaphorical: this is Mal's Mephistophelian moment. Walters wants to expand his Los Angeles operation (he relates this to Mal and Chippie while they're standing in front of a map of California), and Mal has the answer: "relay amplifiers," a new gadget whereby "people in different cities can listen in on a telephone conversation at the same time." Walters is finishing his pitch when a young blonde woman, Trudy Maxwell (Dorothy Patrick), comes down the stairs and Mal's mind is suddenly made up: "I always knew there was some way to beat the races." Out with the telegraph and in with the telephone.

Dissolve via Wright's voice-over—"[Mal's] improvements ran the daily take up to staggering figures"—to a wide shot of a new, markedly more streamlined operation as Trudy comes down the stairs again. Though she's later pinched at the track trying to signal Mal, who's manning a walkie-talkie and binoculars at a house across the way, the two are cruising down the Pacific Coast Highway—this is the American Dream, California-style ("Dames, clothes, automobiles . . .")— when he advises her to "stick around." No ingénue, she replies, "You sound like someone who thinks he's going someplace." Mal's rise to the top is swift: first he engineers a communications crash in order to force Walters to give him a bigger share of the profits (Mal demands and gets 20 percent of the take), then Walters is murdered when a bookie he's been "bleeding" guns him down in his office. Wright, interrogating Mal about Walters's death, reads the tea leaves to him: "It looks like you're gonna be Mister Big over at Tri-State."

Cut from a medium shot of Mal as he exits the police station, where he pauses just long enough to toss away his company ID badge, to a wide shot of him running in the Pacific surf with a German shepherd in the brilliant California sunshine. This is the good life, and the address is 711 Ocean Drive, Malibu. If Mal's new beachfront property and monogrammed robe ("MG") aren't sufficient proof that the old wage slave is dead and buried, Trudy says to him, a note of sarcasm in her voice as she brings him the mail while he's considering which new sports coat to wear that day, "Just wonder if you're the same guy I used to know." "The same," Mal answers, "except for money in my pockets instead of wire, tailored suits instead of overalls." Then, since she's about to leave, Mal asks her to "tell the cook to send . . . some OJ and coffee," at which point Chippie arrives and warns Mal, "Right now you have all of California tied up and everyone knows it. You get too big and those big guys back East will move in."

Mal's days as an independent operator are, like his address, numbered. At a corporate-looking meeting at a corporate-looking office building in Cleveland, Ohio, Carl Stephans (Otto Kruger), the avuncular head of the National Wire Service (he complains about having to drink milk because of his perpetually bad stomach), has decided that it's time to expand the organization beyond Kansas City. Stephans asks his lieutenant, Larry Mason (Donald Porter), to travel to California and persuade Mal that it's in his interest to partner with the organization. In order to entice him (Stephans is coded as a pimp here), he also orders Larry to take his attractive wife, Gail (Joanne Dru). At a swimming pool in Palm Springs where, in the background, a sun-glassed Gail can be seen lying out in the sun and seductively rubbing lotion on her legs, Mal can't resist the bait. He likes what he sees. He also likes the fact that Gail is a class act, the sort of woman who—before she met Larry—went to "smart girls' schools" and "belonged to the country club set." While Mal's desire for his superior's wife is an Oedipal cliché of the genre (see, for instance, *Shakedown* [1950], in which ambitious photojournalist Jack Early [Howard Duff] makes a serious play for the wife of his mobster boss, Nick Palmer [Brian Donlevy]), Mal, despite his oft-stated aversion to marriage, falls hard for Gail.

Mal's fall is as swift as his rise: first Trudy informs him that he's getting less than 30 percent of the profits of the bookmaking business rather than 50 percent as promised, then Gail happens to fall down the stairs and ends up in a Hollywood hospital with a black eye and broken nose. After Larry nonchalantly relays the news to Mal at a boxing match that's a blunt metaphor for his marriage, Mal contracts a man named Gizzi (Robert Osterloh), the owner of a Beverly Hills clothing store, to take out Larry. The irony is that if Mal is imitating Stephans (earlier, at the aforementioned meeting, we see Carl casually ordering a hit on a greedy client: "I believe he's a very sick man. I don't think he'll ever get well"), Mal is doing it, at least in part, for reasons of the heart. In other words, it's not just business; it's personal. The effect of this twist is to complicate the mercenary thrust of Mal's character, which has been dominant up until he meets Gail, a sympathetic identification that remains intact even after he murders Gizzi at the Malibu Sport Fishing Pier when the latter threatens to blackmail Mal unless he makes him a "silent partner."

The fact that this sequence constitutes the credit sequence of *711 Ocean Drive* suggests that it represents a point of no return for Mal. Indeed, the credit sequence concludes with a cut from a shot of Gizzi's body breaking the surface of the water to a telephone ringing at police headquarters. Despite the fact that the police have been unable to prove Mal ordered Larry's death, they now seize on Gizzi's murder to build a case against him. Mal himself has previously enacted an elaborate telephonic scenario to prove that he was in Palm Springs when the homicide occurred. Wright, in turn, uses a tape recording of his call (the sound of a streetcar whistle can be heard in the background) to refute his alibi. Cornered, Mal decides to flee to Guatemala but not before trying to make the organization "pay off every cent they owe [him]." His plan: to "past-post all the books that the syndicate owns in Las Vegas."

The sequence in which Mal taps the "main cables of the wire service that lead to all the horse parlors" in order to "electronically set their clocks back" is remarkable not simply because it's narrated by Wright—in, I might add, an oddly conspiratorial tone—but because it's photographed in low-key, high-contrast light. It's as if Mal has suddenly returned to his earlier hands-on, entrepreneurial self, using his electronic know-how to outwit the mob. As in the '50s heist film, everything initially goes according to plan—too well, in fact. Chippie wins so much money that the racetrack has to write him a check that he can't cash until the next morning, and in an echo of Walters's cruel treatment of Mendel Weiss (Sidney Dubin), another small-time bookie that Mal previously snubbed recognizes Chippie and reports back to Stephans.

The spectacular, Hitchcockian dénouement of *711 Ocean Drive* is set up by the film's penultimate action in which Stephans, after sending his henchmen to kidnap Chippie, tips off the police that Mal is hiding out at the Boulder Inn. Since Stephans can't be bothered to greet Wright, Steve Marshak (Bert Freed) and another associate meet the lieutenant at the airport while Carl sits watching from a parked limousine. Wright is disgusted—"The only reason I'm here cleaning up your dirty laundry is because we happen to want Granger pretty bad"—but the very last time we see Stephans, he's temporarily turning over operations to Steve, because he "promised [his] children that [he'd] go back East on the farm with them for a while." And then he strolls off to a waiting airplane.

The Boulder Dam sequence, which recalls the underground ones in *He Walked by Night* and *The Third Man* (1950), is a tour de force of lighting, editing, and camerawork. It's also metaphorically rich because the "electricity the dam produces . . . is what powers [Mal's] particular racket."[9] The dam that dwarfs Mal and Gail therefore provides a quintessential noir foil to his "evil genius." The fact that it's man-made and the result of collective labor also puts Mal's possessive-individualist character as well as the syndicate's criminal-organizational ethos in sharp relief.

The mise-en-scène complements the expressive editing, lighting, and camerawork. The moment that Mal and Gail exit their car and start running toward the dam, they're imprisoned first in a high-angle wire-crossed shot, then in a medium line-cluttered one. While they try to make themselves less conspicuous by mixing in with a group of tourists who have just exited a bus, once Mal and Gail are inside the dam, the uniformed guide's voice—"We're now descending in the elevator 520 feet"—reinforces the sense of entrapment and recollects, in magnified form, Mal's descent at the beginning of the film. Figuratively speaking, Mal is going down.

As the film dynamically cuts between the humming activities of the police above the dam and the desultory progress of the tourists below, the first stop on the tour is a cordoned-off view of the turbine-driven generators in the Nevada wing of the power plant. "Don't worry," Mal whispers to Gail, "we'll get out of here as soon as we get to the Arizona end." However, as with the previous high-angle shot from the police's point of view (POV), the extreme low-angle shot of the group from the outsized perspective of the generators hints that Mal and Gail are subject to forces beyond their control. This motif is reiterated when the group

Trapped: Mal Granger (Edmond O'Brien) and Gail Mason (Joanne Dru), escaping from the police, reenter the interior of the Boulder Dam in *711 Ocean Drive* (1950).

exits the interior of the dam, and Mal, borrowing a pair of binoculars from another man, sees that Wright is already searching the area with a pair of binoculars. The reverse shot from Wright's point of view sutures the scene: Mal and Gail's only chance now is to make a run for it.

After the pair splits off from the group and reenters the dam's interior (Mal pushes a button that closes an enormous metal door behind them, effectively trapping them inside), he tells an exhausted Gail to wait for him while he tries to shake the police; then, to the sound of keening violins and striped by shadows, the two embrace and kiss. The chase is on. Mal runs down one dimly lit, hollowed-out concrete corridor after another until he suddenly reaches a dead end. Sweating like Bigelow in *D.O.A.* after his fatal diagnosis, Mal starts up a steep staircase that appears to get narrower the higher he climbs. When the film finally cuts away to Wright, another policeman tells him that they "can take the elevator and catch [Mal] at the top," and it's as if electricity itself is now actively working against him.

In the meantime, Mal opens a trapdoor at the top of the stairwell and light spills into the darkness. It appears to be the light at the end of the tunnel until Mal sees Gail being escorted to a waiting patrol car, and as he makes a break for it, he's shot down in a hail of bullets. The concluding shots of the sequence put a metaphorical spin on Mal's classically balletic death: in a fixed long shot, Mal valiantly struggles to his feet one final time before he collapses onto the polished terrazzo, astral-decorated floor, his bullet-riddled body falling out of the screen. What remains is a literally awesome sight: the Winged Figures of the Republic, two thirty-two-foot-high bronze seraphim that, sitting majestically on black diorite plinths, overlook the dam.

Needless to say, *711 Ocean Drive* does not end on this poetic note. It concludes, instead, with a dissolve from a shot of a policeman forcefully holding Gail's wrist to a man placing a bet with a bookie: "Give me two to win on Honeycomb in the fifth." The voice-over narrator glosses the transaction:

Winged Figures of the Republic: Mal Granger (Edmond O'Brien) shot down in a hail of bullets at the end of *711 Ocean Drive* (1950).

Only an innocent two-dollar bet, you say. Well, it's just as innocent [insert shot of a black man placing a bet with his barber] as the germs in an epidemic, spreading [insert shot of a woman with a baby carriage placing a bet via a telephone] the worst kind of disease [insert shot of another man placing a bet with a black man who's shining his shoes], the civic disease [insert shot of Carl Stephans and associates in Cleveland] of criminals with an eight-billion-dollar racket corrupting politicians, buying protection [insert shot of newspaper headline "GRAFT EXPOSED Grand Jury Indicts Public Officials"], fostering crime, all with your two dollars.

The very last shot of the epilogue, a young man wearing a "letterman" jacket exchanging money with a bookie on a college campus, supplies the coup de grâce.

While it's not surprising that a film made in the 1950 shows black men involved in gambling, the image of clean-cut "lettermen," not to mention young mothers with babies, doing so is quite another thing. Yet if the interpellation of the white middle class in the conclusion to 711 Ocean Drive possesses a certain egalitarian appeal, it's also patently tautological. The rhetoric of disease is crucial here, mimicking as it does the epidemiological address of anti-Communist noirs in which there's no such thing as rhetorical overkill. In other words, the epilogue, true to the political-libidinal economy of classical Hollywood, retrospectively endeavors to contain the subversiveness of Mal's character, redoubling the fatalism of the film's voice-over flashback even as it retraces the "tragic" arc of his character.

Despite these custodial measures, the audience arguably identifies in the end not so much with the police—or, for that matter, the sensible "good girl," Trudy—as with Mal, who recalls the telephone worker at the beginning of the film who cannot properly care for his family on the "chicken-feed" wages that the telephone company pays him. Mal's decision to dump his day job as a telephone drone and go for broke as the brains of a bookmaking operation is, in this sense, not without logic: crime doesn't pay, but then neither does a hard day's work. In fact, since Mal's character is compelled to pay with his life for his overweening ambition, the film's moral appears to be that the American Dream—a house in Malibu on Ocean Drive with a closet full of beautiful clothes and a servant to bring you coffee and orange juice in the morning—is a total fantasy for working-class Joes and is only tenable for untouchable criminal executives like Carl Stephans.

THE CAPTIVE CITY: UNDERWORLD, USA

Robert Wise's Captive City (1952), which was designed to "capitalize on the public's renewed interest in organized crime" and features both a prologue and epilogue that showcase Senator Kefauver's sudden celebrity status,[10] stars John Forsythe, who had recently been signed to a five-picture contract by Aspen Productions, an independent production company formed by Wise and Mark Robson early in 1952. Forsythe and the production company are pertinent because *The Captive City*, unlike Wise's previous film, *The Day the Earth Stood Still* (1951), is a low-budget picture (approximately $250,000) and the casting of the then unknown Forsythe contributes to the film's semi-documentary tenor. Moreover, since Wise was working for his own company, he had "greater freedom than he had ever had before"—"it was the first time [he] had ever shot anything without a studio base"—and, consequently, the entire picture was filmed in less than a month in Reno, Nevada, which doubles as the "small Midwestern town of Kennington."[11]

In its "synthesis of the noir style with the exposé format," *The Captive City* "is an important transitional film."[12] Indeed, Wise and his cinematographer, Lee Garmes, "almost completely recapture the romanticized style of the earlier noir period" such as Wise's own *Set-Up* (1949) "with lonely cars prowling the night, muffled footsteps in an alley, and frightened faces emerging from the shadows."[13] In "The Syndicate" Carlos Clarens concludes his discussion of *The Enforcer* with the following précis about the 1950s:

> As the fifties progressed and a gradual mood of distrust spread in the wake of the McCarthy hearings, a political conservatism settled on the film industry, the primary effects of which were the blacklist and the banning of social themes. Another, more aberrant, effect was the appearance of the civic-minded hero, turning his back on corrupt or lax institutions to face up to the un-American enemy, be he a Syndicate member, a Communist, or one of the various Invaders from Outer Space.[14]

The generic resemblance between the '50s syndicate picture and both the anti-Communist and science-fiction film can be seen in the chase sequence that frames *The Captive City*, a sequence that recalls *The Red Menace* (1949) and *Invasion of the Body Snatchers* (1956).[15] A cloud formation at dawn, for instance, looks uncannily like a flying saucer.

While these intertextual echoes evoke "the fifties," a structure of feeling that has itself become something of a cliché, they also attest to the generic heterogeneity of '50s noir. As Wise's own career attests, social themes did not disappear from '50s cinema; they assumed, instead, a deep-structural form (as in *Invasion of the Body Snatchers*) or migrated to different subgenres (as in *The Captive City*). *The Captive City*, in fact, engages a "serious social problem": if in *The Set-Up* corruption is "limited, local, and personal," in *The Captive City* it has metastasized to encompass an entire city.[16]

The film's social-problem slant derives from its investigative origins. In a May 1952 article for the *Los Angeles Daily News*, Wise reported that after hearing about

Senator Kefauver's campaign against organized crime and discovering a series of newspaper articles about a local syndicate, he persuaded journalist Alvin M. Josephy Jr. to collaborate with Karl Kamb on a screenplay. Wise reported, moreover, that he was surveilled by underworld hoods while shooting in Reno. The cinema verité angle of *The Captive City* is referenced at the conclusion of the credit sequence when the camera zooms in for a shot of a document, "The Special Senate Committee to Investigate Organized Crime in Interstate Commerce." After an unseen hand turns a page, there's a quote from Kefauver: "Ordinarily, Americans don't think about the existence of organized crime; they know vaguely that it is there, and let it go at that . . . UNLESS PRODDED BY SOME UNUSUAL CIRCUMSTANCES." The implication is clear: "What we are about to see is a true story, straight from indisputable evidence in government files."[17]

The disjunction between the semi-documentary title sequence and the diegesis proper materializes when the score dramatically shifts from the sort of pastoral music used to score a generic '50s Western à la Wise's own *Two Flags West* (1950) to a series of cymbal-crashing crescendos that accompanies a fixed low-angle shot of a car racing down a deserted highway toward the camera. Inside the speeding sedan are Jim (Forsythe) and Marge Austin (Joan Camden), their abject fear highlighted by a tight claustrophobic two-shot of them sitting in the front seat and a reverse, rear-window one in which another speeding sedan can be seen gaining ground in the distance. Jim quickly pulls over to a police station, where, having identified himself as the editor of the *Kennington Journal*, he requests an escort to the "Capitol this morning and alive, preferably." The urgency of this request is mirrored by the headlines of a newspaper that an on-duty sergeant is reading, "SENATE WITNESS MURDERED," and by the reel-to-reel tape-recording machine that Jim commandeers "in case anything happens to [him] before [he has] a chance to tell [his] story in public"—"for the record."

Though the film briefly reverts to the semi-documentary mode ("perhaps I just better tell what happened"), the ensuing flashback and voice-over narration recall, as in *711 Ocean Drive*, classic film noir and suggest that this particular exposé will not be without a certain expressionist éclat. In an extended introductory montage, Jim inventories the "modern schools," "comfortable homes," and "up-to-date business district" as well as "small industry and warehouse sections" that, like "any other American town of the same size," make up Kennington. As Jim later says in voice-over when he arrives at the *Kennington Journal* for the day, "Kennington wasn't just a town; it was our town." If the allusion to Thornton Wilder is consonant with the film's pastoral mood and music, it nevertheless conflicts with the extraordinary passage that concludes the montage: a deep-focus, wide-angle shot of the new, treeless Levittown-style suburbs in which smoke billows from a

Disturbia: establishing
shot of Levittown-style
suburbs in *The Captive
City* (1952).

stack on the horizon and the shadows of the houses on the left side of the street
intrude on two children racing away from the camera in the middle distance.

Cut to: it's morning, and before Jim takes leave of his "comfortable" brick
Cape Cod house with the "woodie" station wagon in the driveway, he opens a
piece of mail and informs his wife that they've been invited to join the country
club. Despite the fact that the invitation is from his business partner, Don Carey
(Harold J. Kennedy), and will be good for business, Marge responds, "When
a girl lets herself be talked into becoming the wife of a country editor, she sort
of forms a mental picture—you know, taking in chickens and string beans and
corn in exchange for subscriptions." Marge's complaint, like the haunting, de
Chirico–esque shot of "disturbia," belies the folksy sentiment of her husband's
opening voice-over. In fact, Marge's pastoral vision is disrupted almost as soon as
Jim arrives at the newspaper office, where he receives a phone call from a private
investigator named Clyde Nelson (Hal K. Dawson), who's looking into the affairs
of real estate/insurance magnate Murray Sirak (Victor Sutherland) on behalf of
his ex-wife, Margaret (Marjorie Crossland). (The conjunction of foreshortened
close-ups and deep-focus shots, enhanced by the Hoge lenses used by Garmes
in the film, reflects the influence of *Citizen Kane*.)

At the country club that night, Jim receives another call from Nelson but,
exasperated, tells him to call back the next morning. The contrast is illustrative:
whereas Jim and Marge are socializing with Don and his wife, dancing to a live
swing band, Clyde is calling from a dive named Tony's where honky-tonk piano
music blares in the background. More ominously, when Clyde leaves Tony's, the
collar of his jacket turned up against the night, he flinches when a hot rod back-
fires, at which point he notices a dark sedan shadowing him.

The straight cut to a deep-focus long shot of Clyde trapped at the end of an alley bisected with shadows as he frantically attempts to open an enormous metal door spells his doom. Clyde attempts to escape by running out of the alley (and toward the camera), but the sedan bears down on him, its headlights harshly illuminating his terrified face from below, until he's crushed. As in a similar, celebrated sequence in *The Set-Up*, the film cuts from one of the sedan's headlights via a low, rising zoom of Clyde screaming to the bell of a trumpet.[18] The note the trumpet player is holding is so distorted that it sounds like a siren, connecting the up-until-now disparate worlds of the bar and country club.

The low illumination on Jim's profile before he passes through the bold, black-lettered door of the morgue marks Jim's first real encounter with the netherworld of Kennington. Later, as Jim's driving an alternately distraught and angry Mrs. Nelson home, she insists that Murray Sirak killed her husband—"or had [him] killed." However, when the police chief refuses to look into the case (it's been ruled a hit-and-run accident), Jim decides to investigate on his own, a decision that codes him as a public investigator (since, as a member of the press, he's working in the people's interest). This decision does not sit well with his partner, as the *Kennington Journal*, like most newspapers, is wholly dependent on advertising: while the paper may be civic-minded, it's first and foremost, as Don continually reminds him, a business. (In this context, see the scene at the very beginning of the flashback when, right before Jim leaves for work, he asks Marge whether she has seen the new, full-page advertisement that a local business has purchased.)

This paradox is forcefully underlined when, in a montage, Jim pays a visit to all of the people on a list of bookies he discovered in Clyde's office. After getting nowhere with his inquiries but suddenly noticing that, like Nelson, he's being shadowed by the police, he drives up to the Krug Distributing Company, which, he notes in voice-over, "was one of our first advertisers." He's talking to Krug outside his warehouse when three men in identical black suits and hats walk past and get into a dark sedan. Back at the office, Jim learns that one of the men, David Fowler, is an alias for Dominick Fabretti. The headline accompanying the half-tone picture in the newspaper Jim is reading reads: "POLICE CRACK DOWN ON GAMBLING CLUB."

That night, in a sequence that rhymes with the one in which Nelson is murdered (there's a flash cut from a front-window forward-tracking shot of the car driving down a deserted street to a close-up of a single headlight), Jim and cub reporter Phil Harding (Martin Milner) are checking out the warehouse—Phil exclaims, "Hey, look at all the phone wires!"—when a man materializes out of the dark and tells them to get lost. Even as Jim and Phil sit plotting in the car, the man is visible through the front window smoking a cigarette and warily watching them. The next day, Jim learns about David Fowler from the librarian at the UP wire service:

> According to police records, a Sicilian US citizen, between 45 and 50 years of age.... Quiet dresser, avoids limelight. Questioned as suspect, Murder, Inc. Last held in connection Florida killing. Present whereabouts unknown, although believed floating field organizer, race-wire gambling syndicate. Please regard highly dangerous, hoodlum type.

Marge, who has just stopped by the office and who, as both a columnist and the wife of a newspaper editor, appears to be conversant with the findings of the Kefauver Crime Committee, puts two and two together: "This puts Kennington right up there with Miami, Los Angeles, and Chicago." (The telegram recalls, of course, the racing news wire racket that propels the plot of *711 Ocean Drive*.)

Subsequently, while eating dinner with Jim at a local restaurant, she declares that "this charming Mr. Fabretti could hardly be right here in Kennington without anyone knowing it"—until she sees Chief Gillette leaving with his wife. "Small world," Marge reflects, suddenly changing her mind: "This brings up many interesting possibilities. Chief Gillette, the mayor, city council, some of our friends, maybe." The very next afternoon Murray Sirak stops by the *Kennington Journal* to make a proposition: if the paper agrees to lay off the Nelson case, he'll draw up a "contract for so much advertising." Jim turns him down and instead returns that night with Phil to the warehouse, where, as they drive past the three men, Phil snaps a photograph. The camera flash not only recalls the illuminated shot of Nelson right before he's murdered; it also suggests that Jim's investigation is finally coming into focus. However, when Phil disobeys Jim and returns to the office to see what they've managed to get on film, two of Fabretti's men beat him up and destroy the negative. For the first time, Jim realizes that the syndicate means business, and for the syndicate the first rule of business is intimidation.

The real terror begins when Jim returns home early one afternoon and notices a sedan with a Florida license plate parked outside his house, then goes inside to find a telephone repairman installing a "new instrument." (Mrs. Nelson previously told him that before her husband died, their telephone had been tapped.) That night, reflecting in voice-over about his life in Kennington, Jim concludes, "Nothing had happened. Nothing probably would happen. Not to people like us." Marge suddenly appears beside him and, after she asks if the car is still parked outside, turns on all the lights and says, "I can see I'll never do as a Western heroine. If the fort's gonna be attacked, it'll have to be with the lights on." "Honey, this is Kennington," Jim replies, "not Chicago."

Suddenly, the doorbell rings. It's not the syndicate; it's Mrs. Sirak, who reveals that it was Fabretti, not her husband, Murray, who killed Nelson: "Oh, not himself. He doesn't have to. He's too smart for that. If anybody gets in his way, he just presses a button. They bring them in from out of town. Different people every time." (Compare this dialogue with Mendoza's description of Murder, Inc. in *The Enforcer*.) Mrs. Sirak then explains how Fabretti strong-armed Murray into partnering with the syndicate before she reluctantly agrees to testify before a grand jury that the "combination owned half of [her husband's] books." When Jim returns to his house after driving Mrs. Sirak home, the same dark sedan is still parked outside. He rushes inside—Marge is safely tucked in bed—though he now knows the score: "If those hoods can park in front of our house, they can park in front of anybody's house."

There's no car parked outside Mrs. Sirak's house when Jim drives there the next morning, but the canary twittering in its cage is a bad omen: Mrs. Sirak, whom Jim and a neighbor find dead in her bedroom, won't be singing. Despite the fact that advertisers are dropping like flies and Don is threatening to abandon ship, Jim forces the chief of police to raid the warehouse, which is abandoned, however, by the time they get there. As a last resort, Jim calls a meeting of the town's ministers at a local church, where he unveils a chart that diagrams the "chain of command of a three-billion-dollar gambling and bookmaking empire." At the top there's a "handful of ex-gangsters"—"absolute rulers of a state within a state"—then the "regional bosses" like Fabretti, who are in charge of the racing wire service, and, at the bottom, "hundreds of local bookmaking syndicates" like Murray Sirak's.

Reverend Nash, who has been serving as the police chaplain for several years, acknowledges that the chief "can only run the sort of city his superiors tell him to," before continuing: "It's utter hypocrisy and a crime to direct it against a few individual bookies while those who rent space to these bookies, sell them legal services, supply them with telephones and all the other facilities of a legitimate business go entirely scot-free." Nash is about to begin his peroration—this is exactly the sort of impassioned denunciation we expect from a "man of the cloth"— when he stands up from where he's been leaning against a windowsill to reveal a sedan parked outside on the street. "I for one would be very happy to participate if you'll agree in advance to expose all the so-called respectable elements in this town who make Sirak and his activities possible," Nash declares on the way out, adding, "Frankly, I have no faith in that happening. I don't think any of us are in a position to take on our own congregations." This moment, one of the most subversive in *The Captive City*, makes perfectly clear that even the religious leaders of Kennington are more concerned about their economic well-being than cleaning up the town.

Cut to Jim returning at night to the *Kennington Journal*—the building is deserted and populated with shadows—where he wanly concedes in voice-over that his "legs have been cut off at the knees." When he turns on a desk light, though, he sees a UP day wire: "KEFAUVER CRIME COMMISSION OPENS

Live to Tell: Jim Austin
(John Forsythe) and
his wife, Marge (Joan
Camden), hurrying to a
crime committee meet-
ing in *The Captive City*
(1952).

IN CAPITOL." No sooner has Jim hit upon a new course of action than Murray Sirak appears out of nowhere like Mephistopheles himself to offer him "one more chance to make a deal." Jim tells him to "go fly a kite," then leaves that night with his wife for Washington, DC, trailed—as he learns at a Mobil gas station the next morning—by Fabretti's hoods.

Cut to Jim in the Warren—not, it's important to note, the Kennington—police station, where we see him winding up his tape-recorded story—"That's the story. . . . My only feeling . . . is that this must be told to somebody, someone big enough to do something about it"—just as two state troopers arrive to escort Marge and him to Washington, DC. At the Capitol, Jim climbs a flight of stairs on his way to a crime committee hearing already in progress when an anonymous man bumps into him and slips a handwritten note into his hand: "*DON'T TALK* YOU CAN NAME YOUR OWN PRICE." On the public address system, an anonymous male voice announces, twice, "Mr. Austin, please report to the committee room."

After a shot of a placard—"U.S. Senate Special Committee to Investigate Crime in Interstate Commerce"—the film dissolves to the familiar face of Estes Kefauver sitting behind a desk:

> I'm happy to report that the real-life James Austin. . . . is still alive. . . . As a consequence of [his] bold action and the resulting glare of publicity, the aroused citizens of Kennington demanded and now have an honest and responsible administration. I'm sure we all realize by this time that no big-time, organized public gambling is possible anywhere unless some susceptible . . . local officials have been paid off. By these payoffs the underworld creates a vicious circle. Gambling yields large profits. These profits make more money for payoffs.

> More payoffs mean a deeper and deeper penetration by the underworld into our political and economic system.

While this epilogue, as in *711 Ocean Drive*, puts an optimistic spin on the main body of the film, the mere fact that there is one suggests that the diegetic ending remains inconclusive. The question is, What is it about the body of the film that's so disturbing?

In *Somewhere in the Night*, Nicholas Christopher speculates about why Kefauver's postscript seems so inadequate: "If the iron-fisted, totalitarian control that the mob so easily imposed upon Kennington is a barometer, the political infrastructures of American cities after the war were in far more dire straits than Kefauver let on."[19] I would only emend Christopher's observation by reiterating, as Kefauver himself does in the epilogue to *The Captive City*, the significance of the syndicate's impact on the "economic system." In other words, American citizens engage in what Kefauver calls a "little organized gambling," "a little harmless local vice," because they "recognize that such illegal activities are often merely shadow forms of much larger and more successful activities on the part of those who control society."[20]

It's in the last economic instance that the note Jim receives should be understood, as it demonstrates that the syndicate can get to anyone, even if he or she is already inside the Capitol, and that, to recall Kefauver, the underworld has penetrated into the very heart of US society. So even as the message threatens Jim (*"DON'T TALK"*), it directly appeals to his economic self-interest: "You can name your price." Austin is, of course, beyond reproach, yet the fact that the PA announcement is repeated twice hints that it's addressed in part, like Kefauver's epilogue, to the audience: "Cut off the crime dollar at its source, and *your* town and the syndicate will shrivel and die. But it's up to *you*."

The conclusion of Kefauver's speech, which recollects the rhetoric of the World War II "Uncle Sam" recruiting campaign, is particularly barbed because in *The Captive City* the town of Kennington—"our town"—"seems to have been infiltrated, invaded, and annexed by a hostile external force."[21] Hence Christopher's verdict on Wise's film: "*The Captive City* is the most claustrophobic of films noirs about 'occupied' cities—that is, a nameless, ostensibly upright American city which beneath its placid, orderly surface is found to be a chaotic, venomous, criminal environment, from the Chamber of Commerce to City Hall."[22] In the end, the enemy in *The Captive City* is not so much foreign as domestic. Which is to say, it's not them, it's us.

THE BIG COMBO: BETWEEN MEN

Syndicate films such as *711 Ocean Drive* and *The Captive City* "developed as a re-sponse to the Kefauver hearings and offered a vision of gangs in America where there is only one gang organization with different branches in different cities."[23] Still, as Fran Mason points out, the "particular concern of the Kefauver hearings—the apparent pervasion of the United States by gangs—becomes in syndicate films a concern with wider issues."[24] It is precisely because of these wider issues—spe-cifically, cultural paranoia and emerging corporatization—that syndicate films, part gangster picture, part "suspense thriller," should be understood as examples of gangster noir. In fact, the determinate ambiguity and the generic heterogeneity of the syndicate picture is reflected in the Kefauver Committee's conclusion that organized crime had assumed a "totalitarian structure"—"everyone is trapped in the system of reified social structures"—and in HUAC's conspiratorial paranoia about the "combination as an alien 'other.'"[25]

From this dual perspective, *The Big Combo* (1955) is a classic syndicate film in which the "size and power of the 'combination' is outlined, as is the comparative weakness of the representative of the liberal state (the police), who simply don't have the resources to oppose it."[26] Thus, when near the beginning of the film, Capt. Jeff Peterson (Robert Middleton) stops by Lt. Leonard Diamond's (Cornel Wilde) office, he chastises him for spending $18,600 of the taxpayers' money in the last six months to investigate "one man, a single man," the generically named Mr. Brown (Richard Conte). Though Diamond insists that "Brown's not a man. He's an organization," Peterson snaps, "You're dealing with the largest pool of money in the world. You're fighting a swamp with a teaspoon." (The lively pulp dialogue is courtesy of Philip Yordan.)

If the word "combo" in *The Big Combo* is shorthand for "combination," the word "big" suggests not only a classic '50s gangster noir such as *The Big Heat* but a slew of other noirs as well, such as the Hollywood exposé *The Big Knife* (1955). In fact, while the word "big" has some denotative purchase in the case of *The Big Combo*—if only in the diacritical sense of, to adduce the language of jazz, a small as opposed to big combo (for an example of the former, see Leo Morse's indepen-dent "bank" in *Force of Evil* [1949])—it's also pleonastic, not to say exploitative in tenor.

Of course, *The Big Combo* is itself something of an exploitation picture in the strict, production sense of the term. As Chris Hugo has delineated in "*The Big Combo*: Production Conditions and the Film Text," Joseph Lewis's film was made at a particular moment in the history of Allied Artists, which was originally one of the "constituent subsidiaries of Monogram," the notorious—and I want to say "big"—Poverty Row studio.[27] In 1954 Allied Artists was attempting to compete in the "temporarily more open feature film market" (the province of the A picture) at the same time that it pursued the "newly emergent and younger market for exploitation films."[28] The keys to this hybrid, A/B formula were the exploitation component (i.e., sex and violence), the "B film noir look," and a star cast—Wilde, Conte, and Brian Donlevy—the last of whom plays Brown's lieutenant in the film, Joe McClure.

As the eventual failure of the above strategy suggests (upon its initial release, *The Big Combo* was neither a critical nor commercial success), Lewis's film may have been intended as an "intermediate" picture, but in reality it looks and sounds like a classic B movie. Consider, for instance, the star cast, which was only possible by "using the money saved on sets and locations."[29] According to Hugo, the featured players "gave the production an A-film gloss" and were "useful selling points."[30] This may well have been true circa 1954, though in retrospect the male principals were, at least at this point in their careers, "typically B," "aging, not quite stars."[31] As for sets and locations, one of the rhetorical contradictions of *The Big Combo* is that despite the titular stress on the bigness of Brown's combo, the "all-powerful syndicate is depicted," true to the aforementioned cast-driven economic imperative, "entirely through suggestion."[32] The Bolemac Corporation is represented, for example, by Brown, McClure, and two bodyguards, while a "sole plaque in an elevator bears the legend 'Bolemac Hotel,' hinting at the combination's vast assets, which we never see."[33]

Yet if the production values of *The Big Combo* do not rival those of—to cite a later, canonical example—*The Godfather* series, the noir style and the ensemble cast offer real, compensating aesthetic values. Consider the film's inventive sense of audio-vision, which is the very definition of late classical expressionist noir. The director of photography was John Alton, and his work on *The Big Combo*—Todd McCarthy isolates the single-source lighting, "dramatic use of silhouettes," and "severe black-and-white contrasts"—constitutes his "crowning post-Oscar achievement."[34]

Alton's style is at its most expressive and economical—he was famous for being both—in the condensed scene in which Brown's henchmen, Fante (Lee Van Cleef) and Mingo (Earl Holliman), mistakenly execute Diamond's sometime girlfriend, Rita (Helene Stanton), a B-girl who dances at the burlesque club across the street from his apartment. In the first shot, the camera pans up from a low-angle night shot of a curtained window in which a perpendicular neon sign ("BURLESQUE") is blinking on and off. (Note the breeze-stirred curtain and the ambient sound of traffic.) Cut to a medium shot of a hallway marked by another neon sign ("EXIT") into which Fante and Mingo enter. Once the two start down the hall (note here the offscreen sound of a light being clicked on), the film cuts to a full shot of Fante and Mingo, who, turning a corner, stop in front of a door, their faces lit up garishly from below. After Mingo yells "Go!" Fante kicks open the door and starts blasting away, his machine gun erupting like fireworks in the semi-darkened hallway. Cut to a lit cigarette bouncing off a dark carpeted floor, then a woman's braceleted hand, white as a glove from the light in the open doorway, dropping lifelessly into the frame. Finally, in a close rhyme of the opening shot of the scene and as a mournful passage from David Raksin's score, burnished by brass, cuts in, the camera rapidly climbs past the body shrouded in darkness to the "BURLESQUE" sign blinking on and off.

The sound track of *The Big Combo* is equally expressive. Raksin's score for *The Big Combo* with its "jazz voicings" has been justifiably celebrated,[35] as has been the sonic ingenuity of the extended sequence in which Brown orders McClure's execution. McClure has persuaded Fante and Mingo to rendezvous with him at Bolemac's private airport, where the latter have agreed to execute Brown. When the two hit men emerge out of the shadows with their machine guns drawn and aimed at Brown (Fante has signaled their presence to McClure by setting a match to a cigarette, the flame of which—in a classic Alton touch—illuminates his face), the aging, hard-of-hearing Irish mobster unleashes all the feelings that he's kept bottled up inside since being demoted to number two in the combo:

> MCCLURE: Mr. Brown, how do you feel now? Not so big, huh? You took my job. You took my hotel. You thought you could push me right off the earth. You punk. You accountant. You bookkeeper. (Addressing Fante and Mingo) Let him have it. Let him have it right now.

Fante and Mingo, instead of obeying McClure, slowly swivel their guns away from Brown and toward McClure. As McClure backs away, the revolving beam

Button Men: Fante (Lee Van Cleef) and Mingo (Earl Holliman) execute Joe McClure (Brian Donlevy) in *The Big Combo* (1955).

from the watchtower periodically sweeps over him, harshly exposing him in its bright white light as he pleads first with the two killers—"Don't do it, Mingo!... Fannie, don't do it!"—then with Brown: "Please, Mr. Brown, I don't wanna die!"

Brown reaches over and, in a "rare gesture of compassion,"[36] removes the hearing aid from McClure's ear. Just as Raksin's brooding score is about to crescendo, the sound suddenly cuts out and the camera changes to a low-angle eyeline shot from McClure's POV of Fante and Mingo cut off at the neck and dressed in matching dark suits and ties, their machine guns lighting up like thunder-less lightning. The scene is extraordinary not simply because of its use of subjective sound and camera but because it recalls the equally celebrated scene in *The Big Combo* in which Brown tortures Diamond by sticking McClure's hearing aid into his ear and turning up the volume on a radio that's playing "crazy" music.[37] (Lewis heightens the impact by showing McClure's deeply ambivalent reaction.)

The expressionism of *The Big Combo* is a direct result of Alton's and Raksin's contributions, though this expressionism would be merely decorative if it were not wed to the film's "exploitative" theatrics and libidinal politics. Lewis's film was by no means the first film to pit a "lone wolf" policeman mano a mano against a big-time hoodlum. In the early 1950s, *The Big Combo* was notably preceded by such films as John Cromwell's *The Racket* (1951) and *The Big Heat*, the latter of which *The Big Combo* has frequently been compared to.

Still, one striking difference between *The Big Heat* and *The Big Combo* is that, thanks to Yordan (who adapted the screenplay from his own short story), Lewis is able to invest the primary triumvirate of characters—Brown, Diamond, and Susan Lowell (Jean Wallace)—with a bristling sexual psychopathology. Diamond, for instance, is "far kinkier than the straitlaced Bannion."[38] While Dave Bannion in *The Big Heat* claims that he wouldn't touch Debby Marsh with a "ten-foot pole," Diamond is patently obsessed with Susan.

Diamond's sexual obsession is explicitly referenced in the same scene in which Peterson chastises him for wasting the taxpayers' money. When the captain reminds Diamond that the detective put a tail on Lowell for six months and personally shadowed her to Cuba and Las Vegas "out of his own pocket," Diamond responds he did it because the department refused to authorize the trip. Peterson retorts, "I'm not in love with her. You are!" "Love," as in the sort of emotion that Bannion feels for his wife, Katie, both when she's alive and after she's killed in a syndicate bombing, may not be the right word to describe the confused and compulsive nature of Diamond's feelings for Susan. Accordingly, Diamond, momentarily stunned by both the bluntness and truth of Peterson's comments, gets up from his desk, on which a pot of coffee is boiling (compare with *The Big Heat*), and walks around the captain's desk to a sink where he picks up an electric razor and begins shaving. Since Peterson has previously warned him that he "can't touch Brown because he's clean," Diamond's shaving reads like a defense mechanism, an oblique acknowledgment that he has already managed to get his hands dirty trying to nail Brown and, moreover, that there's something not so clean about his attraction to Susan.

Peterson forces Diamond to face this fact when he comes up behind him and says, "between friends," "You can't bear to think of her in the arms of this hood. Forget her. You're a cop. There are seventeen thousand laws on the books to enforce. You haven't [got] time to reform a wayward girl. She's been with Brown three and a half years. That's a lot of days . . . and nights." Peterson's tone is sympathetic: he completely understands the appeal of a "society girl" gone to seed like Susan. However, he also knows that Diamond's quest is quixotic. Diamond wants to be the knight in shining armor who gallantly comes to Susan's rescue, saving her from the villainous kingpin Brown. The only problem is that Susan doesn't want to be saved; she's a slave to Brown just as Diamond is enslaved by his chivalrous fantasies about Susan.

The base nature of Diamond's romantic fantasies is reflected in his on-again, off-again relationship with Rita. In fact, Rita's relationship with Diamond mirrors Bannion's with Debby Marsh in *The Big Heat*—with the proviso that Bannion never acts on whatever sexual feelings he may have for Debby. In *The Big Combo*, Diamond enjoys a sexual relationship with Rita, yet it's almost completely compensatory and, to be blunter than Peterson, masturbatory. The surrogate character of their affair is established in the scene in which Diamond waits for Rita, the ultimate "backstreet girl," outside the burlesque joint where she dances. (Evocatively scored by Raksin and atmospherically lit by Alton—cue fog—it's the epitome of the sort of "dark alley" for which film noir is famous.) When Rita finally appears, Diamond, revealing just how clueless he can be, asks her if she'd "like to go dancing." After she states the obvious (that she's *been* dancing), she caustically reminds him that he hasn't been around for the last six months, which, of course, is the same amount of time that he's been chasing the elusive Susan Lowell.

Although Rita reluctantly agrees to go to Diamond's two-person party, their postcoital dialogue (he has a half-finished beer in one hand, she has a cigarette in hers) is desultory at best:

DIAMOND: Why do you waste your time with a cop?
RITA (leaning her head on his shoulder): Could get a nice rich hoodlum. You should be able to recommend one with your connections.
DIAMOND: What is it about a hoodlum that appeals to certain women?

Backstreet Girl: lobby card of Police Lt. Leonard Diamond (Cornel Wilde) and Rita (Helene Stanton) backstage at a burlesque joint in *The Big Combo* (1955).

> RITA: Hoodlums, detectives, a woman doesn't care how a man makes his living—only how he makes love. Who is she, Leonard? I'm stupid, Leonard, about everything but men—them, I know.

Rita's remarks about detectives and hoodlums make explicit the film's seditious equation between "cops" and "robbers," as if the only difference between them—money aside—were charisma or, as Brown later puts it, "personality." Furthermore, to the perennial question "What do women want?" Rita's answer is not "love" but lovemaking or, more precisely, sexual satisfaction.

Before I address the last issue, it's worth noting that the above reflective scene with Diamond and Rita concludes when she abruptly announces, "Give me my shoes. I'm going home." Diamond is about to hand them to her when she lifts her leg and orders him to "put them on for [her]." Leonard does as he's told, at which point Rita grabs his arm and, as a tenor saxophone keens on the sound track, tells him, "When she hurts you again, don't wait six months." If Leonard is figured here as a masochist to Rita's sadist, he's also, as the close-up of the Gilda-esque poster of her that concludes the scene suggests, a fetishist.

This fetishism is first suggested in the second sequence of the film when, after Susan collapses while dancing with her former piano teacher, Mr. Audubon (Roy Gordon), Diamond's associate, Sam Hill (Jay Adler), picks up her purse and brings it back to the lieutenant. That the real object of Diamond's fetishism is not the déclassé "dark woman" Rita but the rich blonde one with the purse is retroactively confirmed in a speech he later makes to Sam in the wake of Rita's execution. Standing before a window in his apartment, his back to the camera, he holds up a pair of Rita's shoes and rues, "Saks Fifth Avenue. She came to see me in her best shoes. . . . I treated her like a pair of gloves."

In other words, whereas (to return to the difference between *The Big Combo* and *The Big Heat*) Rita is for Diamond a "poor" substitute for Susan Lowell, for Bannion there can be no substitute for his dead wife, Katie. Another difference between the two films is that whereas Diamond is in direct competition with Mr. Brown for the trophy that is Susan Lowell, in *The Big Heat* Debby is intimately involved not with the boss, Mike Lagana (Alex Scourby), but with his combustible right-hand man, Vince Stone (Lee Marvin). In short, Lewis's film represents a double displacement of the psychosexual dynamics of Fritz Lang's film, the net effect of which is to point up the significance of the core triangular relation that animates the gangster noir: police detective, criminal kingpin, and moll/femme fatale.

Consequently, if, in Diamond's one intimate scene with Rita, he wonders what it is about hoodlums like Brown that's catnip for a certain class of women like Susan, Mr. Brown recognizes not only Diamond's identification with him but also the difference between the two. The critical exchange occurs in the antique shop of Nils Dreyer (John Hoyt), a former "skipper" Brown has had eliminated because he knows too much about how, as it were, Brown became Brown. (In 1946 Dreyer skippered a private boat, the S.S. *Grazzi*, from which, according to former associate Bettini [Ted de Corsia], Brown's first wife, Alicia [Helen Walker], mysteriously disappeared.) Although the secret is inscribed on the ship's log, which was previously hidden in an antique bin in Dreyer's store, by the time Diamond and Sam arrive, it has already been reduced to smoking ashes by the prescient Brown. Diamond immediately orders Sam to contact the district attorney—he wants to arrest Brown on the spot for arson—but the "big man" has already procured a court order stating that "all the deeds, papers, and properties" of Dreyer's shop belong to the Bolemac Corporation. As Brown declares, in the process ratifying Diamond's earlier rejoinder to Peterson that Brown is not a person, "he's an organization," "I'm the Bolemac Corporation." In this seemingly incidental but emblematic scene, Brown displays the cunning and panache of the post-Prohibition mobster who's able to manipulate the legal system for his own ends and, at the very same time, flaunt his influence in the face of the law.

The real heart of the scene, however, is Brown's soliloquy about the difference between flatfoots like Diamond and diamond dogs like himself:

Diamond, the only trouble with you is that you'd like to be me. You'd like to have my organization, my influence, my fix. You can't, it's impossible. You think it's money, it's not. It's personality. You haven't got it, lieutenant. You're a cop—slow, steady, intelligent, with a bad temper and a gun under your arm and a big yen for a girl you can't have.

As in the earlier scene in which Diamond and Brown fight over Susan's body at a public hospital after she has collapsed at a restaurant, Brown is seated with his back to the lieutenant the whole time that he's talking to him. The paradox (one exploited by Francis Ford Coppola in the scenes with Michael Corleone in the *Godfather* films) is that despite the fact that Brown is compositionally dominated in both scenes by Diamond, his command of the discursive situation makes him the more dominant figure. In this, Brown is an exemplar of the syndicate "prince" who doesn't carry a gun, rarely loses his cool, and possesses the sort of women that working-class stiffs like Diamond can only dream about.

If the primary difference between Diamond and Brown is, according to Brown himself, personality, the film insinuates that the real reason he's able to attract and keep women like Susan—and, for Brown, there's a direct correlation between power and the capacity to possess women—is rather more particular. In fact, delivering on its exploitation promise, *The Big Combo* is as explicit as a Hollywood picture could get in 1955 about the secret of Brown and Susan's relationship. Foregrounding the difference between Diamond's and Brown's lovemaking, the film cuts from the police detective in his apartment putting Rita's shoes on her feet to Susan alone in her apartment, cocktail in hand, listening to classical piano music on a record player.[39] Susan's predilection for classical music, which is also depicted when we later see her at a private piano recital, "is placed in sharp opposition to the big-band jazz to which Rita performs her striptease routine."[40] That said, the classical piano music that Susan is associated with in *The Big Combo* is something of a red herring, because it reflects not so much who she is as her ideal alter ego, the bright respectable girl she was *before* she met Mr. Brown.

This music is, needless to say, anathema to Brown, who orders her to turn it off as soon as he enters her apartment, as if it represents—not unlike the hearing aid–amplified concert that Diamond is forced to listen to—a veritable assault on his sensibility. Brown doesn't approve of Susan's taste in clothes, either (she's wearing, among other things, black pants): "I like you better in white. You've got a dozen white dresses. Why don't you wear them?" Susan's response—that the color "doesn't please [her] anymore"—suggests, like her drinking, that she understands she's no longer the classic "woman in white" she once was: she's become another sort of woman, a fallen, red-letter one. Still, when Brown orders her to change—"A woman dresses for a man. You dress for me. Go put on something white"—she refuses.

At the same time, Susan can't, for the life of her, refuse his expert physical ministrations. After he grabs her head, he holds her neck with one hand and her face with the other, then roughly kisses her. He's still holding her head in a vise-like grip when he pauses to inquire what's bothering her: "Susan, tell me, c'mon." Susan, violently twisting her head away, hisses, "I hate, despise you." While Susan's animus reflects the change in her feelings about Brown (she previously told him she was listening to the piano music because she was trying to "remember how [she] fell in love with [him]"), the film itself—via the charismatic character of Brown—has already recoded the word "hate" so that it's no longer a simple antonym of "love."

Earlier, in a scene set in a locker room, Brown is interrogating a boxer (who has just been beaten badly in a fight) about the difference between McClure and him. Brown's disquisition, which presages his later monologue to Diamond, is addressed in part to McClure, who's sitting below him conspicuously wearing his hearing aid. It sheds light, moreover, on Brown's considered sense of himself—of what differentiates him from other, lesser men—as well as, not so incidentally, what it is about him that's so attractive to women:

> Take a look at Joe McClure here. He used to be my boss. Now I'm his. What's the difference between me and him? We breathe the same air, sleep in the same hotel. [Yelling into McClure's hearing aid] HE USED TO OWN IT! Now it belongs to me. We eat the same steaks, drink the same bourbon—look [holding up McClure's hand], same manicure, same cufflinks. But there's only one difference: we don't get the same girls. Why? Because women know the difference.

The difference is, in a word, hate, which in *The Big Combo* is inextricably bound up, as it is in Freud, with the life drive or eros.

Therefore, the fact that Susan says she hates Brown cannot be taken at face value. As the 1971 Persuaders' song has it, there's a thin line between love and hate, and since Brown knows this better than anyone, when Susan says the word, it's not a deterrent. It's an incitement to action. Brown, excited, starts to kiss her neck and ear, pleading as he does, "What do you want, Susan, tell me? I'll do anything you want. Tell me." Though Susan murmurs, "Nothing," Brown, still kissing, goes down, his head disappearing from the frame while the camera pushes in for an extreme close-up. Susan's tilted face and shuttered eyes, tremulous voice and drowsy, drugged-like speech, say everything: "nothing, nothing, nothing, nothing, nothing. . . ."

It probably goes without saying that, from one perspective, Susan's surrender is bad: she's a sexual slave to a man who's not only a mobster but who personifies the oppressive, patriarchal norms of the 1950s. From another perspective, though, her surrender lays bare the dirty little secret of female sexuality in the 1950s. We now know what Rita was talking about, what Susan was willing to throw it all away for, and what at least some women want—to twist Mick: satisfaction. In *The Big Combo* Susan is drawn "like a socialite moth to the hot flame" of the gangster, and as the above suggestive scene, not to mention final shot, intimates, the main reason is that Mr. Brown knows how to please her.[41] But since he can only "perform this taboo sexual practice because of his outlaw status,"[42] the corollary is that Susan's jouissance or enjoyment is transgressive as well. In this sense, *The Big Combo* insinuates a connection between sexuality and criminality and, more to the point, degradation and eroticism in which Susan's precipitous descent from her former elevated class position is a by-product of sexually disreputable acts.

In an interview with Peter Bogdanovich, Lewis, referencing Nob, not Bunker, Hill, recounts how he tried to explain to Jean Wallace why her character would "throw herself at Richard Conte's gangster": "Had it ever occurred to you that you're attracted to this man because of his lewdness? . . . This is what attracts you: no respectable man from Nob Hill is going to love you the way this gangster's going to love you."[43] Lewis's explanation of Susan's motivation captures one of the dominant performative contradictions of the embattled relation between the sexes in the 1950s: that because no respectable man—like, say, Dave Bannion or Leonard Diamond—would make love to a woman like Mr. Brown would, women were effectively condemned to being either happy but sexually unsatisfied homemakers or social distaff like Susan.

In this sociocultural matrix, it's worth noting that a number of critics have commented on the retrospective character of *The Big Combo*. For instance, in 1998, in his book *More Than Night*, James Naremore, comparing Lewis's film to the ultra-stylish *Killer's Kiss* (1955), remarked that Kubrick's film, "in its style and mode of production (if not its sexual politics)," "is ahead of its time, whereas *The Big Combo* is relatively antiquated."[44] The material passage here is Naremore's parenthetical cavil, because if it's true that the style of *The Big Combo* is regressive, its sexual politics are—in the precise, performative sense I've indicated above—progressive. This progressivity is not limited to the film's dynamic representation of female sexuality but encompasses its depiction of homosexuality as well.[45]

For example, the only bedroom scene in *The Big Combo* features Brown's torpedoes, Fante/"Fannie" and Mingo, whom Tom Flinn describes as "subtly linked homosexual 'partners.'"[46] In a classically low-key shot, Fannie is fast asleep in bed when he's awakened by a phone call. When he sits up to turn on the lamp, his naked, finely defined torso—cut off at his waist by a white sheet—becomes the main focal point within the frame. Still, it's only when Fannie gets up and puts his feet on the floor that we realize that Mingo is in the same room with him. In fact, their beds are so close together that when Mingo wakes up, his head appears in the same space as Fannie's. (Compare this passage with, for example, the opening scene of *The Brothers Rico*.)

The intimate character of Fannie and Mingo's domestic arrangement is reprised later in *The Big Combo* when McClure comes to their apartment to outline his ill-conceived plan to take out Brown at the airport and the two gunmen are wearing bathrobes. Subsequent scenes are even more explicit. When the "big heat" starts to come down on Fannie and Mingo for murdering Rita, Dreyer, and McClure (Diamond has issued warrants for their arrest), they hole up in Grazzi's former Prohibition safe house. When Mingo becomes stir-crazy, guzzling whiskey straight out of a wooden barrel, a concerned Fannie tells him to "lay off that stuff."

While Fannie's name is not without obvious nominative and anatomical resonance, it's nevertheless Mingo who is stereotypically coded as the "punk" in *The Big Combo*. Thus, despite the fact that the two men overpower Diamond outside the club where Rita dances, Leonard somehow manages to shoot Mingo in the hand with Mingo's own gun, and Mingo not only cries out in pain but also holds up his wrist. (The former action recollects the seriocomic scene in *The Maltese Falcon* [1941] in which Sam Spade [Humphrey Bogart] takes both guns from the gunsel Wilmer [Elisha Cook Jr.].)

Later, Mingo asks Fannie whether Diamond's case against them will hold up in court, and Fannie, in an echo of the scene in which Brown "kisses" Susan, puts his hand behind Mingo's head to reassure him, then keeps it there. Mingo, in turn, puts his hand on Fannie's arm, and despite the fact that Fannie looks as if he's about to say something—there's a long pause—he doesn't. Instead, Mingo voices the sort of utopian fantasy familiar from lovers on the lam like Bowie (Farley Granger) and Keechie (Cathy O'Donnell) in *They Live by Night* (1949) or, closer to home, Bart Tare (John Dall) and Annie Laurie Starr (Peggy Cummins) in Lewis's *Gun Crazy* (1950): "When we get out, let's never come back."

As in the above *amour fou* films, the high romanticism of Fannie and Mingo's relationship means, of course, that it's doomed. Since the police have already identified Fante and Mingo as the persons responsible for the murder of Rita and McClure, Brown knows that the former "soldiers" lead straight to him. Consequently, in order to keep them appeased, he personally delivers food and a cigar box full of money to the safe house; when Fante opens the box with a penknife, it blows up in the two hit men's faces. Fante is already dead when Diamond later tries to extract a confession from Mingo, who's dying of third-degree burns. Cradling Mingo's head in his arms, he orders an attendant to lift up the sheet covering Fante's body. (As with other, potentially graphic scenes in the film, Lewis leaves what Mingo sees to our imagination. However, since Fannie was caught holding the box, we can safely assume that it's not pretty.) Mingo, horrified, breaks down: "Fannie, don't leave me, Fannie!"

Though this passage may not represent, as one critic has opined, the "one true expression of love and loss in the film" (Diamond, for instance, breaks down and weeps after Rita's death), Fante and Mingo arguably have the "strongest romantic relationship in *The Big Combo*" as well as, not so incidentally, the least perverse one in a picture in which perversity is the norm.[47] In this, Fante and Mingo's "more than friends" relationship trumps the film's dominant heterosexual romance narrative, which is composed of the classic triangle of Brown, Susan, and Diamond.[48] This inversion or reversal is prefigured in the famously kinetic opening sequence of *The Big Combo* set at a boxing arena, in which Susan is chased by Fante and Mingo. When the two men finally catch up with her, she's trapped in a medium three-shot between Fante on the left and Mingo on the right, a triangular relation that's reiterated—in a looser, more relaxed composition—in the following scene set at an upscale restaurant where she's fled to get away from Brown or the boxing match or, more probably, both. (The brutality of the boxing match mirrors, as in *711 Ocean Drive*, her abject relationship with Brown.) While Susan sits at a table—with, it appears, absolutely no intention of ever touching the enormous steak set out on the plate before her (a sly allusion to the bruising sport from which she has just escaped)—Fante and Mingo dig in.

Unlike Susan, who, at the beginning of the film, is literally running away from Brown and, unlike Diamond, who is with Rita only because he can't have Susan, Fante and Mingo are always pictured together in *The Big Combo*: "They work together, sleep under the same roof in very domestic twin beds, dine together, and, ultimately, die together."[49] Equally important, if, as Eve Sedgwick has theorized in *Between Men*, sexual rivalry between two men for the same woman is a screen for repressed homosexual attraction, the however subtly expressed male-to-male desire between Fante and Mingo in *The Big Combo* can be said to constitute the film's central dynamic.[50] Indeed, it may not be too much to suggest that the orality in the kissing scene in Susan's apartment is itself a screen for even more forbidden sexual practices and lifestyles. In this sense, Susan and Fante/Mingo—the good-bad society girl and the buddy/buddy "button men"—invert and reflect each other.[51]

In addition, while Susan may well look the part of the ultimate woman in white—pure and unattainable as an angel—she ultimately has more in common with Rita, as the burlesque dancer's "bluesy soprano saxophone" theme suggests,[52] than the sweet, redeemer figure of classic noir. Fante and Mingo may be assassins and "yes-men," indentured like Susan to Brown, but in the Hobbesian, dog-eat-dog world of *The Big Combo*, they're also emblems of male-to-male desire, not to mention models of domestic harmony. More generally, if in *The Big Combo* Lewis uses the syndicate film to explore the political-libidinal unconscious of mid-century America, his film is less a vehicle for the sort of social critique of organized crime that informs *711 Ocean Drive* and *The Captive City* than an exposé of the psychopathology of everyday life.

The result is well-nigh diagnostic: the cop, the very embodiment, or so the argument goes, of law and order in the 1950s, has gone rogue and is less interested in getting justice than in getting into the moll's and even, perhaps, his rival's pants. The hoodlum may look ethnic—that is to say, Italian American—but he's no spaghetti-eating "mustache Pete";[53] rather, he's a well-spoken, well-respected man, legally beyond reproach, or, in Captain Peterson's words, "clean." Finally, if, like pre-retirement Eddie Rico in *The Brothers Rico*, Mr. Brown is nominally an accountant (in reality, he's engaged in "laundering" and loan-sharking), his mantra that "first is first, and second is nobody" means that anybody and everybody is expendable, a philosophy that reflects the congruence in *The Big Combo* between "gangster methods, the capitalist ethos, and the American insistence on success."[54]

Although, unlike *The Big Heat*, the heterosexual romance narrative of Lewis's film flirts with an upbeat conclusion when Diamond walks off into the airport fog with the former bad girl (compare with *Casablanca* [1942]), Susan's affair with "bad boy" Mr. Brown is not driven by the typical moll's desire for, say, clothes or a penthouse apartment but sex of the sort that ostensibly respectable men like Diamond are constitutionally incapable of. However, the transgressive refiguration of mid-century feminine sexuality in *The Big Combo* should not obscure the film's equally transgressive representation of Brown's gay male torpedoes, Fante and Mingo. Indeed, the intense relation between Diamond and Brown in *The Big Combo* suggests that the film's same-sex economy or narrative is not so much a subtext as the main story, posing the question, one long endemic to both the gangster and film noir genres, "of whether any relationships are possible outside the homosocial bonds of the police force and criminal syndicates."[55]

2

THE PHENIX CITY STORY

HISTORY AND FICTION (FILM), CIVIL RIGHTS,
AND THE LAST DAYS OF POMPEII

"JUST THE FACTS"

The Chattahoochee River—deep, dark, and murky, like Albert
Patterson's murder—flows as it always has.

—Alan Grady, *When God's Men Do Nothing*

I want to begin with a couple of facts. On May 17, 1954, in *Brown v. Board of Education of Topeka*, a landmark hearing on five civil rights cases that was argued by Thurgood Marshall, the US Supreme Court overturned the 1896 *Plessy v. Ferguson* decision, whose "separate but equal" doctrine had provided the devil's backbone for the "Jim Crow" system of segregation. At 9:00 p.m., on June 18, 1954, Albert L. Patterson, the Democratic nominee for state attorney general of Alabama, left his law office in Phenix City's Coulter Building and walked to his car, parked in a lot off Fifth Avenue. A moment later, after "four pistol shots rang out in rapid succession," Patterson "walked fifteen steps with a bullet in his brain and two more in his chest before he fell, face-down on the pavement, at the bottom of the stairs leading to his office."[1]

In his essay on *The Phenix City Story*, Jonathan Rosenbaum remembers first hearing about "Pat" Patterson's assassination:

I was eleven at the time . . . watching something like *Our Miss Brooks* or *The Life of Riley* with my grandfather, when an announcement of the murder interrupted the show. I can remember my grandfather telling me the next morning that he hadn't slept all night—the same reaction he'd have nearly three years later, September 1957, when Bart Floyd, a prospective Klan captain just outside of Birmingham, decided to prove his mettle by castrating a Negro "boy" at random, settling on a thirty-four-year-old house-painter, Judge Edward Aaron.[2]

Although there's no necessary link between the assassination of Albert Patterson and the extraordinary violence visited upon Judge Edward Aaron, Rosenbaum's recollection suggests that there is a connection, however subterranean, between the two events and that this connection is central to the force—or, if you will, reality effect—of *The Phenix City Story*.

I will explore this subterranean connection in both the body and the epilogue to this chapter, but it's clear that the above events contributed to Rosenbaum's opinion that when *The Phenix City Story* was first released, it not only "looked, sounded, and felt to me like Alabama in 1955," but it was the "best [movie] ever made in the state, as well as the most authentic."[3] That said, Rosenbaum also admits that the film's semi-documentary epilogue, which features actor Richard Kiley—not Albert's son, John Patterson—seated at his desk in the attorney general's office in Montgomery, "confused [him] so much when [he] was thirteen that [he's] remained confused about John Patterson ever since."[4] Hence Rosenbaum's question: Does the "movie's so-called realism" count, in the final analysis, "more than the reality it purports to depict?"[5]

In an earlier, seminal essay on the films of Phil Karlson in *Dreams and Dead Ends*, Jack Shadoian observes that the film's power "rests not on 'reality' but on its being a well-made fiction making imaginative use of the genre's structure and elements."[6] The question is, What sort of genre picture is *The Phenix City Story*? Is it a gangster film, as the title of Shadoian's book suggests, or is it, say, a film noir?

I raise the issue of genre here not to muddy the waters of interpretation to the point where it resembles the Chattahoochee River but to suggest that Karlson's film is, generically speaking, peculiar. Which is to say that if *The Phenix City Story* is, to adduce the specific subgenre of which it's a species, an exposé or syndicate picture, it is also, rather less simply, a gangster noir where this determination indicates the fusion of film noir and the gangster picture in the 1950s.[7] Put another way, part of the peculiarity of Karlson's movie is attributable to the fact that although it constitutes a classic example of the semi-documentary strain in the American crime film, the picture's expressionist elements cannot be reduced to this neorealist register because, "however timely and true," *The Phenix City Story* is ultimately a "triumph of craftsmanship, of artistry, of economy of means."[8]

While this judgment almost certainly refers to the film's director, it also references the picture's determinate conditions of production. Consider, in this context, the producing studio. The semi-documentary thrust of *The Phenix City Story* would appear to be the diametrical opposite of the full-blown expressionism of *The Big Combo*. However, both films were made at Allied Artists and benefited from that studio's desire circa 1955 to produce pictures that were more "prestigious" and that attracted a wider audience than those made by the company's impoverished predecessor, Monogram. Indeed, Karlson is central to this production history as *Black Gold* (1947), which was photographed by Harry Neumann (who also shot *The Phenix City Story*), marked the "change of the name from Monogram to Allied Artists because it was their first, they thought, important picture."[9] Not so incidentally, it was also "the most expensive picture [Monogram–Allied Artists] had ever made"—approximately $450,000.[10] The difference between *The Big Combo* and *The Phenix City Story* is that whereas *The Big Combo* relied on A-list stars, the "B *noir* look," as well as sex and violence, *The Phenix City Story* was predicated on violence and the "B *noir* style" in conjunction with a "social problem" and semi-documentary ethos.[11]

The docu-noir and social-problem elements of *The Phenix City Story* can be attributed to the film's screenwriters, Crane Wilbur and Daniel Mainwaring. Wilbur, who wrote the story for and co-scripted *He Walked by Night*, was renowned for his "in-depth factual and procedural approach."[12] If the semi-documentary slant of *The Phenix City Story* derives from Wilbur's contribution to the picture, the noir sensibility can be attributed to Mainwaring, who wrote the novel and, under the nom de plume Geoffrey Homes, the screenplay on which the most atmospheric classic film noir is based, *Out of the Past* (1947). (Mainwaring scripted, moreover, the quintessential '50s paranoid film, *Invasion of the Body Snatchers* [1956].) Commenting on the making of *The Phenix City Story*, Mainwaring remembers that the documentary prologue "was done after [he] was gone"; more to the point, he addresses the semi-documentary epilogue that so confused the thirteen-year-old Jonathan Rosenbaum.[13] In the ending that Mainwaring originally composed for Karlson's film, John Patterson's character goes to his wife and says, "This is what they want me to do, and this is what will happen if I do."[14] Flash forward to: "His kids have to be guarded by guys with machine guns, he never [goes] anywhere without a pistol, when he [comes] into the house at night he check[s] the windows, [and] he put[s] the pistol where he [can] find it."[15]

Still, if the "Crane Wilbur–Dan Mainwaring screenplay laces the cold facts of the Phenix City story with cold hard fiction" (the aim, according to Mark Bergman, "is not documentary but drama"[16]), *The Phenix City Story*'s status as a *docu-noir* must be attributed as well to Karlson, who opined in an interview, "Every successful picture I've ever made is based on fact. Sure, plenty of fiction enters into it, but the basic idea is true."[17] This statement tempers Carlos Clarens's assertion that, as opposed to the director's "most typical work," in *The Phenix City Story* "journalistic fact imparted credibility to Karlson's brand of genre fiction," an assertion that's premised on Clarens's delimitation of the director's films as "well-crafted B-pictures."[18] Yet as Karlson himself has stressed, even when he was only a "mechanic" working on the Monogram assembly line, he was always trying to sneak "little pieces of truth" (i.e., social commentary) into the "entertainments" that the studio was cranking out like so many cars.[19]

However (and here I'm trying to do justice to the tension or performative contradiction between fact and fiction, semi-documentary and gangster noir), Karlson's film displays a distinct noir style *and* sensibility. Thus, while *The Phenix City Story* concludes, not unlike a number of syndicate films, with an optimistic epilogue (one that, in the case of Karlson's picture, reiterates the sanguine tenor of the prologue), the totalitarian subtext problematizes the film's already severely compromised happy ending: just as henchman Clem Wilson (John Larch) is the agent of most of the violence in Phenix City, so his boss, Rhett Tanner (Edward Andrews), is a "tool of higher-ups."[20] This "unobtrusive pessimism," as Bergman points out, "is just one of the vestigial noir elements that permeate the film: low-angles, light hanging low from ceilinged sets, sleek cars on wet streets, and an all-pervasive paranoia."[21]

THE LAST DAYS OF PHENIX CITY

> Bright and gigantic through the dark, which closed around it like
> the walls of hell, the mountain shone—a pile of fire. . . . Below,
> the nether part of the mountain was still dark and shrouded
> . . . adown which poured, serpentine and irregular, rivers of the
> molten lava.
>
> —Edward Bulwer-Lytton, *The Last Days of Pompeii*

The title sequence of *The Phenix City Story* opens with a series of magazine covers—*Time, Look*, the *Saturday Evening Post, Life, Newsweek*—that emerge from a pitch-black background and sail toward the viewer. The credit sequence concludes with a crawl of written text superimposed over a collage of covers that evokes not the mythological creature of the Phoenix, as in the alternate title cards ("From the ashes of Phenix City has risen the symbol of democracy"), nor the forever twinned biblical cities of Sodom and Gomorrah explicitly alluded to in the diegesis of the film, but another ancient city and historical narrative: "There is no other place in the world as Phenix City, Alabama. In almost one hundred years it has been the modern Pompeii, where vice and corruption are the order of the day." The remainder of the text elaborates on this dire script—"Unlike Pompeii it did not require a Vesuvius to destroy it, for Phenix City is now a model community, orderly, progressive, and a tribute to freedom-loving peoples everywhere"—introducing a classical note that situates the city within the larger history of Western civilization even as it advertises that Phenix City's "vice and corruption" are the very stuff out of which the daily news is made.

While the invocation of Pompeii would appear to be a classically rhetorical one whereby the "wickedness" of contemporary Phenix City is effectively sublimed by yoking it to history, one of the ironies of *The Phenix City Story* is not simply that it appears to invoke Pompeii in order to promptly disavow it but that the decadence ascribed to Pompeii is not so much historical as mythological. In this "decadent" mythology, what began as a "purely natural disaster" was displaced in time by a cultural narrative in which the citizens of Pompeii were seen to have "colluded in their own destruction."[22] As John Seydl writes in "Decadence, Apocalypse, Resurrection," "The cities in the shadows of Pompeii were seen as sites of excess that portended, deserved, and caused the disaster, their stories merging with the biblical accounts of Sodom and Gomorrah."[23] The locus classicus of this revisionism is Edward Bulwer-Lytton's *The Last Days of Pompeii* (1834), a canonical historical romance that implies that the city's destruction was "retribution for a slave-holding society."[24] Not unlike the 1935 RKO production of *The Last Days of Pompeii*, *The Phenix City Story* actively participates in this fiction.[25]

Before I turn my attention to the documentary prologue of *The Phenix City Story*, it's worth noting that the trope of Pompeii is also exploited in the body of the film—in, to be precise, the mise-en-scène where if pre-eruption Pompeii signifies "vice and corruption" à la Sodom and Gomorrah, post-eruption Pompeii is associated in the popular imagination with bodies embalmed in lava and, figuratively speaking, petrifaction or immobilization.[26] In other words, if, to twist the latter trope, the populace in Phenix City has become somnolent, what will it take to wake them from this nightmare?

"REAL PEOPLE"

> Connections, like the tentacles of a giant octopus, reached into other counties as well as the marbled halls of state office buildings in Montgomery, site of the capitol.
>
> —Edwin Strickland and Gene Wortsman, *Phenix City: The Wickedest City in America*

The Phenix City Story opens with a thirteen-minute, black-and-white documentary narrated by Clete Roberts, a nationally recognized TV anchor and roving broadcast journalist who worked at the time out of KNXT in Los Angeles. Titled "Eye Witness Report from Phenix City" the documentary features interviews with a number of the real-life participants in the Phenix City story. The newsreel, which was "offered to exhibitors at no extra charge" and "did not have to be included when showing the picture,"[27] begins with a classic "talking head" shot of Roberts addressing the audience: "This is Clete Roberts reporting from Phenix City, Alabama. I'm here to learn the truth about Phenix City. Like many other

Americans and people throughout the world . . . I had read of it in the pages of national news magazines such as *Life, Time, Look,* and the *Saturday Evening Post."*

In this, the first part of the newsreel, Roberts not only alludes to the national and international interest in the Phenix City story, but he also introduces an opposition between the tale and the truth, fiction and nonfiction film. Roberts's investigative-journalist angle aside ("I'm here to learn"), the citation of the above sources intimates that the story we're about to see is real:

> The criminal syndicate here in Phenix City . . . prompted me as a reporter to come down here to find out what really happened, to learn how the good people of Phenix City had triumphed over evil and how democracy had successfully asserted itself over a very real dictatorship. I learned many shocking facts from the people who lived the Phenix City story, the real people involved. You will meet them in a moment as I talk with them, and I warn you that what you hear them say you will find hard to believe, but they speak the truth. I warn you too that what you are about to see in the picture which follows my news report will shock you too. It is brutal, it's shocking, but it is based upon the actual story of what happened here in Phenix City.

Here, in the second part of the newsreel, Roberts's appeal accentuates, like his persona, the reportorial thrust of the documentary and sets up another, intra-diegetic antinomy that will be dramatized in the body of the film: that between the "good people" of Phenix City and the syndicate, between democracy and the organization's "evil dictatorship."

While the newsreel can be said to let the proverbial cat out of the bag—the eventual triumph of good over evil and the successful reassertion of democratic principles—the repeated warnings about and emphasis on the "brutal," "shocking" nature of the facts betray the rhetoric associated with the B exploitation picture. At the same time, if the recourse to the sensational language of the low-budget picture whets the audience's appetite for the lurid and the melodramatic, the unadorned, not to say prosaic, character of the interviews indexes their authenticity.

In the first interview—with Ed Strickland, a *Birmingham News* reporter who coauthored *Phenix City: The Wickedest City in America* with Gene Wortsman of the *Birmingham Post-Herald*—Roberts bluntly asks Strickland if the story about Phenix City has been exaggerated, and Strickland asserts, "It has not been exaggerated; it could not be exaggerated." The improvisational quality of the interview, which attests to its verisimilitude (townsfolk can be seen ascending and descending the steps of the Russell County Courthouse in the background), is reflected in the fact that Roberts asks Strickland to look at the camera, instructing him, "Look right straight at the United States of America

Cinéma Vérité: ad for *The Phenix City Story* (1955) comparing events of "movie" to those of "real life."

now." When Strickland continues to look at him, Roberts points to the camera and says, "I want you not to tell me but tell those people right there." Roberts's direction, which equates the viewer with the nation, effectively abolishes the distance between the interviewer and the audience, as if despite Roberts's own on-camera instructions, the truth is transparent and is not being mediated by the cinematic apparatus.

Unlike Strickland, Hugh Bentley, a member of the Russell (County) Better-ment Association,[28] speaks in a distinct Southern accent and, when asked why he has continued to live in Phenix City after the "constant acts of terrorism" (his house was dynamited by the syndicate), replies, "Well, I was born and raised here." Bentley, who teaches Sunday-school class and talks about winning children to Christ, stumbles but eventually manages to articulate a metaphor that may not be as vibrant as Joseph's famous coat but brings some color to his testimony. Referring to Phenix City's "ugly" reputation, Bentley avers that the community "will rise up and throw off this . . . dirty, filthy coat that [he] inherited from [his] father and [doesn't] wanna hand down to [his] children."

Like Bentley, Hugh Britton is a member of the Russell Betterment Associa-tion and, prompted by Roberts as he stands outside his home in the daylight, "imparts a piece of folk wisdom": "When I was a boy, we—just for a pastime, at night—used to take flashlights and broomsticks and go down to the city dump to hunt rats. Kill some big ones! And . . . if you turn a light, a bright light, in a rat's face, that he will run for cover and it doesn't make any difference whether that rat is in the city dump or in the city hall."[29] Britton's demotic conceit and halting, colorful language bespeak, like Bentley's, the truth of his tale.

Roberts's next subject is Quinny Kelly, a janitor at the Russell County Court-house, where the interview takes place. Kelly is also a deputy sheriff and a wit-ness in the current murder trials being held in Birmingham. Unlike Bentley and Britton, Kelly has no use for metaphors. When Roberts asks him about being threatened by the syndicate, he recalls how an anonymous man phoned him and told him to "remove [his] pistol and badge": "Said if I didn't remove my pistol and badge, I wouldn't live." Kelly's occupation and appearance—when we first see him, he's wearing glasses, a straw fedora, and dressed in a dark uniform with a badge—do not inspire confidence that the forces of law and order are up to the task of combating a "very real dictatorship."

But however mechanical Kelly's answers (and Roberts's questions) may be, he's completely unflappable:

ROBERTS: You're gonna go down there and tell the truth, are you?
KELLY: I'm gonna tell the truth and, if I tell anything, it's gonna be the truth.
ROBERTS: Is anybody, is there any guard on you, anybody trying to help you
    stay alive until you get to the trial?
KELLY: No, sir, they are not.
ROBERTS: You carry a gun?
KELLY: Yeah, I carry a gun.
ROBERTS: Know how to use it?
KELLY: Yeah, I know how to.
ROBERTS: Will you use it?
KELLY: Yeah, I'll use it.

After Kelly recalls another incident in which an anonymous caller told him that the "time [for] runnin' [is] now" and that if he doesn't run, he won't live to testify in the trial, Roberts thanks Kelly for the interview and it appears to be over.

Roberts, though, can't resist further probing the issue of fear, as if he can't quite believe that this small, unassuming man with the glasses is not deathly afraid of the syndicate:

> ROBERTS: Not afraid?
> KELLY: No, I ain't afraid.
> ROBERTS: How about your family?
> KELLY: Well, my wife's upset, been upset ever since I talked to her the first time— been under the cure of a doctor ever since I went down and talked to her.

As Roberts goes to shake Kelly's hand, the janitor–deputy sheriff is already starting up the stairs to the courthouse. The fact that his wife is "under the cure of a doctor" suggests that his fearlessness, while admirable, has exacted a very real price.

The final interview of "Eye Witness Report from Phenix City" is, appropriately enough, Mrs. Albert Patterson, the widow of the slain Democratic nominee for state attorney general of Alabama, whom Roberts interviews on the patio outside her home. A "grand Southern woman" of "great courage," Mrs. Patterson, like her simple black dress and white lace collar, is a model of manners and understatement. Asked about where she got the strength to carry on after her husband's murder, she responds, "Well, Mr. Roberts, I suppose I got the courage from being in this fight so long." When asked about the history of elections in Phenix City, she invokes not so much the letter of the Bible, like Bentley, as its spirit, situating the recent tragic events—not unlike the title sequence—in a larger, historical context: "[The] good people in this town . . . were under bondage and they had to have freedom. And it just took something terrible to get people to wake up." I will return to the issue of bondage and "waking" later in this chapter, but if Mrs. Patterson's remark alludes to the Israelites' storied time in Egypt, it also evokes the rather more recent and less mythologically embroidered history of American slavery.

In the brief epilogue to "Eyewitness Report from Phenix City," Roberts rehearses the disposition of the preceding documentary:

> We have been dealing in fact, fact about the Phenix City story. The people with whom we have talked are real people, involved in what has been described as an infamous, sordid chapter in American city politics. There has been no careful rehearsal of speech, no careful phrasing. People have spoken from the mind and from the heart as they felt they should. . . . I return you to your city.

Even as the negative constructions here—"no careful rehearsal of speech, no careful phrasing"—foreground the veracity of the Phenix City story, the closing, second-person direct address ("your") insinuates that what happened in Phenix City can happen anywhere in the United States. Here, the documentary draws on the paranoid, conspiratorial atmosphere that was so pervasive in mid-century America in the aftermath of the A-bomb, the "red menace," and the Kefauver Committee on organized crime. Or, as Shadoian puts it, the "state of generalized paranoia" that pervades *The Phenix City Story* leaves the viewer "unprepared to deal with criminal syndicates, delegations from outer space, and Communists."[30] Hence the manifest antagonist of *The Phenix City Story*, Clem Wilson, a cretinous, toothpick-chewing redneck who's as "soulless as any commie-cum-space monster."[31]

A TALE OF TWO CITIES

> Downward the voices of Duty call—
> Downward, to toil and be mixed with the main
> The dry fields burn, the mills are to turn,
> And a myriad of flowers mortally yearn.
>
> —Sidney Lanier, "The Song of the Chattahoochee"

In the opening voice-over sequence of *The Phenix City Story*, John Patterson (Richard Kiley), the son of Albert Patterson (John McIntire), tells a tale of "two cities," Columbus, Georgia, and Phenix City, Alabama, which are connected by two bridges under which the Chattahoochee River, memorialized by poet Sidney Lanier, flows. The montage that depicts Columbus, Georgia, is composed of a series of elevated wide shots of the open downtown area (note the Sears store) where men are at work on "lathes and drill presses, looms and spinning machines" and where recruits can be seen marching on the parade grounds of Fort Benning, where "boys become soldiers."

By contrast, the initial view of Phenix City is a low-angle shot of Fourteenth Street with the Poppy Club—not Sears—clearly visible in the left background of the frame. "This is Phenix City," John Patterson states, not without pride, "my father's town, my town." If the initial view of Phenix City suggests that it's the antithesis of Columbus, Georgia, the subsequent voice-over montage evinces that the story of Phenix City is itself a tale of two cities. In the first part of the montage, the camera tilts up to encompass a church spire, then pans past neighborhoods and schools as John Patterson continues in voice-over: "It has more churches than any city of its size in the state of Alabama. Twenty-four thousand people live here, send their kids to school here just like they do in the city across the river. Decent, God-fearing people, most of them, who practice law, medicine, tend store, keep house." In this part of the montage, the film mirrors the synoptic, chamber-of-commerce view of Columbus, Georgia, before it turns its attention—via a high-angle shot of a bridge over which traffic is coursing only one way (toward Phenix City)—to the other side of the Chattahoochee River, as if the camera were crossing over to Hades.

In the second part of the montage, the laterally tracking camera details in exacting, semi-documentary fashion both the principal, industrial section of the city, Fourteenth Street, which generates $100 million in annual revenues, and the factories and labor that produce the "industry's tools":

> Dice shaved by skilled hands or loaded with mercury; slot machines rigged to pay off one cent on a dollar, if at all; whiskey that looked like bonded stuff, but wasn't; cards marked with tiny pinpricks or trims so dealers could recognize the aces and face cards. Tools of an industry that flourished for half a century because the good men looked the other way, an industry run by men I went to school with, their fathers ran it, and their fathers' fathers before them, an industry that made Phenix City the most vicious town in the United States. That industry was vice.

After a rapid track-in to a close-up of a young man sealing a deck of marked cards, the film cuts to the Poppy Club, where, in an inverse rhyme of the church shot in the first part of the montage, the camera tilts down as a torch singer dressed in a black tulle corset and three-quarter-length black gloves rises into the frame, holding her hands over her head like Gilda as she performs the "Phenix City Blues": "You've got to kiss me sweet / Cause when you kiss me oh so sweet / I shiver from my eyebrows / Right down to my feet."

"Phenix City Blues" and "Put the Blame on Mame" are, as John Patterson says about Columbus, Georgia, and Phenix City, Alabama, "worlds apart." Meg Myles is not Rita Hayworth, nor is she backed by an orchestra as Hayworth is in *Gilda* (1946). In short, there's a world of difference between the postwar, cosmopolitan atmosphere of Ballin Mundson's Buenos Aires casino in King Vidor's 1946 film and the provincial, déclassé Poppy Club, located as it is in the red-light district of a small town in Alabama circa 1955. Karlson's picture punctuates the contrast by cutting from Patterson's hortatory voice-over narration to the torchy burlesque of the "Phenix City Blues." Forget about Buenos Aires. Forget about Las Vegas. This is "sin city, U.S.A.," which—to quote the all-male bandmembers' chorus—is all about "fancy women, slot machines, and booze."

The second sequence of *The Phenix City Story* cuts from the sleaze and spectacle of the "Phenix City Blues" to the gaming tables at the Poppy Club, where the narrative proper is broached in the form of a serious romance between Fred Gage (Biff McGuire), the son of anti-vice crusader Ed Gage (Truman Smith), and Ellie Rhodes (Kathryn Grant), a young woman who works as a blackjack dealer at the club. Though Fred visibly disapproves of Ellie's job (he's studying for a law degree and plans to work for Albert Patterson for fifty dollars a week once he graduates and passes the bar exam), she's already making "two hundred bucks" a week and is resigned, like the rest of Phenix City, to the status quo: "This place has been here since we were old enough to climb up on an apple box to reach the handles of the slot machines." (Ellie's retort about their not-so-Edenic childhood highlights just how naturalized gambling is and has been in Phenix City.)

Still, when the club's goons, overseen by Clem Wilson (his heavily shadowed face says all we need to know about him) beat up a soldier for complaining that his cards are marked—"You cheated me!"—Ellie becomes alarmed. Later, outside the club, as two cops hustle the formerly noisy but now decidedly subdued man into a cruiser, Zeke (James Edwards), a black man who works as a janitor at the Poppy Club, tells Fred to stay away. Meanwhile, the floor manager at the club, Cassie (Jean Carson), warns the owner, Rhett Tanner, about the blossoming romance between Fred and Ellie. Rhett, who's busy amusing himself with some turtles in a terrarium—"Havin' a turtle race, you know? If I could just figure out a way to fix the winner"—dismisses Cassie's concerns, saying, "She brightens up the joint." Tanner then leaves to have a little talk with Pat Patterson, pausing along the way to say hello to the town's elderly "madam," Ma Beachie (played by herself), and to confer with an associate named Mac about the reformers meeting that night. As Tanner makes his way, first by foot, then by car, to the Coulter Building, the tracking camera and ambulatory pace capture the leisurely rhythms of small-town Southern life. Tanner is cordial, even genial. However, despite his ingratiating "good ol' boy" persona, it's clear that he controls Phenix City, a Bible-belt town where mammon or, as Ellie puts it, "profit" is king and even turtle races can be fixed.

The subsequent three sequences dramatize the relationships between Tanner and Pat Patterson; between Pat and his son, John, who's due to arrive with his wife, Mary Jo (Lenka Peterson), and their two children from Germany, where he has been stationed in Nuremberg prosecuting war criminals; and between the Patterson men and the new reform association led by Ed Gage and Hugh Britton (George Mitchell). In the first sequence, set at the Coulter Building, Tanner laments the current reform campaign—"Half the trouble with the people in the world today is they just don't want to let things stay the way they are"—before, after fiddling with Pat's cane, he offers him twenty-five thousand dollars a year to represent the syndicate. Patterson, who's peeling an orange and has worked for the syndicate in the past (he once saved a couple of Tanner's men from a murder charge), politely declines Tanner's offer. Pat assures Tanner that he intends to "mind [his] own business" and that, like Rick Blaine (Humphrey Bogart) in *Casablanca* (1942), he's "not stickin' [his] neck out," though the mise-en-scène—in the background, a framed picture of Patterson's uniformed son sits atop a bookcase filled with law tomes—hints that his mind may not be as made up as he claims. Patterson's built-up shoe, which is propped up on the edge of the desk in the foreground of the frame (he sustained an injury in the First World War from a German machine gun), reflects this ambiguity: on one hand, the shoe signifies that, as Pat remarks later in the film, he's done fighting the syndicate; on the other hand, it also speaks to his bravery in combat, for which he received the Croix de Guerre with Gilt Star.

Later, at the airport, Pat welcomes his son and family home (John is still in uniform), then, while they are crossing the tarmac, Pat announces that John will be a partner in his law firm—we've previously see a workman stenciling his son's name onto Pat's office door before Tanner enters—and that John's family will be settling down outside Phenix City. When Mary Jo looks askance, Pat insists that the city has changed: "Schools are better, more decent people moving in all the time, three new churches." The camera, however, tells another story: on Fourteenth Street the neon signs ("QUICK MONEY"), loitering couples (in reality, prostitutes soliciting servicemen), and drunks (one man can be seen trying to stand up by embracing a lamppost) attest that some things never change in Phenix City. In fact, the change in lighting—at the airport, the sun is shining while, during the drive, it's not only dark but raining—casts a sudden pall on the Pattersons' homecoming and betrays Pat's boosterish claim about a changed Phenix City.

The running conversation between John and Mary Jo while Pat is driving down Fourteenth Street on the way to his house in the suburbs indicates that John's wife, at least, isn't buying her father-in-law's story about Phenix City:

MARY JO (sarcastic): Three more churches? I see Fourteenth Street's still here . . .
JOHN: I was born and raised in this town, and I didn't turn out too bad, did I?

The two-shot of John and Mary Jo's baby daughter sitting in the backseat, together with Mary Jo's rejoinder to her husband ("You once told me you cut your eyeteeth on a slot-machine handle"), emphasizes the generational nature of corruption in Phenix City. Recollecting as it does Pat's earlier response to Tanner ("I want to sleep nights, too"), the sight of the Pattersons' son, Johnny (Ricky Klein), fast asleep in the backseat suggests that Phenix City, like Harper, Connecticut, in Welles's *The Stranger* (1946), remains in a complete state of somnolence.[32] The last shot of the sequence—a low-angle night-for-night shot of Tanner's club—recalls the film's opening montage and confirms that the Poppy Club is the epicenter of "sin city."

In the third sequence, set at the senior Patterson's home in the suburbs, Pat and John are taking a postprandial stroll outside when Ed Gage and Hugh Britton drive up. Ed's encouraging Pat to come to the reform association meeting that night when, in the process of getting out his pipe, he casually removes a revolver and lays it on a table. Pat rehearses his position—"[Tanner] wanted my services. They didn't buy me. You gentlemen can buy my services any time you want"— but when Mary Jo appears and tells her husband that she needs some baby oil, John decides to ride back to town with Ed and Hugh. If the gun represents the very real danger that the members of the reform association face, the reference to baby oil echoes the startling, even obscene close-ups of the Pattersons' daughter at the airport. Since we've previously seen Tanner make a threatening remark to Hugh Britton after seeing him on the staircase outside Patterson's office—"That's a nice-lookin' boy you got there"—the implication is that John's children are fair game.

The abrupt shift in the film's tone is marked by a canted shot of the car—absent John, who has left to pick up the baby oil—as Britton pulls into a driveway next to the Elite Café. Though Clem Wilson initially blocks the car's progress, he eventually lets the sedan pass and, in tandem with some cronies, trails it into an empty lot where they yank Gage and Britton out of their car and administer a sustained beating. The silhouettes on the wall of the building next door throw the action into brutal relief. Eventually, a man who is pulling into the driveway sees what's happening and cries out for the police. A woman screams, "They're killing him. Do something! Stop them!" A policeman *is* on the scene (we've earlier seen him phoning his wife to tell his "Momma" that he'll be late), but he just stands there doing nothing until John enters the fray, at which point he threatens to take him in.

Once the remaining members of the reform committee arrive, they escort Ed, Hugh, and John back to the Gunter Insurance Agency. There, Jeb Barrett (Allen Hourse) counsels "direct action": "I'm for going down to Fourteenth Street and putting a torch to it." John strenuously disagrees with Jeb's tactics—"I don't like vigilante action any more than my dad does"—but he nevertheless proceeds straight to the Poppy Club, where, after warning Fred Gage to stay away, he engages in a knock-down, drag-out fight with his "old school chum" Clem Wilson. A patron is about to hit John over the head with a chair when Fred belatedly joins the fight. The coda to the scene foreshadows the film's climax: as John and Fred are leaving the club, Clem, armed with a sap, staggers to his feet and starts after them until Zeke, who has been watching from the sidelines, trips him up with a broom, and the three men escape just as a police cruiser pulls up outside. If the impromptu confederation of John, Fred, and Zeke represents the next, integrated generation of reformers, Fred and Zeke's actions also embolden John to wage war against the syndicate. As soon as he arrives at his father's home, bloodied and tattered, he tells him, "We're going to the meeting!"

SHOCK CUT

At the subsequent meeting of the Russell Betterment Association, John, not Pat, does most of the talking, passionately arguing that the committee has underestimated the "intelligence and the decency of the voters in this state." Ed Gage demurs, predicting that on the next election day the ballot box will be stuffed, as usual, "like turkeys." Pat, who first started fighting against the syndicate in 1948, remains unpersuaded as well: "I fought and I lost, and I'm not gonna fight again." John continues to protest, arguing that what they need to do is "find a man that [they] can elect," and then, looking right at his father, adding, "trust him to do the job." The scene concludes on a sober, portentous note. "We're gonna win if it kills us," John pronounces, to which his father grimly replies as he's about to walk out the door, "Yeah, it could do just that."

Pat's words resonate like gunshots in the very next scene, set at the Phenix City Athletic Club. Tanner, a towel wrapped around his substantial waist, is heading to the steam bath when he sees Barton's (Arthur Tell) holstered pistol hung on a peg. When Jeb joins the other men already assembled in the steam room, he reports that John Patterson has "gone in" with the reform association, and Tanner, sharing a knowing look with Barton, declares that it's time to give John the "full test." Cut to Zeke's daughter skipping across a bridge carrying a bag of groceries when a dark sedan appears. After a whiplash pan to a menacing, low-angle shot of Clem Wilson—"Ain't you Zeke Ward's daughter?"—there's a shock cut to the girl's body being tossed like garbage onto the front lawn of Pat Patterson's home, where Johnny's playing next to his little sister in her playpen. The car continues to careen down the road, swerving wildly to the right and hitting a newspaper boy on his bike. When the film cuts back to the Patterson home, John rushes out and gazes, paralyzed, at the dead child until his father identifies the girl as "Zeke's baby" and we see the note pinned to her lifeless body: "THIS WILL HAPPEN TO YOUR KIDS NEXT."

Inside, Mary Jo is already packing to leave for her mother's house in Georgiana with the children while John is on the phone with the police, telling the officer on duty there—between clenched teeth—"I said get out here and get out quick, or I'll be down there with a gun!" "Okay, I'll send somebody right over," the officer replies, then turns to another officer and flatly says—"Somebody just threw a dead nigger kid on Patterson's lawn. Go out and have a look"—before taking another bite out of his sandwich. Back in the bedroom, the children are crying and Mary Jo is hysterical. John tries to reason with her: "There's a war on." Mary Jo, however, has seen enough: "I've waited for you through one war, and I'm not waiting through another." The irony, as Mary Jo says at one point, is that their children were safer in postwar Germany than they are in Phenix City. The analogy

Shock Cut: Zeke's daughter skipping across a bridge as Clem Wilson's car bears down in *The Phenix City Story* (1955).

is patent: the Phenix City syndicate is a form of domestic fascism, and no one, absolutely no one, is safe from its murderous violence.

The latter theme is vividly dramatized in the following sequence in which Fred Gage, shadowing the car that hit the newspaper boy, tails it to the Poppy Club's garage. He has just discovered a sedan with a broken headlight and is searching for the car's license when Clem Wilson smashes him in the face with the butt of a gun. Later, Ed and Ellie, desperate to locate Fred (his car has been found on Fourteenth Street with a ticket on the windshield), drive to city hall, where the sergeant there informs them that Fred was found in a ditch just outside of town—"unconscious but still alive"—and has been taken to the hospital. Unlike the utterly callous sergeant at police headquarters who takes John's call about Zeke's daughter, the nurse at Cobb Memorial Hospital is solicitous: "I'm so glad you came in. We've been trying to get in touch with you. I just can't understand how such a thing could happen to that boy." When Ed and Ellie ask to see him, she adds, "There's just one formality—you know the red tape in a hospital. Where do you want us to send the body?" The utter banality of the woman's response, as Rosenbaum notes, "provides a chilling counterpoint to the atrocities being revealed."[33]

In the aftermath of the newspaper boy's death and in response to John's outrage—"I tell you, Dad, it was murder. There's no question about it. They killed that boy because he saw the car. Do you still say we shouldn't stick our necks out?"—Pat, musing out loud that he's been a lawyer all his life and is still one, decides to try to prove that Gage was murdered. At the inquest, the policeman who found Fred's body agrees with the coroner's opinion that Fred "died of a fracture of the skull caused by a fall from a speeding car"; the policeman also testifies that the location of Fred's body was a "rough, rocky ditch in which a violent fall could cause a fracture of the skull." In response, Pat introduces into evidence a photograph showing that the roadside ditch, which borders a sawmill, was in fact "filled with sawdust—not a rock within a mile—soft as any bed in town, softer than most." Next, Pat introduces the rear seat cushion of a car as evidence—he first apologizes for stealing it—and Clem concedes that it's from his car, after which Pat calls James Kirby, the officer in charge of the laboratory at the Birmingham Police Department, who testifies that the blood on the seat cushion is the same type as Fred Gage's. The case appears to be an open-and-shut one—until, that is, Tanner and two of his cronies conspicuously enter the courtroom right before the verdict and the jury finds that Fred Gage's death was "accidental."

The verdict—a clear travesty of justice—is the final straw for Pat Patterson. When Tanner approaches him outside the courthouse as he's leaving with John, he disingenuously says that he's been thinking about setting up a fund in Fred's memory, and Pat tells him right to his face, "I've changed my mind. . . . I'm gonna fight you. . . . I'm running for attorney general of Alabama." Suddenly, for the first time since the beginning of the film, John's voice-over can be heard: "The decision had been made. From here in it was war." Cut to Mary Jo's mother's house, where John is about to return to Phenix City when his wife runs after him and says she wants to go with him. Their kiss—a photograph of Mary Jo's grandmother can be seen hanging on the wall in the background—bookends the earlier four-shot of the Patterson family in extremis. Just as Pat's decision to run for state attorney general heals the rift that has opened up between the generations (John has earlier, angrily called his father "defeatist") Mary Jo's decision to return to Phenix City—John: "You know how rough those boys can play?" / Mary Jo: "Then it'll be rough for both of us"—repairs their marriage and figuratively reintegrates the Patterson family.

For the first time since the beginning of the film, Karlson also employs montage to convey the syndicate's ruthless modus operandi:

> I'd said they'd play it rough. Well, that would be the understatement of all time. . . . Dad's campaign began to get more violent every day. Men who had the courage to defend him were beaten half to death in broad daylight. And they didn't stop with men. When the free press cried out, they tried to silence it. When a parson raised his voice, they tried to drown it out. But they didn't stop Dad. He lit across the state of Alabama telling the bitter truth in the cities and villages of sixty-seven counties.

In the accompanying montage, a car pulls up, tires squealing, in front of a barber shop window plastered with campaign posters ("VOTE FOR AL PATTERSON"), and three rocks, one after the other, shatter the glass; a group of Tanner cronies turn over a campaign truck that's been set on fire; a syndicate thug punches a Patterson supporter, then pushes him down a steep, exterior flight of stairs; another car, tires squealing, turns a corner, and a woman, her face covered in blood, is violently shoved out onto the pavement; a Tanner man on the sidewalk slaps a newspaper boy in the face, takes his papers, and throws them into the street;

finally, a parson is preaching to his congregation when a rock sails through the stained-glass window behind him.

The contrapuntal dynamic that drives the narrative of *The Phenix City Story*—civic resistance swiftly followed by violent reprisal—continues apace. A high-angle shot of Pat Patterson vigorously campaigning outdoors in front of a large audience at night and vowing to produce evidence to "convict and condemn the murderers of Phenix City" is succeeded by a wide-angle shot of his office, where a gasoline fire can be seen destroying the evidence.[34] The same cause-and-effect dynamic obtains in the next sequence, albeit with a self-reflexive, mediatic twist. The recto is a deep-focus wide shot of a WDAK camera operator in the left foreground of the frame; in the background, Hugh Bentley is addressing the citizens of Alabama: "My friends, I bring you news from hell." The verso is a wide-angle shot of a living room where Mrs. Bentley and her two sons are watching the telecast of the event as a man steals up to the house and lights a stick of dynamite. The bomb explodes and the screen disintegrates.[35]

The last, "dynamite" sequence recalls the documentary prologue to *The Phenix City Story* and simultaneously lays bare the film's dominant device: Karlson's tele-visual style. Even more so than *The Brothers Rico*, which also presents an unsparing portrait of the syndicate, *The Phenix City Story* reflects the impact of television on American society and, in particular, the motion picture industry. The influence of TV can be seen not only in Karlson's recourse to both cinema verité and the semi-documentary genre—location shooting, nonprofessional actors, and so on—but also in the flat, post-expressionist lighting associated with late '50s gangster noir. More specifically, *The Phenix City Story* alternates between the new low-contrast look of television and the graphic language of gangster noir that are dramatically on exhibit in the silhouette shadows in the Elite Café beating scene.

As in the wake of Fred Gage's death, the classic expressionist mode returns with the force of the repressed in a montage accompanied by John Patterson's voice-over narration:

> This was Phenix City on election day. My Dad asked the statehouse to proclaim martial law, and others asked but there wasn't any answer, so the day was like all other election days all over the years. The strong-arm boys were out in force to keep in line the citizens who thought they had a right to vote for whom they pleased.... Votes were bought and sold, and sex was often used in lieu of money but was no guarantee you could vote. No one who voted for Al Patterson was guaranteed that right.

In the accompanying montage, a Tanner crony shoves a Patterson supporter as he walks up to a polling place; another Tanner crony trips a Patterson supporter as he exits; a woman snakes her arm around a would-be Patterson supporter and presses him up against a wall; a man punches a male voter in the face as a woman, her left leg provocatively cocked, stands in the foreground of the frame; a Tanner man slaps a female Patterson supporter in the face with the back of his hand; and, in the most graphic passage, a male Patterson supporter, his face bloodied, wobbles in the foreground as, in the background, two syndicate men rough up two other male Patterson supporters.[36] When, in voice-over, John Patterson sardonically queries, "Where were the police?" the camera cuts to the Phenix City police station, where the officers on duty are "keeping a sharp eye on things"—playing cards.

ASSASSINATION: "THOU SHALT NOT KILL"

Given what we have just witnessed, it's no surprise that Pat Patterson loses Russell County and that the syndicate celebrates at the Poppy Club with drinks—"the good alcohol"—on the house. Patterson, though, goes on to win the remaining sixty-six counties in the state to become the Democratic nominee for attorney general, and since Alabama regularly voted Democratic in the 1950s, his election is a fait accompli. Consequently, at the Phenix City Athletic Club, Tanner and his posse contemplate their next move. Although Jenkins (Reese Taylor) philosophically observes, "Well, he hasn't been sworn in yet," the suppositional thrust of Tanner's reply—"*if* he is sworn in"—has a fatalistic ring, one that's reinforced when Pat is leaving his house at night to go to the office and John asks him if he told the Phenix City Ladies Club that he didn't "believe [he] stood a chance in a hundred of living to be sworn in." Pat laughs the question off, but it hangs in the air like a noose.

Ellie has been acting as the "bright eyes" for the reform association at the Poppy Club (in this she mirrors Jeb), so when she notices that "something's going on" one night, she reports back to Pat before stealing off to a back room. Sequestered in the dark, she watches from above, through the bright square of a window, as Tanner and Clem descend a staircase to a posse of men waiting below, the high-contrast light casting sharp diagonal shadows across their bodies. Tanner's upset that Jeb has come to the club; Jeb, however, insists, "It's gotta happen tonight." Just then, Cassie catches Ellie spying, and despite the fact that Ellie manages to escape and phone the Patterson home to warn Pat, John tells her that his father has already left for his office.

Cut to a low-key wide-angle shot of Albert Patterson exiting his office building in downtown Phenix City. While Ellie pauses to watch from across the street, a silhouetted figure joins Patterson—a virtual silhouette himself—as he makes his way to his car, which is parked in the same lot where Ed Gage and Hugh Britton were attacked. Ellie starts across the street to warn Pat when two gunshots ring

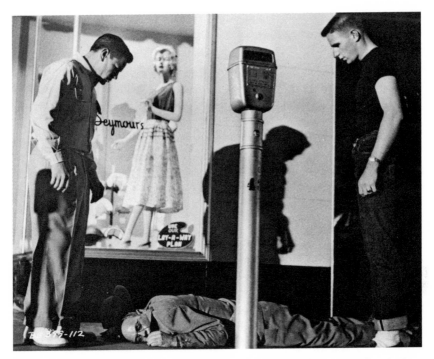

Mannequin Regard: passersby gaze upon the lifeless body of Albert Patterson (John McIntire) in *The Phenix City Story* (1955).

out, the camera cutting on action to a close-up of a pistol firing twice as Pat's body jerks backward. Ellie screams and the camera cuts again on action to a close-up of Pat's shadow-halved face, blood trickling from his mouth. As people spill into the street, Pat lurches into the light, staggering like Frankenstein toward the Coulter Building, where he drops to his knees in front of the Seymour dress shop. The female mannequins in the shop's brightly lit window—perfectly coiffed and costumed—seem like figures from another, pristine world in which bodies never bleed and darkness has been banished forever.

Later, at the Colonial funeral home, where Pat's body has been taken, the leaders of the reform association are trying to incite the crowd that has gathered—"the only law the Phenix City mob respects [is] the muzzle of a gun"—when John, still dazed, appears on the steps. Rousing himself as if from a deep sleep, he declares that the "days of the vigilantes are over" and that what's needed now is not "riots and bloodshed" but the "good opinion of decent people all over the state." John, like his father before him, knows all too well that violence begets more violence and is the mirror image of the syndicate's methods: mob violence is mob violence, whether perpetrated by "the people" or the syndicate. At the same time, there are limits to his sense of tolerance. When the crowd becomes restive, he climbs to the top of the staircase and announces, "If the law doesn't find [the murderer of my father], I will. And if the law doesn't take his life, I promise you I'll do it myself." The clash between two modes of civic response to senseless violence—the cathartic release associated with vigilante action and the slow, sometimes painful process of democracy—is embodied here in all its performative force in the conflicted person of John Patterson.

John is still addressing the crowd when the funeral director informs him that there's an urgent call for him. It's Ellie Rhodes, who relays that the men who murdered his father are hiding out at Zeke's place. In a rhyme of the earlier scene in which Zeke's daughter is kidnapped and murdered, John races across the bridge and enters Zeke's darkened house. Someone switches on a light—Zeke is prostrate on the floor and a man has his hand over his wife Helen's (Helen Wilson) mouth—when Clem attacks Patterson with a sap. In the ensuing fight punctuated by Zeke's wife's terrified screams, John knocks Clem unconscious, then, after breaking a chair over the head of Zeke's assailant, rushes to the basement, where he discovers Ellie's body. While Zeke's wife stops her husband from using a rifle to smash in his assailant's head, John proceeds to the porch and, seeing Tanner standing below him on the lawn, throws himself at him. The two men tumble down a steep incline into a creek and thrash around in the water until Tanner confesses, "I killed Ellie, John, I . . . I didn't kill your Dad." John, unable to control himself any longer, pushes Tanner's head under the water—an act that's not without a certain baptismal intimation—and is about to drown him when Zeke appears and pleads:

> Listen to me. Back there two minutes ago, I was gonna beat a man's brains out. I was gonna take his body and throw it out of the car like he did my little girl. But my wife, she took my hand and she said . . . "'Thou shalt not kill,' the Lord said." And I stood there looking at her—she was crying and all bloody where he beat her—and I was gonna do it anyway, but she said, "No, Zeke, no. We've been fightin' against things like this. All our life we've been fightin' against people takin' the law into their own hands."

A two-shot of Zeke and John—Zeke has dragged Tanner, still alive, onto the bank—sutures the sequence and suggests that John's fight has finally, righteously been conjoined with Zeke and his wife's.

Bloodied and tattered, not unlike after his first brush with the syndicate at the Poppy Club, John returns to the Colonial funeral home, where, after decking Jeb, he uses the telephone inside the front entrance to call the state capitol. When the governor refuses to respond to the emergency, John asks him to listen and, holding up the receiver to the people outside, shouts, "I need your voices.

... You want this city cleaned up?" The crowd roars and John tells the governor that "by tomorrow morning when they hear about [his] father's death, you'll hear ten thousand times that sound—the voice of Alabama!" John then holds out the receiver once again and, after the crowd roars, listens to the governor's answer before announcing to them that the state is "sending the militia" and that "tomorrow Phenix City will be under martial law."

Cut on action to a wide shot of city hall, the site of the miscarriage of justice that was the coroner's inquest into Fred Gage's murder. As army jeeps and trucks pull up, armed soldiers leap out; at the Poppy Club, the soldiers enter the gaming room and smash the slot machines or cart them outside to be stacked against a wall; at a dump outside the city, the slot machines and roulette wheels are burned, the smoke from the bonfire rising Phoenix-like into the air. Over the preceding montage, John Patterson observes:

> So the law came to Phenix City at last. It took my father's death to bring it. It wasn't the kind of law my father fought and died for. But it was the only law the men who killed him could understand—the law with a loaded gun in its hand. . . . We won a battle, but had we won the war?

Not unlike other syndicate pictures such as *711 Ocean Drive* and *The Captive City*, *The Phenix City* closes with a semi-documentary epilogue.

The camera tracks in to a medium shot of John Patterson, the newly elected attorney general of Alabama, who, sitting behind a desk "in his father's place" (this is the scene that so confused the thirteen-year-old Jonathan Rosenbaum), states that he has "two sacred duties to perform": to "seek out and bring to justice the murderers of [his] father" and to "keep the gambling hells of Phenix City firmly closed forever." In this biblically inflected conclusion, which echoes both Hugh Bentley's television address ("I bring you news from hell") and Zeke's injunction to John ("The Lord said, 'Thou shalt not kill'"), John Patterson looks "right straight at the United States of America" and says, "With God's help I shall not fail."

CROSS OF FIRE

As Howard S. Berger and Kevin Marr observe in their blog entry on *The Phenix City Story*, the citizens of Phenix City are under the thumb of Tanner's syndicate and have become totally immobilized, as petrified as Lot's wife or the victims of Mount Vesuvius.[37] This state of petrifaction or ossification is mirrored in the film's mise-en-scène in two scenes. In the first, Tanner's making his way to the Coulter Building to talk to Pat Patterson when he pauses to chat with Mr. Seymour in front of his dress shop. (Seymour's shop is located to the right of the Coulter Building and next to the parking lot where Clem Wilson and his men attack the members of the Russell Betterment Association.) As Seymour is telling Tanner about the new preacher's fire-and-brimstone sermon at that Sunday's service ("The text was Sodom and Gomorrah"), a female mannequin can be seen in the display window in the background of the frame. In the second, rhyming scene, Albert Patterson, having been shot, staggers and collapses in front of the dress shop, in the front window of which two female mannequins are visible. The full high-contrast shot—Patterson's body forms a horizontal in the foreground while the mannequins form a vertical in the background—illustrates the fate of those citizens who acquiesce to the syndicate, somnolence, and those who defy it: death.

The theme of somnolence first materializes in *The Phenix City Story* when Tanner visits Patterson's law office, and in response to Tanner's complaint about the reform movement ("I don't like trouble. I despise it, keeps one awake at night"), Pat responds, "I don't think at all. I don't wanna. More relaxin' and safer.... Sorry, I wanna sleep nights, too."

> TANNER: Lots of people don't lose any sleep on our account.
> PATTERSON: You keep quite a few awake—Gage, Britton, Bentley.

Later, in the immediate aftermath of the murder of Zeke's daughter, Mary Jo voices what happens when—to cite the title of Grady's book—"good men do nothing": "What's there to cry about? Rock-a-bye baby, go to sleep. Go to sleep forever."

The act of waking associated with resistance to the syndicate is epitomized by John Patterson. Right before he attempts to stop the beating of Gage and Britton, he goes to a drugstore to buy baby oil and, on his way in, passes a Johnson & Johnson "baby" advertisement that comments, like Mary Jo's outcry, on the syndicate's corruption of innocence. If John Patterson is an agent of change in *The Phenix City Story*, not least because he's initially an apologist, an anonymous man and woman are the first people to respond to the beating. In other words, if the people of Phenix City are, as Shadoian says, a "society of sleepwalkers,"[38] they're finally, collectively, waking up from their long slumber.

The turning point in the film—a "real" shock effect—is the murder of Zeke Ward's daughter, which revives the issue of bondage in addition to the buried mythological connection between slaveholding and the fall of Pompeii. On one hand, the murder of Zeke's daughter is plainly intended to intimidate John Patterson since the little girl's body is thrown onto the front lawn of his father's house in plain view of John's children. On the other hand, it's also intended to send a message to Zeke for intervening on behalf of Fred Gage and John Patterson at the Poppy Club. The latter insinuation is confirmed when, during the trial for Fred Gage's murder, Clem Wilson testifies that he's "got nothin' against niggers long as they behave." Wilson's testimony suggests that the killing of Zeke's daughter is an act of racial terror of the sort practiced at the time in the Deep South by the Ku Klux Klan.

In fact, the Klan was an active presence in Phenix City at the time:

Local law enforcement and city officials were members of the Ku Klux Klan. Locals remembered that the Klan held annual torch light parades through Phenix City to intimidate blacks. Robed Klansmen walked or rode the fenders of slowly moving cars; they were so easily recognizable under their sheets that people along the route called them by name. The parades always concluded with a raucous rally south of town at Ku Klux Hill, where a cross was burned in sight of the black community.

This was life in Phenix City, when Albert Patterson made his first political bid for political office in 1946.[39]

Things had not changed appreciably by 1954. Around the same time that John Patterson returned to Phenix City, Howard observes, "white folks around town took comfort in knowing that blacks knew."[40]

Despite the fact that the Production Code Administration repeatedly objected to the "specific item of the murder of the Negro girl,"[41] the filmmakers refused to cut the offending scene. In other words, the killing of Zeke's daughter is essential to *The Phenix City Story* as a fiction film qua fiction film; it's also integral to the film's political-libidinal economy in which the syndicate's supremacy is not so much separate from as equal to the racial violence of Phenix City. Hence Rosenbaum's take on the murder of Zeke Ward's daughter: "What made the film believably convincing as well as Southern was the *racist* killing of a little black girl to scare the Pattersons away from challenging the mob—an incident that I only recently figured out must have been invented."[42]

Equally or more importantly, the murder of Zeke's daughter is central to the film's narrative, prefiguring the dramatic climax of *The Phenix City Story*, which, like the penultimate funeral home scene, is also invented. If the brutalization of Zeke's wife registered in her beaten and bloodied face viscerally reinscribes the violence visited on the men, women, and children of Phenix City depicted in the campaign and voting sequences, Ellie's actions counterpoint the impassivity of the female mannequins in Seymour's shop window, who gaze blindly upon both Tanner and Patterson alike. Just as Ellie's death remembers the murder of Fred Gage, who is killed, like Ellie, for opposing the syndicate, the location of her body in the basement of Zeke's house suggests that her death is a displaced double of Zeke's daughter's. In this displacement, the white heterosexual romance of Fred and Ellie is sacrificed for the symbolic marriage, made under the sign not of the Ku Klux Klan but of the Christian cross, between Zeke Ward and John

Patterson—between, that is, the incipient civil rights movement and the gospel of nonviolence preached by both Albert and John Patterson.

CODA: DE POST FICTION

Commenting on the prescience of *The Phenix City Story*, Rosenbaum notes that Karlson's film

> was released less than eighteen months after racial segregation was ruled unconstitutional in *Brown v. Board of Education of Topeka* but this was still over a month before Rosa Parks refused to relinquish her seat on a Montgomery bus, thereby launching the civil rights movement. Yet the nonviolent activist position of Martin Luther King Jr. that first became widely known during that protest is already implicitly present in this movie, in the *fictional* character of Zeke Ward.[43]

Rosenbaum's reading captures the way in which *The Phenix City Story* crosses fact with fiction, invention with documentation, a chiasmus that accents the racial deep structure of *The Phenix City Story* in which the (white) '50s syndicate or gangster film is crossed with the repressed of *film noir* understood as "black film."

To advance such an argument is not, of course, to make a historical claim about *The Phenix City Story* or, in particular, John Patterson, whose career in public service in the wake of his father's death would be increasingly motivated by political expediency in the form of an intransigent anti-integrationism. Although it's now perfectly clear that with respect to the issue of civil rights, John Patterson was on the wrong side of history, the screenplay for *The Phenix City Story*, including and especially what the PCA referred to as the "murder of Zeke Ward's daughter,"[44] had been completed by late 1954—before, that is, Patterson became attorney general of Alabama.

It might not be too much to say, then, that the fictional John Patterson—the one who, embracing Zeke Ward's ethos about nonviolence, marries Martin Luther King Jr.'s message with his father's own anti-vigilante philosophy—was ultimately betrayed by the real, historical John Patterson. In other words, the historical record does not diminish the liberatory promise of *The Phenix City Story*, which, as scripted by Wilbur and Mainwaring and directed by Karlson, sneaks a "little bit of truth" into the B syndicate picture that is the dark heart of '50s gangster noir.

3

THE BROTHERS RICO

SUNSHINE NOIR AND THE '50S SYNDICATE PICTURE

Oh! Blessed rage for order, pale Ramon,
The maker's rage to order.

—Wallace Stevens, "The Idea of Order at Key
    West"

In his entry for *The Brothers Rico* in *Film Noir*, Carl Macek asserts that Phil Karlson's 1957 film is a "thriller deeply rooted in the postnoir style": "In these films the subtly ritualized violence and dark ambience of the film noir was replaced by an overt emphasis on crude violence and a dull, almost flat style. This type of film became the heir apparent of the rapidly declining noir output of the 1950s."[1] With the exception of the adjectives "crude" and "dull," this is a reasonable description of classic noir circa 1957. However, these same two adjectives betray the author's negative, stereotypical take on *The Brothers Rico* vis-à-vis classic noir:

> The conventions of *true* noir film making—which emphasizes a world devoid of order and possessed of a sentiment rejecting compassion and sensitivity—had long since wasted away for lack of usage. *The Brothers Rico* is a simple thriller that displays very little in the way of noir ambience, a film constructed from archaic conventions and petty obstacles that strongly point to the decline of the noir series during the 1950s.[2]

I have cited this critique at length because it epitomizes the sort of thinking about "true noir." From the last perspective, *The Brothers Rico* can only be a faux or false noir, a "simple thriller," whose violence is "crude" and style "dull," its obstacles "petty" and conventions "archaic."

I want instead to suggest that *The Brothers Rico* is a complex thriller and that its style is—to the trained eye—anything but dull. Moreover, precisely because it illustrates how a resourceful director can mine the genre's not-so-archaic conventions, Karlson's film not only is, to cite Andrew Spicer's judgment in *Film Noir*, a "masterpiece" of late '50s gangster noir but also represents a direct link to modernist noirs such as *Point Blank* (1967).[3] As for "petty obstacles," I will leave it up to viewers to decide whether the obstacles that Eddie Rico (Richard Conte) has to face in *The Brothers Rico* are petty.

On the DVD commentary Martin Scorsese is—in the very best sense—predictably articulate about the virtues of *The Brothers Rico*, observing that "many of the pictures shot in the late '50s had a flatness to them."[4] Scorsese attributes this flatness to the "influence of fast-shooting television crews" in addition to the recognition on the part of directors and cinematographers that the contrast in these pictures was preferable to the "expressionist shadows" associated with film noir. As an example of this style, Scorsese cites both the "last few American movies" made by Fritz Lang and Hitchcock's *Psycho* (1960). I will return to these formal issues in the conclusion of this chapter, but I would only note that Scorsese also observes that this "flat" style "allows the tragedy [of *The Brothers Rico*] to cut even deeper than it would have if the film had been more beautifully photographed, beautifully composed."

Part of the interest of *The Brothers Rico* derives, as Scorsese remarks, from its source material, Georges Simenon's *Les Frères Rico* (1952). After the war Simenon moved to the United States,[5] settling at one point at Shadow Rock Farm in Lakeview, Connecticut, where he wrote *La mort de Belle* (1961) and *Les Frères Rico*. While living in the United States and before returning to France, Simenon spent time in Florida, and his acute sense of place is conveyed in the opening pages of *Les Frères Rico*, which is set on the western coast of the state. The protagonist of the novel, Eddie Rico, lives there with his wife, Alice (Dianne Foster), and their three daughters. Simenon's concise, clipped prose captures the milieu of an upper-middle-class Floridian suburb in the early 1950s: "They had a nice house, brand-new, modern, dazzling white, in the most fashionable section of Santa Clara, between the lagoon and the sea, just a few steps from the Country Club and the beach. Eddie had given it a name he liked: *Sea Breeze*."[6] It is, as the narrator later waxes, "paradise itself": "Everything was beautiful. Everything was bright and clean. Everything bathed in light. At times it felt like living in the middle of a travel poster."[7]

This is the same world—bright, clean, beautiful—that Eddie Rico inhabits at the beginning of the film. In Simenon's novel, Eddie wakes up every morning to the sound of blackbirds or, more precisely, "Eddie didn't quite wake up any more: there was only a vague awareness of day breaking," but "because of the blackbirds the world cut a little more deeply into his sleep and mingled shreds of reality with his dreams."[8] Though Eddie is indeed living the "good life," the travel poster and the strident cackle of the blackbirds intimate that this life is too good to be true, that it's a dream or illusion from which one day Eddie will be abruptly awakened.

This portent assumes a slightly different configuration in Karlson's film that can be said to begin with the credit sequence and consists of a single abstract image: a dark, starlike splatter encircled by a darker, triangular-shaped ring that's set against a mottled-gray, impasto background. The image is reminiscent of an Abstract Expressionist painting (which movement was dominant in the United States at the time), and the dark stain or splatter looks like blood.[9] The image can be seen as a figurative transposition of the blood that appears on Eddie's face at the beginning of the novel when he nicks a mole on his left cheek while shaving. Eddie has worried about the mole in the past, and when he questions his doctors about it, one says, "If it weren't so deep, a flick of the knife would take care of it. As it is, it would leave a scar."[10] Simenon's metaphor suggests that Eddie's relation to the mob is more than skin-deep and is, in fact, cancerous.

In both the novel and the film, the precipitating action is a phone call from Phil (Paul Dubov), the right-hand man of Eddie's former boss in the syndicate, Sid Kubik (Larry Gates), that wakes Eddie in the early morning. The diegesis opens with a wide shot of the Ricos' master bedroom, the morning light slanting through the screen doors and highlighting Eddie and Alice in their beds, which are set close enough together so that Eddie can reach over in his sleep and place his palm on his wife's breastbone.

When the phone rings, Eddie gets out of bed to answer it, pausing as he's leaving the room to look back longingly at Alice, her face peacefully reposed in sleep, the ring on her right hand glinting in the light. It's been ten years since the Ricos were married and three years since Eddie went clean, breaking with the organization to start his own laundry business. Now, out of the blue, Phil has called "asking" him to take in a "boy" named Joe Wesson (William Phipps). When his wife suddenly appears in the living room, where Eddie has taken the call, he insists that he's "through with them," but Alice, who has twice "almost been the mother of [his] children," is worried about the child that they've talked about adopting. Eddie reassures her that "nothing's gonna happen" before sweeping her up in his arms and carrying her, like a bride, back to the bedroom.

The connubial mood carries over to the next sequence, where the couple banters as Eddie stands before a mirror shaving and Alice reads aloud from a letter in which Eddie's mother is saddened by the fact that her son Gino (Paul Picerni) "is going away for a long time" and the "baby," Johnny (James Darren), has had to "go away, too." Alice senses a connection between Phil's call and Mama Rico's letter. Eddie, however, dismisses her fears: "Darling, you sound like a superstitious peasant from the old country." While the sequence, like the previous one, ends on a bright note when Eddie pulls Alice into the shower with him, in the final shot Eddie's image is distorted by the pebbled-glass shower door, the aluminum frame of which splits the screen in two, separating the couple. The shower door, like the mirror, reflects the duality or ambiguity of Eddie's character: on one hand, he's associated with a compulsive cleanliness—once he gets in the shower, he asks his wife for a bar of soap; on the other hand, the phone call and letter hint that the past may not in fact be past, that Eddie "may have quit the rackets" but he's still "smeared with its dirt."[11]

The past begins to aggressively reassert itself when Eddie arrives at work, and the hoodlum that he's supposed to be hiding is lurking behind his desk reading his papers. More troubling still, Eddie's driving to the Flamingo club when a car bumps into him at a stoplight. The man in the dirty—make that, filthy—car is his brother Gino, who signals to him to pull over. Gino gets into Eddie's immaculate convertible, and they drive to a palm grove where the seagulls shriek like the sleep-disrupting blackbirds in Simenon's novel and the grove itself is a miracle of symmetry, the planted trees as orderly as cadets at attention. The telephone call and letter are, Eddie soon realizes and as Alice intuited, connected: Gino was the "gun" in the killing of a mobster named Carmine, Johnny was the driver, and Joe Wesson is the new "gun" that the organization has brought in from Kansas City. Worse yet, Johnny has disappeared—there's talk on the street that he has already talked to the DA—and Gino has been sent against his will to St. Louis. Gino wants to escape to Cuba or South America or "any place where [he] can get lost," but Eddie persuades him, despite his brother's distrust of Sid, to go to St. Louis—to continue to play, like Eddie, by the rules.

When Eddie returns to his office, there's more bad news, delivered again via telephone by Phil: Eddie has to fly to Miami to meet with Kubik, which means he won't be able to sign the adoption papers that day with Alice. Earlier, when Eddie arrived late to work, a deliveryman in a company truck happily complained to him that his "new kid could keep this laundry busy all alone." A magnanimous boss, Eddie replies, "Give him all the diapers he needs." The irony, of course, is that Eddie's not only childless but because of the Family, he must now indefinitely postpone starting a family of his own.

The following sequence set at the Excelsior Hotel in Miami attests to Karlson's keen sense of space and composition, mise-en-scène and choreography. Sid's ocean-view suite, richly appointed in the most au courant, Oriental décor circa 1957, is as expansive as his mood: he welcomes Eddie like a prodigal child—"You're as close as I'll ever come to having a son"—and Eddie responds in kind, "How do you think it'll feel being a grandfather?" The mise-en-scène suggests, though, that the relation between the two men is not as amiable as it appears. Sid and Eddie sit next to each other conversing on the balcony, but the partition of the sliding glass door directly behind them puts them on either side of the frame. This sense of separation is exacerbated when Sid, slipping off his silk smoking jacket, goes to his bedroom to change. (He's scheduled to go deep-sea fishing that afternoon.) While Sid sits on a bed with his back to Eddie, Eddie remains standing next to an empty chair:

EDDIE: What did you want to see me about, Sid?
SID: How's your brother doing?
EDDIE: Who, Gino?
SID: No, no, Johnny, the kid. Heard anything from him lately?

Changing both his shoes and the subject, Sid asks about Eddie's mother, claiming, "Everything I've got, what I am, I owe to her because of what she did for me." (We later learn that, in the past, Mama Rico [Argentina Brunetti] took a bullet in the leg for him.) Standing up, Sid turns to face Eddie and, pointing to his heart, declares, "My name is Kubik, but in here I'm a Rico."

It's only after Sid leads Eddie back into the living room and pours a drink for him that he returns to the subject of Johnny: from his sources, and to Eddie's genuine surprise, Sid has learned that Johnny has married a young woman named Norah Malaks (Kathryn Grant) and that her brother, Peter (Lamont Johnson), has talked to the DA. Sid sits down on the edge of a desk, and the mise-en-scène—the geometrical shadow of a '50s "atomic" lamp is visible on the wall behind and between the two men—cues the audience that subtext is paramount: "Our connection at the DA's tells us that Malaks is asking the DA that if a witness could be produced who would turn state's evidence, would they give that witness a break?" Sid, placing a hand on Eddie's shoulder, says that he knows Johnny would never talk, but "our friends are nervous. They like to have everybody present and accounted for."

The mise-en-scène figures prominently in the final scene of the sequence as well. Right before Eddie is about to leave, he and Sid pause before the door to his apartment, where they shake hands and Sid wishes him good luck. On the wall directly behind them there's a large Asian-style picture of an ornately dressed man sitting in a chair. The picture points to Sid's regal status and, given the Orientalist codes of the day, his inscrutability: Is he telling the truth? Can Eddie trust him? Though Sid's first act after he closes the door is ambiguous—he walks over to a tackle box that's open on the desk and yanks on a large lure, as if to see if it'll hold—the brief, shocking scene that follows glosses the meaning of the previous one.

After putting on a white captain's cap (an article of clothing that, like his two-tone shoes, momentarily gives Sid a comically incongruous appearance), he makes his way down an empty, well-appointed hall to another room. There's a straight cut, accompanied by the offscreen sound of grunts and groans, to a shot of Phil standing inside the room looking at something. Phil opens the door for Sid and there's the sound of someone being hit. Cut again to an anonymous man in a rumpled white shirt standing behind a chair in which another man is bent over at the waist. The man who's standing yanks the other man's head up by his hair, and as the camera zooms in for a close-up, we see that it's Gino, his sweat-stained face bruised and bloodied: "Thanks, Uncle Sid."

Unaware of Sid's perfidy, Eddie flies straight to New York, where, after Peter Malaks rejects his request for help (because, he says, he doesn't "help gangsters"), Eddie's forced to return to the past—that is, to his childhood home in Brooklyn. The camera cuts from Eddie standing outside his mother's candy store on Mulberry Street at night to a low, extremely dark shot of Mama Rico limping toward the door. The subsequent, extended sequence contrasts with the one set at the Excelsior Hotel: compared to Sid's ultra-contemporary, tastefully decorated apartment, Mama's flat is cramped and cluttered with tchotchkes and religious artifacts. At the same time, it's also lived in and intimate—familiar.

Mama escorts Eddie through the candy store and kitchen to the den, where Eddie's grandmother (Mimi Aguglia), despite the fact that she doesn't speak a word of English, is watching TV. The reverse shot is startling: on the silver screen, gunshots ring out as a flying saucer passes overhead. It's an uncanny, even surreal image. While Eddie stands to the left, talking to his grandmother, his mother stands to the right, gazing at a triptych of her sons, the brothers Rico: Eddie,

UFO: TV movie playing in Eddie Rico's (Richard Conte) childhood home in *The Brothers Rico* (1957).

Gino, and Johnny. Like the TV and the brand-new refrigerator that Eddie has bought them, he's an alien element, unlike Gino and Johnny, in this Old World environment.

Accordingly, when Eddie joins his mother at the kitchen table—he eats the salami and sips the Chianti she puts out for him—it's plain that he's not there for business and pleasure, as he just told her; he's there strictly on business: to find out where Johnny is. Mama, though, doesn't trust Sid (in this respect she's like her son Gino) and staunchly refuses to tell Eddie where her youngest son is: "I keep my mouth shut—like this [pointing to her lips]—they don't like it, so they kill me." If Mama's silence represents an ironic inversion of the Mafia code of omertà, her recognition of the part she has played in her sons' fates also differentiates her from Eddie, who remains in a total state of denial.

Previously, when Eddie told Peter Malaks that Johnny might be killed if Peter didn't help him, Eddie asked him, "Do you want that on your conscience?" Betraying the ease with which he's able to use rhetorical force if necessary to get what he wants, he browbeats his own mother: "Okay, you have Johnny's blood on your hands." Mama drops to her knees before a statue of the Virgin Mary and changes her mind only when Eddie starts to leave, revealing that the last time she heard from Johnny he was living in El Camino, California, "on a farm with some people whose name is Felici."

If Eddie now has what he wants, the fact that he has had to emotionally extort his own mother to get the information suggests that he's operating from a position not of strength but of weakness, that however much he might actively disavow the knowledge, he's a pawn of the syndicate. The organization's power is reflected in a gaze that's even more ubiquitous and omnipotent than it is in *The Enforcer*. The audience, like Eddie, becomes aware of this gaze and the utter dread it inspires as soon as he leaves the familiar confines of his mother's home. Eddie's walking down Mulberry Street at night when a car door opens onto the sidewalk, stopping him in mid-stride: it's a hood from the "hood" named Vic Tucci (Richard Bakalyan) and he's out on the town, or so he tells Eddie, with two blondes, Jean and Nellie. While Jean doesn't have to be encouraged to make nice with Eddie ("Hi there, handsome"), the composition is restricted—the camera is tight on Eddie, who, sitting in the backseat of the car, is pushed to the left side of the frame—and Vic's questions are offhand but freighted, like Kubik's: "Heard anything from your brothers?"

The sense of claustrophobia is sustained when Eddie slips into a diner to book a flight to Phoenix, a telephone-booth call (the first is to Alice) that, in the course of the film, becomes the most pervasive audiovisual trope of Eddie's increasing isolation and alienation. In Phoenix the camera pans from Eddie striding across the tarmac to a man dressed in a white cowboy hat and contemporary Western

Under Western Eyes: Eddie Rico (Richard Conte) talks to an American Airlines representative while, in the background, mobster/"dude cowboy" Pete Selsun (George Cisar) stands watching in *The Brothers Rico* (1957).

garb standing inside the airport, watching him. In the next, deep-focus three-shot, Eddie is making a reservation with a ticket agent in the foreground while the man stands smoking in the middle ground. In the immediate foreground, a desk model of an American Airlines plane sits on the counter; to the right and rear of Eddie, a sign reads "BACK IN THE SUN PHOENIX." If the model airplane is a figure of flight—of, that is to say, Eddie's desire to flee—the "urban cowboy" standing between the ticket agent and Eddie represents a symbolic block on Eddie's fantasies of escape. In fact, the unassuming-looking mobster not only bears witness to the syndicate's presence in the West but also gives the lie to the booster poster of Phoenix, which, with its sunny, cloud-swept landscape, references the sunshine state from which Eddie's becoming ever more estranged.

When the man finally introduces himself, as we know he will, he says his name is Pete Selsun (George Cisar), though Eddie doesn't recognize him until he says that he's originally from Chicago and used to be the bartender at the Shoreline Tavern. Pete, like Vic, tries to talk Eddie into staying the night and sampling the "action" ("roulette, blackjack, poker") before he remarks, "It's a funny thing. Last night at the joint someone got to talking about you and your brother." Ignoring Pete's comment, Eddie turns down his offer to stay the night and enters a telephone booth. However, even as he's standing inside the sound-insulated booth, waiting to talk to Alice, Pete can still be seen standing in the background, looking quizzically at him.

The trap tightens when Eddie arrives at the El Camino Hotel. The same triangular composition obtains here as at the Phoenix airport, but this time Eddie is the object of both the desk manager's and the bellhop's gaze. While the El Camino, according to the taxi driver, is the "best hotel in El Camino," it's a far cry from the Excelsior, not to mention Eddie's home, a stark contrast that's reflected in a plangent passage in George Dunning's score when he first sees the room. The Felicis' home promises to be more hospitable. But when Eddie approaches the front door, Norah's sister's daughter, Mary (Mimi Gibson), fearfully asks her mother as she's locking it, "Is he the man, Mommy?" as if Eddie is some sort of monster (which, of course, he is).

The colored-glass lamp in the left foreground and the cluttered décor associate the Felici residence, despite the country location, with Mama Rico's flat, as does the presence of women, not merely Mary and her mother but Norah herself, who, as she turns from the stove (we see that she's pregnant), puts her hand to her forehead. (The gesture could come straight from a John Ford Western.) Norah's smile turns to a frown, though, when she sees who it is: Norah has absolutely no illusions about who Eddie is or why he's there. As she stands united with her sister and Mary in a three-shot, the first thing she says is "How did you find us?"

As the sequence plays out, it rhymes with Eddie's encounters with Sid Kubik and his mother. Thus, once Norah's sister and Mary absent themselves from the room, Eddie and Norah stand, separated by a beam, talking in the living room. As soon as they start to argue, Mary calls out from the kitchen, "Aunt Norah, is he the man I'm not supposed to talk to?" and, as if to answer her question, Johnny comes through the front door. For a moment, Eddie and his youngest brother are joined together in a spirit of fraternal affection even as Mary's apostrophe—"That's him, the man I mustn't talk to"—functions like a chorus. The composition and tone alter dramatically when Johnny grabs a bottle of wine and they sit down at a table. While Eddie and Johnny converse about their respective families—"We're thinking of adopting" / "I see there's gonna be another Rico soon"—Norah stands above and between them, her arms wrapped around the beam, eventually sweeping down to force her husband to ask Eddie why he's there.

Eddie, parroting Kubik, blames Norah for clouding his brother's judgment when Johnny suddenly stands up from the table:

We didn't make any deal with the DA or anybody else. I'll tell you why I ran out. Norah had something to do with it, not that she even asked me to or told me to. No, Eddie, it's because she's clean and good, the first decent thing that ever happened to me. And when I found out we were gonna have a kid, I wanted to make sure that there'd be one Rico [who] could grow up free of all the things that you, Gino, or I ever grew up with.

Johnny, unlike Eddie, is perfectly willing to accept the consequences of his actions. But when he fatalistically asks his brother, "When do you think the executioners will come?" Norah faints, and in a disturbing echo of the opening scene of the film, Johnny carries his pregnant wife into their bedroom, where he lays her on the bed. When she comes to and still sees Eddie standing in the doorway, she pleads with her husband, "*Please* get rid of him. *Please* get rid of him." Johnny does as she asks and, after showing Eddie to the front door, again reverts to a fatalistic mood: "So maybe I am gonna die, but then you got even bigger troubles—you gotta live." Unlike Eddie's earlier, self-serving admonishments to Peter Malaks and his mother, Johnny's rebuke has the sting of truth.

Norah's anxiety and Johnny's warning come to fruition the moment that Eddie enters his hotel room at the El Camino. The cue, as in the "beating" scene at the Excelsior Hotel, is an offscreen sound—in this case, a deck of cards being shuffled. Eddie, startled, turns to see a man sitting in a chair and dressed like Pete Selsun in an off-white hat and jacket. The man, whose name is Mike Lamotta (Harry Bellaver), says that he's "in charge." Eddie insists on phoning Miami immediately, but he soon discovers that Sid has checked out of his hotel, that Lamotta is acting on his orders, and that Kubik has used him "like a bloodhound to track down [his] brother"—in other words, that Gino, Johnny, Norah, and his mother were right and he was wrong. In a dramatic but futile gesture, Eddie vents his rage on the phone—"The dirty, stinkin' animal!"—since, as in *Force of Evil*, it's the syndicate's dominant means of communication and because, like Kubik, it's inanimate. In other words, as much as Eddie desperately wishes it were otherwise, it's not personal; it's business. Feelings, as Eddie himself previously said to Gino—"Feelings . . . are for old women"—are wholly beside the point.

In a compelling, understated performance by Bellaver, Lamotta, who's the epitome of bemused detachment, acts not unlike a psychoanalyst. In response to Eddie's histrionics, he waves his cigarette in the air and says, "If it makes you feel any better to scream your head off, go ahead," then, with an air of finality, "but it changes nothing." Suddenly there's a knock at the door and Lamotta's right-hand man, Gonzales (Rudy Bond), enters and announces that the hit man has arrived and is "sober." Lamotta glances at his watch and says, "Let's say ten thirty then," and Eddie, indignant, cries out, "How can they do a thing like that?" At the beginning of *The Brothers Rico*, Eddie is the picture of robust mid-century masculinity—successful, attractive, well-groomed, virile. Now he's the picture of abjection, having become what he earlier derided—feckless, emotional, feminine.

As soon as Gonzales leaves, Eddie tries to appeal to Lamotta's better instincts: "You sit there and talk about Johnny like you're getting rid of some garbage. This is a human being." Eddie's humanism is, needless to say, not only misplaced but hypocritical, as Lamotta is only too well aware: "So he's your brother. We're all brothers, aren't we? Has that ever stopped anything?" Lamotta's rhetorical question pricks Eddie's pretense like a balloon. The crux of the scene occurs when

Eddie disingenuously claims that he "was never in on that end"—in on, that is, the mob's inveterate recourse to violence and murder. Lamotta is merciless as a judge: "Don't give me that. You knew it was going on, so don't start playing holy with me now." As if the word "holy" has triggered some lost religious impulse in Eddie, he gets off the bed and, like his mother, drops to his knees before Lamotta to plead for his brother's life, offering him one hundred thousand dollars and a business "that's worth more than that." La Motta isn't even tempted: "What good is money or a business to a dead man?" Instead, he gives Eddie some advice— "Stop tearing yourself apart, boy. Figure like it's ten thirty. Figure like you've already lost him"—before taking off his jacket and saying, "I'm gonna call down for something to eat. You want anything?" Eddie is aghast:

> EDDIE: Something to eat? You just sentenced a man to die. How can you think about eating?
> LAMOTTA: You think it's crude that I should eat at a time like this. Wake up, Eddie, Johnny's already spoken for; he doesn't count anymore. But you, you're alive. Did you hear that? You're alive.

In existentialist terms, Lamotta is authentic whereas Eddie, at least until this particular moment, has been asleep. In fact, Lamotta, despite appearances, is arguably Eddie's conscience or daimon. Accordingly, after he retrieves the lamp that Eddie has knocked off the night stand and right before he picks up the receiver to call for room service, he asks, "Are you listening to me or am I just talking to myself?"

The transactional, epiphanous nature of the encounter between the two men is marked by Eddie's switching places with Lamotta, sitting down in the chair that the other man has just vacated. Awake at last and resigned to his fate, which is to facilitate his "baby" brother's death, Eddie slumps against the chair as the film cuts to a long night-for-night shot of two sedans, headlights ablaze, pulling up in front of the Felici farmhouse. When the film cuts back to the hotel room, the jumble of dirty plates, beer bottles, and cigarette butts registers not only that time has passed but also that Eddie's once perfectly ordered life has devolved into chaos.

It's 10:24 and while Gonzales telephones the Felici house, Lamotta, in another echo of Sid, pours Eddie a drink. When Eddie refuses both the drink and the receiver, Lamotta pulls him up from the chair. The telephone motif and Karlson's use of three-shots are expressively married when Eddie's forced to talk his brother into giving himself up. Johnny is jubilant: "I'm a father! I'm a father! He's a boy and we're gonna name him after Papa, Antonio Rico. You're an uncle!" The ironies are multiple and ferocious: just as one Rico has entered the world, another one is about to go out; Johnny, the kid brother—not Eddie, the eldest Rico—is the first to perpetuate the family name; and Eddie, by talking to Johnny, is acting in

Sid's, the Family's, interest. Indeed, for all intents and purposes (and as Johnny's address insinuates, "You're an uncle"), Eddie *is* Sid.

Eddie finally, belatedly rebels against the organization—at least in the film, where he elbows Lamotta and screams to Johnny to call the police. It's too little, too late, however. Gonzales saps him mid-sentence, and Lamotta, grabbing the receiver, tells Johnny to "go out and meet the boys on the road," alone and unarmed, if he wants his "wife and kid to stay in one piece." Offscreen, a baby cries. In *Les Frères Rico* Eddie plays by the rules to the bitter end: "They had fooled him. Or rather, with him too, they had been enforcing the rules. They had used him to track down Tony. He had never had any illusions, had done his best to find his brother, and played the game."[12] Later, Lamotta calls him to relay, word for word, Sid's message: "*Tell Eddie it's all right.*" Eddie's reward for his supreme act of obeisance: "They didn't ask anything else. They never asked him anything difficult again."[13] Though Eddie's initially a zombie—"Things were still dull, without color, without taste, almost without life"[14]—the novel ends on a surprisingly expectant note. Eddie flies back to Florida, but instead of calling his wife to tell her when he'll arrive or going directly home, he has his chauffeur drive him to his business—in the novel, a fruit and vegetable emporium—where his right-hand man, Angelo, welcomes him back with one word: "Boss." This simple salutation gives Eddie hope that one day the color and taste will come back into his life. The last sentence of Simenon's novel is exclamatory: "He had worked hard, so very hard, since the store in Brooklyn, to get there!"[15] Eddie's brothers are dead, yet here, "in his own territory," he's still a boss.[16]

Whereas in *Les Frères Rico* Eddie is still working for the syndicate, in *The Brothers Rico* he has been completely out of the business for three years. Consequently, once Johnny's dead, he can't go back to being a boss, nor can he continue to pretend—as he does at the beginning of the film—that when he was part of the organization, he was only an accountant. In the conclusion to *The Brothers Rico*, Eddie—unlike his character in *Les Frères Rico*, who submits to his fate—is a changed man, the film cutting from an agonized Johnny going alone and unarmed to his death to Eddie waking up in the hotel room with Lamotta and Gonzales. (Gonzales, in a striking gesture, walks out of a bathroom toweling his hands.) When the phone rings at last, it's not Phil calling Eddie to give him Sid's blessing, as in the novel; it's just one of Lamotta's men tonelessly reporting that everything is "fine." Then Lamotta orders Gonzales to escort Eddie back to New York City.

Jack Shadoian has observed that the "true climax" of *The Brothers Rico* occurs "when Eddie realizes that he has been used and that he is powerless to prevent Johnny's execution."[17] After this, according to Shadoian, "the tragic potential of the film is exhausted."[18] Shadoian is right about the climax of Karlson's picture, but he's wrong about the hotel scene exhausting the film's "tragic potential," because Eddie's painful enlightenment does not end in his hotel room in El Camino.

On the flight back to New York, Gonzales, petulant because Eddie won't make small talk with him, acknowledges that it "was pretty rough back there in El Camino." However, as he says, "Ya gotta play the game according to the rules, not like your brother Gino." The fact that Gonzales voices Eddie's mantra in the novel—"He had chosen to belong to the organization and to play the game, and follow the rules"[19]—suggests that the rules no longer make any sense to Eddie. Equally or more importantly, Eddie picks up on what Gonzales, relishing his position of superiority, is really telling him: "What happened to Gino?" Gonzales: "Didn't you know? He tried to get out of the country against orders. Tough, real tough. Two of the brothers Rico gone." Overcome with anguish, Eddie covers his face with his hands as the stewardess, entering the frame, reminds him to fasten his seatbelt. In a haunting echo, the last thing we hear before the film cuts to the lounge of the Phoenix airport is the stewardess repeating, as in a dream, "Fasten your seatbelt, please." It's an order, as it were, of a different order—a beneficent as opposed to malignant one—and reintroduces a dimension that's been excluded from the film since the concluding scenes at the Felici farm, a woman's voice.

At the Phoenix airport, all clean lines and bright lighting, it's as if Eddie's back in the quotidian world—a sailor is dozing in a chair, a black man is mopping the floor—back on earth, back on his own turf. In the bathroom he meticulously washes his hands as Gonzales tries to make nice: "Listen, pal, let's get this straight. I got nothing personal against you. Just got my orders to get you back, so if you got any other ideas in that head of yours, forget about it. They'd only find you anyway. [Laughing to himself] Even if there ain't another Rico to send after you."

The setting is significant: the floor sparkles as do the chrome hand dryers and white porcelain sinks, while against the back wall a row of chrome-and-leather chairs rests on an elevated shoeshine stand, empty as the chair in Sid's apartment. Earlier in the film, in the bathroom, in his pristine home in Florida, Eddie was trying to forget his past, trying to wash away his sins. Now, standing before another mirror and confronted yet again with his own complicity in his brothers' deaths—Gonzales's cruel jest is the catalyst—he finally washes his hands of the organization, using his clasped hands to knock Gonzales out.

The straight cut from Eddie walking out of the bathroom and exiting the airport to a tight shot of the door of a police cruiser—the insignia reads "Arizona Highway Patrol"—officially signifies he has switched sides. When the cruiser pulls away, Eddie is standing in an exterior telephone booth, a palm tree swaying in the breeze. He's telling Alice to leave the house immediately and wait for him in "that place where those two people spent their honeymoon" (an allusion to the hotel in New York City where they stayed after being married) when a man jerks open the door and says, "Been looking all over for you." The syndicate, it appears, has caught up with Eddie, but in fact it's a truck driver who has agreed to give him a lift back East. The shot of Eddie fast asleep in the cabin of a trailer truck carrying new cars to market is a rich one, reflecting both his sudden fall in fortune and, as in the later traveling shot of him in an open railway car, his heightened awareness that, like his brothers before him, he's a wanted man.

Sid, mobilizing the vast resources of the organization, sets the bloodhounds on Eddie, but Eddie, at least for the moment, is free and it's as if Karlson's hand is freed as well. The film explodes into an extended montage, the film cutting from Phil on the telephone getting out the word that Eddie is "loose" to two men in dark suits and hats ripping open the screen door to the Ricos' bedroom. (This scene, given the film's opening sequence, reads like a violation.) In addition to the kinetic action and rapid-fire editing, the montage is littered with noir-inspired images and compositions: a low-angle canted shot of an anonymous man scanning passengers below a sign that says "Track 19"; a slow descending pan to another anonymous man vigilantly posted below a neon sign that reads "AIRPORT BAR"; and a wide shot of a neon sign "RENT A CAR $2.50 A DAY" superimposed over a close-up of Sid talking on the phone. The *plan américain* shot, superimposed over running trains and railroad tracks, of Eddie turning around to face the camera marks his fugitive status.

At a hotel in New York City, Alice is scanning a newspaper and pacing the room—a bed situated slightly off-center grounds the frame—when Eddie knocks. After he breaks the news to her about his brothers' deaths—"it was too late"—she

Mob Dragnet: dissolve from anonymous mobster searching for Eddie Rico (Richard Conte) to another anonymous mobster checking track 19 in *The Brothers Rico* (1957).

corrects him: "It was always too late from the first day you and Kubik . . .," then begins to backtrack: "You had no choice." Eddie quickly corrects her: "Twenty years ago when Kubik offered me that job, I should have thrown it in his face." Alice again tries to let him off the hook—"You had nothing to do with all that filth and corruption and killing, you didn't, you were just their accountant"—but Eddie, pacing now, knows better, insisting that he "stamped" himself "property of the organization."

Vowing to quit the syndicate, Eddie contacts Norah's brother, Peter, who agrees to help him get Alice out of the country and arrange a meeting with the DA. The next day at the Gotham National Bank—in a triangular three-shot that's reminiscent of the syndicate's surveillance of Eddie before Johnny's death—a young Italian-looking male clerk recognizes Eddie and makes a phone call. However, the ensuing three-shot of Eddie, Alice, and Peter sitting together in the backseat of a cab indicates that Eddie's actions are constructive rather than, as in the past and however unwittingly, destructive. This is confirmed when, once Alice and Peter depart for Idlewild, Eddie turns to see the young man standing outside the entrance to the bank, tapping a cigarette against a pack. The fact that he catches the young man unawares suggests, as in his earlier sighting of Vic standing watch outside Malaks' apartment building, that he's now in control of the gaze.

The shift in specular relations is dramatized at Fasoli's, an Italian restaurant where Peter has set up the meeting with the DA. In a remarkable matte shot, Eddie's standing inside the kitchen to the right of a swinging door with a circular window that looks out onto the dining room, and precisely because Eddie commands a view of the restaurant, he's able to see that Vic is tailing Peter. An equally remarkable composition occurs when after Eddie escapes through the restaurant's back door, he stops long enough to see if anyone has followed him. In the deep-focus reverse shot—the most intricately lighted in the film—there's a ladder of shadows in the right foreground, an empty chair in the middle, and, in the left foreground, a man hiding behind a stairwell, down which a meowing cat descends. The man appears to be Vic, but when he emerges from the shadows, we see that it's Eddie. The ambiguity not only suggests that Eddie's being pursued by himself but that the past may finally be catching up with him. Hence the evocative image of the empty chair, which recollects the early scenes in Kubik's suite and the later one in the men's room at the Phoenix airport.

Having outwitted the syndicate, Eddie returns to his childhood home on Mulberry Street and embraces his mother, who, after confessing it was all her fault—"I'm to blame"—plaintively asks her son, "What's there to live for?" Eddie, echoing Johnny's last, hopeful words on the phone (note the statue of the Virgin Mary in the background), replies: "There's another Rico, a new Rico, Antonio, who'll live without fear like a decent human being." Eddie then crosses the living room to the candy store—presumably to call the DA—where he's about to put a coin in the wall phone when a familiar voice calls out to him from offscreen: "Hello, Eddie." As Sid approaches from the right, another man with a gun is approaching from the left. In an expressive variation on the three-shot that Karlson has employed throughout the film, Eddie's momentarily caught between the gunman's shadow on the right and his own shadow to the left. Sid tells him to "take it easy," but Eddie, face-to-face with his "uncle" for the first time since both of his brothers were executed, bellows, "You dirty, rotten stinkin' animal!"

Sid, sporting a homburg (see, for example, Mr. Brown in *The Big Combo*), is, as always, measured: "I've got things to say, but not here." Eddie himself seems paralyzed until Mama, screaming "Murderer!" comes between the gunman and him, at which point Eddie calmly takes out the revolver he took from Gonzales in the bathroom at the Phoenix airport and—in a shocking because graphic cut—shoots the gunman in the temple. After another lightning cut to a low-angle shot of the gunman falling backward against a display case, shattering the glass, Mama falls to her knees, screaming hysterically at Sid, who shoots and wounds Eddie. Eddie, though, returns fire, killing him.

The headline of the *New York Chronicle*—"CRIME ORGANIZATION EX-POSED District Attorney Aided By Rico"—is the anticlimactic, semi-documentary transition to the film's epilogue. The wistful score, brightened by the sound of a xylophone, accompanies a long panning shot of Eddie and Alice driving down a palm-lined street and pulling up in front of the Bayshore Children's Home. It's a sunny day, the sky scudded with clouds as in the travel poster of Phoenix, and the children are outside on recess. Eddie parks the convertible and goes around to open the door for Alice, whose white gloves match the color of his tie, before fumbling for a moment as he looks for the recommendation letter from the DA. In the final wide shot, which rises inexorably toward the heavens, Eddie and Alice walk arm in arm toward the entrance of the orphanage, past a nun in a habit watching over a gaggle of small children moving clockwise in a circle playing Ring around the Rosie.

CODA: THE IDEA OF ORDER AT BAYSHORE

It's tempting to say that Richard Conte was born to play Eddie Rico in *The Brothers Rico*. If his "subdued characterization" of Martin Rome in *Cry of the City* (1948) reflects his ability to invest hoodlums with humanity, his performance as Max Monetti in *House of Strangers* (1949) as the family patriarch's "favorite son" at odds with his two brothers prefigures the intense fraternal dynamics of *The Brothers Rico*.[20] Similarly, while Conte's role as Mr. Brown in *The Big Combo* is a direct precedent for his portrayal of syndicate boss Eddie Rico in Karlson's film, Conte's sympathetic interpretation of mob assassin Nick Magellan in *New York Confidential* is the ultimate ironic pretext for *The Brothers Rico* as in the former Russell Rouse film, Eddie's completely at the mercy of the methodical mob violence that propels both narratives.

In the Jack Lait and Lee Mortimer exposé on which Russell Rouse's *New York Confidential* is loosely based, the authors evoke the new, post-underworld organization: "The rattle of the sawed-off tommy-gun, the whining whistle of the leaden slug, and the thud of its impact against flesh are no longer the sound effects in the orchestration of the gangsters' theme song."[21] The cinematic accent is not accidental, as Lait and Mortimer underline: "Everything is now organized into an institution, a hundred times the proportions of any outfit dramatized by Raft and Robinson."[22]

The crucial event in the time between the publication of Lait and Mortimer's exposé and *New York Confidential* was the Kefauver Committee hearings on organized crime. In fact, in *Washington Confidential* Lait and Mortimer "claimed that Senator Estes Kefauver of Tennessee, looking for a book to put him to sleep, picked up a copy of *Chicago Confidential*, and was shocked into action by the revelation it contained."[23] In Rouse's *New York Confidential*, the Kefauver Committee is explicitly referenced: the syndicate's attorney, Robert Frawley (Barry Kelley), warns Nick and mob boss Johnny Achilles (Onslow Stevens) about "rumblings in Washington of another Senate investigative committee like the Kefauver thing."

While the mobsters in *The Brothers Rico* conform to the new criminal paradigm sketched in Lait and Mortimer's *New York Confidential*, the Kefauver Committee is conspicuous by its absence in Karlson's film. As opposed to *711 Ocean Drive* and *The Big Combo*, in which the DA and police have a prominent role, law enforcement—except for the fleeting shot of the Arizona police cruiser—remains completely offscreen in *The Brothers Rico*. The law in Karlson's film is, to cite the prologue to *New York Confidential*, the "law of the syndicate" and, as in Rouse's film, it's pitiless. Anticipating Mr. Brown's maxim in *The Big Combo*, Charlie Lupo's precept in *New York Confidential*—that the "organization always comes first"—prefigures his own eventual demise. Thus, when Lupo himself becomes a liability, he's taken out by Nick Magellan; the irony is that Lupo originally brought Nick to New York from Chicago to eliminate an associate who "made an unauthorized hit." When Nick himself is executed by an anonymous assassin, the circle is viciously closed.

The conclusion to *The Brothers Rico* mimes the intrafamilial conflict of *New York Confidential* when, in the conclusion of Karlson's film, Eddie kills his surrogate father, Sid Kubik. However, unlike Nick Magellan, Eddie lives to see another day. Whereas Nick's assassinated at night on a New York City street, Eddie is blessed by the bright morning sunlight as he makes his way with his wife to adopt a child at the Bayshore orphanage. Compared, then, to the grim, disenchanting conclusion of *New York Confidential*, the happy ending of *The Brothers Rico* functions as a form of eucatastrophe in which the fairy-tale dénouement does not so much deny the catastrophic events that have preceded it as furnish a brief glimpse of joy, "poignant as grief," beyond this world.[24] Hence the statue of the Virgin Mary in Mama Rico's flat and the salvific presence of the nun in the final scene (see the sober image of the sister tolling a bell at the end of *Vertigo*), the mise-en-scène of which is not only consonant with the Catholicism of Italian American culture but also presages a sacramental notion of the family, a holy one distinct from the resolutely secular, murderous rituals of the Family.

The world therefore seems particularly grievous and life infinitely precious in *The Brothers Rico*, Eddie's redemptive actions notwithstanding, because both films remain unleavened by the consolatory pleasures of style. Writing about Fritz Lang's "nearly telegraphic clarity of narrative technique" in his '50s American crime films, Tom Gunning remarks that it "begins to resemble camouflage: the films strive to resemble the very environment they critique. Lang's classicism cloaks a distance and irony which penetrated to the cold rage for order that underlies the emotional expressivity of '50s culture."[25] Similarly, Karlson's style in *The Brothers Rico* perfectly models Eddie's clean, well-ordered life and the increasingly sanitized world of the syndicate, of which his own sunny, Floridian life is a hollow simulacrum.

This is the scrubbed-clean, denuded world of late '50s gangster noir: it may be sunny outside, there may be light, but there will be blood and, eventually, darkness. The gleaming bathroom at the Phoenix airport in *The Brothers Rico* leads straight to the shower sequence in *Psycho*, as if Hitchcock's postclassic noir, which originates in Phoenix, picks up right where Karlson's film leaves off. The horror of it all is that it happens in a perfectly nondescript hotel room, the sort frequented by impulsive young women on the run as well as former mob accountants turned suburban businessmen for whom sunshine turns out to be the ultimate mode of bewitchment.

PART TWO

THE ROGUE COP FILM

4

WHERE THE SIDEWALK ENDS

THEFT, ADAPTATION, PROTOTYPICALITY

> We were born to tread the earth as angels, to seek
>   out heaven this side of the sky
> But they who race alone shall stumble in the dark
>   and fall from grace
> Then love alone can make the fallen angel rise
> For only two together can enter paradise.
>
> —June Mills (Alice Faye), *Fallen Angel*

The first, if not prototypical, "rogue cop" film of classic American film noir is H. Bruce Humberstone's *I Wake Up Screaming* (1941), which was previewed for the trades only a little over a month after *The Maltese Falcon* (1941). Humberstone had directed a number of Charlie Chan movies in the 1930s, but *I Wake Up Screaming*, which was adapted from a Steve Fisher novel that was itself an homage to Cornell Woolrich (the investigating detective of both the novel and the film is named Ed Cornell), is a horse of a different color.

The plot of *I Wake Up Screaming* is a mix of *My Fair Lady* and *Peeping Tom*: sports promoter Frankie Christopher (Victor Mature) conspires with a couple of social associates to turn diner waitress Vicky Lynn (Carole Landis) from a "hash slinger" into a "celebrity." However, when she suddenly ends up dead after informing her sponsors that she's going to Hollywood, Frankie becomes the prime suspect. Though Cornell (Laird Cregar) knows that switchboard operator Harry Williams (Elisha Cook Jr.) is the culprit, he's intent on framing Frankie for stealing the girl of his dreams. In the meantime, Frankie and Vicky's sister, Jill (Betty Grable), become romantically involved and then act as amateur detectives à la Nick (William Powell) and Nora Charles (Myrna Loy) in *The Thin Man* series.

After the couple extracts a confession from Williams, Frankie goes to Cornell's apartment, where he discovers a shrine, complete with pictures and flowers, to the murdered femme.

Ed Cornell in *I Wake Up Screaming* prefigures one variation on the rogue cop formula in which the "contaminated law officer" abuses his position of authority and responsibility for a woman.[1] The film also introduces more than a note of "dark perversity" in the form of both voyeurism (Cornell "peeps" at Vicky through the front window of the diner like, according to Jill, "the wolf looked at the three little pigs") and "repressed homosexual passion" (see the creepy scene where Frankie wakes up in his apartment to find Cornell seated in a chair at the foot of his bed).[2] As the latter memes indicate and as Edward Cronjager's moody, high-contrast lighting attests, *I Wake Up Screaming* is, like *Stranger on the Third Floor* (1940), a seminal proto-noir, but is it a prototypical rogue cop film?

I Wake Up Screaming is, I want to argue, a *proto*-prototypical rogue cop film, and the reasons are at once formal, industrial, and historical. If the first, formal reason is something of a quodlibet, it's also one reason why Humberstone's picture is a proto- rather than full-fledged noir: the sound track. I'm referring to the film's periodic recourse to "Over the Rainbow" as Jill's theme. While one might argue that the Harold Arlen music is employed as a whimsical counterpoint to Frankie's big-city motif, Alfred Newman's "Street Scene," the persistent and ultimately distracting use of "Over the Rainbow" underscores the film's debt to the 1930s MGM musical just as Dwight Taylor's dialogue is more reminiscent of later rather than early Dashiell Hammett—that is to say, of *The Thin Man* (1934) rather than *The Maltese Falcon* (1929).[3]

The industrial and historical arguments against Humberstone's film are interrelated. *I Wake Up Screaming* is something of a one-off in that it did not initiate a subsequent cycle or series. As for the historical angle, the cultural-political conditions of possibility for the rogue cop film did not materialize until the late 1940s, a period marked by, among other things, the aftereffects of the war and the rise of anti-Communism. Though a case could be made that *The Bribe* (1949) is the prototypical rogue cop film—in this MGM production, federal agent Rigby (Robert Taylor) abdicates his duty when he falls in love with raven-haired siren Elizabeth Hintten (Ava Gardner)—his abdication, like Elizabeth's blackmail-induced bad turn, is momentary. (Elizabeth agrees to drug Rigby and thereby aid the war-surplus racketeers with whom her dying husband has been in league so that he won't be arrested and die in prison.) In the final analysis, Robert Z. Leonard's *Bribe* plays more like a noir-inflected melodrama than a classic rogue cop film.[4]

DETECTIVE STORY: IN THE LINE OF FIRE

"You think you're on the side of the angels."
—Mary McLeod (Eleanor Parker), *Detective Story*

The Bribe's status as a prototypical rogue cop film can be gauged by comparing it to a picture that appeared one year later, *Where the Sidewalk Ends* (1950), which benefits from a piratical relation to an acknowledged model of the subgenre, *Detective Story* (1951). In fact, *Where the Sidewalk Ends* has an unusually complex textual and production history because it's not only based on a pulp novel, William Stuart's *Night Cry* (1948), but it was substantially revised in light of Sidney Kingsley's prizewinning Broadway play, *Detective Story* (1949). *Where the Sidewalk Ends* was initially adapted from *Night Cry* by Victor Trivas, Frank P. Rosenberg, and Robert E. Kent, while Ben Hecht was engaged to write the screenplay. Hecht submitted a final script in December 1950, but Darryl Zanuck, the head of production at Twentieth Century Fox, "recommended several ways to mitigate the guilt of the main character,"[5] Mark Dixon, a rogue cop who accidentally kills a suspect, then endeavors to cover it up. (The copy for one advertisement reads: "This is the story of Mark Dixon, a tough cop . . . who could kill a man with his fists—*and one night he did!*")

Hecht submitted a revised final script later that December, and principal photography commenced on December 27, 1949, in New York City. Shooting concluded in Los Angeles on March 3, 1950, but on March 10, Zanuck, viewing the completed picture, insisted on extensive retakes. "One of Zanuck's motives in demanding the retakes," according to Chris Fujiwara, "may have been to capitalize on the similarity between [*Where the Sidewalk Ends* and *Detective Story*], knowing that *Where the Sidewalk Ends* would reach theatres before *Detective Story* and hoping to *steal* the competition's thunder."[6]

Detective Story, which Paramount produced and William Wyler directed, is a faithful adaptation of Kingsley's play. There are a number of brief exterior scenes, though the film is primarily set, like the play, on the second floor of the 21st Precinct police station in New York City, and most of the action takes place either in the main squad room or in the lieutenant's office. (Wyler and director of photography Lee Garmes utilize long takes and deep-focus compositions to animate what is essentially a stage set.) Jim McLeod (Kirk Douglas) is a police detective who's not above violating the constitutional rights of his "collars" by using a rubber hose. In the course of the film, he's busy booking Arthur (Craig Hill), a young ex-serviceman who has embezzled $480 from his employer, as well as helping to question two "cat burglars," Lewis Abbott (Michael Strong) and Charley Gennini (Joseph Wiseman). However, McLeod is obsessed—a police reporter refers to him at one point as Captain Ahab[7]—with a "black-market baby" doctor, Karl Schneider (George Macready). One of the doctor's patients, Miss Anderson, is in critical condition at Bellevue Hospital. In a police wagon on the way there— McLeod hopes that she'll be able to positively identify Schneider—the detective learns that Anderson has died and, after threatening the doctor ("You butcher one more patient and, law or no law, I'll find you and I'll put a bullet in the back of your head and drop your body in the East River"), McLeod punches Schneider in the gut, putting the doctor in the hospital.

Despite the fact that Schneider, unlike Anderson, manages to survive, his attorney hints that they have something on McLeod, and when Lieutenant Monaghan (Horace McMahon) interrogates a hood who owns a "creep joint in the Village,"[8] the lieutenant discovers that McLeod's wife, Mary, was impregnated by the "pig" (McLeod's term of abuse) before she asked Schneider to farm out the baby. McLeod has idealized his wife—"I thought you were everything good and pure"—but he now believes that she's a "tramp." (In Kingsley's play he calls her a "whore."[9]) The discourse of insanity circulates throughout the film—an "elderly, aristocratic-looking woman" claims a man is using radar to surveil her from the top of the Empire State Building[10]—and Mary's revelation brings McLeod to the breaking point. Mary, devastated, walks out on her husband. However, when she returns to the station to inform him that she's leaving (a taxi is waiting outside), McLeod tells her that he'd blow his brains out if she weren't waiting for him every day when he got home.

McLeod, whose moral indignation verges on the messianic, is—as Schneider's attorney remarks—a "law unto himself" or, as Monaghan puts it, "judge and jury." When a police reporter makes a case about the importance of proof, McLeod invokes his ability to sniff out the "stench" of evil, which, he claims, he learned to do as a child: "Every day of my childhood, I saw and heard that father of mine abuse and torment my mother with that criminal mind of his and drive her straight into a lunatic asylum. . . . Every time I look at one of these babies, I see my old man's face!"

McLeod never does resolve his relationship with his dead father. First, Mary walks out on him when he can't forgive her—in a paranoid spasm, he questions how many other men she's been with—then Gennini grabs an officer's revolver and McLeod suicidally tries to take the gun away from him. McLeod dies in the line of fire, passing away while reciting the Act of Contrition and, crucially, before he can be redeemed. In the end, it's as if the "justice of the streets" has come back, like a boomerang, to exact its own, violent form of revenge.[11]

For Dennis Broe, Wyler's *Detective Story*—unlike, say, his earlier *Wild Boys of the Road* (1933), which "lionized working-class survival"—codified the '50s police procedural by refocalizing the "working-class characters of the fugitive crime film into an array of suspects," cementing the "station house as the central location of working-class life," and modeling the parameters of the "now strictly regulated contours of the crime film."[12] By contrast (and Broe's related critique of *Where the Sidewalk Ends* notwithstanding), Otto Preminger's film radically reframes the antagonistic relation between the fugitive and cop; it also situates the sympathetic fugitive cop within the proletarian milieu of the metropolis and, in the process, reconfigures the limits of the rogue cop film.

WHERE THE SIDEWALK ENDS: HATE AND THEFT

> Paine had not stopped living like those thousands who were dead. He was beginning to come alive.
>
> —William Stuart, *Night Cry*

Where the Sidewalk Ends, which was the first in a series of noirs that Otto Preminger made in the 1950s, was succeeded by *The Thirteenth Letter* (1951) and *Angel Face* (1953). *Where the Sidewalk Ends* reteamed Preminger with a number of key Fox creative personnel, such as art director Lyle Wheeler, set decorator Thomas Little, editor Louis R. Loeffler, and, in particular, director of photography Joseph LaShelle. Equally or more importantly, it re-paired Dana Andrews with Gene Tierney, who had graced *Laura*, a singular picture that put the eponymous heroine, played by the ravishing Tierney, on a pedestal and then brought her swiftly back down to earth. When Laura enters her apartment midway through the film, having ostensibly been murderously disfigured, detective Mark McPherson (Dana Andrews) wakes up from a dream about the woman in the portrait only to see the dream girl herself, very much alive, standing before him like a veritable apparition.

Where the Sidewalk Ends is set, as the title indexes, "in a gritty, naturalistic milieu far removed from the glamor of *Laura*."[13] The opening credit sequence, in which the film's title is spelled out on a sidewalk with the same sort of white chalk used to outline a dead body, concretizes this difference. A man who's whistling Fox's perennial go-to tune, "Street Scene" (we see only his trousered legs and shoes), steps off a curb where rainwater sluices into a debris-littered gutter. The body of the film opens with a Times Square process shot of Detective Mark Dixon (Dana Andrews) and his partner, Paul Klein (Bert Freed), driving to the 16th Precinct station, where Detective Thomas (Karl Malden) is being promoted to lieutenant.

Although Dixon started out in the department at the same time as Thomas, he's being demoted, as Inspector Nicholas Foley (Robert Simon) informs him in his office, because of "twelve more citizen complaints against [him] this month for assault and battery."

DIXON: By who? Hoods, dusters, mugs, a lotta nickel rats.
FOLEY: You've gotta learn what's expected of a police officer and what isn't.
DIXON: I'll try to learn not to hate hoods.

FOLEY: You don't hate hoodlums. You like to beat them. . . . Your job is to detect criminals, not to punish them.

Dixon, it's plain, is a bad cop, one who's prone not simply to sarcasm but to sadism. Which is to say that he may as well have HATE tattooed on *both* hands.

Cut to the 43rd Street Hotel, where a floating crap game is in progress. Rich, out-of-town Texan Dick Morrison (Harry von Zell) is winning big to the dismay of Tommy Scalise (Gary Merrill) and the mobster's confederate, Ken Paine (Craig Stevens). However, when working girl Morgan Taylor (Gene Tierney), the decoy that Paine has used to lure Morrison to the club, tells her estranged husband it's time to leave, Ken slaps her twice across the face. For those viewers familiar with *Laura*, it's a shocking scene: Tierney may be beautifully dressed by Oleg Cassini (her husband at the time), but Morgan Taylor is not Laura Hunt, and this is definitely not the beau monde. Though Morrison gallantly intervenes, in the ensuing fight Paine punches him out like a clock.

Later, after Dixon and Klein arrive at the hotel and discover that Morrison has been knifed to death, Dixon grabs Scalise by the lapels and pulls "Dream Boy" up from a bed on which he's been reclining. The censorial Breen Office, referencing Hecht's stage direction about Scalise speaking in a "dreamy voice," commented that any suggestion that the mobster "is under the influence of narcotics" could not be approved.[14] Despite this caveat, Scalise is constantly putting an inhaler to his nose, and it's not because he has a cold. (It was common knowledge at the time that soldiers used Benzedrine inhalers during the war to stay alert.)

There's not a little bad blood, needless to say, between Dixon and Scalise: Dixon has been trying to take Scalise down for four years, and two years earlier the mobster made a "monkey" out of the detective by beating a murder rap:

DIXON: You're still a killer.
SCALISE: Why are you always trying to push me into the gutter, Dixon? I got as much right to the sidewalk as you have.

When Scalise proceeds to mention Dixon Sr.—"Your father liked me"—Dixon tells him to shut up. The detective is hot to handle Scalise (which, in Dixon's case, means manhandling him). However, Lieutenant Thomas, who has just entered the room, orders him to track down Paine instead.

Paine's address, 58 Pike Street, is an apartment building that sits in the shadow of the Manhattan Bridge. After Dixon pays the cabbie, he looks through a window where an old woman, Mrs. Tribaum (Grayce Mills), sits asleep at a table on which a radio is playing "Eine kleine Nachtmusik," then enters the building and stands outside the open door to Paine's apartment. (The detective is dressed in a dark

Cop/Killer: Detective Mark Dixon (Dana Andrews) stands over the body of Ken Paine (Craig Stevens) in *Where the Sidewalk Ends* (1950).

fedora and overcoat, and the low-angle shot foregrounds the darkness his figure cuts.) Paine is so drunk—he's on the phone trying to locate Morrison—that he remains completely oblivious of the detective. When Dixon finally interrupts him, Paine tells him to get lost, and when the detective doesn't budge, Paine springs up off the bed and slugs him. Dixon, whose pugilistic instincts have become second nature by now, punches him in the stomach, then lands a big uppercut that drops him like a tree.

Checking on Paine, Dixon lightly slaps his face, places a hand on his heart, and when Paine doesn't respond, feels his pulse. As the score rises, the strings trilling, the camera dollies into a medium close-up of Dixon, his face edged with shadow. Cut to a POV shot of a phone. Before Dixon can decide what to do, it rings (it's Klein), and while the camera tracks in again, he learns that Paine was an ex-syndicated columnist with a "head full of metal and a lot of friends." Dixon slumps against the wall—in the close-up his eyes are edged again with shadow—and his stunned expression registers the impact of Klein's communication: Dixon hasn't inadvertently killed a "nickel rat." He's killed a "war hero."

The POV shot of Paine's corpse splayed out on the floor decides the issue for Dixon: after he retrieves the ex-serviceman's kit bag from the closet, he empties out the dresser, stuffs the contents into the bag, and yanks the overcoat off the dead-heavy body. When we next see Dixon, he's dressed in Paine's trench coat, he has a bandage under his left eye, and he's carrying the dead man's bag. (For the noir locus classicus, see Walter Neff [Fred MacMurray] impersonating Mr. Dietrichson [Tom Powers] in *Double Indemnity*.) Dixon's about to get into the cab he previously called when he glances over at the window where Mrs. Tribaum, now wide-awake and wide-eyed, returns his gaze.

Dead Man Walking: Detective Mark Dixon (Dana Andrews) impersonating dead "war hero" Ken Paine in *Where the Sidewalk Ends* (1950).

In *Film Noir* Andrew Spicer observes that the "maladjusted veteran ceased to be a topical figure by the end of the 1940s, replaced by the rogue cop, another figure trained to kill, skilled in covering up his tracks, and a similarly destabilizing social force."[15] *Where the Sidewalk Ends* literalizes this replacement because, in the above paradigmatic sequence, the rogue cop transforms into the maladjusted veteran. In other words, in impersonating the dead man, Dixon not only effectively becomes Paine but metaphorically assumes his wound, as if his own distemper were a function of the war.

If the shot of Dixon-as-Paine standing before a barred ticket counter at Pennsylvania Station does not bode well for the detective, he's nevertheless determined to evade detection at all costs. When he returns to Paine's apartment, Klein is already there and has just checked a closet where the ex-serviceman's hat and uniform still hang. Dixon, however, gets to the other closet first, inside of which Paine's body is propped up against the wall like a dummy. Later, Dixon carries the dead man out over his shoulder, momentarily hiding behind a stairwell when Morgan's father, Jiggs (Tom Tully), comes looking for the man who hit his daughter. (In the wide low-angle shot where Dixon unloads Paine's body into the backseat of a car, a train on the elevated track above screeches to a halt.) Still later, at the precinct station, Dixon stands conspicuously in the background of a deep-focus shot—he's centered in the frame to the left of a diamond-patterned window, a fedora shading his face—as Lieutenant Thomas interrogates the taxi driver who drove "Paine" to Penn Station.

The same diamond-patterned window in front of which Dixon has been perched on a desk surfaces in the locker room scene that follows, in which Dixon and Klein retire for the night. The camera pans past a picture of a woman taped to a locker, after which Dixon pauses before the window—the camera is tight on his wasted face—beyond which the "dark city" lies, the windows lit up like little boxes of light. Dixon's face suddenly drops out of the frame, and in a striking time-lapse shot, night turns into day. When the camera eventually pans down to

Dixon, past the boxing pictures taped to the wall behind him, he's sitting up in bed, smoking, an ashtray full of stubbed-out cigarettes on the table next to him.

The above "girlie" and boxing imagery provides a sub rosa commentary on the next, dressing-room scene—we've just seen Morgan showing an outfit to a department-store buyer (the designer is played by Cassini)—where a blonde model is lecturing her about Ken as she applies pancake makeup to Morgan's bruises: "You keep thinking of him as a glamor boy—you won't see him for what he is. . . . So he won the war. . . . Does that entitle him to spend the rest of his life drinking barrels of whiskey and punching girls in the nose?" Therefore, there's no little irony when Dixon—"Mister Tough Guy"[16]—shows up, accompanied by Klein, to interview her.

Preminger's feeling for blocking and choreography—of bodies in repose or moving in space—is amply in evidence in the interrogation scene set in a back room where drawings of models, not "dames," decorate the wall: first Dixon's standing in front of and with his back to Morgan, who is seated (Morgan: "Ken and I separated three months ago"), then Dixon's standing to the left and rear of her (Morgan: "Kenneth was drinking and we had a quarrel" / Dixon: "I understand he hit you"); then he's standing in front of a Venetian-blinded window as she sits on a desk (Morgan: "My father went down to Ken's place after he dropped me. . . . He told me before if Ken ever hit me again, he'd beat [him]"); and, finally, Dixon's standing next to Morgan when he tells her, "Morrison was killed last night."

This is the "noir whirlpool": at the very same instant Morgan learns that Morrison was murdered, Dixon learns that the man he killed was married to her and, moreover, that the taxi driver who came to Paine's door when he was hiding in the stairwell was her father.[17] Is this why Dixon stops Morgan on the street as she's leaving for the day and asks her out to dinner? It's no coincidence that this scene—the first exterior, daytime one in the film—features Dixon and Morgan alone together for the first time. When the two return to her apartment so that she can change, Jiggs reminds the detective that he received a diploma from the mayor "for aiding Mark Dixon in a time of danger." (Jiggs picked up Dixon in his cab when the detective was chasing some thieves in Central Park.) The irony, of course, is that while Jiggs's anecdote speaks to Dixon's reputation as a good cop, Morgan's father, thanks to Dixon, is about to become the prime suspect in Paine's murder. The irony is redoubled when, as Morgan and Dixon are about to leave, Jiggs gives the couple his paternal imprimatur, remarking that at least his daughter is going out with someone who won't, unlike his current son-in-law, "land her up to her neck in crooks."

The film's coupling of Morgan with the man who, unbeknownst to her and Jiggs, killed her husband is reprised in a domestic scene set at a restaurant owned by a middle-age woman named Martha (Ruth Donnelly). She's obviously fond of Dixon, no doubt in part because he sent up her "wife beater" husband. (While Dixon's quick to use his fists, he does not appear to be disposed, like Morgan's estranged husband, to hit women.) Martha's affection for Dixon also mirrors Jiggs's unabashed admiration for him. In fact, if Jiggs, figuratively speaking, is a positive paternal figure for Dixon as well as a potential father-in-law, Martha is a surrogate maternal figure who wants Dixon to lay off the "dizzy blondes" with whom he usually consorts and settle down with a "lady" like Morgan: "Fella like him ought to be married to a beautiful girl—have a home, kids." Moreover, the fact that Martha relays this advice to Morgan *after* Dixon has left—Klein has just informed him on the phone that they've discovered Paine's body in the East River—sharpens the contrast between the detective's warring personalities: the rogue cop who has never married because he's too busy punishing crooks and the policeman who may finally have found something to live for besides trying to exorcise his father's ghost.

Earlier, at Martha's restaurant, Morgan, musing about her estranged husband, laid the blame for their present separation partly on his unemployment—"too much pride"—and partly on her inability to understand "what made him so mean and impossible."[18] While the first, economic predicament was not uncommon for ex-servicemen returning home after World War II, Morgan's allusion to Ken's meanness and obstinacy applies to both Dixon and Paine: Dixon, not unlike Morgan's husband, doesn't understand why he acts out the way he does and therefore remains totally subject to his psychic demons.

The doubling of the two men is literalized again, dramatically so, when Morgan and Jiggs are brought to Paine's apartment, where Lieutenant Thomas has summarily concluded that the taxi driver killed the ex-serviceman. The critical moment occurs when Thomas orders Dixon to pretend to be the dead man—to put on the ex-serviceman's hat and raincoat, tape adhesive under his left eye, and carry his traveling bag—so that Mrs. Tribaum can verify the identity of the man who got into the taxi the night that Paine was murdered. And, in fact, Mrs. Tribaum remembers that the man did not wave to her as Ken always did, which means that Jiggs, as Foley suspects, killed him. When Foley arrests Morgan's father, Dixon finds himself on the horns of a dilemma: if he confesses, he'll exonerate Jiggs, but he'll lose Morgan; if he doesn't, Jiggs may go to jail.

For Dixon, who's still driven by the desire for self-preservation, there's only one option. Meeting up with his partner at a bar, he announces he's going to make Scalise confess to both murders, and when Klein reminds him of Foley's orders, Dixon, his hand curling into a fist, threatens to hit Klein if he tries to stop him. Cut to a Turkish bath where Scalise's right-hand man, Steve (Neville Brand), is giving his boss a massage. Although the Breen Office was concerned about the script's inclusion of a "'pansy' character" in the department-store scene, it was not evidently troubled by Scalise's "penchant for surrounding himself with young muscular men, . . . his use of a sauna as a hangout, and his habit of receiving visitors lounging in bed" (as in the initial interrogation scene at the 43rd Street Hotel), all of which "carry strong gay connotations."[19] As in the earlier, hotel interrogation scene, Dixon grabs Scalise, who's wrapped up in a sheet like a mummy, and when Steve tries to restrain him, Dixon hits him so hard that he sends Steve staggering backward against the wall. What follows is not especially surprising, so much so that Dixon's aggression appears to mask a deep masochistic desire to be punished: Scalise's goons beat him to a pulp. What *is* surprising is that before the gang leaves out the back door (in a wonderfully atmospheric passage, they're briefly enveloped in a cloud of steam), one of Scalise's men has to talk him out of smashing Dixon's head in with a chair.

Dixon, who has literally been battered senseless, ends up at the Taylors' apartment, where Morgan answers the door in her robe. (The still-made bed in the living room indicates that her father's out.) As soon as Mark enters, holding a bloodied handkerchief to his chin, he sits down on the bed and says, as if to himself, "Where the devil am I? I keep coming and going." He stands up and is about to leave when he falls back against a wall:

DIXON: Why did I come here? I must have had something on my mind.
MORGAN: What happened to you?
DIXON: A run-in with Scalise and his pals.
MORGAN: Shouldn't I call the police?
DIXON: Let's leave the police out of this. I made a big idiot out of myself to-
    night, bigger than usual. . . .
MORGAN: I'll fix your head. Come with me.
DIXON: I suggest you use an axe.

Instead of taking an axe to his head, Morgan shows Dixon to the bathroom, where she cleans his wounds, applies a bandage to his jaw, and gives him a wet towel, which he presses against his forehead. The scene is a rich one: Morgan's the nurse and Dixon, like Paine, is suffering from a head wound so severe that he doesn't even know where he is or what he's doing. At the same time, if the bandage on Dixon's jaw is a "visual symbol of [his] inner damage,"[20] the fact that Morgan applies it suggests that if anyone can fix him, she can.

Dixon's temporary amnesia evokes certain '40s "tough" thrillers such as *Somewhere in the Night* (1946), *Crack-Up* (1946), *High Wall* (1947), and *The Crooked Way* (1949) in which the returning veteran's illness is a figure for a profound existential crisis.[21] In *Where the Sidewalk Ends*, it's also a trope for an equally profound moral crisis. In this sense, Scalise's men can be said to have knocked some sense into the detective, because Dixon eventually remembers why he came to the Taylors' apartment—to tell Morgan and Jiggs that they should hire a "big-time lawyer"—before confessing (it's obvious that he's talking about himself and Morgan's father): "Innocent people can get into terrible jams, too. One false move and you're in over your head." Dixon here voices the quintessential noir condition of being, the archetypal noir (anti-) hero "existentially adrift and trapped by circumstance."[22]

Dixon's liminal status—part cop, part killer—is highlighted when he returns to the precinct station. After Inspector Foley chastises him for going after Scalise and driving him underground, the inspector "invites" him to take a week off out of his annual vacation: "I want you to go someplace and get hold of yourself. Look at you—all bunged up like a barrelhouse vag! First thing you better do is get your head fixed up, inside and out." The scene ends, though, on an ironic, not to say ambiguous, note when Foley instructs Thomas to "try talking to Steve like Dixon would." This directive represents a remarkable about-face on Foley's part—with the proviso that one of the roles of the rogue cop in the police procedural is to forcibly remind the authorities that it's necessary at times to bend the rules.

Previously, in an exterior scene—only the second daytime one in which Dixon is shown on the sidewalk—the detective and Morgan are leaving Martha's café after the owner has "made love" to her because, according to Martha, he doesn't know how to. Morgan exclaims, "It's a wonderful day! No job, everybody against me, my poor Dad sitting in a cell, and it's a wonderful day!" (Morgan has been fired from her job because of the negative publicity surrounding her father's arrest.) Morgan's optimism is borne, it appears, of the blossoming romance between Dixon and her as well as the fact that she's off to see Ackerman, an expensive defense attorney whom Mark has raised the necessary down payment for. (The brief but telling scene where Dixon wakes up his partner in the middle of the night for a loan and Klein asks his long-suffering wife to pawn her jewelry testifies to the deep bond between the two policemen as well as the scant wages on which they're forced to live.)

Later, as Mark and Morgan are returning to his apartment, her earlier romantic enchantment seems to have vanished with the light: Ackerman has informed her that he won't take the case because he's too busy, though she suspects it's because her father may be found guilty. Now it's her turn to articulate the archetypal noir scenario: "I thought because Dad was innocent nothing could happen to him, but it will." Mark reassures her with a force that startles her that "it won't," at which point her suspicions are immediately aroused: "You know something you haven't told me." Mark turns away—he's about to tell her the truth about Paine's death—when, in the deepening silence, Morgan speaks instead:

MORGAN: You don't know what it's like to have your father in trouble.

DIXON: My father was a thief. He's dead now. He died when I was seventeen trying to shoot his way out of jail. I've worked all my life to be different from him.

Morgan's reaction represents a decisive turning point in the film: true to her post-separation epiphany, she first says Mark's name, then as "Street Scene" swells on the sound track, they kiss.

When Mark abruptly breaks it off—"You'd better go home. You're a sucker for wrong guys like Ken and me"—she insists, "You're not wrong. . . . I'm glad you told me about your father. You're not like him, I know." Is Morgan right? How different, really, is Dixon from his father? Mark may be on the "side of the angels" (as Mary McLeod says to her husband in *Detective Story*), but he has also crossed the thin blue line in the past, and having killed Paine and hidden the body, not to mention allowed an innocent man to go to jail, his behavior has been, strictly speaking, criminal. When push comes to shove, Mark does not—and, perhaps, cannot—confess to Morgan that he killed her husband. Instead, he confesses to the prime, if largely unconscious, cause of which Paine's death is an effect. In this light, Dixon's crusade against Scalise can be seen for what it is—a displaced act of violence against his father or, in a word, patricide: Dixon doesn't want to avenge his father's death. He wants to kill him.[23]

As Morgan lies down to sleep, Mark sits at a desk and composes a letter to Inspector Foley "to be opened in case of death":

> I didn't have the guts to tell you this when I was alive because I didn't want to end like Sandy Dixon's kid. That's what every hood in New York calls me— Sandy Dixon's kid. . . . I wanted to end up as a cop and that's what I'm going to do. I killed Kenneth Paine. It was an accident. I went in to pinch him, he slugged me, I hit back. How was I to know he had a silver plate in his head? But I covered it up like a mobster because I couldn't shake loose from what I was. Now I'm shaking loose. I'm going to get Scalise for you. He's a hood like my old man was. You won't have to worry about pinning the Morrison killing on him. You can pull him in for mine.

While Mark's composing the letter, we can hear his voice on the sound track, and a lamp casts his still bruised and bandaged face, shot in extreme close-up, half in light, half in shadow: the cop who still wants to do good and the cop who has acted like his old man—like, that is to say, a hood, like Scalise. In the letter Mark lays bare the root cause of his rogue behavior: that, for all his good intentions, he hasn't been able to come out of his father's shadow and that, in some profound sense, he's "still Sandy Dixon's kid." Consequently, in his own mind at least, the only way to shake loose of the past, to square his killing of Paine and Scalise's murder of Morrison, is to sacrifice his own life—to die, like McLeod, in the line of fire.

Though Fujiwara claims that Dixon "writes from the perspective of one who is already dead" and it's this foreknowledge that "finally liberates him to act against Scalise,"[24] Dixon, as we've seen, has already acted against Scalise and been severely punished by the mobster in the process. The difference this time is that Dixon knows he may die. At the same time, this knowledge is intimately bound up with another kind of foreknowledge. Before Dixon composes his letter to Inspector Foley, he leaves his apartment to meet with a stoolie, Willie (Don Appell), who agrees to sets up a rendezvous with Scalise. When Dixon returns, there's a "startlingly erotic" shot of Morgan,[25] a 3rd Avenue Athletics blanket thrown over her sleeping body. In other words, Dixon's death wish (to invoke the later, notorious 1974 rogue cop film starring Charles Bronson) is tangled up with his equally intense desire for Morgan.

Dixon's waiting under a streetlamp on East River Drive when a car driven by one of Scalise's hoods picks him up. (The shot of the sedan as the elevator ascends to the mobster's hangout located at the top of a parking garage—Dixon's sitting in the backseat next to one of Scalise's hoods—is an inspired one: a frame, as it were, within a frame.) Dixon immediately turns over his gun, and once he's frisked, he's escorted to Scalise, who is reclining, as usual, on a bed. (In what appears to be a sop

The Sleeping City: Detective Mark Dixon (Dana Andrews) gazes at Morgan Taylor (Gene Tierney) fast asleep in his apartment in *Where the Sidewalk Ends* (1950).

to the censors, a poster that reads "GIRLS" is plastered to the wall behind him.) Scalise is planning to leave the next morning, but Dixon will be left locked inside the room, an embarrassing situation that, Scalise adds, will give them "something to laugh about": "Maybe it will give the department a laugh, too." Dixon, needless to say, is not laughing: when the camera cuts away for the reverse shot, his face is halved in shadow and his eyes are narrowed with hatred.

When Dixon stands up (Scalise has previously ordered him to sit down), the mobster warns him that if he starts "mussing [him] up, [he's] gonna get it": "You'll only throw one punch and they'll let you have it." The audience understands that it's a fait accompli: in a reprise of the earlier, locker-room scene, Dixon punches Scalise in the face and, in response, one of Scalise's hoods shoots him in the shoulder. The hood is about to shoot Dixon again when, in a reversal of the sauna scene, Scalise stops him because he realizes that the detective has come there to frame him. Instead, Scalise orders Kramer (David Wolfe) to fix Dixon up so that he *doesn't* die.

While Kramer administers to Dixon's wound (in yet another echo—this time, of the bathroom scene at the Taylors' apartment), Scalise thinks aloud, and it's clear that he understands Dixon better than the detective understands himself:

> It's a fancy way of trying to frame somebody—getting yourself knocked off. A guy's gotta be out of his head for that. I didn't know a guy could hate that much, not even you, and all because your old man set me up in business. I got it added up now, Dixon. . . . You found Paine and slugged him and killed him and you took the body to the river. . . . And you've been walking around ever since, half cop and half killer. The man who hates crooks, the law that works by itself, the cop who can't stand to see a killer loose. So what is he? A hood and a mobster like his old man.

When the phone rings, one of Scalise's men reports that the police have beaten the truth about Morrison out of Steve. Scalise starts for the door, after which Kramer mutters, "What about the bandage?" Scalise's retort is short as a shotgun blast: "Let him bleed."

Once Scalise and his men have departed, Dixon tries the door—it's locked— then, noticing a staircase, climbs to the roof, where the elevator works are located. As the hand on the elevator "clock" winds down floor by floor, Dixon pulls the switch on the power, trapping Scalise's getaway car in the lift. There's the sound of a police siren, and Scalise, looking up, swears, "That dirty cop!" an apostrophe that's not without irony, as Dixon's identity as a clean cop was predicated on his own death and the written confession that he left for Foley.

The coda to *Where the Sidewalk Ends* introduces one final turn of the screw. After the inspector congratulates Dixon, whose arm is in a sling—"Always have to break orders, always have to do things your way"—Morgan walks in with the news that her father's about to be released. There's more good news as well: the inspector is recommending a promotion for Dixon. Foley then hands Mark's letter back to him, but Morgan is shocked when she sees the instructions on the envelope ("You expected to die"). Foley explains that Dixon was pretty sore at him and, after telling Mark to tear it up, suggests that he take a rest—"until [his] arm heals." "Dad's waiting," Morgan adds. "Will you come home with us?" A happy ending of the sort that Martha envisioned and Dixon could only have dreamed about before now appears to be in the offing.

The camera stays on the couple for a pregnant pause (it's a medium two-shot) before Mark finally asks Foley to read the letter. "What is it?" Morgan asks, and when Foley looks up before continuing to read, she adds, "Mark?" Even though the latter interrogative recalls her earlier, romantic address to Dixon in his apartment, one that can be said to have blocked, however unintentionally, his full confession, Mark still can't look at or answer her. Rather, his silence directs Morgan's attention to Foley, the embodiment of the law, who declares, "That clears up both cases. You're under arrest."

Morgan can't believe her ears and, pleading with Mark, says, "What is it? Please tell me." However, Dixon's still unable to tell her the truth and asks Foley if she can read the letter, at which point the inspector hands it to Mark, who, turning to face Morgan, hands it to her. Morgan reads it, then, looking up, eyes brimming with tears, softly says his name. Although Mark preemptively tells her good-bye, in the reverse shot Morgan's face is lit like an angel's:

MORGAN: Anybody can make a mistake.
DIXON: You mean you're gonna give Sandy Dixon's kid another chance?
MORGAN: Every chance in the world.
DIXON: That's enough to live for.

CODA: *NIGHT CRY*, OR RINGING THE CHANGES

In William Stuart's *Night Cry*, the rogue detective's name is Mark Deglin, and he has a "look of coolness and bitterness and cruelty about him."[26] At the scene of the first crime—a brownstone mansion where Morrison's found dead, knifed in the heart—Deglin complains to the medical examiner that "he's one of the best detectives on the force" and therefore shouldn't have been passed over as captain.[27] In other words, the novel draws an explicit connection between Deglin's resentment and his rogue propensities: an item in a tabloid opines that "he'll be taking it out on [the seamy side of the underworld] for what he didn't get in the recent Civil Service advances."[28]

In Preminger's film Dixon is, of course, demoted. Moreover, whereas in *Where the Sidewalk Ends* he's single, in the novel he's involved with a "canary," Janie Corby, who sings at a "fashionable and expensive" club called the Flamingo. A key scene in *Night Cry* occurs when Deglin returns to his apartment to find Janie curled up in an easy chair. When she flings herself at him and starts backing him into the bedroom, he slaps her "so hard in the face with his open palm that the impact rang in the apartment."[29] The difference between the novel and film is striking: the fact that it's Paine in *Where the Sidewalk Ends* who slaps Morgan effectively displaces the violence against women from the detective to the husband—from, that is to say, the explosively violent cop to the separated, ex-serviceman husband. This displacement, together with Martha's reference to her ex-husband as a "wife beater," makes Dixon's character more sympathetic than Deglin's.

In *Night Cry* Morgan Taylor's character is also substantially different than it is in Preminger's film. In Stuart's novel she's more reminiscent of the eponymous heroine of *Laura* than the working-class "mannequin" in *Where the Sidewalk Ends*. For example, her "comfortable and respectable parents" live in Greenwich, and after the row with Ken at the private gambling club and before she discovers that he has been murdered, she takes a taxi to her parents' house, where, the following morning, she takes a "bay mare" out for a ride at a local stable: "The clouds in the sky were higher and thinner. . . . A pale sunshine broke through, occasionally touching the trunks and branches of the huge, shedding trees with a hint of gold."[30] This idyllic autumnal moment has no real parallel in Preminger's film, which, set in the guttered environs of the city, studiously avoids any pastoral references. In Stuart's novel, by contrast, the country in the guise of nature is employed to mirror the decline of Ken and Morgan's marriage. So when Morgan comes to Deglin's apartment late at night to talk, she recounts how throughout the spring she had been watching a tree outside the back window of Paine's apartment, and "it was as if it was our tree."[31] In fact, the evening that Ken died, Morgan went to his apartment to tell him "maybe she was wrong," and even though he wasn't there, she went to the back of the room, where "the light shone from the window full on [the tree], and it seemed as though it was dying."[32]

In *Night Cry* Deglin's fascinated with Morgan—"He had watched her clear, pure profile, the way her eyes lowered, and lifted, the movement of her body in the chair, . . . the sudden trembling of her pale hands."[33] A romance between them never blossoms, however. When she comes to the precinct station with her father to talk to the captain (the DA thinks her former lover, Pete Redfield, killed her husband and Morgan disposed of the body), Deglin listens to her until she begins explaining why she went to the window ("I—I was watching a tree") before he gets up and walks out. Later, at a bar, Deglin gives the receipt for the incriminating kit bag to the bartender (it's stashed in a cardboard box at a Chelsea storage company) and asks him to give it, in turn, to the captain. In the final scene of the novel, Deglin returns to his apartment, where he borrows some money from Janie, then flees without her. The final words of the novel are "Run, Deglin. RUN!"[34]

The dénouement of Night Cry, in which Deglin goes on the lam, differs considerably—to understate the matter—from the complex, morally complicated happy ending of Where the Sidewalk Ends. While Deglin undergoes a moral crisis in the novel and puts into motion an act that will dispel what he calls the "illusion of truth,"[35] he does not turn himself in and therefore remains an outlaw. That is to say, he's still motivated by the desire for self-preservation, a drive that connects with his earlier, expressed resentment about not being promoted. It's here that the superiority of Hecht's screenplay becomes apparent, as Dixon's desire for self-preservation in Preminger's film is fueled not by advancement—he's nonplussed when Inspector Foley informs him that he's being demoted—but by an overweening desire to punish criminals. More important, a minor subplot in the novel—the Scalise brothers' waterfront robberies—becomes, in Where the Sidewalk Ends, a classically antagonistic relation between cop and criminal (this is the "Hecht touch") in which the cop's father can be said to have fathered the gangster. In this sense, Dixon and Scalise are, figuratively speaking, both siblings and, when the detective covers up his killing of Paine, brothers in crime.

Finally, the elimination of Janie's character and the attendant development of Dixon and Morgan's relationship in Where the Sidewalk Ends foregrounds the role of the family romance in the film. In the novel Deglin is effectively framing Redfield and Morgan. In Preminger's film the family romance compounds Dixon's guilt because he's framing not only a man who admires him, Jiggs Taylor, but also the father of the woman with whom he's falling in love. Moreover, Deglin's final description of Morgan in Night Cry—"It was incredible that someone like Morgan . . . should be touched by even so much as the edge of violent death"—applies more to the character in the film than the one in the novel. In Stuart's novel Morgan was formerly an army nurse—she met Ken while he was convalescing in a hospital—and her ostensible guilt hinges on a "War department photograph which had been released in the general news pool following the bombardment of an American hospital" and in which she could be seen "carrying a wounded man."[36]

The casting of the "ethereally beautiful" Gene Tierney in Where the Sidewalk Ends, paired with Dana Andrews for the final time—they had previously appeared together in Tobacco Road (1941), Belle Starr (1941), Laura, and The Iron Curtain (1948)—is critical.[37] On one hand, Tierney is too beautiful to be true, a being who appears to have been transported from another, alien world ontologically distinct from the "succession of downbeat boarding houses, diners, and gangster hideouts" that everyone in the picture seems to inhabit.[38] On the other hand,

Tierney's otherworldly beauty is essential to her character, her open-book face a direct counter to Andrews's grim, tight-lipped countenance, what one critic has nominated the "face of noir."[39]

Only such a seraphic figure could annul the fatal revenant that is Dixon's dead father and thereby tender a rogue cop the promise of redemption. Only a seraph could love someone who has just confessed to killing the former "war hero" she married. It defies belief. Yet just such suspension of disbelief is as much a part of gangster noir as, say, private detectives and femmes fatales. In *Fallen Angel* a con-man falls in love with the object of his con, and the cop, not the con man, kills the dark woman who, like Vicky Lynn in *I Wake Up Screaming*, is a waitress at a roadside diner. If Mark Dixon in *Where the Sidewalk Ends* is Mark McPherson five years after *Laura*, then the ex-cop who, mad for the girl, goes rogue in *Fallen Angel* is Dixon three more years down the line, the "bad cop" who wasn't lucky enough to have met a fallen angel who happens to look just like Gene Tierney.

5

THE THIN BLUE LINE

Surely this is not the best of possible worlds since
we can easily conceive of possible worlds that are
better.

—Gottfried Wilhelm Leibniz, *Theodicy*

If it's true that in 1950s Hollywood cinema "cultural politics shifted away from
working-class concerns," it's also true that the "protagonists of the now dominant
police procedural" who "surveyed and policed the neighborhoods" were anxious
about their place in the pecking order in an age when Americans were fast becoming "status seekers."[1] While *The Prowler* and *Shield for Murder* are not nearly
as well known as *The Big Heat*, they are provocative in their own right, shedding
shadow, as it were, on the rogue cop genre and the contentious issue of class in
mid-century Cold War America.

William McGivern's novels—*The Big Heat* (1953), *Rogue Cop* (1954), and *Shield
for Murder* (1951)—are especially significant in this regard, since the métier of his
protagonists tends to be law enforcement and the milieu of his fiction proletarian.
For instance, *Rogue Cop* mobilizes the familiar and familial trope of two brothers—one a veteran, one a rookie; one bad, one good—in order to explore the lure
of easy money for law-enforcement officers trying to survive on sixty-five dollars
a week. However, whereas *Rogue Cop* depicts the protagonist's abrupt about-face
and eventual redemption, *Shield for Murder* tracks a detective who, embittered at
being on the outside of the high life, goes from bad to worse when he murders a
bookie and steals his payoff in order to pursue the American Dream in the form
of a suburban tract home. In fact, the protagonist's ignominious death in Edmond
O'Brien and Howard W. Koch's film complicates the received wisdom about the
glorification of law and order in the 1950s crime film even as it calls into question

the middle-class-based consensus of the Cold War, as if the rogue cop were an inverted or displaced symptom of the "red" or alien other in all of us.

THE PROWLER

CAR CULTURE

It's almost impossible to overestimate the importance of automobiles and single-family homes in the evolution of the American Dream as well as the social space and class with which it's most associated in the twentieth century: the suburbs and the middle class. In the consumer republic that emerged in the aftermath of World War II, "first and foremost on the consumer's wish list was a private home."[2] As early as 1950, as a consequence of the Veterans Administration and Federal Housing Administration, this dream wish was realized to an unprecedented degree: "Single-family housing starts spurted from 114,000 in 1944 . . . to 1,692,000 in 1950."[3] In *Crabgrass Frontier*, Kenneth T. Jackson documents that these federally insured and mortgaged homes were located not in the cities but in the suburbs, so that by 1950 the "national suburban growth rate was ten times that of central cities."[4]

Of course, to get from the suburbs to the city and back (jobs and industry were still primarily located in urban areas), it became increasingly necessary to own an automobile. The car therefore became number two on the American consumer's wish list, a heretofore luxury commodity that, with cheap credit and plentiful fuel, a new national highway system and ever more efficient advances in mass, Fordist production, finally became available to the average American family. Although "as late as 1950, 41 percent of American families did not own a car," by the end of the 1950s, "75 percent of homeowners had bought [one]."[5] Americans went from taking the bus or train to being—to invoke a paradigmatic novel of the period—"on the road."

Automobiles became virtually synonymous with the American experience in the twentieth century, not unlike horses and the Western frontier in the nineteenth. Accordingly, the story of the American auto industry is not only "one of the most important dramas in modern American history" but also "defined who we are": "mobile and prosperous."[6] And *the* fantasy car for most mobile and prosperous Americans in the 1950s was a Cadillac. In *Fortune* magazine's annual survey of readers in 1950, "nearly half of all automotive owners in the United States would select a Cadillac if given their choice of a new automobile."[7] If, as Cadillac itself acknowledged in 1950, "only a small percentage of American motorists have ever owned or driven a Cadillac or, for that matter, so much as enjoyed a ride in one,"[8] a Cadillac was, as the conclusion to *Plunder Road* illustrates, the ultimate commodity-body-sign.[9] Dream wish and fantasy object, it was something to aspire to and even, in some exceptional cases, kill for.

CADILLAC

Joseph Losey's *The Prowler* (1951) is, as was immediately recognized upon its release in France, a *policier*, but the real generic prototype is the quintessential film noir, *Double Indemnity*. Losey had seen Billy Wilder's picture "many, many times" and considered it "one of the best films of its sort ever made."[10] While the resemblance is apparent in the plot—in both pictures, a man gets involved with a married woman and the husband dies—it's perhaps most obvious in the faux Spanish house in which the majority of the action in the first part of the film takes place. This house—one of "those expensive Hollywood imitations" that were not so much beautiful as status symbols—was, for Losey, "a horror."[11]

Before shooting on *The Prowler* commenced, a composite set was built and the director worked with John Hubley on what he called the "pre-design" of the film.[12] The crucial influence here, in addition to Hubley, was Bertolt Brecht. Losey had staged a famous version of *Galileo* with Charles Laughton in Hollywood in 1947, but it was on *The Prowler* that he learned how to combine theater and film. The aim, according to Losey, was to "perfect the visual aspect of a visual medium, also its auditory aspect, so as to show only the things you wanted to show for a specific effect or specific purpose."[13] This notion of "selective reality" is reflected in the way Losey and Hubley refined the set design, "reducing and particularizing the horror."[14]

It has been remarked that Susan Gilvray (Evelyn Keyes) is not a spider-woman like Phyllis Dietrichson in *Double Indemnity*.[15] Rather, Susan is seduced by Webb Garwood (Van Heflin), a spider-man or *homme fatal* who is not an insurance agent like Walter Neff (Fred MacMurray) in Wilder's film but a policeman. Webb, moreover, is less interested in "crooking the house," as Walter memorably soliloquizes at one point, than in having everything that it symbolizes: "the essence of the American dream."[16] Part of the allure of the postwar version of this dream was, as I've noted, the promise of a home in the form of a detached, single-family house. Consequently, when Webb and his partner, Bud Crocker (John Maxwell), responding to a call, approach the Gilvrays' home, Bud remarks, "Quite a hacienda," a comment that establishes a distinct class difference between the policemen and the house's inhabitants. Susan answers the door, and while Bud confers with her—she had just gotten out of the bath when she saw a man in the window—Webb, flashlight in hand, checks out the empty lot next door.

This split between interior and exterior action is critical to the film's political-libidinal economy and is foreshadowed in the film's pre-title sequence. In this stunning prologue, the camera is positioned outside the house and the audience

Viewer Voyeurism: exterior window shot of Susan Gilvray (Evelyn Keyes) après bath in *The Prowler* (1951).

can see—through a curtain-framed window—a blonde-haired woman, the top half of her body wrapped in a towel à la Phyllis Dietrichson in *Double Indemnity* as she looks in the mirror and removes a shower cap. After checking her hair, she briefly absents the frame; when she returns, she suddenly gasps in terror—she's looking to the right of the camera's perspective—and slams down the blind. The fact that this sequence appears, in conjunction with Lyn Murray's fanfare, superimposed on the blind—"HORIZON PICTURES PRESENTS"—suggests that the filmmakers were not unaware of the exploitative element of the pre-title sequence. (The film's original working title was "The Cost of Living," which is a reference to John Gilvray's [Sherry Hall] radio sign-off, though it was changed to *The Prowler* at the insistence of producer S. P. Eagle, aka Sam Spiegel.)

Even though the audience's POV in the pre-credit sequence is not perfectly aligned with that of the prowler, we nonetheless share his voyeuristic, "peeping Tom" point of view. So when Webb, checking out the premises, looks in at Bud questioning Mrs. Gilvray, we are aligned with his gaze. Susan's explaining to Bud that she saw the prowler not in the bedroom but in the bathroom window when Webb looks to the right, and the camera tracks laterally in the same direction, then to a medium, low-angle shot of Mrs. Gilvray opening the blind. The straight cut to Bud and Susan—the now "naked" window visible between them—sets up the older, happily married man's word to the wise: "Well, if I was you, from now on I'd keep the curtain closed. Did you ever notice in a bank they always keep the account room out of sight so the customers won't get tempted?"

No sooner has Bud completed his little lecture than Webb's face materializes in the window and Susan gasps again. When Webb suggests that "maybe the lady is

Peeping Webb: Officer Webb Garwood (Van Heflin) surprises Susan Gilvray (Evelyn Keyes) as she is conversing with his partner, Bud Crocker (John Maxwell) in *The Prowler* (1951).

just imagining things," she bridles, insisting to Bud, "He was just as plain as your friend's face right now," before slamming the blind again—this time in Webb's face. Bud's speech introduces, as Reynold Humphries observes, the "twin themes of sex and the commodification of the woman's body."[17] Unlike the audience's initial, sexualized view of Susan, which is aligned with the prowler's and is marked by a decided prurience, Webb's is mediated by the interior of the "hacienda" in which he first envisions her. From this architectural perspective, Susan's body—as in a window display—is defined less by her sexuality than by her conspicuous, upper-middle-class status.

The intimate relation between character and mise-en-scène is reiterated when once Bud and Webb leave the house, they pause and converse—notably, at cross purposes—by their patrol car. Whereas Bud encourages Webb to cultivate a hobby like his and his wife's rock collecting, Webb uses the detachable car lamp to play the light across the façade of the Gilvray house, commenting, "Pretty plush if you can get it." It's not entirely clear whether he's referring to the house or to the Gilvrays' lifestyle, but when Webb asks him what Susan's "angle" is, Bud answers, "Her? No angle—they're well-heeled." And when Webb then asks whether she's married, Bud replies, "Yeah, sure she is. Some crackpot. Squeezed enough dough to retire, then works for the fun of it." The concluding exchange between Webb and Bud before they depart—"That house must have set him back plenty" / "Yeah, maybe thirty-five, forty grand in this market"—recalls Bud's opening appraisal even as it reduces the Gilvray home to the strict, market-driven calculus of capital.

Susan's lying across her bed, sipping a cup of coffee and listening to the radio (an instrumental version of Dick Mack and Lyn Murray's "Baby") when a light starts to play across the room and a car door can be heard closing outside. The doorbell rings and it's Webb again, who has stopped by, he says, to see if she's all right. Susan asks (the question is loaded), "Do prowlers generally come twice in the same night?" and Webb answers by walking straight into the living room, where he promptly makes himself at home, plunking down on the couch. While she gets him a glass of milk (Webb claims he has to "keep in shape"), he learns, picking up a photograph, that she was once an actress but that it didn't work out. Susan: "I was a little short of talent." Webb's impromptu visit seems to have run its course when he mentions his name and Susan remembers that he was a star center for a high-school basketball team near Terre Haute, Indiana, where she grew up. In response, Webb recounts that although he went to college, he was benched by the coach and lost his scholarship because he wasn't a team player. Webb attributes what happened—with not a little bitterness—to "just another one of [his] lousy breaks"; otherwise, he would have a "nice soft job at one of those big bond houses" and would be "eating lunch every day at the university club." Now he's "just a dumb cop."

Susan, discomforted, tries to redirect the conversation by returning to their shared past in Indiana. After Webb asks her which street she grew up on, she says, "Lakeview," and he reminisces:

> You had sidewalks and lawns out in front. I lived down in Covington. My old man's idea of success was buck twenty an hour, union scale. He was a mainte-nance worker in the coalfields. He must have had a dozen chances to cut loose and make himself some real dough wildcatting. He was too yellow to risk his buck twenty an hour. He never made it.

From this confession, it's clear that Webb has not managed to substantially im-prove upon his father's way of life. The key word is "union," in the sense that Webb's notion of success is predicated not on collective or class interests but self-aggrandizement.[18]

When we next see Webb, he's at the Gilvray house again; however, this time he's in the kitchen, peering over Susan's shoulder into the well-stocked refrigera-tor and helping himself to a cold beer. As Susan carries a tray with cold cuts and a stack of bread into the living room, he crows, "If they could only see me now, I'd be the envy of the force," before scoffing at his fellow officers' preference for "hamburgers" on their night off. Susan immediately picks up on his derisive tone:

SUSAN: You don't like being a policeman, do you?
WEBB: Why should I?
SUSAN: Well, for one thing, you look nice in a uniform.
WEBB (referring to his natty suit): This is the only uniform I like.

Webb's quip anticipates the rebellious, antiauthoritarian structure of feeling epitomized by films like *The Wild One* (1953) and *Rebel without a Cause* (1955) that would bedaze mid-century America.

Webb and Susan are conversing in front of the radio cabinet—she's showing him the recordings that her husband makes of his programs "to improve his diction" (Mr. Gilvray, unlike Webb, not only enjoys his job but is an exponent of the Protestant work ethic)—when Webb abruptly reverts to the issue of his profession:

SUSAN: There's nothing wrong with being a policeman.
WEBB: Nothing wrong with digging ditches either or delivering the mail. I'd
    rather be one of those guys who shows up at ten in the morning after having a big argument with himself over whether he'll drive the station wagon today or the convertible.

As Bud's wife says about Webb when he later cuts out after having dinner at their house, he "hates being a cop," a blue-collar, working-class occupation that conflicts with his inflated notion of himself.

While Susan never encourages Webb's sexual overtures, she does solicit his desire for transgressive behavior and, in this sense at least, plays the part of the "bad girl" to his "bad cop." Thus, when Webb runs out of cigarettes, Susan tells him that her husband keeps a carton locked up in his desk, and with her blessing, he picks the lock with a bobby pin he plucks from her hair—without, however, asking for permission for the latter, presumptuous act. Webb's leading question to Susan—"Does he keep everything locked up?"—makes explicit what has already become implicit: that, for Gilvray, Susan is a prized possession locked away in the house like money in the bank.

Webb, having expertly picked the lock, lights up one of the stolen cigarettes when Gilvray's voice suddenly resounds on the radio, mirroring his behavior— "When I lean back from the table, I take the first puff of my cigarette"—and it's as if, as Webb himself says, Susan's husband is watching him. In fact, given Gilvray's ubiquity in the first half of *The Prowler*, it's striking that he only appears offscreen as a DJ on the radio. Yet as Susan herself dimly recognizes, she's subject to a form of sonic surveillance that is perverse precisely for being so incorporeal. Echoing her earlier admission that she has to listen to her husband's broadcast every night "because he always asks [her] how he was," Susan tells Webb that her husband "always knows what [she's] doing."

Initially, Susan married her husband because she wanted a "big home" and a "family," but now, without any children, the house radiates, as Foster Hirsch notes, "an atmosphere of defeat."[19] Susan's alienation is mirrored in the Diego Rivera print, *The Flower Carrier* (1935), that decorates the dining room wall. For example, while Webb's surreptitiously exploring her husband's papers, Susan goes to the kitchen to get him another beer, and when she reappears, she's momentarily framed in the doorway, the Rivera print to her right above a bouquet of flowers on the table, a composition that links her with the "domesticated proletariat . . . destined to be exploited by the men in her life."[20] The script underlines the theme of romantic exploitation when Webb tries to kiss Susan. Mortified, she manages to fight him off—"You're a real cop, you want everything for free"—and then, when he tries to kiss her again, slaps him three times: "What do you think I am? I told you to leave me alone. Now, get out of here."

When Webb later returns to the Gilvray house, as we know he will, he comes in the official guise of a policeman and ostensibly to apologize. But as "Baby" plays softly in the background ("The right time, baby, to fall in love"), he claims to suffer from "homesickness"—a pregnant word, this, given his itch for the Gilvray house—and wonders out loud what would have happened if, in the past, they had crossed paths at a school dance in Terre Haute. Turning up the radio, he asks Susan to dance, and despite the fact that she pleads with him not to kiss her, he does, the camera cutting to a shot of his hat sitting on the phonograph on which her husband plays his "diction" recordings: as cosseted and radio-friendly as John Gilvray's voice is, it's no match for Webb Garwood's insidious terms of endearment.

On Webb's next visit to the Gilvray home, his fifth, he tells Susan that his two-week vacation begins the next day and asks her to accompany him to Las Vegas to see a "motor court" that he's dreamed about owning. With this real estate "working for him twenty-four hours a day," Webb claims, a man "amounts to something—he's got some position in the community." Susan, of course, can't get away for a day, let alone two weeks, so when she doesn't show up at the airport, Webb drives to her house, where he shines the car light on the exterior and repeatedly hits the horn to make her come outside.

There's bad news. Susan's husband, suspecting the affair, has quit his job and threatened to kill both of them. Worse yet, at least for Webb, she feels "rotten." Webb, defeated, returns to his single, sparsely furnished room at the Angela Hotel, where, when Susan calls, he tells her that "it's quits" and hangs up. For Pierre Rissient, action in Losey is "inscribed in décor"[21]—here, the human target riddled with bullet holes hanging on the wall above the bed on which Webb lies, shaving with an electric razor. When Susan later shows up unannounced at his room— "Take me away now!"—Webb, referencing her Lakeview past, insists that even if she did leave her husband, she would start to hate him because she would "miss the things [she's] used to," the "easy life stuff" like the maid and the house. Standing at the end of the bed, Susan acquiesces: "I've been wrong. I've forgotten what it was like to have self-respect," and as soon as she's out the door, Webb falls back on the mattress, a big smile breaking out on his face. In the overhead, high-angle shot that follows, he tosses a balled-up piece of paper, a version of the "Dear Susan" letter he was composing, and tosses it two-handed, as if it's a basketball, into the bowl-shaped ceiling fixture, a *gestus* that contradicts his repeated insistence to Susan that their romance is, as he just said to her on the phone, "finis." In fact, Webb has only just begun his scheme to lure Susan even deeper into his web of deception.

It's night, and after dropping off Bud, he drives to the Gilvrays and pretends to be a prowler, slashing a screen window with a knife, then opening and shutting a gate to make it squeak. Webb waits patiently in his cruiser until the "prowler" report has been relayed on the car radio and he can return to the Gilvray home. When Susan's husband, armed with a "popgun" purchased because of the original prowler, comes outside to look around, Webb, who's hiding in the bushes, shouts "Halt!" and shoots, killing him. At the coroner's inquest, Webb maintains that the shooting was an accident and that he's never met Susan before. (Bud, who's sitting in the audience next to him, is so astonished that he tells Webb he "must be getting old": "I've known you to forget faces but not a figure like that!") Susan herself blurts out at one point that Webb's a "murderer," but when she testifies— her voice is so faint that the coroner hands her a microphone—she disavows ever having seen him, and the shooting is ruled an "accidental homicide."

Acquitted, Webb immediately retires from the police force and begins his campaign to insinuate himself back into Susan's life. First, he approaches Susan's brother-in-law, William Gilvray (Emerson Treacy), and offers to give her seven hundred dollars—his "entire life savings," as Gilvray later recounts to Bud—to tide Susan over until she's back on her feet. Moved by Webb's magnanimous gesture, Gilvray refuses to take the money but promises to talk to Susan on Webb's behalf. When we next see Webb, he's returning to the scene of the crime, dressed in a sharp suit and carrying a box of flowers.

The scene is pivotal not simply because Webb manages to persuade Susan that he didn't kill her husband in cold blood—according to him, "the whole thing turned on a freak accident"—but because it demonstrates the role of décor, costuming, and blocking in *The Prowler*. Carpets are rolled up on the floor, white sheets are draped over the furniture, the shelves are bare, and Susan, who's wearing white gloves, is packing John's diction recordings. (The fact that the gloves are dirty hints that while Susan may be innocent, she's not without culpability.) Still, as with so much else in *The Prowler*, the most evocative aspect of the mise-en-scène is more a matter of absence than presence: in this particular case, the ashen outlines of the frames of the prints, pictures, and paintings that formerly adorned the walls. These blank spaces point to the hollowness at the heart of petit bourgeois interiority. The house has died, as Hirsch notes, "and the literally bare rooms only reinforce the barren quality that emanates from the house when it was 'full.'"[22]

This said, the room, pace Hirsch, is not literally bare. In fact, early in the scene, the console radio, which has been moved from against the wall to the middle of the room, now stands between the couple like Gilvray's ghost, and as they're conversing, Susan picks up a bunch of wilted flowers and idly sets them on the cabinet. These dead flowers evoke Rivera's *Flower Carrier* and her former, radio-mediated life with John Gilvray; they also suggest, since Webb has brought flowers, that even as Susan is saying good-bye to one relationship, she's about to enter into another, even more exploitative one. Therefore, after Webb swears on what he says is the "only thing [he] ever really cared about"—his love for Susan—that he didn't kill her husband, he insists that she, in turn, reconfirm her belief in him. Her rhetorically extravagant response—"I do, I do, I do, I do"—is the segue to the following nuptial scene and Susan's desire to believe, despite considerable evidence to the contrary, that Webb's telling the truth.

Cut, via the sound of a tolling bell, to a crane shot of a church where a funeral is in progress, then to another church across the street—not in shadow, as the first one, but in sunlight—from which newlyweds Webb and Susan Garwood are happily exiting. (The tour de force camerawork—the 180-degree shot captures both the funeral and the wedding in one continuous take—is, as Losey himself recalled, the beginning of his "baroque style."[23]) Gilvray, responding to a reporter's question—"How do you feel about this union?"—comments that it's time to "forget the past" and, appropriately enough, the newlyweds' car is wrapped like a wedding present. However, the concluding, overhead shot of the car's roof—there's a white ribbon bow in the shape of an X—hints that their future together will be vexed.

Though Raymond Lefevre observes that with *The Prowler* "Joseph Losey becomes Joseph Losey"—"the lucid painter of a progressive disintegration within a décor"[24]—this disintegration is not immediately apparent. In fact, the score is blithe (a particularly lyrical version of "Baby"), and once the Garwoods arrive at the motel court, Webb picks up Susan and carries her over the threshold of the brightly lit owner's apartment. When a buzzer interrupts their homecoming, Webb, however, quickly abandons his new wife to check out how his business is doing. The flashing neon "VACANCY" sign is, like the X, portentous. Webb bounds into the front office, where the Talbots, an attractive young woman and a much older man, have just registered and where Webb stares at the woman so intently that her husband hustles her out of the office. In the meantime, Susan's unpacking Webb's suitcase only to discover his service revolver (after the inquest, he insisted that he "couldn't bring [himself] to touch a gun as long" as he lived) while in the front office, Webb's busy playing a slot machine.

When he eventually strolls into the bedroom with two glasses to make a toast, Susan queries, "Haven't you noticed I haven't been drinking much lately?" Webb, realizing that she's pregnant, begins to cry, but it's difficult to say whether he's genuinely moved that he's going to be a father or whether he's already worried that, since his wife's four months pregnant and Gilvray was impotent, their testimony at the inquest will now be subject to intense scrutiny. In this extended sequence, which exhibits Losey's flair for "intimate, small-scale theatricality,"[25] the director marshals all the elements of classical sound cinema to convey the Garwoods' anxiety. Not only is the bedroom furnished with twin beds (a convention, of course, of the period), but Webb and Susan are also physically separated by a radio. The radio is not playing, yet as in the post-inquest sequence at the Gilvray house, it speaks volumes: Gilvray is one ghost who will not be silenced. Losey's acute sense of audio-vision is reflected, moreover, in the constant rumble of traffic and the periodically flashing lights from the trailer trucks rumbling past on the highway outside, a ceaseless din that indicates just how far the Los Vegas motel court is from the family-friendly peace and quiet of the Los Angeles suburbs where Susan previously resided with her husband.

In fact, it's as if the outside world, like the siren that stops Webb and Susan's conversation cold at one point, has already encroached on their increasingly fugitive dream of happiness. Despite the easy life that the motel court promises— "even when you're sleeping," according to Webb, "it's making money for you"—the move to the motel court is a distinct regression. Since the "plain white walls of the owner's apartment and its arched doorway . . . repeat the dominant architectural motif of the house," the motel court is the "architectural equivalent of Webb's soullessness."[26] That motif is imprisonment, one that's mirrored in the bars of the bed against which Webb rests his head after he learns Susan's pregnant, as well as the doorway in which he's framed when he retreats to the living room to smoke a cigarette and brood on this sudden reversal of fortune.

As Lefevre has observed, the locations in The Prowler detail a progressive deterioration from an expansive home in the suburbs to a motel court in Las Vegas to an abandoned shack in the Mojave Desert. In Los Angeles, Webb was bored to death by Bud's stories about his rock-collecting adventures with his wife; now he remembers his former partner's anecdote about a "rip-roarin' mining town" called Calico, the site of one of the "worst Indian massacres in the history of the Southwest."[27] If, according to Bud, Calico is the "tail end of creation," it's also the ungodly place where the Garwoods' baby—with Webb as the unlikely midwife— is about to be born.

And yet, as Susan's rose-tinted attitude upon arriving in the desolate ghost town betrays—"Should we take the penthouse or the bridal suite?"—it might as well be Niagara Falls. The dissolve to Webb polishing his new Cadillac sedan while Susan's inside washing the dishes is a perfect, if parodic, "version of 1950s domesticity."[28] When Webb, whistling, goes inside, he throws the dirty dishwater out through a gaping hole in the wall, then, in an echo of their initial, fateful coupling, puts on another record before he asks Susan to dance. (The song is "Baby," which has acquired a new "double meaning."[29]) Later, as they stroll and watch the sunset, Webb is ebullient, waxing about all the "good breaks" that their "kid," unlike "his old man," will have: "That kid's gonna be on the beam the moment he's born!" Webb's fantasizing about the next time that Susan is pregnant—she'll have the "biggest private room, in the best hospital in Vegas, nurses around the clock, flowers, doctors, nothing but the best"—when the booming sound of John Gilvray's voice (theatrically amplified) shatters this reverie: "I'll be seeing you, Susan."

This ghostly, beyond-the-grave address is the beginning of the end of Webb's dream. Suddenly, Susan's beset by stomach pains (and, perhaps, pangs of guilt), and as a storm blows in, the wind whips through the shack, ripping a white bedsheet that has been acting as a temporary wall off its nail tacks. The cutaway to the Cadillac outside, now coated with dust, suggests that all of Webb's labors have come to naught. When Susan screams in pain, Webb decides it's finally time to go for a doctor, but before he leaves, he takes out his suitcase and removes his revolver. As Susan suspects, he plans to kill the doctor if he recognizes them.

Doctor James (Wheaton Chambers) safely delivers the baby—not a boy, as Webb had hoped, but a little girl. However, when Webb goes inside to check his wife (the father-to-be has been nervously waiting outside), the doctor drives off with the baby and the key to the Cadillac. As Webb frantically searches for the spare key, Susan, who has warned the doctor and hidden the key underneath her, assails Webb: "You murdered my husband! You would have killed a doctor!" Webb doesn't even bother to lie this time:

> So what? I'm no good. But I'm no worse than anybody else. You work in a store—you knock down on the cash register. You're a big boss—the income tax. Ward heeler—you sell votes. A lawyer—take bribes. I was a cop. I used a gun. . . . How am I any different from those other guys? Some do it for a million, some for ten, I did it for sixty-two thousand.

Now that Susan knows the truth and the doctor has had enough time to get away, she throws the key at Webb.

Though Webb races off in the Cadillac, in a poetically just twist of fate his escape route is blocked by another car, the Crockers', who have come looking for the Garwoods. Bud's overjoyed to see his former partner, but Webb, blind with desperation, repeatedly smashes his car into the Crockers' until he notices police cruisers in the distance, at which point he abandons his beloved Cadillac and literally runs for the hills, scrambling up a mountain of gravel, slipping as he goes. He's about to reach the summit when one of the policeman calls "Halt!" and when Webb doesn't obey, the officer fires and Webb falls, his lifeless body sliding back down the hill.

The fact that Webb dies just like Susan's husband is not lost on the audience, whose gaze is now aligned not with Webb but with Susan, who watches from inside the shack, her face pressed against the glass. For all his exertions, Webb ultimately ends up back where he began: on the outside, his precipitous fall from the man-made mountain a product of his "get-rich," "gold-digging" dreams and a testament to the "Ozymandian delusions of a society grounded in the pursuit of wealth."[30] That the dénouement of *The Prowler* is set in the Mojave Desert, the same location as the conclusion of *Greed* (1924), is not accidental. In his "analysis of human behavior and in the scale of his themes," Losey, according to Paul Mayersberg, is the "von Stroheim of post-war cinema."[31]

Equally important, *The Prowler* is indelibly marked by the tumultuous cultural-political period in which it was produced. In 1945, while Losey was employed at MGM, he became a member, like Dalton Trumbo, of the Communist Party. By 1951 the second wave of hearings instigated by HUAC was about to begin, and in the intervening years the FBI had been tracking Losey's activities. (The file would eventually run to eight hundred pages.[32]) When Losey learned that he was about to receive a subpoena to appear before the committee, he fled the country. It's in this light or shadow—what the French call *la chasse aux sorcières*—that *The Prowler*, the screenplay of which was written by Trumbo and credited to soon-to-be-blacklisted writer Hugo Butler, appears as a *film gris*.[33] While the film's indictment of greed—"$100,00, a Cadillac and a blonde"—is one part of its critique of the American Dream, another, rather less obvious part is the way in which the surveillance and persecution of American citizens in the "age of affluence" is intertwined with the politics of class. The latter, "gray" aspect remains one of the most plangent attributes of *The Prowler*, not least if one remembers that—in a truly subversive touch—John Gilvray's voice in the film was dubbed by none other than its famously blacklisted writer, Dalton Trumbo.

THE BIG HEAT

SOMETHING

The Big Heat, with the possible exception of *The Big Combo* and *Touch of Evil*, is the most celebrated rogue cop film. The source material is William McGivern's novel of the same name. In general, Sidney Boehm's screenplay is a faithful adaptation of the novel—in both texts the protagonist is detective Dave Bannion—but there is, at least in retrospect, one striking difference. Whereas the opening of Fritz Lang's film rack-focuses on the suicide of Tom Duncan and the ripple it causes in city government and civil society, McGivern's novel includes a subplot: the murder of a gas station attendant that occurred the previous week in Northeast Philadelphia.

Bannion's partner, Gus Burke (Robert Burton), has arrested a "Negro" suspect in a "cheap, brown suit" who claims he "didn't kill nobody."[34] When Bannion arrives at the station for his shift, Burke smiles at him and says, "I could find out in ten little minutes if you'd just let. . . ." Bannion stops him cold, "There won't be any of that stuff on my shift."[35] Bannion then walks over to the man and tells him, "We just want the truth from you. . . . If you've done nothing wrong, you've got nothing to worry about."[36] Later we learn that a beat cop has in fact verified the Negro's alibi. It turns out that the "man's record looked good": "He was employed as a body-and-fender man around town, had never been in any trouble with the police, and his family were respectable people."[37] "We've got the wrong guy," Burke admits. "Well, we can let the right one go," Bannion replies, "which is something."[38]

The Negro, as the man has been called up to this point, disappears from the novel until Bannion's wife, Katie, is killed by a car bomb intended for her husband. In the deep wake of her sudden death, Bannion becomes obsessed (Burke tells a fellow cop, "He's going off like a bomb") with tracking down the syndicate criminals responsible for her murder. Desperate for any sort of lead, Bannion goes to the home of the body-and-fender black man:

> The house, an ace-deuce-trey type on Pine Street, with three rooms stacked on top of another, was shabbily furnished but clean. There was a warm pleasant smell of stewing meat and rice. . . . The front door opened. . . . This was Ashton Williams, the young Negro Burke had had in two weeks before as a murder suspect.[39]

The house's warm smell reflects Bannion's immediate positive reaction to the black working-class family who lives there. The house may be poorly furnished, but it's "clean," a cardinal epithet in a novel about police corruption.

Compare McGivern's capsule description of Ashton Williams's home with the apartment building where Larry Smith, the young hood who hired Slim Farrow to wire Bannion's car, resides: "a huge but elegant apartment house that featured uniformed doormen and a discreetly lavish atmosphere for anyone who could afford its prices."[40] The apartment itself is equally lavish: "a modern, four room apartment . . . brilliant now with the morning sun. Everything was glinting in it; the bright yellow drapes, the blond, maple-wood furniture, the cocktail shaker on top of the big combination bar and record player."[41] Larry's on top of the world, but his boss, Mike Lagana (Alexander Scourby), is anxious about the "loud-mouth reformers."[42] Not Larry, whose only real worry is how to persuade Lagana that it's good business to peddle "horse": "You always have them around, do-gooders, busy bodies, their pants in an uproar about slums, garbage collectors, colored people being kept out of polling stations . . . and all the rest."[43] If Selma Parker (Edith Evanson) provides the link in Lang's film between Slim Farrow and Larry Smith, Ashton Williams is the vanishing mediator in McGivern's novel between the haves and the have-nots, the privileged few and the disenfranchised many.

NOTHING

William McGivern's novel opens, like Lang's film, with a policeman's suicide. However, his name is not Duncan but Deery, and he lives in an apartment, not a house. At the same time, the Deerys' apartment is, like the Duncans' home in the film, understated. About the room in which Deery kills himself, the narrator says, "It was a pleasant room, a luxury that a man without children could provide for himself in a small, city apartment."[44] The bedroom where Dave Bannion talks with the widow, Mrs. Deery, is slightly more luxurious: "Bannion turned the knob and entered a very clean, very neat room, furnished with fragile elegance. . . . Mrs. Deery was seated on a brocaded sofa. . . . The legs and back of the sofa were bright with gilt."[45] If the key word in the first passage is "luxury," one of the key terms in the second passage—in addition to "clean" and "gilt"—is "fragile." In other words, the Deerys appear to be better than middle class, but this class status is precarious.

This uncertain class status is confirmed when Bannion returns to the Deery apartment to confer with Mrs. Deery after he has talked to Lucy Carroway, a "hostess" at the Triangle Bar who was once involved with her husband when he owned a summer home in Atlantic City. At the end of Bannion's visit, having learned nothing new from the tight-lipped widow (except, of course, that Lucy Carroway is a "liar"), he casually asks, "Do you still have your place there?" Mrs. Deery answers, "No, we had to sell it years ago. . . . With the prices, we just couldn't afford it."[46] The question is, How could an honest cop afford a summer home in Atlantic City in the first place?

In Sidney Boehm's adaptation of McGivern's novel, the initial action has been moved from the city to the suburbs. The décor is, again, understated. However, the bedroom in which Dave Bannion (Glenn Ford) talks to Mrs. Bertha Duncan (Jeanette Nolan) features a triple-paned mirror that not only suggests that he's under her spell—that is to say, he only sees what she *wants* him to see[47]—but also initiates the complex play of mirrors in *The Big Heat*. The prologue to this interrogative scene in Lang's film is Tom Duncan's suicide: there's the sound of a gunshot and Bertha rushes downstairs. However, after the initial shock, she seems less concerned about her dead husband than with the letter that he has left for the district attorney.

Bertha opens and reads it, then, after closing the blinds, phones Mike Lagana, who, in McGivern's words, has the "police department, the whole city, in his hands."[48] In the novel we never see Mrs. Deery contact Lagana; the phone call is therefore significant in Lang's film because it introduces the audience to Lagana *before* Bannion goes to the Duncan house. Cut to a young man in a white robe handing a phone to Lagana, who, having just been wakened, props himself up in bed to take the call. After Lagana speaks elliptically to "the widow," the young man lights his cigarette and dials the number of Vince Stone (Lee Marvin) for him. The portrait of Lagana is stereotypical (he's wearing silk pajamas and is framed by an enormous oak headboard), though there's also a homoerotic subtext, one that can be traced back, like the trope of the "languidly luxurious" crime lord, to classic gangster pictures like *Little Caesar* and *The Public Enemy*.[49]

Dissolve to Vince Stone's apartment, where Debby Marsh (Gloria Grahame) is sitting on the couch in the living room, her back propped up against the arm and her legs sticking straight out. (Her hieratic posture, we soon learn, is as unconventional as her personality.) Vince's apartment is decorated in an aggressively modern style with a built-in bar; an abstract, faux-Cubist painting; and numerous mirrors for, among other things, Debby to admire herself in. Compared to the previous scene, in which Lagana's face is initially halved in shadow, Stone's apartment is so brilliantly lit that it glitters.

In McGivern's novel Stone's apartment is "expensively furnished" but "impersonal"—"His idea of class was a suite in a good hotel"—and is used for both "business and entertainment": "The manager was pleased with the arrangement; Stone's parties in the penthouse were insulated from the rest of the building. He was a valuable tenant; the management realized that when they got their tax bills from the city."[50] Stone's penthouse apartment is proof positive of the archetypal young hood's rapid rise to the top and attests to the organization's stranglehold on city government. When, in Lang's film, Stone comes to the phone, he's wearing a light-colored shirt with white cuffs and collars, and his diamond ring and tie pin, gold cufflinks and watch chain, are conspicuous as he stands talking to Lagana. If clothes and accessories make the man, he's made it. Clothes also make the woman. In McGivern's novel Debby's "wearing a gold lamé hostess gown . . . and high-heeled golden sandals"; in the film, she's dressed in a white Grecian number—more negligée than gown (the costumier is Jean Louis)—that's slit down the front.[51] Like the young man who lights Lagana's cigarette and dials the phone number for him, Debby is coded as a servant or slave. However, unlike Lagana's valet, her sarcastic tone and manner—"Oh, Vince, it's him!"—mark her, narcissism and moll costuming notwithstanding, as an independent spirit with a mind very much her own.

The first three locations in *The Big Heat* are connected via class status and phone calls to the syndicate. While the "real purpose of these calls is to block the suicide's note"—"the letter of public confession becomes repressed as a new message system sets up a detour through private lines"—the Bannion home and its image of "lower-middle-class felicity" provide a distinct counterpoint to the "series of well-appointed interiors that opens the film."[52] This said, the Bannion residence, especially if one takes into account that he's a sergeant rather than a beat cop like Webb Garwood in *The Prowler*, reads as middle rather than lower-middle class. In fact, the interior of the Bannion house—in this sequence, we see the living room and kitchen—is almost as brightly lit as Stone's penthouse, albeit the décor is modest: this, the film seems to say, is an honest detective's home.

Dave and Katie's (Jocelyn Brando) relationship also provides a distinct counterpoint to Vince and Debby's. Unlike Stone, who, after taking Lagana's call, orders Debby to "shut the door and see if anyone needs a drink," Dave puts down the newspaper—he's reading about Tom Duncan's suicide—to help his wife set the table. Moreover, whereas Stone dominates Debby, or at least tries to (in this he can be said to be overcompensating for his own abject subservience to Lagana[53]), Dave and Katie's marriage—she sips his Scotch and takes a drag from his cigarette—appears to be an egalitarian, companionate one. The ensuing exchange, like a lot of the dialogue in Lang's film, is lifted directly from the novel:

DAVE: How you manage steaks on my salary—you know, downtown, they
    just don't believe me.
KATIE: Tell them you married an heiress. Next year, when Joyce starts kindergar-
    ten, you're gonna have to kiss the steaks goodbye until she finishes college—
    unless you become police commissioner in the meantime.

As opposed to the fast, high living ostentatiously on display in Stone's penthouse apartment, the Bannions, who are already thinking about their daughter's future education, are associated with classic middle-class virtues like thrift and foresight. Katie's mocking reference to her husband's reliance on the "book" to raise their daughter (the allusion appears to be to the sort of child-development handbooks popularized in the 1950s by Dr. Benjamin Spock) points to Dave's cooperative role in the work of child rearing even as it depicts the couple as quintessential '50s middle-class suburban parents.

If the Bannion marriage represents the "domestic tranquility that the '50s saw as ideal,"[54] two phone calls disturb this picture-perfect scenario. In the first, Lucy Chapman (Dorothy Green) calls during the above steak-and-potatoes dinner and asks to meet with Bannion. Cut to The Retreat, another brightly lit space like

Vince Stone's penthouse, where the men outnumber the women and the booze flows freely. In McGivern's novel the nightclub is called the Triangle and it's suffused with a "nervous," sexual excitement: "The long, oval bar, which imprisoned a colored trio on a tiny bandstand, was crowded with sailors, soldiers, and sharply dressed young men, who were covertly eyeing the chorines from the next-door burlesque house."[55] (As with the elision of the character of Ashton Williams, the fact that the James Meehan Trio is elided in Lang's film—except for a sign outside—represents a determinate erasure.) This underworld environment—both the bartender and the slick customer at the bar eyeball Bannion—defines Lucy Chapman. (In the novel when Bannion asks Lucy if she's a hostess, she replies, "Well, that's putting it pretty fancy.") Lucy relates that she was seriously involved with Duncan and that he had asked his wife for a divorce; Lucy also mentions that he "owned a summer place" in Lakeside. However, not unlike the scene set in Bertha Duncan's bedroom, Bannion can see Lucy only in the light of The Retreat, and in this harsh artificial light (see the series of pinups on the wall), her insistence that the police department is "covering up for a cop's widow" is blasphemous; for Bannion, there can be no possible comparison between a B-girl and a policeman's widow. Lucy flatly disagrees: "The only difference between me and Bertha Duncan is that I *work* at being a B-girl."

Bannion's contempt for Lucy is tangible, but he returns—good cop that he is—to interview Mrs. Duncan, who's stiffly posed on the couch next to a photograph of Mr. Duncan. Bannion begins by warning her that Lucy might try to blackmail her about her husband's affair, adding, "She probably thinks you're wealthy." "A wealthy policeman," Mrs. Duncan rejoins, "would be a novelty." However, when Bannion inquires about the Lakeside home, Mrs. Duncan, provoked, refuses to answer the question in the interest of preserving, she claims, her dead husband's "good name."

The teletype that Bannion reads when he returns to his desk at the station broaches the first, offscreen act of violence in the film:

UNIDENTIFIED WOMAN FOUND DEAD 6.26 AM OFF COUNTRY PARKWAY. THROWN FROM CAR AFTER BEATING AND TORTURE. DRESS AND SHOES LABELED LAKESIDE FASHION SHOP.

At the county morgue, the coroner, who couldn't be more blasé about Lucy Chapman's death—"trouble always catches up with a girl like her"—concludes that it was a "sex crime" perpetrated by a psychopath: "You saw the cigarette burns on her body?" "Yes, I saw them," Bannion responds, "every single one of them." In both McGivern's novel and Lang's film, the heat is produced by both the police and the syndicate, though Bannion, unlike the coroner, already knows that Lucy's murder is not a "sex crime." It's a "hit."

Still, as soon as he returns to the station, Lt. Ted Wilks (Willis D. Bouchey) calls him on the carpet for "pestering" Mrs. Duncan before asking, then ordering him to lay off the Duncan case. When Bannion mentions Lucy Chapman's death, Wilks describes her as a "barfly," the same metaphor that the bartender at The Retreat uses to describe women like Lucy: "They come and go like flies. . . . They're floaters—not much more than a suitcase of nothing between them and the gutter." If social prestige in *The Big Heat* is predicated on one's residence, then Lucy's death amounts to—to italicize one of the most charged words in *The Big Heat—nothing*.

The baby carriage that Bannion finds abandoned on the sidewalk outside his house when he returns home evokes both the "baby boom" associated with the '50s suburban nuclear family—see the subsequent three-shot of Bannion with his wife and seven-year-old daughter, Joyce (Linda Barrett)—and projects the kind of future that Bannion's daughter, unlike Lucy, can look forward to, one in which family and homemaking are, at least for women, the foundation of happiness. But unlike Lieutenant Wilks, and despite the manifest class differences between Joyce and Lucy Chapman, Bannion remains haunted by the death of the B-girl, so much so that when he tries to add a block to the toy police station that his daughter has been building, he inadvertently knocks it down. (The fact that Bannion refers to it as a "castle" and Joyce says it's a "police station" indicates the inextricable link in *The Big Heat* between home and civil society, the private and public spheres.)

Bannion is still ruing his bad mood and behavior when the phone rings and Katie relays the expletive-laced message. While Lucy's brutal death retrospectively confirms the intrusive, disquieting character of the first call, the second, obscene one is a direct threat to the Bannions' domestic well-being. Incensed, Bannion goes straight to the source, Lagana's private residence. In McGivern's novel, it's located on the city limits: "Mike Lagana lived out here, in a sixteen-room house with an English country tone to it. His home was boxed by six acres of land, impeccably cleaned and pressed by a Belgian gardener, and sat sturdily and prettily in the cup of a shallow green valley."[56] The fact that the estate is "impeccably clean" recollects McGivern's description of the Duncans' bedroom—no working-class, *How-Green-Was-My-Valley* milieu here. Although Lagana's Tudor estate reflects the "grandeur of an upper-class lifestyle,"[57] the police detail denotes his privileged, inviolate social status and the wholesale corruption of the city's law enforcement:

POLICEMAN: Who do you wanna see?
BANNION (showing his badge): Mike Lagana.
POLICEMAN: Oh, sorry, I didn't recognize you, Sergeant.
BANNION: How many men on the detail, officer?

POLICEMAN: Three of us on the day and night shift, four after midnight.

BANNION: Ten cops to watch over Mr. Lagana. One hundred bucks a day of the taxpayers' money.

POLICEMAN: Well, Mr. Lagana kinda runs things. I guess that's no secret.

BANNION: No, that's no secret at all.

After Bannion pushes past the butler, he pauses in the foyer, gazing at the adjoining ballroom, where Lagana's daughter's party is raucously in progress, complete with a swing band, jitterbugging teenagers, and servant-served refreshments.

Eventually, Lagana, who's dressed in a suit with a carnation pinned to the lapel, appears and escorts Bannion into a wood-paneled study furnished with books and tapestries, chinoiserie and Old World paintings, a room fit for a prince—or a big-time hoodlum. Standing beneath a portrait of his mother hanging above the marble fireplace, Lagana boasts, "She lived here with me in her own suite of rooms, her own bath, everything," before he asks Bannion if he needs help with the police "benefit dance" or the "pension fund drive." The detective replies, though, that he's there to discuss Lucy Chapman's murder: "It was an old-fashioned killing, Prohibition kind." (Bannion's description of the killing points up the embourgeoisement of the criminal class, which has moved "out of the shadowy stairwells and back alleys" of the metropolis to "luxurious estates."[58]) Now it's Lagana who's offended: "I've got an office for that sort of thing. This is my home, and I don't like dirt tracked into it." Then, miming Wilks, he sits down behind his desk (note the two phone lines) and, assuming the full weight of his authority, declares, "I've seen some dummies in my time, but you're in a class by yourself."

The preceding and ensuing exchange between Bannion and Lagana can only be called, as Gunning puts it, an "argument about class":

BANNION: We don't talk about those things in this house, do we? Oh, it's too elegant, too respectable—nice kids, party, painting of Mama up there on the wall. No place for a stinkin' cop. It's only a place for a hoodlum who built this house out of twenty years of corruption and murder. I'm gonna tell you something. You couldn't plant enough flowers around here to kill the smell.

LAGANA: I warned you to get out.

BANNION: Cops have homes too, only sometimes there isn't enough money to pay the rent, because a cop gets hounded off the force by your thievin' cockroaches for trying to do an honest job.

LAGANA (pressing a button): George!

BANNION: What's the matter, you think I live under a rock or something? Your creeps have no compunction about phoning my house, giving me orders, talking to my wife like she was . . .

If the last, dramatic ellipsis punctuates, like Bannion's demotic language and brush-off of the butler, his defiance of the protocols of polite society, Lagana, by contrast, is the epitome of the '50s, post-Prohibition mobster: he honors his mother's memory, dotes on his daughter, and appears to be a respectable businessman. The stink of Murder, Inc. is, pace Bannion, nonexistent. The only thing that Lagana's "castle" reeks of is money.

Bannion's dressed down again by Wilks for busting into Lagana's house and punching out his bodyguard, though the critical sequence in *The Big Heat* occurs that evening at Bannion's home. After finishing the dishes in preparation for a night out at the movies, he's having second thoughts about being a police detective when Katie encourages him to stay on the force and not to compromise. The close-ups as they kiss are unusually intimate for Lang, and Dave whispers, "Let's stay home." (This union is both romantic and sexual.) Then, while he puts Joyce to bed, Katie leaves to pick up the babysitter. Suddenly an explosion rocks the house, and Dave races outside to see his wife trapped in his car, which is burning and mangled from the blast.[59] The bomb has killed not only Katie but also any possibility of happiness for Dave Bannion. In an era when "tomorrowland" was the watchword, his future's already embalmed. This, too, is "the big heat": the suburban, nuclear-familial American Dream embodied by the Bannion home and marriage incinerated in a flash.

In the following scene, set in the commissioner's office, Higgins (Howard Wendell) behaves not unlike Lagana, proffering Bannion a loan from the police fund to tide him over. Sounding even more like Lagana, Higgins informs Bannion that "Wilks has eight men on it, full time"—"Don't worry, there'll be a payoff"— adding, "Why, there isn't a man in the entire department [who] wouldn't give a month's pay to break this case." Bannion cuts him to the quick: "What about you, Commissioner?" While the police detail that Higgins has assigned to protect Bannion's daughter is ironic, recalling the police contingent at Lagana's house, the commissioner's recourse to the word "payoff" is equally, not to say more, ironic (since he's being handsomely paid off to look the other way), as is the last part of their exchange—"How much would you give?"—which echoes the Red Cross poster "Give Blood Now" in the main office of the police station.

The dissolve to Bannion's house, empty now except for the baby carriage and a single phone line, emphasizes the very real price that Wilks's and Higgins's corruption has exacted. Because the mover's still there and a taxi's waiting for Bannion, we see the house in the "process of being stripped bare, shot from a high angle which captures its stark, almost geometrical emptiness": "Lang's X-ray vision into the emptiness at the heart of things."[60] The mover, gesturing to the carriage, reminds Bannion that it will be billed, like the rest of his possessions, "quarterly on the storage charges." Dave's about to walk out when his partner, Burke, walks

A House Is Not a Home: POV shot of Detective Dave Bannion (Glenn Ford) contemplating an emptied-out house after the bombing death of his wife in *The Big Heat* (1953).

in and reports that Wilks "feels lousy about what happened": "He said any off-the-record help is yours." "Tell him to stop bleeding for me," Bannion snaps, "it will run all over his pension." Then, before he leaves, Bannion takes one last look at what once was and now will never be, tears welling in his eyes. It's a devastating moment, a glimpse at the fragility of the American Dream and life itself.

The dissolve to Debby dancing and humming a rhumba to herself as she stirs a goldfish-bowl-size glass of martinis at the built-in bar at Stone's penthouse apartment highlights the violence—the loss and pain and suffering—on which Stone's extravagant lifestyle is predicated. Contemplating her (not, I might add, without a certain wonderment), Vince describes her "career" to Larry: "Six days a week she shops. On the seventh she rests." Debby's conspicuous consumption offers a vivid contrast to McGivern's description of Bannion gazing at his home for the final time: "It was strange and familiar to him now, as impersonal as a furniture arrangement in a shop window."[61] If Debby's hyper-consumption references the rogue materialism of postwar American capitalism, she also represents an active counter-motion or mode of resistance to Stone and Lagana's practice of death in life. Pretending to be a circus ringmaster with a big hat and hoop, cracking a whip and putting his animals through their paces, Debby mimics Vince—"Hup and sup, Larry! Hup and sup, Larry!"—until Lagana walks in the door and Vince cuts her off: "Check the kitchen, baby, will ya." Debby resumes her act, though this time as the object of her impersonation: "Now it's Debby. Hup, Debby! Hup, Debby!"

In the meantime (in the literal sense of the word), Bannion, consumed with finding out who murdered his wife, goes to a junkyard where, in the background, sparks fly from a welding torch. McGivern writes: "The 'graveyard' was a mile long

Mirror Double: Debby Marsh (Gloria Grahame) primps as she and Vince Stone (Lee Marvin) share a cocktail in *The Big Heat* (1953).

stretch of automobile junkyards . . . that crawled like a rusty ugly growth along the border of the city. . . . Every yard had small mountains of bodies, democratic heaps of smashed-up Cadillacs and broken rusty Fords."[62] The owner of the junkyard patiently listens to Bannion—he's sympathetic—but refuses to help him: "Nothing here for you, mister, nothing at all. You see, I've got a wife and kids, too." While the smashed-up cars at Victory Auto Wrecking evoke Katie's violent demise—death as the ultimate form of democracy—the exchange between Bannion and Atkins foregrounds the impact that the syndicate has had on working-class citizens who, like the junkyard owner, are too scared, in Bannion's words, "to stick out [their] big fat neck." Still, as Bannion's departing, an older, crippled woman, Selma Parker, hobbles over to the chain-link fence—the shot–reverse shot imprisons both characters in its crisscross pattern—to tell him about Slim Farrow, a recently deceased mechanic who may have rigged Bannion's car.

Now that Bannion knows the name of the person who hired Slim Farrow, Larry Gordon (Adam Williams), he returns to The Retreat, where Gordon's sitting at the bar playing craps. Bannion, however, doesn't know that it's him and has just ordered a beer when Stone burns a cigarette into a woman's hand for picking up a pair of dice too quickly. Debby, who's also sitting at the bar, is impressed with the way Bannion puts her sadistic boyfriend in his place—"You like workin' girls over, don't you?"—and, once Vince leaves, offers to buy him a drink. Bannion doesn't mince his words: "With Vince Stone's money? I'd choke on it." Debby nevertheless runs after him, and despite the fact that Bannion insults her again— Bannion: "Aren't you Vince Stone's girl?" / Debby: "The way you ask it, it sounds like a bunch of dirty words" / Bannion: "Well, that was the general idea"—she goes back with him to his hotel.

Her reaction upon seeing his desolate hotel room—"Say, I like this, early nothing"—not only recalls Bannion's emptied-out house and the junkyard owner's plea ("Nothing here for you...") but also exposes Bannion's metaphysical homelessness, a condition closer to nothingness than being. As Debby sits on the bed propped up against some pillows, Bannion asks her if her luxe life with Vince Stone is worth it:

BANNION: Is the good good enough?
DEBBY: Clothes, travel, expensive excitement, what's wrong with that?
BANNION: Nothing, if you don't care where his money comes from.
DEBBY: The main thing is to have the money. I've been rich and I've been poor, and, believe me, rich is better. Did you think I was an heiress before I knew Vince?

This conversation, like the earlier one between Bannion and Lagana, can be said to constitute an argument about class; the difference is that Debby's rhetorical question about being an heiress hints that she may be more like Katie Bannion than Lagana.

Though Debby's perfectly happy to talk to Bannion, albeit not "out of school," as soon as she chides him for being as "romantic as a pair of handcuffs" he puts her in a cab. Bannion's blunt rejection of Debby—"I wouldn't touch anything of Vince Stone's with a ten-foot pole"—has, however, fateful consequences. When she returns to Stone's apartment, he asks Debby where she has been (Larry followed her to Bannion's hotel room), and when she lies, Stone throws a pot of boiling coffee in her face. Stone's savage act of violence is reminiscent of his behavior at The Retreat and points to him as the psychopath behind the murder and torture of Lucy Chapman.

In *The Big Heat* the women who are the object of violence (with the exception of Katie Bannion) are all B-girls and associated with a gangster retreat rather than a suburban home—a bar, as it were, rather than a kitchen, alcohol rather than coffee. The film's ambivalence about working women is symbolized by Debby's hideously disfigured face, the left side of which is scarred. The good or innocent side is associated with Katie Bannion; the bad or corrupt one with Bertha Duncan.

Duncan's perfidy is demonstrated in the scene where Bannion returns to her house, his third and final visit, to interrogate her: "The furniture's the same, nothing's been changed, you haven't started living the high life yet." (In fact, Bertha's wearing what appears to be a new pearl necklace and matching earrings.) The dialogue between the two bristles with their mutual contempt for each other:

BANNION: You protect Lagana and Stone for the sake of a soft plush life.
MRS. DUNCAN: The coming years are going to be just fine, Mr. Bannion.
BANNION: There aren't going to be any more coming years for you—none at all.

In McGivern's novel Bannion's about to shoot Mrs. Deery when his arm suddenly drops and the "muzzle of the gun [is] pointed at the floor": "I don't have the right to kill you." In the film, Bannion's strangling Mrs. Duncan—an act that rhymes with his previous, near-strangulation of Larry Gordon—when the police, alerted by Lagana, arrive.

The difference between the novel and film is considerable: while Debby later assures Bannion that he couldn't have killed Bertha Duncan—"If you had, there wouldn't be any difference between you and Vince Stone"—Bannion's final interaction with Debby in Lang's film is fraught with ambiguity. When Bannion receives yet another disruptive phone call and learns that the "relief detail" at his brother-in-law's apartment building hasn't arrived as scheduled, he tosses his revolver onto the bed—"Keep this for company"—before rushing out the door.

The moment that Bannion enters the apartment building where his sister and husband reside, a man in a slouch hat puts a gun in his back: "Okay, Mac, get 'em up high." The man, it turns out, is a friend, not a foe—an ex-serviceman, like the other men who have come to his brother-in-law's aid—but the military atmosphere conveys, as in *The Captive City*, just how embattled American civil society had become circa 1953, as if the war over there had migrated here, to the home front, in the guise of organized crime.

Dissolve to Debby, dressed in a mink coat, standing outside Mrs. Duncan's house, the right, still immaculate side of her face profiled in the window. Bertha, who's about to leave, answers the door in pearls and *her* mink coat:

BERTHA: Were you in an accident?
DEBBY: Yes. You have a nice home.
BERTHA: Did Mr. Stone send you?
DEBBY: No. I've been thinking about you and me—how much alike we are, the mink-coated girls.
BERTHA: I don't understand you. What are you here for, Miss Marsh?
DEBBY: Debby. We should use first names, Bertha. We're sisters under the mink.

The initial non sequitur here is revealing, suggesting a causal relation between Debby's accident and Bertha's home in which Debby's disfigurement is a direct function of the dirty money behind the "nice" bourgeois façade. (Thanks to blackmail, Mrs. Duncan's now the beneficiary of a "million-dollar trust fund.") More important, perhaps, Debby's emphatic identification with Mrs. Duncan—"We're sisters under the mink"—acknowledges her own complicity in the syndicate's reign of violence.

Not surprisingly, Bertha Duncan refuses to acknowledge Debby's sisterly address and instead walks around the desk to call Vince Stone. That this is the very same spot where her husband committed suicide is no accident: the film has now viciously come full circle. As Bertha's dialing Vince's number, Debby shoots and kills her. In McGivern's novel Bannion hears about what Debby has done on the phone from Debby herself: "I'm a tough guy. I did what you couldn't do, Bannion."[63] The fact that Debby repeats her boast—"I'm proving I'm a tough guy"[64]—indicates the extent to which Bannion remains constrained by the law while, as an ex-moll and therefore doubly an outlaw, Debby's able to access the phallic prerogatives associated with the masculine regime. The irony is that in repudiating her moll persona and becoming in effect a femme fatale, Debby also metaphorically kills off her other, criminal self.

In Lang's film the dissolve from a wide shot of the gun that Debby has just tossed on the floor to Bannion standing before a shop window watching Vince Stone park outside his apartment building indexes the displacement that has just occurred. The mise-en-scène, as elsewhere in Lang, is eloquent. As Gunning remarks, "Bannion does not look into [the window]: there is nothing there he wants."[65] In other words, Bannion is the direct antithesis of both Bertha Duncan and pre-accident Debby, not to mention Lagana and Stone, characters for whom the soft, plush life is everything. Yet if it's true that Bannion's character is devoid of desire for sex or commodities, his desire for revenge—to be, as Colin McArthur says, an "avenging angel"[66]—has not been sated. Moreover (and I'm thinking here, as in *The Phenix City Story*, of the female mannequin in the display window), it may well be that since his wife, Katie, is dead, all women are dead to him and therefore only a means to an end, subject as they are to the instrumental logic of ratiocination associated since Poe with the classic detective figure.

At the same time, Debby, as her "tough guy" persona epitomizes, is not simply a tool of Bannion's instrumental reason but a very real agent in her own right. In fact, before Bannion can track down Stone in his penthouse, she has already thrown a pot of boiling coffee in the latter's face, payback for ruining her single most important attribute in a man's world—her face: "It'll burn for a long time, Vince. . . . The lid's off the garbage can and I did it." Debby's retributive act of violence mirrors both the violence that Stone has perpetrated against her—an "eye for an eye" or fire for fire—and the cleansing action associated with the law ("the big heat"). Not so incidentally, it also figuratively throws back in Vince's face his earlier order ("Check the kitchen, baby, will ya"). In other words, it's precisely because Debby's not a '50s "everywoman," a homemaker or domestic *femme atrapée* domiciled in the kitchen with all the newest labor-saving devices, that she can avenge both Lucy Chapman's and Katie Bannion's deaths.

Though Vince eventually manages to fatally wound Debby, Bannion's able to catch up with him as he's climbing a fire escape on the balcony of his apartment, the same one where Stone and Lagana—in a shot familiar from countless classic gangster pictures—previously stood looking out over the city. Still, unlike Webb

Garwood in *The Prowler*, Stone does not die at the hands of the law. Despite the fact that he screams at Bannion to fire—"Go on, shoot! Shoot, shoot!"—the rogue cop ultimately renounces his once exorbitant desire for revenge. In the novel Bannion confronts Stone in the garage of his apartment building as Stone's escaping for a "vacation" somewhere in the sun. Bannion's waiting for Stone to shoot so that he can exchange fire—"You're not going anywhere. I can't wait . . . to make it legal"—when Burke appears out of nowhere and shoots him. The narrator records the impact of Stone's death on Bannion: "He had lived with anger and sadness for an eternity, it seemed. Now the anger was gone, and there was nothing but sadness."[67]

In Lang's film Stone survives, hauled away—his face still burning—by the police, but both the novel and the film resist the consolations of a classically romantic happy ending. In McGovern's novel Debby dies in a hospital; in the film she dies in Vince's penthouse, the "sinister" side of her face turned away from the camera and swathed in fur as Bannion tenderly attends to her as she passes away. Holding her hand, he finally opens up and reminisces about his dead wife:

> BANNION: You and Katie would have gotten along fine. She was a sampler— she'd take sips of my drinks and puff on my cigarette. Sometimes she used to taste the food off my plate.
> DEBBY: I like her. I like her a lot.

A number of critics have remarked, not without reason, that in the end Debby is only redeemed because she does Bannion's dirty work by killing off Bertha Duncan and, equally or more importantly, because she dies. Still, death itself, as I noted earlier, is the great agent of democratization in *The Big Heat*: in its cleansing fire, the former—for Bannion—insuperable class differences between Debby and B-girls Lucy and Katie (note the chiming "feminine" endings) are dissolved.

The coda of *The Big Heat* is, as critics have also remarked, darkly ambiguous. For example, in the conclusion to the film, we do not see Dave Bannion reunited with his daughter, Joyce, or ensconced with her in a new suburban home. Instead, he's back at his desk, back at work, seemingly reintegrated into the police force, if not the world of the living. However, as soon as he sits down, the phone rings— it's a hit-and-run accident—and he's off. As he exits the station, striding past the "GIVE MORE BLOOD" sign, he tells Hugo, "Keep the coffee hot." Question: Has coffee, that icon of domesticity, been returned to its proper place in the order of things, or is Bannion's directive a portent that the forces of chaos and disorder have only been temporarily pacified? There's another, even more disturbing possibility: that Bannion has not completely exorcized his rogue impulses—that, due to Katie's death, he will remain haunted by his coffee-throwing alter ego. In the last, traumatic instance, Bannion, unlike Katie and the B-girls, will have to continue the hard work of living, in which living itself is sometimes indistinguish-able, like analysis, from the interminable work of mourning.

SHIELD FOR MURDER

DIRT

There's a distinct class difference between Dave Bannion in *The Big Heat* and Barney Nolan in *Shield for Murder*. Both are police detectives, but McGivern's *Shield for Murder* elaborates on Nolan's past—in particular, the forbidding urban environment in which he grew up: "Nolan had been born in the section of Phila-delphia called Brewerytown and had grown up fighting the Jews from Strawberry Hill and the Italians that came from South Philly in loud arrogant gangs. Nolan's father, a brawling, blustering laborer, championed Barney's fights, and threatened to beat him senseless if he ever took any dirt from what he called the foreign ele-ment."[68]

In the novel we also learn how Barney became a policeman, and this back-story—necessarily elided in the film—is tangled up not with reform elections, as it is in *The Big Heat*, but ward politics: "His break came in the '34 Mayoralty campaign, when the Ward Leader had been genuinely worried for the first time in twenty-nine years. Barney had weighed one-ninety then, had a minor reputation as a street brawler, and used his physical endowments to chase the Democratic canvassers off the street. He put two of them in Jefferson Hospital, and pretty soon the Democrats were afraid to step into the ward."[69] As recompense, the ward leader advised him to "take the exams for the police department," and "six months later he received his appointment."[70] Then he "accidentally got in right with old Mike O'Neill"—he let O'Neill's brother go after stopping him for drunk driving and running a red light—and the "fluke had landed him on the detective force."[71] He was with "Foot Traffic," a beat cop, for ten years and then in Germantown, a "monotonous dead end," for six more before being transferred to Center City:[72]

> But even in Center City, Barney's on the outside looking in:
> Everybody had money, but there wasn't a chance for him to get at it. Some cops, just a few to be sure, were in on the take from the night-club owners, racket men, and gamblers. But not Nolan. He had lived on the fringes of a set that enjoyed easy money, easy living and easy women.... He had gone along as usual on forty-eight dollars a week; and, as usual, the smart people had written him off as another dumb cop.[73]

The last part of this passage recalls Webb Garwood's lacerating description of himself at the beginning of *The Prowler*—before, that is, he gets smart and kills Mr. Gilvray. Like Garwood before he turns rogue, Barney Nolan is a good, clean cop—at least in terms of corruption—but he fantasizes about the fast set, the easy money and women and living. And like a lot of gangster noir characters, he's laboring under the yoke of necessity: "Luck, fate, God's will. . . . What was it that jerked him around like the dummy on the end of a string?"[74]

CASTLE HEIGHTS

Directed by noir stalwart Edmond O'Brien and producer Howard W. Koch, *Shield for Murder* opens with Barney Nolan (Edmond O'Brien), not God, jerking the string and turning the wheel of fortune. In the first, pre-credit sequence in the film, the camera tracks laterally in reverse as Nolan strides down a street before slipping into the shadow of a doorway in order to screw a silencer onto the barrel of his service revolver. A bookie, Kirk Martin, stands on the curb talking to two men in a car. Martin finishes his business and is walking away when Nolan catches up with him and, throwing his arm around his shoulder like an anchor, steers him into a dark alley. Nervous, Martin offers Nolan more and more money to pay him off, but Nolan, who has been tipped off that the bookie has twenty-five thousand dollars on him, shoots him in the back. After Nolan unscrews the silencer from the handgun, he rifles through Martin's pockets for the money, then screams, "Stop or I'll shoot!" and fires his gun twice into the air. Unbeknownst to him, an elderly man who is both deaf and mute, Ernest Sternmueller (David Hughes), has seen everything from an apartment window that looks out onto the alley. As passersby crowd noisily into the alley, the film cuts to the title: *SHIELD FOR MURDER.*

In McGivern's novel the narrator notes bookie Dave Fiest's "slender, neatly tailored back."[75] Later, Barney remembers that the first time he met Fiest, the bookie was wearing a "beautiful, light-weight gabardine [suit] with hand-stitched lapels; and when [he] waved for drinks, he'd seen the flash of gold cufflinks and a diamond ring."[76] Like Vince Stone in *The Big Heat*, Fiest's clothes and accessories signify his membership in the smart set. One notable difference between Mc-Givern's novel and the film, though, is that in the book Barney doesn't know how much money the bookie has on him; he just knows that "Fiest, like all bookies, carried his assets in a liquid form and close at hand."[77] The difference is important because whereas in the novel fate still has a hand in Nolan's fortunes, in the film Barney already knows that the money—"the payoff on a big bet"[78]—belongs to Packy Reed (Hugh Sanders), a small-time mobster who, however much he might be unlike Lagana, is principled when it comes to his money: he'll want it back on the pain of death.

Another difference between the novel and the film is that while Barney's antagonist in McGivern's book is newspaper reporter Mark Brewster, in O'Brien and Koch's picture Brewster (John Agar) is a young detective who's Nolan's protégé.

Killer Cop, Dames, and Dough: pressbook for *Shield for Murder* (1954), starring Edmond O'Brien and "introducing" Marla English, "sizzling new screen sensation."

There's an investigative reporter in the film, Cabot (Herb Butterfield), but the investigation proper is conducted by Brewster, who, despite his affection for Barney, is determined to follow the case where it leads him, even if it means taking his mentor down. In fact, Brewster's investigation is mediated, as in the novel, by Nolan's girlfriend, who, like Mark, wants to believe that Barney's not guilty of murdering a man in cold blood for money.

In the novel Barney's girlfriend, Linda—Patty Winters (Marla English) in the film—is central to McGivern's exploration of the politics of class and Nolan's desire to change his proletarian station in life, forever on the outside looking in. Linda is a singer at the Simba. The Simba, "a fashionable nightclub with an elegantly dressed doorman and a green-and-white canopy that extended from the club's double-glass doors to the street,"[79] as well as Linda's occupation, "canary," are the stuff of pulp fiction.[80] If the Simba is an object of Barney's class resentment— "He saw [the politicians and racket men], night after night, sitting around . . . and heard them talking about big days at the track, watched them pick up fifty-dollar dinner checks, listened to their stories of money, women, vacations"[81]—Linda's not only a good girl but the embodiment of a different, better class of people and way of life. The opposite of everything that is dark and dirty and mean, Linda's a dream wish, a sexual-romantic fantasy reflected in Barney's first, pristine vision of her: "She was wearing a white net gown with a billowing skirt, and her finely molded shoulders were bare. Her skin was lightly tanned, and he had never seen anyone in his life who looked so shining and lovely and clean."[82] Linda is like Debby Marsh in the last, redemptive light of *The Big Heat*. Which is to say that, in a certain light, she also could be Katie Bannion.

At the same time, unlike both Debby Marsh and Katie Bannion, Linda for Barney is a revenant, a sublimated reminder of his past impoverished, bruised, and bruising life. Before he dropped out of school, he had admired a girl in chemistry class "who wore soft wool sweaters, tweed skirts, and even a string of pearls."[83]

> She came from a family with money, obviously, because she lived in Haddington and, just as obviously, she was a high-class sort of girl. She represented a type Nolan had never known at all, but one which he instinctively resented. . . . However, the ambivalence of his relationship to her was such that while resenting her and hating her he also wanted her to be his girl."[84]

In McGivern's *Shield for Murder*, as in *The Big Heat*, issues of class are intertwined with issues of race. In high school Barney worked "setting pins in his neighborhood bowling alley": "He hated setting pins because most of the regular pin boys were colored, and Nolan's father had always warned him against working with colored people. It gave them ideas, his father said, with mysterious emphasis on the word 'ideas.'"[85] For Barney, Linda is the ultimate embodiment of white society and femininity, her lightly tanned skin a signifier—by virtue of the fact that it's a function of choice, not nature—of her superior, unblemished class status.

One day, having purchased a gardenia with the money from his pin-setting job, Barney asked the Haddington girl out and, when she refused, he grabbed her by her finely molded shoulders, then, "in a frightening rage," "shook her until the books she was carrying tumbled to the floor."[86] The chemistry teacher, who was one of Barney's "few heroes," berated him and made him clean up the classroom that afternoon, but what really "hurt was being treated like a criminal because he had presumed to date a little bitch from the fancy section of Haddington."[87] In other words, there's an explicit, if elliptical, connection between Barney's feeling of being a criminal and the motivating incident of the novel and film. If Linda, the rematerialization of the formerly unattainable object of Barney's desire, motivates him to buck the system, his cold-blooded killing of the bookie is the moment when he irrevocably crosses the line from being a violent but, technically speaking, clean cop to an irreparably bad one.

While Linda in McGivern's novel is a "good bad girl"—if only because she's a singer at the Simba and, for Mark at least, because she's dating Barney—in the film Patty's the "good girl" as ingénue. Barney has just gotten her a job at the Blackout. Yet when he sees her dressed as a cigarette girl in a strapless, black-satin corset with a sweetheart neckline, he grabs the club owner by the lapels and rails, "Haven't got enough legs here? Gotta put her in a peep show!" Nolan's intemperate behavior is reminiscent of Johnny Farrell's (Glenn Ford) in *Gilda* when he drags the eponymous, post-striptease character off the dance floor, although the only thing that Patty does to displease Barney is to put on a Playboy Bunny costume minus the collar, cuffs, and white cotton tail.

Patty's bewildered by her beau's violent, unpredictable behavior: "What makes you hate like that?" Barney promises that "things are gonna be different": "You'll see in a minute. Think I'm gonna be a cop forever?" As proof, he drives her to a new housing development in the suburbs called Castle Heights to show her a "model home" that's "all furnished" and "ready to go." (The set decorator is Alfred E. Spencer.) It's dark, and after turning on the lights and flooding the interior of the house, he points out the living room, complete with cabinet TV; a dining room, the table already set with plates, silverware, cups and saucers; a guest bath; a master bedroom; and, best yet, a "Beauty Queen Kitchen." About the last regal space, Barney enthuses like a salesman: "Everything's automatic. Electric garbage disposal. Dishwasher. Up here we have an electrical stove, three burners." "Special cooker," Betty chimes in before Barney resumes his pitch: "And there's a refrigerator, deep freeze. Rotisse-a-mat." Then, while Patty toasts an imaginary guest with one of the cups and lies down on the couch, kicking off her high heels, Barney steals outside, where he buries the twenty-five grand in some dirt. Later,

Scene Stills Make Complete Home Furnishings Window Display

The four stills shown below can be used as a complete home furnishing window display or used separately with each type of furnishings. Suggest you work out tieup with large furniture or department store supplementing a window display with use of these same stills in their newspaper advertising.

Table Service	Living Room	Kitchen	Electric Appliances
Still SFM-LB-1	Still SFM-LB-2	Still SFM-LB-3	Still SFM-LB-4

Page Four

Model Tract Home: "home furnishing window display" available to movie-theater exhibitors of *Shield for Murder* (1954).

as he's dropping Patty off at her apartment building, two of Reed's hoods, Fat Michaels (Claude Atkins) and Laddie O'Neill (Larry Ryle), notify Nolan that the boss wants to see him. Before Barney leaves with them to see Packy, he tells Patty to "sleep tight and dream about our little house."

The model home sequence in *Shield for Murder* is an invention of screenwriters John C. Higgins and Richard Alan Simmons, but it's a brilliant evocation of the mid-century, middle-class suburban dream. While a "tract home" in "Castle Heights" may be an oxymoron, for Barney Nolan—haunted by the Haddington girl and, as Cabot says about one of the cops, "too little money in [his] pockets"— it's to die for. As Patty later laments to Mark, "He wants to carry me through the door with a ring on my finger." With his girl by his side and an "automatic," ready-to-move-in home, Barney will have realized his dream of leaving behind the mean streets for the sweet suburban life. However, as with the overhead high-angle shot of the ribbon cross that decorates the top of the Garwoods' wedding car in *The Prowler*, when Barney retrieves the key for the model home that the agent has left for him, the tight shot of Patty and him imprisoned behind a crisscross of white clapboards suggests that Barney's dream is a trap.

In fact, the wheel of fortune has already begun to turn. First, Mr. Sternmueller shows up at the police station with a letter, and although Barney is able to intercept him, he is forced to confront the man at his apartment. As in *Where the Sidewalk Ends*, Barney shoves Sternmueller, and when the old man hits his head, he dies. In order to make the man's death look like an accident, Barney drags the body out of the room and throws it down the stairs, an act that makes Nolan seem less like a hot-tempered but essentially good cop like Mark Dixon in *Where the Sidewalk Ends* than a seriously crazed ex-con like Tommy Udo (Richard Widmark) in *Kiss of Death* (1947).

To unwind Barney retreats to an Italian restaurant where he meets a blonde woman named Beth (Carolyn Jones), who, as he puts it in the novel, "let a man do anything to [her] as long as he filled [her] up with booze first." When he notices a bruise on her arm, though, he becomes disgusted and telephones Patty, who informs him that Reed's goons have just tried to force their way into her apartment. Apoplectic (not unlike Bannion in *The Big Heat* after Larry Gordon's obscene phone call), Barney immediately telephones Reed. Cut to Barney and Beth eating a spaghetti dinner. While she's busy cleaning her plate, Barney, who hasn't even touched his, surreptitiously removes a revolver from his holster and slips it into his jacket. The big plates of pasta with red sauce and meatballs echo not only the elegantly set table at the model home but also Barney's bitter description of himself in McGivern's novel after Linda asks him whether Dave Fiest, the bookie he killed, was married and had a family: "I'm a cop, a meat-ball cop from South Philly."[88]

Reed's goons arrive in no time, but instead of handing over Packy's money, Barney pistol-whips the "private detectives" and, as the jazz music on the radio spikes, beats them to a pulp. (For its time, circa 1954, the scene is startling, at once graphic, extended, and surreal—see, for example, the alabaster-white "comedy" masks that look down, grinning, from the wall.) As Barney continues to wail away, a woman screams; Beth covers her face with her hands; a man, a strand of spaghetti trailing from his mouth, recoils in horror; and the matronly Italian American proprietor shouts, "Somebody call the police! Somebody call the police!" "You had the police," Barney quips, strolling out the door as if absolutely nothing has happened.

Earlier, in a seemingly throwaway scene, Beth uses the mirror behind the bar to teach Barney how to look tough. Repositioning the cigarette in his hand, she instructs him, "Now take a puff, square your shoulder, narrow your eyes." It's an odd, parodic moment: even as it self-reflexively foregrounds the film's cognizance of its own generic belatedness, it suggests that Barney's abuse of Sternmueller's body was an aberration—that, like Mark Dixon in *Where the Sidewalk Ends*, Barney Nolan may not be as bad as he seems. But Barney, to quote Gus Burke on Bannion after the death of the latter's wife, is "on a hate binge." Thus, when he returns to his apartment and Mark tries to take him in (Mark has in the meantime discovered another draft of Sternmueller's letter), Barney knocks the pistol out of his protégé's hand and hits him over the head with the butt of his gun. Then, when Patty won't run off with him—she asks him if he took Packy Reed's money and, in turn, he asks her if she's been talking to Mark—he slaps her, hard.

In McGivern's novel Barney doesn't hit Linda; he shoots her, because, having given her the money to hide, he thinks she has double-crossed him: "He fired a shot and saw her spin as if struck by a giant fist, and then he waited . . . until he saw the blood spreading through her robe."[89] Before he shoots her, he goes to the bathroom to wash his face and pauses to gaze at the "bottle of cologne and perfumes and jars of cold cream and bath salts": "The bottles were pretty, and their contents looked gay and colorful. Everything about the immaculate bathroom was her, he thought: clean, dainty, precious."[90] Linda's bathroom—an intimate, feminine space—is a refuge from the dirty, cheap, and coarse masculine world in which Barney has had to make his way. As Linda surmised earlier, defending him to Mark Brewster, "Barney's made a symbol of me. He's put me on a ridiculous pedestal. He's got me confused with success and security and love, and all the things he's missed in life."[91]

Though Captain Gunnarson (Emile Meyer) has already concluded that Kirk Martin's death was a matter of "blue murder," he nevertheless believes, as Mark Brewster reflects in the novel, that "bad cops are nobody's business but the police department's."[92] Now, confronted with the evidence of Barney's crimes, Gunnarson, addressing the detectives assembled in his office, is forced to concede that Barney is a "maniac wearing a city shield" and concludes, "If he gets away, they'll laugh at us. If we nail him, they'll hate us. When this story breaks . . . every police officer in the county will get dirty looks and dirty words. Go out and rub your faces in the mud." The subsequent, wide-angle shot of Barney standing outside a laundry—the word "CLEANED" is prominent in the background of the frame—couldn't, in the context, be more ironic: Barney's shield is not tarnished; it's black.

Barney's transformation from venial to mortal rogue cop is dramatized when, after a motorcycle cop rides up to a call box, then speeds off, Barney, who has been watching from the shadows of the laundry, goes over and listens to the APB:

> The homicide suspect at large is Barney Nolan, detective lieutenant attached to University Precinct. He may be driving precinct detective car eight. His description: five-eleven, two hundred pounds, male Caucasian, thirty-six years of age, wearing a brown suit, brown shoes, possibly tan topcoat, brown hat. This man is armed and dangerous, probably psycho. Use caution.

In a continuation of the film's play on appearances (earlier, when Reed's private detectives appeared at the police station, Mark queried, "Cops?" and Cabot answered, "Robbers"), Barney throws his hat and trench coat into a garbage can and, after disappearing into a basement, reemerges as a uniformed "man in blue." He's strolling up to his apartment when another officer who's staking it out approaches him and asks, "Are you the beat cop?" In this scene Barney's uniform is not a disguise; it's a sign of regression. Barney, like Webb Garwood at the end of *The Prowler*, is not moving forward; he's going backward.

Caught between the police and Packy Reed, Barney arranges to meet a man named Manning (Richard Cutting), who has promised to help get him out of the country. In the upside-down world in which Barney now finds himself—he's hiding out in another basement with a "friend," the Professor, who's studying for an exam that night—everybody's a wise guy. First, the Professor comments that "night school at [his] age isn't easy"—"Business administration is a difficult subject"—then Manning arrives, takes one look at Barney, and comments, "That's quite a deal, a detective dressed in a patrolman's uniform." Still, for "fifteen grand," Manning claims he can deliver the goods: "US passport, charter plane to Cuba, airline tickets to Buenos Aires."

Later, in the locker room at a local high school where Barney has agreed to rendezvous with Reed's detectives, Barney makes the exchange, but O'Neill—his head covered with bandages like Claude Mulvihill's in *Chinatown* (1974)—realizes that the envelope is stuffed with newspaper slips, not money. The ensuing gunfight between Barney and O'Neill, which takes place in a public swimming pool where men and women in bathing suits scurry from the whizzing bullets, unfolds like some absurdist play, in the process commenting, like Barney's demented behavior in the bar, on his utter disregard for human life: reverting at one point to training, he drops to a crouch and, taking direct aim at O'Neill, drops him.

In *The Prowler* Bud Crocker says to Webb that a policeman's job is to protect not things but people. Having given up for good on people, Barney returns to the model tract home to get the only thing that means anything to him at this point in his rapidly downward-spiraling life: money. In McGivern's novel Barney attempts to run Mark down with his car after seeing him exit Linda's apartment. Afterward, he drives through the "middle-class residential streets of the city . . . with no destination in mind": "Outside the sun was shining and wind sang clearly in the trees. Kids from a nearby school ran along the streets shouting to each other and the policeman at the intersection."[93] This impossibly idyllic vision of suburbia—where policemen are an integral part of the good life—is the exterior complement of the felicitous portrait of the middle-class *interieur* in *The Big Heat*. Both films also suggest that such happiness is as elusive as the wind singing in the trees.

Bleeding from a shoulder wound and with the police in hot pursuit, Barney races out to the new tract-home development located on the outskirts of the city. Not unlike Webb Garwood at the end of *The Prowler*, Barney scrambles up a hillside, then after exchanging fire with two officers, digs the cache of money out of the dirt, his not-so-angelic face smeared with mud. With the cash in one hand and his service revolver in the other, Barney staggers around to the front of the house, where he stops next to a sign: CASTLE HEIGHTS TRACT HOMES. When the headlights of the police cruisers lined up across the street suddenly flood the "lawn" with light, Barney goes down in a hail of bullets, '30s gangster-style like Mal Granger in *711 Ocean Drive*, the shots kicking up dirt, the money littering the lawn like dead leaves.

In McGivern's novel Barney decides to escape to Mexico and while hiding out in the city, dreams of seeing Linda there: "He could see her in a white dress, her arms and legs browned by the sun, coming across a hotel lobby to him with the bright quick smile on her face."[94] This passage uncannily conjures the famous Mexican cantina scene in *Out of the Past* when Jeff Markham (Robert Mitchum) sees Kathie Moffat (Jane Greer) coming toward him out of the sunlight; it also confirms just how idealized the "first" Linda—"the bright and smiling one . . . who had stroked his head when he was drunk and ready to explode"[95]—has become in Barney's mind. Later, after catching a private flight to Richmond, Virginia, Barney boards another plane to Dallas, where, as he waits for it to take off, he has another vision of Linda: "happy and smiling, coming to him somewhere, sometime, in Mexico."[96]

In reality the "paunchy little man" with a briefcase sitting in the seat directly behind him is named Tommy, and he has been hired by a South Philly racketeer to whom Barney owes twenty-five Gs, to take care of him somewhere between Dallas and Mexico: "[Tommy] looked at his watch as the plane taxied down the runway. Time for forty winks before they reached Dallas. Settling himself comfortably, he glanced once at the back of Barney's head, and then closed his eyes. The plane climbed into the night."[97] In McGivern's novel Barney is ultimately subject not to the institutional forces of law and order but, as in the syndicate picture, the merciless law of the mob dramatized in '50s gangster noirs such as *New York Confidential* and *The Brothers Rico*. In the end, his mind's eye on the angelic Linda, he never sees it coming.

In Koch and O'Brien's film, Barney, the badge and uniform aside, is less a policeman than a psycho killer costumed as a cop. The fact that he dies like a gangster in a blaze of glory on the dirt outside his dream home rather than somewhere between Dallas and Mexico highlights the film's critique, like *The Prowler*'s, of the "myth of suburbia."[98] In the dénouement to *Rogue Cop*, set in an ambulance as it races, siren blaring, toward a hospital, Chris Carmody (Robert Taylor), haunted by all the things that he'll never get to tell his brother Eddie, a rookie cop who was killed by the syndicate, says to his partner, Sid, that he's a lot like Eddie: "A better cop than I'll ever be." Chris then asks forgiveness, a request that underscores not only Sid's status as Eddie's surrogate and Chris's symbolic reconciliation with his brothers in blue but also the film's Judeo-Christian ethos.

The ending of *Shield for Murder*, by contrast, cuts from a high-angle shot of Barney Nolan—his bloodied hand outstretched as if, in death, he's still grasping for the money scattered next to his corpse—to a low-angle shot of a phalanx of policemen approaching the tract home. The men are collectively appraising the scene when Mark Brewster gets down on one knee and, as the score segues from a bluesy riff to a dramatic swell, removes the "shield" from Barney's uniform. Mark's staring at the badge cupped in his hand when Gunnarson orders Cabot, "Write his story good." Although there's no doubt about the captain's grammar—it's bad—the meaning of his command is ambiguous: Is it aesthetic, as in "Write a good story," or political, as in "Make it right"?

Early on in *Shield for Murder* Cabot refers to the police as "one big secret society," and when Mark Brewster refuses to shed any light on the Kirk Martin killing—"No story. What is done is done"—the reporter laments that his story will get "buried behind a girdle ad." It's no secret, though, that Cabot believes that Barney was fundamentally different than the other good, if "impure," men on the police force who, as he explains to Mark, "don't have to kill and beat up [people] just for kicks." In fact, he's all too well aware and reminds Mark, "Last year Nolan killed two hungry wetbacks in a market burglary. Three years ago it was that tramp on Sullivan Street."

Mark doesn't have to be reminded. He has just returned from Germantown, where he's been looking into Barney's past. A detective named Jerry Spiegel, who "had made the mistake of knocking off too many protected handbooks in the downtown area and had been sent to Germantown to reflect on his sins,"[99] recounts:

> I was working with [Nolan] the night he killed those two colored boys. We come in from different ends of the alley, see, and I get to 'em first. They were scared silly. I calmed 'em down, and then along comes that Nolan with his gun out and swearing like a wild man. The kids were edgy anyway and bolted. Nolan dropped 'em both with shots in the back.[100]

Later, at the Center City station, Barney accuses Mark of being a "snoop" and is about to take a swing at him when the desk sergeant breaks it up.

Mark proceeds downstairs to the call room, where the day's hearings are about to begin and where the room is crowded with "vags and drunks," cops and bondsmen, claimants and defendants, lawyers and witnesses.[101] A black man named Jeremiah Green, dressed in "incredibly tattered clothes" with "no address," has been brought in for being drunk and walking the streets with a brick.[102] The magistrate asks Jeremiah what the brick was for:

"Fo de rat."

There was a murmur of laughter, and the Negro bobbed his head and smiled tentatively.

"What rat?" The magistrate, who had a reputation for wit, leaned back in his chair and regarded the Negro with raised eyebrows.

"De rat is where I sleep, Jedge."

"I thought you told the House Sergeant you had no address?"

"*It* ain't got any address, Jedge. It's a box and I move it 'roun. The rat comes in a hole, and I'se chockin' it wit de brick."[103]

McGivern records Mark Brewster's profound sense of disenchantment, a disillusionment that no amount of Leibniz can ameliorate: "He felt tired and depressed, partly because of the brush with Nolan, and partly because people like the old Negro always made him wonder what in hell was wrong with the best of all possible worlds."[104]

6

TOUCH OF EVIL

GOOD COP/BAD COP

I wasn't the lone wolf in this affair. Nobody is who
believes in the law.

—Mitchell Holt, in Whit Masterson's *Badge of Evil*

Orson Welles's involvement in *Touch of Evil* (1958) has been captured in an anecdote. According to Albert Zugsmith, on the last day of shooting *Man in the Shadow* (1957), Welles asked him if he had anything to direct, and the producer, pointing to a shelf of scripts, answered that Welles could have any one he wanted. Welles allegedly responded, "Which is the worst one?" and Zugsmith pulled out Paul Monash's screenplay for *Badge of Evil*, which was based on Whit Masterton's novel of the same name and which Welles went on to rewrite.[1]

Touch of Evil famously opens with a spectacular murder signed by Welles when "contractor Rudy Linnekar [and] a blonde nightclub dancer [are] killed in an explosion a few yards this side of the Mexican border."[2] This news report is later playing on the radio in a Chrysler convertible driven by Ramon Miguel "Mike" Vargas (Charlton Heston in all his post–*Ten Commandments* glory) and his new wife, Susan (a pre-*Psycho* Janet Leigh). Even though the couple is on their honeymoon, Mike, who's the chairman of the Pan American Narcotics Commission and due any day in Mexico City for the dope trial of Vic Grandi, feels that it's his "sacred duty," as Susan sarcastically puts it, to investigate the murder. Vic may be in jail, but the Grandis are a big family, and his brother "Uncle Joe" Grandi (Akim Tamiroff) is now the boss in Los Robles, the border town where the explosion has just occurred. (If Grandi, according to Susan, is an "old-fashioned, jug-eared, lop-sided Little Caesar"—she tells him that he's "been seeing too many gangster movies"—he's also a monstrously comic double of Joseph "Uncle Joe" Stalin.)

Border Crossing: Miguel "Mike" Vargas (Charlton Heston) and his newly wedded wife, Susan (Janet Leigh), cross the border as Rudy Linnekar (Jeffrey Green) and a blonde sit impatiently waiting in his car in *Touch of Evil* (1958).

While there's some question about jurisdiction inasmuch as Los Robles is located on the border between Mexico and the United States, Police Captain Hank Quinlan (Orson Welles) remarks to District Attorney Adair (Ray Collins) that two "Americans" have, for all practical purposes, been "blown to ash with dynamite . . . in [his] own police station."[3] Vargas, at least at the beginning of the investigation, informs Police Chief Gould (Harry Shannon) that he's "merely what the United Nations would call an observer." Welles, however, sets up an immediate opposition between the two representatives of the law: whereas Vargas is described in the script as a "square-jawed Mexican" who effectively has "Cabinet status with the Mexican government," Quinlan's glossed as a "grossly corpulent figure in an overcoat, a huge cigar in the middle of his puffy face."[4] In other words, if Vargas is a picture of probity, Quinlan, notwithstanding the fact that he has given up booze for candy bars, is the embodiment of excess. In fine, good cop, bad cop.

One way that Welles fleshes out this generic opposition is by metaphorically playing on the difference between being "clean" and "dirty"—with the proviso that circa 1959, and relative to "Americans," Mexicans were stereotypically portrayed as "dirty." So, for example, the DA reminds Quinlan that Vargas is "in charge of some kind of cleanup here on this [the Mexican] side of the border," a remark that suggests that Vargas is a "good cop" even as it insinuates that Mexico is "dirty." And near the end of the film, after Susan has been found drugged and half naked on one of the beds in the Hotel Ritz with "reefer stubs and a heroin fix," Vargas shouts at Quinlan's trusted sidekick, Sergeant Pete Menzies (Joseph Calleia), "How can I leave [Los Robles] until my wife's name is clean? Clean!"

At this late point in the delirious narrative that is *Touch of Evil*, Susan Vargas, it's clear, has been touched by evil, as has her husband, whose name echoes Francisco de Vargas, a fifteenth-century Spanish detective. (De Vargas was known for his ability to, as the proverb "Averíguelo Vargas" has it, "crack difficult cases."[5]) By comparison, Quinlan has been figuratively knee-deep in "filth" from the opening of the film as he literally is at the end when he has fallen into the dirty, debris-littered water of the canal.

Accordingly, when Vargas and Quinlan rendezvous at Marcia Linnekar's apartment to interrogate her "boyfriend," Manolo Sanchez (Victor Millan), about her father's death—Quinlan has intuited from his bum leg that the shoe clerk is the primary suspect—Sanchez turns to Vargas and asks, "How do we begin? Do we play around first with a few nasty questions, or does [Quinlan] get out the rubber hose right away?" Sanchez also tells Vargas in Spanish, and Mike in turn tells Quinlan (Vargas translates) that Sanchez "thinks he's in for some sort of third degree." Despite the fact that Vargas assures Sanchez he has "nothing to worry about," when Sanchez continues to speak in Spanish, Quinlan slaps him because he doesn't "speak Mexican." Finally, while Vargas is searching the bathroom for evidence and inadvertently knocks over an empty shoe box, Quinlan can be heard saying to Sanchez, "What are you scared of, boy? I'd only slap you again if you got hysterical again. Wouldn't be anything brutal. Why, even back in the old days, we never tried to hurt people in the face. It marks 'em up. We gave it to 'em like this." Offscreen there's the sound of a punch and Sanchez can be heard groaning.

Quinlan is aggressively acting on his "intuition" that since Marcia stood to inherit a "million bucks" and Linnekar "objected to having a Mexican shoe clerk for a son-in-law," Sanchez murdered her father. Yet if Quinlan has established, however speciously, a motive, it's imperative, as Vargas reminds him, "to put Sanchez at the scene of the crime" and, equally important, to present evidence. The evidence, such as it is, turns out to be two sticks of Black Fox dynamite that Menzies subsequently discovers in a shoe box in Marcia's bathroom, the very same box that—"in a rhyming long take"[6]—Vargas previously found to be empty of both shoes and dynamite.

Vargas knows that his own word may not be enough, so he wants proof positive that "[Quinlan] framed that boy." Cut to his hotel room, where he hands Adair a document showing that Quinlan purchased seventeen sticks of Black Fox dynamite at Hill's Hardware in Los Robles. In addition, Deputy DA Al Schwartz (Mort Mills) has discovered that a hired hand at Quinlan's turkey ranch used fifteen sticks of dynamite, which leaves two missing—the same number that Menzies found in the shoe box in Marcia's bathroom. Quinlan, who in the meantime has arrived at the hotel after a tête-a-tête with Grandi, is predictably outraged, taking out his badge and, not unlike Dave Bannion in *The Big Heat*, tossing it on a desk. "Thirty years!" Quinlan blusters to Adair and Gould as he storms out of the room, down a hall, and into a deserted ballroom: "Thirty years of poundin' beats, ridin' cars. Thirty years of dirt and crummy pay."

In fact, the only thing that Quinlan has to show for three decades on the police force is a two-acre turkey ranch. In this sense (and opposed to other rogue cops like Webb Garwood in *The Prowler* and Barney Nolan in *Shield for Murder*), he's not corrupt, financially speaking. (Gould cries out, "Hank Quinlan never took a dollar in his life!") Quinlan's corruption is, instead, "a form of vanity, the vanity of those who believe themselves infallible."[7] This vaingloriousness is reflected in the people who surround the police captain like so many courtiers. For example, when Gould, Adair, and Schwartz are taking an elevator to Vargas's hotel room for the conference, Gould complains that "this Mexican," Vargas, "is bringing criminal charges against one of the most respected police officers in the country." And Schwartz, indirectly commenting on Gould, pejoratively describes Quinlan as the "idol of the police force."

The pivotal moment in *Touch of Evil*, at least with respect to Quinlan's character, occurs during the aforementioned tête-à-tête with Grandi at a bar as Menzies looks on sadly from inside Marcia Linnekar's apartment. Though Quinlan has been on the wagon for twelve years and has no intention of striking a deal with Uncle Joe, at one point he looks down at the double bourbon that Grandi has bought for him and suddenly sees that it's half empty. It's a brilliant moment, gesturally speaking: before Quinlan realizes what he has done, he's already drunk to Gould's proposition of a "sweet setup." Therefore, by the time Menzies arrives, it's too late: Quinlan's already "fried," recalling that when he was a "rookie cop," his wife was strangled by a "half-breed." "That was the last killer," Quinlan mutters, as if more to himself than Menzies, "that ever got out of my hands." In other words, the real, remote cause of Quinlan's rogue behavior is revenge: "revenge on the race that killed his wife, a loss that we are given to understand has destroyed his life."[8]

One cannot, I think, overestimate the significance of this loss, not because it explains or excuses Quinlan's abuse of power (it doesn't) but because it figuratively mirrors (I'm thinking here of the "magic mirror" scene in *The Lady from Shanghai* [1947]) Vargas's relation with Susan as well as Sanchez's with Marcia Linnekar. In other words, the "legal" and "sexual plots" are inextricably mixed or crossed in *Touch of Evil*, in which the navel of Welles's picture is what Stephen Heath calls the *hors-la-loi* or, to accent the specific sort of mixing that motors the film's libidinal economy, *el mestizo*.[9] This notion is reflected not simply in incidents and relations—Vargas/Susan, Sanchez/Marcia, "half-breed"/Quinlan's wife—but in the borderland itself. (A sign in the film refers to Los Robles as the "Paris of the Border.")

So, to take the "mixed party" at the Mirador Motel, Grandi's gang, which is made up of black-leather-jacketed pachucos and "proto-dyke Chicanas,"[10] molest and drug Susan, thereby polluting her pure image so that by the end of the film, when she has been transported to the Hotel Ritz, she resembles her dark "gypsy" other, Tanya (Marlene Dietrich). Similarly, in order to avoid being blackmailed by Grandi (who has engineered Susan's hallucinatory debasement), Quinlan strangles the "Mexican, American, Italian Grandi" to death.[11] The fact that Quinlan strangles Grandi in the same hotel room where Susan has been deposited and, not so incidentally, with one of her stockings suggests that the captain is simultaneously avenging his wife's death, fantasmatically murdering the "half-breed" who murdered his wife, and figuratively doing what Vargas, despite the "hot Latin lover" stereotype, never gets around to doing in the film: consummating his relationship with Susan.

However, lest it seem that Welles has merely muddied stereotypical racial antinomies, Vargas himself concedes to Quinlan at one point that enforcing the law is a "dirty job." Moreover, when he discovers that Susan isn't at the Mirador and that his gun is missing from his briefcase, he rushes off to the Rancho Grande, where he breaks a glass, bashes the head of Grandi's nephew Pancho (Valentin De Vargas) against a jukebox,[12] and, after hauling Risto (Lalo Rios) down the full length of the bar, barks, "Listen, I'm no cop now. I'm a husband! What did you do with her?" Vargas receives his answer when, during the ensuing mêlée, the police arrive and Schwartz informs him that Susan has been charged with Grandi's murder—Susan is just another "jane" for Quinlan—as well as with possession of narcotics. Consequently, in order to clear or "clean" Susan's name, Vargas is forced to fit Menzies with a wire so that he can get Quinlan on record confessing to Grandi's murder. Vargas's earlier concession that law enforcement is a "dirty job" notwithstanding, he's not happy about having to resort to such dirty tricks: "You think I like it? I hate this machine. Spying . . . Creeping about."

The conclusion to *Touch of Evil* is appropriately rife with irony. Right before Quinlan emerges from Tanya's "brothel," Menzies tells Vargas that somebody could have planted the captain's cane, which he found at the scene of the crime "beside Grandi's corpse." "You know better," Vargas replies. "You're an honest cop!" Menzies's response is not only contrary to the point of paradox—"Sure I am. And who made me an honest cop? Hank Quinlan"—but exemplifies the sort of performative contradictions that energize *Touch of Evil*. For example, despite the fact that Quinlan appears to realize that Menzies is wired—"What's it called, that thing you're wearing?"—he's not referring to the "bug" (what Stephen Heath wittily describes as a "walking Mike"[13]); he's referring to the "halo" over Menzies's

Tercio de Banderillas: Police Captain Hank Quinlan (Orson Welles) waiting for the end in Tanya's bordello in *Touch of Evil* (1958).

head, as if Vargas had managed to turn the police captain's former right-hand man into what Quinlan calls, on mike, "one of these here starry-eyed idealists." At the same time, Menzies himself is no angel—his wings have long since been clipped—nor, for that matter, a common crook. Tired of Quinlan having played him for a "sucker" all these years by planting evidence for him to find, Menzies presses his suit:

> MENZIES (on mike): Grandi was strangled.
> QUINLAN (on mike): Grandi was a crook.
> MENZIES (on mike): You're a killer, Hank.
> QUINLAN (on mike): Partner, I'm a cop.
> MENZIES (off mike): Yeah, yeah, yeah. Drunk and crazy as you must have been when you strangled him, I guess you were somehow thinking of your wife. The way she was strangled.
> QUINLAN (off mike): Well, I'm always thinking of her. Drunk or sober. What else is there to think about? Except my job. My "dirty" job.

Even though Quinlan here tacitly confesses to killing Grandi, this confession does not stop him from shooting Menzies once he realizes that his former confidante is a "walking microphone." He's also about to shoot Vargas at point-blank range when Schwartz arrives with Susan. Instead, while Quinlan's momentarily distracted, Menzies shoots him. Quinlan, mortally wounded, staggers to his feet and pauses to look up at Menzies's body slumped over the bridge, at which point the blood from Menzies's hand drips onto his hand and Quinlan falls backward into the dirty, debris-littered canal.

Schwartz is replaying the recording—Menzies: "How many did you frame?" / Quinlan: "Nobody that wasn't guilty"—when Tanya arrives and he tells her, "[Hank's] famous intuition was right after all. He framed that Mexican kid, Sanchez. But he didn't need to. The kid confessed about that bomb." The subsequent exchange between Schwartz and Tanya—"Hank was a great detective all right" / "And a lousy cop"—suggests it may in fact have been Sanchez who planted the bomb that killed Rudy Linnekar and his companion, Zita (Joi Lansing).

Still, the question of Sanchez's innocence or guilt remains an open-ended one, inasmuch as both Sanchez's confession and Quinlan's status as a "great detective" can't be taken at face value. Consider, for instance, Quinlan's physically abusive interrogation of Sanchez in Marcia Linnekar's apartment, not to mention the captain's last exhortation to Menzies: "Break him! Break him!" Consider as well Vargas's discovery in the Court of Records that "in every case where [Menzies] and Quinlan uncovered the principal evidence," the defense denied the existence of the evidence. Consider, finally, that Quinlan has just tried to frame Vargas for Menzies's death and, failing this, is about to murder the "lousy foreigner" when Menzies shoots him.

AFTERWORD: IN THE NAME OF THE LAW

> QUINLAN: Lawyer! I'm not a lawyer! All a lawyer cares about is the law.
> VARGAS: Captain! You *are* a policeman, aren't you?
>
> —*Touch of Evil*

In 1958, in a *Cahiers du cinéma* interview about *Touch of Evil*, Welles remarked that the "most personal thing [he] put in the film was [his] hatred of the abuse of police power."[14] Welles's comment is a reminder that Quinlan is eerily reminiscent of Joe McCarthy. (McCarthy died on May 2, 1957.) Just as Quinlan has a bum leg, McCarthy famously used to limp, having falsely claimed that it was a "result of a bombing mission."[15] McCarthy was also, like Quinlan, overweight, a "terrible lush" (he died of sclerosis of the liver), and, after the US Senate censured him in 1954, frequently appeared in public disheveled and sporting a five o'clock shadow.

Most to the point perhaps, Welles, speaking about *Touch of Evil*, appeared to be thinking of the notorious senator from Wisconsin when he essayed that "Quinlan does not want to submit the guilty ones to justice so much as assassinate them in the name of the law, using the police for his own purposes, and this is a fascist scenario."[16] In light of this remark, Vargas's retort to Quinlan that the "policeman's job is only easy in a police state" evokes not only the fascist threat posed by the Axis powers in World War II and the postwar climate of hysteria stoked by HUAC and McCarthy but also the cultural-political conditions of possibility of *film gris*, which was hatched in the "big heat" of the Hollywood "witch hunt."

PART THREE

THE HEIST MOVIE

THE ASPHALT JUNGLE

THE CITY UNDER THE CITY

The modern gangster film can be said to begin with *Little Caesar*, an urban, ethnic "rags to riches" story made against the coal-black background of both the Depression and Prohibition and charged by the electrifying performance of Edward G. Robinson as Rico Bandello. Rico fantasizes about becoming somebody, about making it big like bigger-than-life, newspaper-headlining Legs Diamond, and since there's no future for him in gas station heists, he moves from the country to the city, a "symbolic passage from innocence to corruption" that foreshadows his eventual, inevitable, and precipitous "fall from grace."[1]

W. R. Burnett wrote *Little Caesar*; he also wrote *High Sierra* (1941), a novel that extends the author's "vision of a culture in declension."[2] However, *High Sierra* reverses the metropolitan impulse of *Little Caesar*. In Raoul Walsh's film, Roy "Mad Dog" Earle—Humphrey Bogart in a career-changing performance—is a former Dillinger associate who hails from the Dust Bowl. But Earle, for Burnett, is not a gangster or a member of organized crime but represents, instead, a "reversion to the western bandit."[3] When Earle's released from prison after Big Mac (Donald MacBride) has purchased a pardon from the governor, the world has passed him by. Before he meets up with the other, younger members of the heist gang at Shaw's Camp high in the Sierra Mountains, "Mad Dog" visits the family farm, and it's as if he's mourning his life even as he's living it. Later, during the Tropico Springs Inn heist, he's forced to kill a guard and flees to the "high sierra," where he's gunned down by the police.

If *High Sierra* is the "twilight of the American gangster," Earle is a representative of "rural America and a simpler time."[4] In Burnett's *Asphalt Jungle* (1950), composed almost a decade after *High Sierra*, the grassroots America signified by the combination of self-reliant farmer and Midwestern bank robber has hardened into an "asphalt jungle." While Dix Handley is not a "big shot," he's a man out of time, and in his desire to "crash out," he's "rushing toward death" like Roy Earle.

In *The Asphalt Jungle*, Dix dreams day and night about returning to his childhood home in Kentucky. In the first dream, he's sound asleep despite the sunshine streaming through the window and the sound of the city outside:

> The snow was falling lightly over the cornfield—first snow of the year. He and Lou Sally went out to gather pumpkins for Halloween. It was toward evening and dark; thin smoke was rising straight up from the farmhouse chimney. The sky was the color of slate, and a big, rayless red autumn sun was going down just beyond a rise in the flat farm land. Big, fat orange-colored pumpkins were scattered all over the field among the corn shocks.[5]

The passage is significant precisely because Dix is asleep. In other words, in this "scene" Dix's unconscious speaks, and it's all about a "safe pleasant field" far removed from the reality of his environs, Camden Square, the "immense downtown slum beyond the river where there was one bar at every intersection, prowl cars by the dozen, and harness bulls working in pairs" and where, at night, the rain slicked the "streets and pavements, turning them into black, fun-house mirrors that reflected in grotesque distortions the street lights and neon signs."[6] The difference between the past and present—Boone County and Camden Square—is, in brief, the difference between day and night.

In the second dream, Dix has just reviewed the plan for a heist of a jewelry store named Belletier's. He's lying in a cot in a bunk room behind his friend Gus's hamburger joint and staring out a high window at a "small patch of sky, jeweled with a star."[7] The "clatter of dishes, laughter, [and] desultory talk" gradually fades away, replaced by a bucolic vision of "home country":

> blue grass, crows in the woods, mares heavy with foal nuzzling you at the fence corners, good fishing in the creeks and good swimming, good company, too, of an autumn evening when there was frost in the air and a wood fire was jumping in the hearth.[8]

In this reverie Dix is not sleeping but day- or, more properly, night-dreaming. This is the good life—in the best, Platonic sense—and Burnett's use of the second-person pronoun captures the urgency and immediacy of Dix's "blinding desire."[9] Sitting up suddenly, Dix is disoriented and feels that "he had been lifted up in the night by unknown hands and carried to this place of exile, this alien city . . . far from home, far from sense and meaning."[10]

The third dream occurs in medias res—in, that is, the middle of the heist. The prompt for Dix is the faint whirring sound of the small electric drill that the "boxer," Louis, is using to break into the safe at Belletier's. The sound reminds Dix of the happiest time of his life:

Katydids! Little devils, singing all the summer night while the full moon rose above the hill at the edge of the cornfield, laying a pale-blue drugget over the countryside, the frogs plucked bass strings in the pond where the cattails waved and the bluish witch light of the will-o'-the-wisp flickered overt the stagnant water, and the cows rubbed their sides against the fences and sometimes lowed plaintively in the darkness as if afraid. Dogs barked from farm to farm, answering one another, and keeping up a wordless conversation far into the night, and freight trains hooted lonesomely at the far edge of the horizon, trailing a long plume of gray smoke streaked underneath with red reflections from a firebox.[11]

The final image of "freight trains hooting lonesomely at the far edge of the horizon" condenses time and space in a chronotopic figure structured by the paradoxical logic of the *après coup*. Even as Dix is looking out onto a city square, standing watch on a heist that, if everything goes as planned, will allow him to realize his heart's desire, he's lost in a reverie. The image of the freight train, though, marks the limits of his fantasy. As in the classical pastoral, his harmonious vision of nature is predicated on industrial culture, as if his reverie were a diorama in a natural history museum. In this diorama the "long plume of gray smoke" is a synecdoche of the smokestacks and dark satanic mills of the mid-century Midwestern American metropolis, and the epithet "lonesomely" is an index of an existential aloneness from which, short of death, there is no sanctuary.

Dore Schary, during his second tenure as head of production at MGM, purchased *The Asphalt Jungle* in manuscript form from Burnett himself. Though MGM as the producing studio was an anomaly ("To MGM a 'crime' picture was not," according to the author, a "major picture"[12]), producer Arthur Hornblow Jr. was wise enough to hire John Huston to write the screenplay with Ben Maddow. While Maddow had previously adapted *Intruder in the Dust* (1949) from William Faulkner's novel of the same title, Huston had already worked on *Law and Order* (1932), an adaptation of Burnett's *Saint Johnson* (1930), as well as *High Sierra*, and as his direction of *The Maltese Falcon* demonstrated, he respected the source material. Huston and Maddow's script for *The Asphalt Jungle* stayed, as Burnett noted, "close to the action, the characters, and the atmosphere."[13] "Quite a few of my novels and stories have been turned into motion pictures," Burnett observed; "not one of them pleased me as much as *The Asphalt Jungle*, neither *Little Caesar* nor *High Sierra*."[14] Burnett took issue, however, with two aspects of Huston's direction: the beginning and the end. With respect to the beginning,

Burnett wanted the picture to start, as the novel does, with the "horrific news of the nightly toll of crime coming over the Commissioner's radio, the voice of the asphalt jungle."[15] The picture "instead starts as any small-time crime story might": "night, slums, an individual pursuing his individual way."[16]

I will return to Burnett's complaint in the conclusion to this chapter, but it appears that he was displeased that Huston had made a genre picture—that is to say, a gangster noir—with the requisite semantic elements (night, slums, etc.). In fact, *The Asphalt Jungle* begins not at night but in the early morning daylight as a police car prowls a "poor neighborhood" (read "slums") of an anonymous Midwestern city. Visually speaking, the introductory scenes of the film are unremarkable, but the sound track—both the score (Miklós Rózsa's pulsing music) and the ambient sound (the police car radio that counterpoints the score)—is at once animated and atmospheric.

Cut to a prowl car climbing a hill past a dilapidated rooming house (a wide shot that, due to the terrain, appears canted) succeeded by a wide shot of a man in a dark suit and fedora who, hearing the police radio, dodges behind a column before walking straight toward the camera. The man is Dix Handley (Sterling Hayden), and in the novel the narrator remarks that there was something about the bones of his face that was a "little alien, as if he had an ancestor who was part Indian."[17] The bones of Hayden's face may not look alien, but his character, Dix, definitely looks alienated, dominated as he is by an arcade whose enormous concrete columns dwarf even this tall, big-boned man with the stern, no-nonsense countenance. Dix's destination is a run-down café that advertises "HOME COOKING" and "AMERICAN FOOD," although the sign next door—"PILGRIM HOUSE"— gestures to America's colonial origins and suggests that Dix is not so much an Indian as a pilgrim, not unlike Ethan Edwards (John Wayne) in John Ford's *The Searchers* (1956). Here, Huston's film invokes the American jeremiad, in which the big city is seen as a machine that represents a fall from the Edenic innocence of the garden or country.[18]

The transition from the first to the second sequence of *The Asphalt Jungle*— and from the exterior to the interior—is effected via a sonic cue: a radio that Gus (James Whitmore), the café's proprietor, turns up as he slips Dix's gun into the cash register when two cops walk through the door searching for the person who held up the Hotel de Paris the previous night. If Dix is a vagrant (the charge that the cops, failing to find a gun, haul him in on), Gus is socially ostracized because he has a humped back. (Later, a truck driver who's "stealing looks at the girl pictures in a movie mag"[19]—a bit that foreshadows the later, calendar scene with Erwin "Doc" Riedenschneider [Sam Jaffe]—calls Gus "Humpty-Dumpty," at which point Gus Spanish-walks the truck driver out the front door.)

In *Public Enemies, Public Heroes* Jonathan Munby argues that the heist or caper film reiterates, as in the American jeremiad, the conflict between the "civic community" (gemeinschaft) and society-as-corporation (gesellschaft).[20] In other words, unlike a classic gangster picture like *Little Caesar*, the heist film is less about the individual gangster than the gang, where the latter functions as a surrogate family diametrically opposed to the alienating forces of modernity and legitimate society. In *The Asphalt Jungle* legitimate society is represented by Commissioner Hardy (John McIntire), who, in the novel, is the new, reformed face of a corrupt city administration. Lou Farbstein, a middle-age reporter for the *World* whose point of view informs the first chapter of Burnett's novel, has been looking "like Diogenes for an honest man for a long time, and had begun to feel that the flame in his lantern would sputter out before he found him. But, though the flame had shortened almost to nothing, here he was at last. Hardy!"[21] In Huston's film we're introduced to Hardy as he's lecturing Lieutenant Ditrich (Barry Kelley) about the Fourth Precinct: "thirty-four thefts, thirty-three burglaries, eighteen robberies, seven assaults, five morals offenses in the last thirty days. That's a record." Now, Hardy continues, "one of the most dangerous criminals alive is . . . at large in this city."

Cut to a taxi cab pulling up in front of a warehouse. Out steps a little man in a dark overcoat and homburg, "one of the most dangerous criminals alive." Huston sharpens the disjunction between the commissioner's hyperbolic rhetoric and the object of his outrage when the little man, Doc, introduces himself to Cobby (Marc Lawrence), the ferret-like man—"a parvenu among aristocrats"[22]—who runs the establishment. "Herr Doktor," with his slight, German-accented voice and exquisite sense of politesse, "possesses a cosmopolitan air that's at odds with the derelict surroundings."[23] Still, the first thing that Doc does when Cobby pours a drink for himself is to peruse the Vargas calendar on the wall. If Cobby, with his bowtie and pencil mustache, is an "amateur in a society of professionals" who dreams about "prestige and status," Doc is a "wise man of the underworld" who fantasizes about "escape and girls."[24]

Still, Riedenschneider, unlike Cobby, has a scheme to realize his dreams—a detailed plan for a half-a-million-dollar caper ("a ripe plum ready to fall")—and needs only fifty thousand dollars to put it into operation. While Cobby repairs to his office to telephone the "Big Fixer," Alonzo D. Emmerich (Louis Calhern), Doc steals another look at the calendar—there's a close-up of a young girl with her hands tied behind her back—just as Dix arrives to place a bet. The connection is subtle but unmistakable: just as Doc's Achilles' heel is girls, *young* girls, Dix's weakness is the horses. When Cobby "bones" Dix—"Your tab's good to twenty-five hundred. But that's the limit"—Dix leaves in a huff. "My book beats him and beats him," Cobby crows, "but he keeps coming back for more." Dix is a big-time loser (he owes the book twenty-three hundred dollars); at the same time, he can't bear to be in debt to a small-minded man like Cobby. The good news is that since Gus wants him to lay low for a while—"the Happiness Boys are on the rampage"—he's willing to stake Dix a thousand dollars and hits up a friend, Louis Ciavelli (Anthony Caruso), for the rest.

Unlike every other character in the film, Louis has a family—a wife, Maria (Teresa Celli), and a baby boy, Louis Jr. However, the deep-focus shot of Louis in striped pajamas on the phone in the foreground of the frame and, in the background, the brass bars of a bed on which his wife lies wide awake conveys a feeling of entrapment: "I got mouths to feed and rent to pay and all that stuff." The ensuing shots—the first a medium, slightly low one of Louis tattooed with shadows, the second a high, chiaroscuro-drenched one of Maria rocking Louis Jr.'s crib—only reinforce the sense of imprisonment. While Louis in Burnett's novel is an "expert trouble-shooter for a big electrical-appliance store" and makes "pretty good money," this front is absent in Huston's film. Hence the attraction for Louis—as for Dix, Gus, and Cobby—of a big score.

Cobby, "the biggest, non-syndicate bookie in the city,"[25] is the liaison between Doc, the mastermind, and Emmerich, the "front man." In Burnett's novel a "big shiny Cadillac" is parked outside Emmerich's "cottage"; in the film an interior three-shot establishes the power relations among the three men.[26] Cobby stands, drink in hand, between Doc, who's sitting with his back to us, and Emmerich, who's dressed in a well-tailored dinner jacket and seated in a leather, brass-tacked wingback chair that frames his large, key-lit face. Despite the fact that Doc's fresh out of prison, he's figuratively allied with Emmerich because of his cosmopolitanism and proposes that the personnel—a driver, a "boxman" (safecracker), and a "hooligan" (gunman)—"will be paid like house painters." Here, it's as if the other members of the crew are mere craftsmen—that is, working men with a specialized, labor-intensive trade or skill set.[27] In the novel Doc adds that these men "will have no part in the division of the take,"[28] a locution that emphasizes the division of labor between the personnel and the bank (Emmerich) or "brains" (Riedenschneider). In other words, the driver, gunman, and safecracker are depicted as "functional units" in a hierarchical structure "based on the Fordist division of labor," in which the workers are hired hands who are just as alienated from "criminal" as from "social" labor.[29] The heist gang therefore appears less like a family and more like a mini-corporation, an inflection that suggests just how deeply the organizational ethos had penetrated American society at the beginning of the 1950s.[30]

In this top-down criminal hierarchy, Emmerich is the putative head; as a "top-notch criminal lawyer,"[31] he also mediates between the heist gang and legitimate society. This said, one of the ironies of *The Asphalt Jungle* is that Emmerich is actually a front for a front: the Cadillac and expensively furnished cottage notwithstanding—"Why, in this 'cottage,'" Doc reflects, "the furnishings alone must be worth nearly fifty thousand"[32]—he's flat broke. The audience discovers this only later when Emmerich confesses his secret to Bob Brannom (Brad Dexter), a private detective he has phoned to collect whatever outstanding debts are owed him, but the film makes perfectly clear the cause of his financial woes.

Thus, after Emmerich shows the men to the door—on the way Doc remarks that, once the job's over, "it's Mexico for me" ("Mexican girls are very pretty. I'll have nothing to do all day long, but chase them in the sunshine")—he proceeds down a hall to the living room, where Angela Phinlay (Marilyn Monroe), a curvaceous young woman with blonde hair, is fast asleep.[33] (Compare this passage with, for example, the scene in Robert Siodmak's *Criss Cross* where Anna [Yvonne DeCarlo]—the prize in the masculine rivalry between Steve Thompson [Burt Lancaster] and Slim Dundee [Dan Duryea]—is sound asleep on a couch while the rest of the gang is busy planning the caper.) "I had the market send over some salt mackerel for you—best grade they could find," Angela, suddenly waking up, says brightly, "I know how you love it for breakfast." "Some sweet kid," Emmerich says, as if to himself.

In the novel, however, Emmerich reflects bitterly and at length on his relationship with Angela:

> She'd cost him a fortune. He'd furnished this cottage for her; he'd given her money by the handfuls; he'd sent checks to her mother and several other relatives; he'd bought her a car, a mink coat, a diamond bracelet. And now he was sitting here drinking his beer and wondering why the hell he had done it.[34]

Monroe's abbreviated performance as Angela is indelible and provides a pretty good idea about why Emmerich has done it. The Hustonian antihero is a dreamer (see *The Maltese Falcon*): if Doc dreams about nubile Mexican girls, Emmerich's fantasies have foundered on the "doll" with the "beautiful hair" and "lovely body" curled up on the couch.[35]

As opposed to Doc's and Emmerich's dreams of escape, Dix's fantasy life does not revolve around women; he's obsessed instead about "making a killing" on the ponies, a dream that's fueled in turn by another, deeper dream wish: to buy back the Kentucky bluegrass farm where he was born and bred. Thus, when Gus phones him about the heist, Doll Conovan (Jean Hagen), a woman whom Dix has reluctantly taken in like a stray (the club she works at has just been raided), wakes him up. Dix has been talking in his sleep, although the only words she could make out were "Corn Cracker." Dix, as if he's still under the spell of the dream, recalls:

"Some Sweet Kid": "Uncle" Alonzo D. Emmerich (Louis Calhern) wakes "niece" Angela (Marilyn Monroe) in *The Asphalt Jungle* (1950).

He was a tall, black colt. . . . I was on that colt's back. My father and grandfather were there, watching the fun. The colt was back-jumpin' and pitchin'—and once he tried to scrape me off against the tree, but I stayed with him, you bet. Then I heard my grandpa say, "He's a real Handley, that boy—a real Handley!" And I felt proud as you please.

When Doll asks Dix if it really happened just as he said it did in the dream, he continues:

Not exactly. The black colt pitched me into a fence on the first buck, and my father came over and prodded me with his boot and said, "Maybe that'll teach you not to brag about how good you are on a horse."

If the difference between Dix's dream and the reality of what happened turns on paternal validation ("He's a real Handley"), his post-dream reverie pivots on his ancestry and the Handley name, both of which indicate a certain breeding or class. Dix, continuing to reminisce, tells Doll that "one of [his] ancestors imported the first Irish thoroughbred into our country" and that the Handley farm—160 acres ("thirty in blue grass, the rest in crops, fine barns, seven broodmares")—"was in the family for generations":

Then everything happened at once—my old man died, we lost our crop, the black colt I was telling you about broke his leg and had to be shot. . . . The mares were sold to save the farm, but we lost it anyway. I'll never forget the day we left. Me and my brother swore we would buy the farm back some day.

However, at the beginning of *The Asphalt Jungle*, everything is not lost—yet. Dix tells Doll about how, betting on the horses, he was once on the verge of having enough "moo" to buy back Hickory Wood: "Twelve grand would have swung it, and I almost made it once. I had more than five thousand in my pocket—Whirlaway was running in the Preakness. I figured he couldn't lose. I put it all on the nose. He lost by a nose." Now, despite the string of bad luck, Dix figures that his "luck's got to turn."

Unlike the '50s syndicate picture, the heist film as a subgenre centers on the preparation and the execution of a robbery: "The pièce de résistance . . . is often an elaborate presentation of the heist itself, at great length and detail, in order to display its intricacy, precision, and fine workmanship."[36] Depending on the picture, the heist film also reveals the motivation of the individual gang members. The Asphalt Jungle is a paradigmatic heist film not simply because it details the planning and execution of a heist but because it exemplifies the crisscross of plot and intention that's the "ultimate law" of the subgenre.[37] Here, as J. P. Telotte observes in "Fatal Capers," the heist film generates the sort of tensions and pleasures that exemplify the "noir project" and isolates them for examination.[38] In sum, if the classic heist film is a transgressive fantasy whose pleasures mime those of classical realist film, "fatality writes an end to the fantasy and its transgressive pleasures."[39]

Accordingly, when Emmerich realizes that he can't raise the fifty thousand dollars necessary to fund the job (Brannom has been unable to bleed any money from Emmerich's debtors), he confesses that he's been "dreaming up a double cross." Moreover, he claims he can fence the jewels, then disappear: "Take a plane to another country—to another life. Melt down the gold and platinum and sell it as bullion. Dispose of the rocks, one by one . . . they'd last a lifetime." Emmerich's double cross—a plot turn that's central to both The Killers and Criss Cross—is therefore critical to the fatal libidinal economy of The Asphalt Jungle because when Dix, Doc, Louis, and Gus rendezvous at Gus's diner to rehearse the plan, the audience already knows that, despite Doc's meticulous, "beautifully worked out" scheme—"from the observed routine of the personnel to the alarm system, the type of locks on the doors, and the age and condition of the main safe"[40]—the heist is compromised, fatally so. At the same time, one consequence of this dramatic irony is that the audience is encouraged to identify even more with the tradesmen who will actually carry out the heist, allied as they are against the law and a would-be thief turned traitor. (Needless to say, there is no "honor among thieves" in The Asphalt Jungle.)

The fact that the access to the Belletier jewelry store is an "old storm tunnel" that leads to the store's furnace room—the subtitle of Huston's film is "The City under the City"—literalizes the notion of an underworld. As soon as Louis drops down a manhole, having handed the "soup" to Dix (who, in a wonderfully resonant gesture, gently places the explosive in the crease of his fedora), he's trapped by pipes that funnel, as in Renaissance perspective, to infinity. This horizontal

Safe Work: "boxman" Louis Ciavelli (Anthony Caruso) cracks a safe as "idea man" Doc Riedenschneider (Sam Jaffe) checks his watch in *The Asphalt Jungle* (1950).

entrapment is mirrored by the vertical bars of a gate that opens onto the alcove where the safe's located. (The alcove is protected by an "electric eye," novel technology circa 1950.) The gate itself is featured in a pair of deep-focus rhyming shots: in the first, the camera is tight on Louis in the foreground of the frame as he drills into the safe, while in the background and to the right of the gate, Doc sits in the customer's chair, smoking a cigar and glancing periodically at his watch. In the second shot, Doc's standing, a cigar poised in the air like a conductor's baton, as Louis pulls the cork out of the bottle with his teeth, then uses the eyedropper in his gloved hand to extract enough "nitro" to blow the safe.

The explosive works like a charm—there's a heavy, muffled blast—but as Dix reports from his lookout onto the square, it sets off alarms all along the block. (The film's ambient sound track—designed by veteran MGM soundman Douglas Shearer—is expressively audible in the relatively silent, dialogue-free heist sequence.) Though the men decide to proceed, sirens can be heard in the distance when Louis's drill suddenly breaks. Louis calmly fishes a new drill out of his overcoat, and after a couple of sharp hammer blows and with the aid of a skeleton key, the doors of the safe swing open. The overhead shot of Doc emptying tray after velvet tray of precious stones—rubies and star sapphires—into a briefcase provides the audience with a privileged perspective on the climax of the heist.

Now that the gang has the goods in hand, the back door, which opens onto the alley, is the preferred means of escape. However, the bars on the window of the door, which echo the steam tunnel pipes and the alcove gate, foreshadow the appearance of the night watchman, who, noticing that the door's slightly ajar, enters with gun drawn. Dix does what he has been hired to do, knocking the man down, but when the gun flies out of the guard's hand, it strikes the floor and goes off, the errant shot striking Louis. In the novel Doc reflects that "chance, or whatever you wanted to call it, was the kind of thing you could never allow for, no matter how carefully you planned," then, indignant at the futility of it all, he rails:

Why plan at all? Why not blunder about impulsively, trusting in God, like the rest of the chumps and hoosiers? You figure everything out down to the last detail, hours and hours of planning, then . . . what? A burglar alarm goes off for no sensible reason—as if merely to point the finger at you. . . . Then a gun butt hits the floor by chance; the gun, a senseless hunk of metal, fires of its own accord; and a man is shot![41]

Just as the above pointing finger recollects the celebrated fateful conclusion to *Detour* (1945), the slashing bars of shadow on the manhole as the men climb out of the city under the city reiterate the dominant trope of *The Asphalt Jungle*: imprisonment.

If godless chance dogs the heist in Huston's film, human frailty haunts the aftermath. After Gus escorts Louis home to be attended to by a doctor, Doc and Dix go straight to Emmerich's cottage, where, when they balk at his suggestion that they leave the jewels with him, Brannom pulls a gun on them. Dix pretends to go along with Brannom's order, but when Doc tosses the bag onto the floor, Dix shoots and kills Brannom. In an echo of the errant gunshot in the jewelry store, Emmerich manages to get off a shot and Dix, despite jumping sideways, is seriously wounded. Cut—in a classic low-key sequence—to Emmerich dumping Brannom's body into the river.

Warned by Gus that the "dragnet's out" and the police are "combing the district," Doc and Dix hide out in the attic of Donato's, an Italian grocery store. Dissolve from an establishing shot of the store to the interior, where Doc is standing at the top of the stairs listening to Donato (Alberto Morin) talking on the phone, Doc's face framed by the shadow of a barred window etched onto the opposite brick wall. Doc has good news—Emmerich has arranged for the insurance company to buy back the jewels for $250,000, "no questions asked." The chiaroscuro window shot, not unlike the bar imagery during the heist sequence, is not, however, auspicious.

While Doc and Dix wait to hear back from Cobby about the insurance, Dix plays solitaire, an activity that accents the play of chance in the film even as it aligns his character with Emmerich's casino-playing wife, May (Dorothy Tree). In the meantime, Doc, cigar in hand, fantasizes about Mexico: "It's eight thousand feet up. The air is very pure, many first-class clubs and restaurants, a horse track, and girls—plenty young girls." Doc's reference to a horse track is intended to bait Dix, to whom he offers an invitation, "all expenses paid," to accompany him to Mexico. Dix, though, replies that his mind's made up (he's heading south to Kentucky). Doc's philosophical: "Listen, Dix. You can always go home, and when you do it's nothing. Believe me, I've done it—nothing." Doc here is the voice of the city and modernity: the past is past and the idea of home, a prelapsarian place uncorrupted by the vagaries of the present, is an utter illusion. Thomas Wolfe was right: you can't go home again.

If the country as a refuge or sanctuary is a pipe dream in *The Asphalt Jungle*, the city, at least for the heisters, has become a "city of nets." Forced to move, Doc and Dix are making their way to Dix's apartment on Camden Street (the setting—fog, neon, and dark, decrepit buildings—is atmospherically evoked by Hal Rosson) when a cop with a flashlight stops them. In a reprise of the earlier jewelry store sequence, Dix knocks the cop down but not before the "harness bull" splits Doc's head open. Back at Dix's apartment, Doc, blood streaming down his face, cries out, "A broken down old harness bull, no good for chasing anything but kids has to trip over us. Blind accident! What can you do against blind accident!"

That Doc fails to note that the "bull" got a good look at him when he mentioned that a "bunch of hoodlums had been bringing young girls" to the area speaks to his character's weakness, though Doc does acknowledge his complicity in the mess that he and Dix now find themselves in: "I'm not kidding myself. It was the extra dough Emmerich promised. I got greedy. Greed made me blind." Needless to say, the sin of greed is not exclusive to Doc; it also applies to Emmerich and *his* Achilles' heel, Angela, who, having become his alibi, has suddenly become a real liability. Hence his suggestion that she "might like to take a trip." Angela, who's dressed in a low-cut, off-the-shoulder black dress, is lying like a wayward child across Emmerich's lap, chattering about Cuba and the green bathing suit she's going to wear there—"Yipe!"—when Hardy and two cops show up.

Three scenes in quick succession spell the end of the road not only for Emmerich but also for Gus, Cobby, and Louis: first, Angela wilts under Hardy's questioning, then Emmerich commits suicide in his office, the blast from the revolver blowing the torn-up letter he was writing to his wife across the desk blotter like leaves; Gus is being led to his cell when he sees Cobby, who's already behind bars after having been broken by Ditrich, and physically attacks him before he's pulled away; and a policeman and two detectives approach Louis's apartment only to discover a priest, a casket, and a grieving widow. The barred shadow of a window on the wall of Louis's apartment, which recalls the window shadow at Donato's, supplies a graphic epitaph.

Now the only members of the gang who are still free or alive are Doc and Dix, who, despite their mutual respect for each other, decide to separate. In a reverse echo of the film's beginning, Doc gets into a taxi and asks the driver to take him across town to where his relatives live. But once he sees that the driver's name is Frank Schurz (Henry Rowland), he asks him in German if he has any friends in the old country—"*Haben sie Bekannten in Deutschland?*"—and when Frank answers, "*Ach, ja!*" Doc offers him a fifty-dollar tip to drive him all the way to Cleveland. Frank: "How about your relatives?" / Doc: "Forget 'em." Home, for Doc, "is where the money is."

They're on their way out of the city when Frank says they should stop for gas. Doc, having just passed a cop before getting into the taxi, replies that they should wait until they're out of town:

> DOC: Then we can do everything at once: have a little meal, beer, a cigar, and
> go in comfort.
> FRANK: I can see you're a man who likes his pleasures.
> DOC: What else is there in life?

Dissolve to a diner where a dark-haired boy is jitterbugging with a teenage, be-ribboned girl as Doc and Frank sit at the bar. When the song ends, the girl, who could be a younger version of Emmerich's "little niece,"[42] turns to the jukebox and says, "Let's play some more." The only problem is that the two boys who are with her are fresh out of nickels. The girl's complaining—"Where do we go? To a third-rate movie. Then we take a drive and blow two tires. Not one, but two. Then we come in here and he treats me to what? A Coke!"—when Doc takes a roll of nickels the bartender has just given him and breaks it on the table right in front of the girl, saying, "I like music, too." Doc then takes the girl's seat, after which she begins jitterbugging with the other, blond boy until, waving him off, she starts dancing all by herself. Rhythmically waving her hands in the air, she dances past Doc toward the camera, the low angle accenting her tight sweater; in the reverse shot, Doc sits entranced by her exhibitionist abandon. The girl twirls and slaps her hands, dancing backward toward the window of the diner, where two motorcycle cops, their gold badges glinting in the light, watch through the

Snatched: policemen surveil Doc Riedenschneider (Sam Jaffe) as he watches a jitter-bugging girl in *The Asphalt Jungle* (1950).

open bars of the Venetian blinds.[43] It's an extraordinarily suggestive shot: it's not simply that Doc, completely absorbed in the pleasures of the moment, is blind again—this time to the police intently watching outside—but that the repressive, censorious gaze of the law is conflated with the fetishism and voyeurism of classical male scopophilia.

Frank, who has been patiently standing behind Doc, reminds him for the third time that "it's getting late." Doc, though, is in no hurry. Mexico, at least for the moment, can wait: "Plenty of time, my friend, plenty of time." So the girl continues to dance, and Doc continues to watch until the song ends:

GIRL: Don't go. We haven't used all the nickels.
DOC: You use them.
GIRL: Thanks, thanks ever so much.
DOC: The pleasure was all mine.

Doc and Frank are exiting the diner when the motorcycle cops intercept them. While one of them takes Doc's overcoat and slaps the pocket, jangling the jewels sewn into the lining, Doc asks the other one, "How long have you been out here?" The cop pauses, then answers: "We've been watching you through that window for two or three minutes." Doc's reply—"Say about as long as it takes to play a phonograph record"—betrays an acute awareness of the passing pleasures of the moment and an equally acute appreciation of the price such pleasures sometimes exact.

Cut to a sedan where Dix and Doll are stopped in front of a railroad crossing as a freight train passes, the X of the crossbuck bars flashing in the light. When Dix's head slumps against the wheel, Doll jumps out of the car and rushes around to the other side and gets in, then, crossing the tracks, hails the switchman, who directs her to a doctor's house. At the house, the doctor inspects Dix. Doll: "Is it bad?" / Doctor: "It isn't good." Next, the doctor goes into an adjacent room to call the police; when he returns, Dix and Doll are gone, and the doctor tells the switchman that Dix "hasn't got enough blood in him to keep a chicken alive."

In the novel, Dix and Doll drive straight to the farm, where he stands in front of the family house in "blank bewilderment":

There were the trees the bats used to fly out of on summer evenings, hunting their dinner. There was the trampled dooryard and the big oak whose trunk he used to try to span with his outstretched arms. . . . And there, just above him . . . was the room where he'd been born.

In his delirium, Dix seems to have forgotten that his family no longer lives there. In fact, the current owner is a "fat little Polack" with a "slight foreign accent" like Doc's. Dix's family lives, instead, in a "run-down-looking little farm house" with "a light in the window."[44] When Dix and Doll show up, Dix's brother, Woodford, answers the door and his mother cries, "Glory, it's William Tuttle." Dix, meanwhile, is talking again in his sleep:

> Damn foolishness, or just pure greed, as his mother had said, when the old man sold the big black colt to a horseman from Lexington. Tuttle couldn't stand to see him led away. . . . He'd never forget that day. Sunlight was warm in the dooryard, and the hoarse cawing of the crows sounded from the cornfield.[45]

A "vaguely familiar voice" that seems to come from a long distance away breaks in on Dix's dream. It's Doc Carmichael and he's speaking to Dix's brother: "Not much use, Woodford. Do the best I can. But. . . ."

The dénouement of Huston's film represents, as Burnett recognized, a substantial revision. Huston and Maddow not only invert the conclusion of the novel, which ends with Commissioner Hardy sound asleep at his house followed by a coda featuring the reporter Farbstein, but they also reintroduce a critical passage from the first chapter to ironize the commissioner's big speech. The setting is Hardy's city office at dawn, and he has just responded to a reporter's question about Ditrich—"Lieutenant Ditrich is in jail, and he'll go to trial"—when, in the process of defending the police ("People are people, even in blue uniform"), he switches on one loudspeaker after another, the battery channels blinking like traffic lights:

> We send police assistance to every one of these calls. Because they're not just code numbers or a radio beam. They're cries for help: people are being cheated, robbed, murdered, raped [switching on a third channel] and it goes on twenty-four hours a day [switching on a fourth channel] every day in the year.

Hardy's next gesture is equally melodramatic. "Suppose," he says, switching off all four channels on the battery, "we had no police force, good or bad. Suppose we just had silence." The commissioner then answers his own rhetorical question: "No one to listen. No one to answer. The jungle wins. The criminals take over."

The conclusion to Hardy's monologue, composed by Huston and Maddow, recalls the beginning of the film and the commissioner's description of Riedenschneider:

> Well, gentlemen, three men are in jail; three dead, one by his own hand; and one man is a fugitive, and we've reason to think, badly wounded. . . . In many ways he's the most dangerous of them all. A hardened killer, a hooligan, a man without human feeling or human mercy.

Dissolve to a high wide-angle shot of a meadow and a bridge in the distance, while on the far right-hand side of the screen, a dark sedan speeds down a lane toward the camera. Cut to the sedan racing diagonally from left to right past a white picket fence as, in the foreground, horses graze in a meadow. (The color and speed of the sedan are, in the context, incongruous.)

The road crests, then dips—it's a POV shot—and suddenly we're not distanced from Dix, despite Hardy's lecture, but right there in the car with him and Doll. In the subsequent extreme close-up, Dix's unshaven, grizzled face is silvered with shadow and he's lost again in reverie, in a dream of homecoming that has haunted him his entire life:

> I tell you, the black one's the best. The bay is all right, but the black is a real good colt. Prettiest way of going of anything Pa ever bred, easy as thank you, but he's always way out in front of the other yearlings. I sure hope Pa don't sell him. He's a stake horse or I never saw one. That black colt will win Pa out of debt if he only hangs on to him.

Dix pulls the car over to the side of the road and gets out, his white shirt stained with blood as he pushes open a gate that reads "HICKORY WOOD FARM." Cut to a medium shot of Dix in the foreground, his hands hanging at his sides, Doll right behind him in a dark overcoat as he stumbles toward the camera, the clouds above bright with sunlight.

A horse is galloping toward Dix when he falls to the ground. Doll runs toward him, the camera fixed as the eyes of God. Cut to an extremely low-angle medium close-up of Doll turning over Dix's body—"Dix, Dix . . ."—succeeded by a high wide shot of her running toward the farmhouse. In the penultimate shot of the film, a horse nuzzles Dix's neck as he lies faceup on the earth, his eyes and mouth open to the brilliant autumnal air and sky.

What remains arresting about the dénouement of *The Asphalt Jungle*—one deepened by the etymological sense of the word "caper" as a form of horsemanship—is the "stark contrast" between the dead man and the live dumb animals in which the word "dumb" translates, as in Pieter Bruegel's *Landscape with the Fall of Icarus*, the horses' "utter incomprehension of what has happened."[46] At the same time, the film's ending reiterates the opposition in Huston's film between the fatalism associated with film noir and the utopian impulse for social transcendence associated with American realism where (and this speaks to the existentialist strain of the film) the freedom that Dix finds in the end comes only, as it does for Roy Earle, with death.[47]

Though the PCA completely missed the ambiguity of the ending (Questionnaire: "Does the story tend to enlist the sympathy of the audience for criminals?" Answer: "No"), *The Asphalt Jungle*, which was made during the HUAC hearings, is Huston's "swansong to the American crime film," reflecting his "despondency and disenchantment" in the postwar period.[48] Since he was a founding member of the Committee for the First Amendment and, according to Burnett, cast three Communists in *The Asphalt Jungle* (Hayden, Jaffe, and Lawrence), it is therefore no surprise that in 1949, in a review of *We Were Strangers*, *The Hollywood Reporter*, vigorously eschewing understatement, outed Huston as a Communist: "It is the heaviest dish of [revolutionary theory] ever served to an audience outside of the Soviet Union."[49] The writing, as it were, was on the wall. In this hysterical context, both Ditrich's savage beating of Cobby in order to turn him and Gus's subsequent attack on the bookie capture the traitorous climate of the "witch hunt," a Catch-22 that would characterize Sterling Hayden's subsequent encounters with HUAC.[50]

When Emmerich phones Angela to warn her that the police may want to talk to her about his alibi, he offhandedly explains that it's "good old dirty politics." The politics may have been old and they were certainly dirty, but they were not, in the end, good for anyone—except, of course, McCarthy and his gang. The vision of the good life on which the heist in *The Asphalt Jungle* is predicated—New Deal liberalism and a certain pastoral idealism[51]—had, by 1950, vanished in the winds of change like the plume of smoke from a streaking, lonesomely hooting train.

8

THE BIG CAPER

> Men who live outside the law are surprisingly like
> those who live within it. They have their loyalties
> to family and friends to the same degree that the
> butcher, the baker, and the candlestick maker
> have.
>
> —Willie Sutton, in *I, Willie Sutton*, by Quentin
> Reynolds

ARMORED CAR ROBBERY: STRIPTEASE

On August 21, 1934, a West Side hood by the name of John Manning disguised as an ice vendor in a long white apron pushed a three-wheeled cart toward the Rubel Ice Corporation at Bay 19th Street in the Bath Beach section of Brooklyn. At 12:25 p.m., an armored car from the United States Trucking Corporation pulled up in front of Rubel's. One of the guards drew his revolver and stepped out of the cab. When, following procedure, the other guard got out, Manning threw aside the burlap sacks blanketing his cart, grabbed one of the submachine guns hidden there, and "jammed its snout into the driver's compartment."[1] The remaining members of the gang—Percy Geary, Francis Oley, and Archie Stewart—had been lounging in the vicinity and, springing to life, disarmed the guards and driver. After they forced the armored car crew and the milling iceman to crawl under a platform and lie flat on their faces, Joseph Kress and Bernard McMahon moved two sedans, a Lincoln and Nash, respectively, next to the armored car. John Oley, Francis's brother, climbed inside the truck and started tossing bags of money to Kress and McMahon, who put them into the Lincoln. After John Oley had tucked the last bag of money under his arm, he, Kress, Geary, and his brother got into the Lincoln; McMahon, Stewart, and Manning climbed into the Nash; and the two sedans roared off. The men drove to Gravesend Bay at the foot of Bay 38th

Street in Brooklyn, where they boarded a "mahogany-colored speedboat" and a "Sea Bright power dory."[2] No one in the gang had fired a shot, no one had been injured, and everything had gone exactly as planned. The heist itself had taken only two or three minutes and the haul was $437,950, at the time the "largest amount of cash ever taken in the history of American crime."[3]

In 1950 Robert Angus and Robert Lees wrote a treatment of the Brooklyn armored car robbery, and Earl Felton and Gerald Drayson Adams "turned the treatment into an unusually tight, hard-edged screenplay" originally titled *Code 3*.[4] ("Code 3" refers to an emergency police response in which sirens and lights are employed.) Although *The Asphalt Jungle* went into production earlier, in December 1949, both Huston's film and *Armored Car Robbery* were released on the same day, June 8, 1950. Despite the fact that both pictures are heist films, the similarities end there. Whereas *The Asphalt Jungle* was made at MGM, Richard Fleischer's film was a bargain-basement production whose running time is roughly half the length of Huston's—67 minutes versus 112. Destined as the bottom half of a double bill with the Columbia comedy *The Good Humor Man* (1950), *Armored Car Robbery* was shot in sixteen days and "mainly on location in and around Los Angeles."[5] But the biggest difference between the two films, production aside, is that whereas *The Asphalt Jungle* is the prototypical '50s heist film, *Armored Car Robbery* is something of a generic hybrid: a heist picture and "police procedural."[6] Simply put, unlike Huston's film, where our sympathies are clearly intended to lie with the crooks, audience identification in *Armored Car Robbery* is aligned with the law, so much so that, like many semi-documentary noirs, "it highlights the all-encompassing power of law enforcement."[7] This said, Fran Mason contends that *Armored Car Robbery* is "perhaps the most typical film of the heist subgenre" and "looks more modern than the nostalgic romanticism of *The Asphalt Jungle*."[8]

One reason that Fleischer's picture seems so modern today is that, stripped of the "melodramatic" backstories that embroider *The Asphalt Jungle*, it unspools like an action film. *Armored Car Robbery* opens with a low-angle exterior shot of Los Angeles City Hall, an icon of the 1940s and 1950s crime film, then cuts inside to the Records and Communications Division, where male operators can be heard rotely reciting, "Los Angeles Police Department." One of the operators answers a call from Wrigley Field (which, at the time, was the ball park of the minor-league Los Angeles Angels in South Central) and, after jotting down the information—"robbery and shooting"—places it on a conveyor belt that transfers the message to a dispatcher who, in turn, relays it to Homicide. Lt. James Cordell (Charles McGraw) immediately gets up from his desk and puts on his hat, but his partner, Lieutenant Phillips (James Flavin), who is holding a thermos in one hand, complains, "They don't even give you a chance to digest your lunch." The "they," of course, refers to the criminal element.

Cut to another wide low-angle shot, this time of Wrigley Field. Into the frame steps a fedora-hatted man, Dave Purvis (William Talman), as the play-by-play announcer at the ballpark narrates the action on the field: "It's going to be close, there goes Williams, he slides, he's in there—safe!" Suddenly there's the sound of a siren, and after Purvis takes a stopwatch out of his beautifully tailored, double-breasted jacket, a patrol car pulls up and, in a close-up, he presses the button on the stopwatch. Moments later Cordell and Phillips appear, only to be told that it's just another "false alarm."

Since Purvis has been timing how long it takes for the police to arrive at the prospective scene of the crime, his stopwatch action can be said to mirror the technological expertise of law enforcement dramatized in the opening sequence of the film. While the writers' decision to change the location of the heist from an ice company to a ballpark was doubtlessly due to the fact that by 1950 refrigerators had become a common household appliance and therefore ice was no longer a precious commodity, the stadium setting is not coincidental. It's not simply that baseball is the proverbial national pastime but that, as in anti-Communist noirs such as *The Thief* and *The Atomic City*,[9] there's something especially un-American or, in a word, perverted about someone who would stick up an armored car outside a baseball park. Phillips's concluding comment about the false alarm highlights this sentiment: "Some crank wasting the taxpayers' money." Equally important, if baseball is a sport that depends on teamwork, the question then becomes: Which team is tighter, the police or the gang?

Cut to the Bijou, where Yvonne LeDoux (Adele Jergens) appears from behind a curtain wearing a striped bustle, long black gloves, a feathered headdress, and a black leg-baring satin dress accessorized by a white fur stole. (The bustle, needless to say, is the first thing to come off.) Her husband, Benny McBride (Douglas Fowler), sits mesmerized in the audience. When Purvis arrives, we learn not only that Yvonne is "high rent" and Benny's broke but also that she's seeing someone behind his back. (Purvis's reaction, which indicates he may well be the guilty party, begins to answer the above question about teamwork.) The straight cut from a daylight exterior shot of Wrigley Field to the dark interior of the Bijou shifts the gaze from the criminal to the sexual register and suggests that the two are not unrelated. In *Armored Car Robbery* as in numerous heist films, including and especially *The Asphalt Jungle* (vide Emmerich and Riedenschneider), one of the primary motivations for participating in a caper is desire, *sexual* desire. So after Benny brags about what he's going to do to the "creep" who cuckolded him, Purvis responds, "The first thing you need to do is lay your hands on some money." In other words, the role of the Bijou in *Armored Car Robbery* is not merely exploitative, where, say, the men in the audience, including Purvis and Benny, are surrogates for the male spectator but, as I detail below, allegorical.

In "The Big Caper" Stuart Kaminsky writes that sometimes the "man of action" is also the "man who plans the caper."[10] Purvis is that man. At the boardinghouse where Benny resides, Dave broaches the idea of the heist to Benny and his two confederates, Al Mapes (Steve Brodie) and Ace Foster (Gene Evans). The stake, Dave explains, is "half-a-million bucks, cash. Only it's a one-shot deal, all or nothing in three minutes." When Al asks if it's a bank, Purvis replies, "You might call it that, only this bank has wheels under it." Al and Ace are skeptical—Ace says that he's "not ready for a sixty-buck funeral"—but once they learn that Purvis, who pulled off a successful armored car robbery in Chicago three years ago, is the brains behind the job, the odds sound a whole lot better to them.

Purvis explains that he gets one-half of the stake and everyone else will get equal shares, then they repair to the bedroom, where Dave pulls down a window blind on which the layout of the heist has been diagrammed. As Wrigley Field is the final stop on the armored car's route, the "strike" will happen there; the "dough," however, will not come from the ballpark but from the "cash receipts from bank transfers, markets, and theaters" that have already been deposited in the truck. "You're gonna study this routine," Purvis says, as he begins to expatiate on the plan, "until it comes out of your ears."

The heist in *Armored Car Robbery* was inspired by the 1934 Brooklyn armored truck robbery, but cinematically speaking, it owes less to this heist than to the caper in *Criss Cross*.[11] In both the Siodmak film and *Armored Car Robbery*, the men are dressed as laborers—in the Fleischer picture, painters—and the element of surprise is a smoke bomb. In *Armored Car Robbery* Ace drives to Wrigley Field and pulls up behind the armored car in a jalopy whose radiator appears to be overheated; when he gets out to check it, Dave and Al wander over to watch along with one of the armored car guards. Though the crowd inside the stadium, as in the earlier, play-by-play description of the "steal," appears to be cheering on the gang,[12] a restricted, low-angle composition right before the bomb explodes provides a visual counterpoint to the audio track: Ace is bent over the engine in

"Strike": Dave Purvis (William Talman) explains the layout of Wrigley Field in *Armored Car Robbery* (1950).

"Steal": title card for *Armored Car Robbery* (1950) with, on the left from top to bottom, criminal "mastermind" Dave Purvis (William Talman), "burlesque queen" Yvette LeDoux (Adele Jergens), and Lt. James Cordell (Charles McGraw).

the lower left-hand part of the frame, an armored car guard stands above him, and Benny and Ace stand to the right, reframed inside the window of the jalopy.

If in the opening Wrigley Park scene Purvis can be said to have "acted as a police dispatcher," he now "serves as a third-base coach, relaying wordless signals"—for example, tugging his cap to cue Al.[13] Consequently, when the other armored car guards emerge from the stadium with the day's receipts, Dave rubs his cheek and Ace sets off the bomb. In the smoke and confusion (see *Criss Cross*), Ace, Dave, and Benny knock out the guards, and once they put on gas masks, Al pulls up in the getaway car and Dave hits the stopwatch.

Everything is going exactly as Purvis has planned except that when a man inside the stadium calls the LAPD to report the robbery, Cordell and Phillips happen to be cruising in the area, and in the ensuing shootout, Phillips is killed and Benny's seriously wounded. The issue of loyalty versus betrayal is illustrated by Cordell's and Purvis's respective responses to their fallen comrades. At the hospital where Cordell has gone to check up on his partner, he learns that Phillips has died.

Cut to Cordell entering a room where Phillips's wife, Marsha (Anne Nagel), sits wringing a handkerchief in her hands:

CORDELL: Tough break, Marsha.
MARSHA: For you, too.
CORDELL: Yeah.
MARSHA: I know how you feel, Jim. You were partners for years.
CORDELL: Yeah. Kinda get used to the guy.
MARSHA: I know.
CORDELL: Marsha, I just wanna say . . .

Cordell looks up, but when he meets Marsha's eyes, he can't continue and instead gets up to go, saying, "If there's anything I can do for you, you know where I am." The scene is moving in part because it's so understated.

Compared to the close relation between Dix and Gus, Gus and Louis, as well as Dix and Riedenschneider in *The Asphalt Jungle*, the heist gang in *Armored Car Robbery* is, at best, a loose confederation of petty hoodlums that crumbles in the immediate wake of the holdup. Al's driving away from the scene of the crime with Cordell in pursuit, Benny's thrashing in the backseat like Mister Orange (Tim Roth) in *Reservoir Dogs* (1992), and they're approaching the hideout near the Torrance oilfields when a roadblock appears ahead. Dave looks over at Benny—his eyes are closed and his head's slumped against his chest—and screams, "C'mon, snap out of it!" before slapping him twice. Later, at the hideout, Dave refuses to take Benny to a doctor to get patched up: "I don't care if he needs a hospital. All he's gonna get is first aid." (First aid for Purvis is a slug from a bottle of whiskey.) Benny begs Al to talk to him, but as Ace and Dave are putting the loot in a suitcase (the single-source kerosene-lamp lighting is classic "Jimmy Valentine"), Purvis tells Al how he really feels: "We've stalled long enough. We could have been out of trouble and halfway to Mexico if it hadn't been for him. . . . If he kicks off, we'll bury him at sea and [you can] do your moanin' then." Benny suddenly appears in the doorway, one hand holding a gun and the other holding his guts in: "I'm gonna get me a doctor. Don't try to stop me, Dave." Purvis agrees to Benny's demand—"You'll get everything you're entitled to"—but even as he's reassuring him, he reaches behind his back for a gun that's laying on a loose stack of loot and plugs him, twice.

While Ace drives off to dump the body and the car in the harbor ("No loose ends"), Al asks Purvis whether they'll be getting a share of Benny's cut. The answer, needless to say, is no and he offers two reasons. First, Benny's widow will be getting a "full share." Al, his voice thick with sarcasm, replies, "Well, ain't that just dandy. Big-hearted Purvis playing Santa Claus to his pal's widow, a burlesque queen." Dave keeps stuffing the now empty money bags into a furnace, though Al knows that he has hit a nerve. However, when he asks what the second reason is, Dave punches him in the gut and, once he's on his knees, claps his ears like a pair of clash cymbals.

One of the performative ironies of gangster noir is that in a hybrid picture like *Armored Car Robbery*, the parts of the film about law enforcement invariably tend to be less audiovisually engaging than those about the criminals. This said, the most striking procedural passages in Fleischer's film are those that feature Cordell's hard-boiled detective. William Talman is one of the "most reptilian villains" in classic noir (in *Armored Car Robbery* he's also one of the most heartless), but Charles McGraw, who "looks like an armored car draped in a pin-striped suit,"[14] is more than his match. McGraw's pinched voice and taciturn temperament dramatically punctuate the dialogue of *Armored Car Robbery*. For instance, when an investigator named Bronson from the Pacific States Insurance Company shows up at the Harbor Division to inquire about the Los Angeles Armored Car Company's claim—"If they collect their insurance, it'll be the biggest that my company's ever had to pay"—Cordell cuts him to the quick: "Get out of our hair and let us work!" An even better, because more pungent, exchange occurs near the Torrance oilfields, where the police have discovered the abandoned getaway car. Detective Danny Ryan (Don McGuire), examining the backseat, observes that "somebody lost a lot of blood," to which Cordell deadpans, "Not enough to suit me."

In the meantime, at the lumber warehouse where the gang has been hiding out, Al, Ace, and Dave are about to leave—in the high-contrast, night-for-night light, the planks and ladders skew the composition and cast elongated shadows on the wall—just as the police, who have arrived in time to see the car with Benny's body disappearing into the water, are closing in. Al and Dave manage to escape—Al by boat, Dave on foot—but when Ace stumbles noisily as he tries to make it to the boat before Al takes off, Cordell shoots and kills him. Two down, two to go.

Thanks to painstaking, old-fashioned detective work, Al is the first to be apprehended. At Benny's apartment Cordell and Ryan discover a framed theatrical photograph of a woman and a matchbox on which an address—SUNSET 7-2131—has been written. Matchbox in hand, Cordell tracks Purvis to the Valley Motor Court, and despite the fact that Purvis manages to escape yet again, he's forced to leave his clothes behind. Later, at police headquarters, a forensics expert inspecting Purvis's socks and shirts—"Pretty good dresser"—notes that the lipstick smear on one of the shirts is a "theatrical brand." While Cordell's conferring with the forensics expert, Ryan calls from the Star Booking Agency to report that the woman in the photo is Yvonne LeDoux and that she works at the Bijou. Then, before Ryan hangs up, he adds, glancing at a full shot of the burlesque queen in his hand, "Yeah, you should see her in her working clothes. Imagine a dish like this married to a mug like Benny McBride. The naked and the dead." Cordell's wooden response—"Very funny"—is, in its own gruff fashion, eloquent; for Cordell, there's nothing remotely funny about the death of a partner, especially if your partner was a cop.

Cordell's studied indifference to Yvonne's charms also points up his protégé's inexperience. (At one point Ryan exclaims about LeDoux, "That's a lot of woman.") The difference between the two men is demonstrated when they go to the Bijou, where Ryan pauses in the lobby to whistle at a life-size cutout of Yvonne. They're standing at the back of the theater watching her live—Cordell: "Well, there she is with bells on." / Ryan: "And very few bells"—when Cordell asks Ryan if he wants to "kill some time" since she'll be on "for another five minutes." Ryan: "You twisted my arm." As "sweet" Yvonne bumps and grinds to the sound of catcalls and a vamping band, the two detectives are enjoying the show from the rear of the theater—or at least Ryan is—when Al Mapes walks in and takes a seat up front. Al has come there to put the squeeze on Yvonne and find out where Purvis is; instead, Cordell and Ryan, working together as a team, arrest him. Three down, one to go.

Though Al's now in police custody, Purvis is as elusive as he is smart—Cordell knows that to capture him he has to catch Yvonne "off base." The detective therefore decides that Yvonne should be surveilled day and night, which involves shadowing her and installing a Dictograph in her dressing room that communicates with Ryan's and Cordell's cars. Ryan's sitting outside Yvonne's dressing room, monitoring the Dictograph (it's obvious from his demeanor—he's playing with a deck of cards—that it's tedious work), when Cordell shows up. Ryan, not unlike the play-by-play announcer at the beginning of the film, narrates the action: "She's back. She just finished a show. Here come the beads. The clicking sound is her bracelet on the table. Now she's gonna put on her street clothes."

This aural, reverse striptease may appear peripheral to the film's narrative, but it's indispensable to the libidinal economy of *Armored Car Robbery*, laying bare, as it were, the heart of the heist picture. In other words, the kick of this particular genre is not simply the caper or, to recite Ryan, the "naked," but the process or "tease"—say, listening in on the gang as it puts together the job. Hence the de rigueur, prototypically high-contrast shot of the crew assembled around a table—or in Fleischer's film, before a window shade—for the big reveal.

The fact that Ryan's crushed that Yvonne's striptease is not televised nevertheless spells trouble. Thus, when Cordell asks him to go undercover as Mapes to trap Yvonne, he's all in. Yet as Cordell's earlier, impassive reaction to Ryan's jest suggests, it's difficult to outwit Purvis. For instance, the first time we see him at the Valley Motor Court (he's waiting for Yvonne) he's using a razor blade to meticulously remove all the labels from his shirts. Unlike Yvonne, he's also constantly on the move, "changing not only his name" (one of his aliases is Martin Bell) but his address as well.[15]

The telephone, as in *Force of Evil* and *The Brothers Rico*, is part and parcel of Purvis's MO. Thus, when he originally tells Benny he has a new phone number, Benny starts to write it down, but Purvis stops him, saying, "I don't like things written down. Memorize it!" Benny, of course, subsequently writes it down on a matchbox, the same one that Cordell later finds at his apartment. Still, Purvis is a past master of the same telecommunications that the police use to capture criminals (as depicted in the film's opening, semi-documentary sequence). The routine is simple but ingenious: Purvis goes to a bar where he waits for Yvonne until she gets out of work; when she arrives, they go to separate telephone booths and she calls him. Therefore, despite the fact that Ryan, masquerading as Al, corners Yvonne at the bar and forces her to contact Purvis, Purvis is already stationed in a phone booth and tells her, "That guy's not Mapes. That's a cop." Purvis then instructs her to leave through the back door, where he captures Ryan and commandeers his patrol car.

Although the police still have the upper hand, as both Ryan's and Cordell's cars have been installed with telecommunications technology, when Ryan tries one too many times to convey his location to Cordell, Purvis saps him and uses nonverbal signals to give Yvonne directions to a deserted warehouse. Then, before he ditches the car for a cab, he orders Ryan to "walk the plank," and when the rookie cop makes a move to escape, Purvis shoots him. He's about to finish Ryan off à la Benny ("No loose ends, baby") when Yvonne stops him and they race off. While Ryan has been seriously wounded, he proves his mettle when he crawls to the cruiser—his exertions are painfully audible—and calls Cordell to report that Purvis and Yvonne are headed for the Metropolitan Airport. The shot is a classic noir one: as in the pre-heist, window-framed shot at Wrigley Field, the camera angle is low and Ryan's bloodied face is wedged between the steering wheel and the front seat.

At the airport Purvis has chartered a private plane to Mexico and is about to board the plane with Yvonne when the tower instructs the pilot to pull onto the east runway and stand by for orders. Purvis puts a gun to the pilot's head. However, before the plane can take off, a commercial airliner begins its descent. The sound of sirens forces Purvis's hand; grabbing the suitcase, he leaps out of the plane and starts running down a runway. The horrified look on Yvonne's and Cordell's faces reflects his grisly fate; when the camera cuts away at the last moment, it's clear he has run right into the whirring blades of the propellers.

In the final, high-angle shot of the penultimate sequence of *Armored Car Robbery*, Purvis's body lies facedown on the tarmac, the money from the now open suitcase scattering in the wind, an evocative shot that foreshadows the sequence in *Private Hell 36* in which two detectives, Cal Bruner (Steve Cochran) and Jack Farnham (Howard Duff), arrive at a post-chase, post–car accident scene where the money from an elevator caper is blowing in the wind. In the process of trying to collect the rapidly dispersing money, Bruner can't resist pocketing some of it, and Farnham reluctantly agrees to go along with his partner's scheme. (The title of the film refers to the lot number of the trailer park where Bruner stashes the money and where, after he shoots his partner, their superior, Captain Michaels [Dan Jagger], shoots and kills him.)

In the coda to *Armored Car Robbery* (and in a reprise of the scene in which Cordell endeavors to comfort Phillips's widow), the lieutenant returns to the hospital, this time to visit Ryan, who's recuperating. The film ends on a comic note when Cordell hands his partner a magazine in which their exploits have been written up: "How's it feel to be famous?" Because Ryan has to squint to read his name in the small print, the film's minimization of the rookie cop's heroism suggests that, unlike Cordell and his protégé who risk their lives for the public good, Purvis is out for only one person: himself.

A comparison with *Criss Cross* and *The Asphalt Jungle* is illuminating. Whereas Siodmak's and Fleischer's films feature triangular romantic relationships, Purvis—unlike Slim Dundee and Steve Thompson, who are obsessed with Anna— possesses none of the passion that fires the other two men. As for *The Asphalt Jungle*, whereas Dix and Riedenschneider are each motivated by a dream, however unrealistic or perverted, sharing a bond that demonstrates the solidarity that's possible in the improvised community of the heist gang, Purvis is, as Ryan refers to him at one point, a "complete blank." Consequently, if the classic heist film represents a critique of the socioeconomic order, Purvis embodies the emptiness of capitalism, a cold, soulless logic devoid of desire except for the desire for accumulation.

The modernity of *Armored Car Robbery* can also be gleaned by comparing it side by side, as in a View-Master, with *The Hoodlum*, a bottom-of-the-barrel, B heist film directed by Max Nosseck and released by Eagle Lion that Wheeler Winston Dixon has described as a "damned film, a doomed film, a cheap and rotten film about a cheap and rotten world."[16] Lawrence Tierney, reprising the sort of bad-to-the-bone character he perfected in *Dillinger* (1945), a Monogram hit that Nosseck also directed, plays Vincent Lubeck, the mastermind of a scheme to rob an armored car. In a classic passage that recalls the Bijou theater in *Armored Car Robbery*, Vincent first notices the armored car while he's watching a woman returning to her secretarial job at a bank. Though the heist in *The Hoodlum*, like the caper in *Armored Car Robbery*, draws on the Brooklyn armored car robbery (in Nosseck's film a surveyor and fruit-cart vendor just happen to be outside the bank when the armored car arrives for its pickup of Federal Reserve deposits), Nosseck's film capitalizes on the real-estate maxim "location, location, location," as the Breckenridge Mortuary is located next to the bank and right across the street from the gas station where Vincent works. Vincent's scheme, like Purvis's, is ingenious. When he reads about the death of an unidentified man in the newspaper, he sends two members of his gang, Christie (Angela Stevens) and Eddie (Richard Barron), to pose as the dead man's niece and her attorney in order to claim the body. Christie and Eddie's only request is that "Uncle John" be buried at a specific time—"the precise moment of his birth"—so that the post-service procession to the cemetery can be coordinated with the heist and render a failsafe escape from the police blockade.

The heist, as in *Armored Car Robbery*, is successful, though in an inversion of Fleischer's film, Vincent refuses to give Christie a full share, and the gang members not only turn on him but, together with Christie, abscond with the money. The most striking difference between the two films, however, is that *The Hoodlum* is at once a heist *and* a classic gangster picture, featuring a scene in which Vincent uses toy cars and a cardboard model of the bank to describe his plan as well as tracing Vincent's life from the city dump to juvenile hall ("possession of firearms"), to the reformatory ("breaking and entering"), to the city jail ("petty theft"), to the county jail ("grand theft auto"), to the state penitentiary ("armed robbery"), to parole, to the heist—to, in the final scene, back to the city dump next to which he grew up.

As this extensive character arc and the film's familial dynamics in the form of Vincent's long-suffering mother and his conflicted brother demonstrate (Johnny is played by Tierney's own real-life brother, Edward), *The Hoodlum* is ultimately a gangster melodrama. Moreover, while the penultimate airfield sequence in *Armored Car Robbery* anticipates the penultimate "prop wash" sequence in *The Killing*, the staged cortege in *The Hoodlum* gestures not so much to the rise of organized crime in the early 1950s as the sort of "big shot" funerals associated with such classic '30s gangster films as *Little Caesar*.

THE KILLING: JIGSAW PUZZLE

In the opening chapter of Lionel White's *Clean Break* (1955), set at an anonymous racetrack, we're introduced to Marvin Unger:

> In the course of his thirty-seven years, Unger had been at a track less than a half a dozen times. He was totally disinterested in horse racing; in fact, had never gambled at all. He had a neat, orderly mind, a very clear sense of logic and an inbred aversion to all "sporting events." He considered gambling not only stu-

pid, but strictly a losing proposition. Fifteen years as a court stenographer had given him frequent opportunity to see what usually happened when men placed their faith in luck in opposition to definitely established mathematical odds.[17]

If the classic heist film is predicated on a transgressive fantasy—"the perfect crime"—the fantasy that motivates both White's novel and Stanley Kubrick's *The Killing* is not so much opposed to as premised on its ostensible other understood in the final analysis as the "forces of law and order."[18] As a court stenographer, "a small cog in the metropolitan judicial system,"[19] Unger has seen things from the inside and therefore places his faith not in luck—say, making a killing at the track—but in logic. Despite this principle, Unger has nevertheless placed his faith in a man, Johnny Clay, an ex-con who's fresh out of state prison, where he has spent the last four years and who's beset, according to Unger, "by some sort of definite anxiety complex."[20] Unger, though, reasons that Johnny's "trifle" neuroticism is "natural enough"; in fact, it may be a good thing, because it has made him "unusually cautious," someone who "wanted to take no chances."[21]

It's impossible to appreciate Kubrick's achievement in *The Killing* without seriously engaging White's novel. On one hand, a lot of the film—most obviously, the nonlinear, multiple point-of-view structure—derives from *Clean Break*. On the other hand, Kubrick and Jim Thompson's screenplay rings a number of important changes on the source material. (Kubrick only credited Thompson for his dialogue, but given how important the dialogue is to the film, it only seems fair to credit the pulp-fiction master for his contribution as well.[22]) One difference between the two texts is the introduction in *The Killing* of an omniscient, "voice of God" narrator (Art Gilmore) who periodically comments on the diegetic action. For example, near the beginning of the film, Marvin Unger (Jay C. Flippen) turns away from the bar where he has just left a slip of paper for Mike O'Reilly (Joe Sawyer) with the address of a meeting that night before heading off to the pay-off window to cash his winning ticket. As the camera cranes up to a high wide-angle shot, the narrator intones, "He began to feel as if he had as much effect on the final outcome of the operation as a single piece of a jumbled jigsaw puzzle has to its final design."

The third-person voice-over narration of *The Killing*, like the film's picture-puzzle structure, is not without precedent: in this case, Louis de Rochemont's *March of Time* newsreels; the "News on the March" sequence in *Citizen Kane*; semi-documentary crime films such as *The House on 92nd Street* (1945), which was produced by de Rochemont; and Kubrick's "prizefighter" documentary, *Day of the Fight* (1951), which featured *CBS News* announcer Douglas Edwards as the narrator and which the director had hoped to sell to the *March of Time* series.[23] Originally, Kubrick sent his director of photography, veteran cinematographer

Lucien Ballard, to the Golden Gate racetrack at Bay Meadows, San Francisco, to shoot documentary footage that he intended to use under the opening credits. However, when Kubrick screened the footage, he found it completely unusable and sent Alexander Singer, an associate producer on *The Killing*, back to the racetrack with a "clockwork, fixed-lens Eyemo camera."[24] Kubrick was so impressed with Singer's footage that he subsequently decided to employ it, like the voice-over narration, as a periodic structuring device in the film.

Although the documentary-style footage in *The Killing* looks as if it's stock, it has a dual function—one realistic, one tonal. In conjunction with the public address announcer's communications, it orients the viewer with respect to time and place; in tandem with the voice-over, it simultaneously opens up an ironic space between the narrator and the action, the God-like narration and the heist-minded characters. At the same time, if both the narration and racetrack footage act as "distancing devices" or "alienation effects,"[25] the narration also enjoys a special relationship to the director in that it possesses a certain resemblance to Kubrick's "voice" even as it remains structurally differentiated from its "author" or auteur.

Thus, from one perspective, the narration that accompanies Unger's actions in the opening scene appears to render the character's sense of agency: Marvin may be only one member of the crew, one piece of a puzzle that's still "jumbled" (compare this voice-over with the celebrated picture-puzzle scenes in *Citizen Kane*), but, given the collaborative nature of the heist, his part is integral to the "final outcome" or design of the operation. Still, from another perspective, the past tense and stentorian tone of the narration—consider, for example, the recourse to the "as if" construction—works to complicate the feeling of efficaciousness. Part of the import of the latter agnostic perspective is, of course, a consequence of genre. So, writing about the "criminal-adventure thriller," Frank Krutnik observes that the antihero's "daring gamble against the delimitations of his place within culture is marked . . . by the inevitability of its failure."[26]

Given the inevitability of failure aside, one might therefore ask, What, exactly, *is* the transgressive fantasy that propels *The Killing*? In *Clean Break* White limns the various characters' motivations. Marvin Unger decides to put up the seed money for the heist in part because he considers his current job "far beneath his intellectual abilities."[27] Michael Aloysius Henty, who's a bartender at the racetrack, wants to get away from the "slum" of a neighborhood where he lives and move to the country.[28] (He dreams of a "small, modest little house with a garden."[29]) George Peatty bemoans a "fate which limited his earning capacity to what he could make as a cashier at the track," one that's in inverse proportion to the fate that had made his wife, Sherry, "the sort of woman . . . who wants everything."[30] Randy Kennan (Ted de Corsia), "patrolman first class," owes loan shark Leo Steiner (Jay Adler) well over twenty-six hundred dollars and dreams not only of being able to pay him off one day but also, after he has retired from the force, of catching up with the "fat bastard."[31]

Johnny's motivation in White's novel is in many ways the least legible, although the fact that he's a professional criminal suggests that's all the reader needs to know. Unlike the others, he has long since opted out of the rat race. In *The Killing* we're first introduced to Johnny Clay (Sterling Hayden) at Marvin's railroad apartment, where he has just been with Fay (Colleen Gray) and where he mentally defines the heist, which he's been thinking about for "four damned long years," in opposition to her desire that he "get an honest job" and "settle down."[32] In other words, Fay effectively wants Johnny to become like Mike, George, Marvin, and Randy, each of whom, as Johnny describes them at the meeting to review the heist, is working and has a job: "You got some sort of income, some sort of legit connections."[33]

"The Big Gangster Heist": Danish program for *The Killing* (1956) with Johnny Clay (Sterling Hayden).

Like Johnny, the characters in *The Killing* are roughly the same as they are in *Clean Break* with the exception of Marvin (who's an alcoholic and has more than paternal feelings for Johnny[34]) and Mike (who has an invalid wife to care for). As Johnny puts it in both the book and the film, "[These men] all have jobs, they all live seemingly decent, normal lives. They all have money problems."[35] The heist picture has historically evinced a necessary mimetic relation to the socioeconomic order, necessary because in order to "crook the house" (to echo Walter Neff in *Double Indemnity*), you don't have to be a crook, per Johnny's appraisal of his fellow crew members, but you do have to know how the house works. (I've used the second-person pronoun here because if the viewer doesn't share in the transgressive fantasy that fuels the caper film, then the picture doesn't play—there's no payoff, no pleasure.) Moreover, given the close relation between the caper and the object of desire, whether bank or jewelry store, racetrack or US Mint shipment, heist films tend to mimic Fordist and Taylorist modes of production and management, using such principles as fragmentation (breaking up a job into its constituent parts), division (partitioning the labor into skilled and unskilled or, in the case of *The Killing*, amateur and professional), and synchronization (coordinating actions so that they come off at the proper time).[36]

Since a racetrack heist involves an especially "compressed scale of high risk" (the "idea men" are often "quite risk-averse, preferring to limit the execution of their plan to a time-benefits ratio that yields the most profit with the least amount of risk"),[37] synchronization is key. The narration in *The Killing* insistently dramatizes this preoccupation with temporal precision. For example, when the voice-over cuts into the action for the first time—"At exactly 3:45 on that Saturday afternoon in the last week of September"—it fixes the temporal and seasonal parameters of the film.

While the voice-over narration in *The Killing* reflects the fixation with temporality at the core of the heist picture, one formal or visual analogue of this fixation in Kubrick's film is the recurring dolly shots that track from left to right. The most arresting of these camera movements is associated, not surprisingly, with the idea man, Johnny. After the narrator pinpoints the time—"At seven PM that same day, Johnny Clay, perhaps the most important thread in the unfinished fabric")—walks from the kitchen through the living room to the bedroom, where Fay's dressing. In his expert reading of *The Killing*, Thomas Allen Nelson notes that at the outset of the film, the "characters are more synchronized in space than time."[38] As the word "synchronized" indexes, the duration and fluidity of the lateral tracking shots also possess a temporal dimension. In other words, because these cross-sectional "dollhouse" shots traverse not only the interior of rooms but the walls in between,[39] the net effect is to call attention to the director's mastery of movement—of, that is, time over space, form over matter, motion over picture.

Hence the lateral tracking shot of Johnny striding "like a giant" through Marvin's apartment—Kubrick insisted that Ballard use a 25mm lens, "one of the widest motion-picture lenses available at the time"—a shot that foregrounds the ex-con's confidence that his plan is going to be, as Johnny brags to Fay in the novel, "foolproof."[40]

What James Naremore refers to as the "ostentatious" character of these distorted, short-lensed trucking shots should not, however, be taken at face value.[41] Which is to say that there are any number of cinematic elements that counter the scene's "forward thrust" (to cite the composer Gerald Fried's description of the film's aesthetic[42]). Consider, for instance, the set design or, more specifically, the objects, walls, and window curtains that punctuate the foreground of the frame and vertically counterpoint the general horizontal thrust of the moving camera. Even more to the point, perhaps, consider the lighting and mise-en-scène.

Thus, with respect to the lighting, when Johnny stands with Fay in front of the bedroom window, the dark pleats of the curtain look just like bars. With respect to the mise-en-scène, when Johnny initially enters the room, he sits down on the bed to help Fay buckle the belt on her skirt. Since one of the working titles of *The Killing* was "Bed of Fear,"[43] the significance of this bed shot can be ascertained by attending to the repetition of this figure in the film. For example, in the previous sequence, Mike crosses a bedroom to check up on his wife, who's laid up in bed; moreover, in a subsequent scene, George Peatty (Elisha Cook Jr.), who has just returned home from the track, crosses from the hall to the combination living/ bedroom where his wife, Sherry (Marie Windsor), is lying on a couch like a "pulp fiction dominatrix," reading a magazine.[44]

Despite Sherry's manifest, passive-aggressive disinterest, George is intent on telling her a sweet, if desultory, story about a couple who refer to each other as "Mama" and "Papa." But before George can finish the anecdote, Sherry interrupts him, pricking his ego like a circus balloon: "And the climax of this exciting story— the moral, the punchline?" Sherry's sardonic query anticipates the succeeding scene in which she secretly meets with her "big, handsome, intelligent brute" of a lover, Val Cannon (Vince Edwards), and in which the fade to black, like the cutaway to the gust-opened door in *Out of the Past*, effects a sexual ellipsis. Sherry's self-reflexive dialogue also anticipates the unhappily-ever-after end to their marriage when George, his face pitted with buckshot, shoots her in the stomach and, even though she's dying, she makes sure she gets the last word: "I never had anybody but you. Not a real husband, just a bad joke without a punchline."

Consequently, the fact that a bed is the terminus of the first lateral tracking shot featuring Johnny prefigures the termination of the fantasy in addition to the prime cause of the failure of the entire enterprise: fear crossed with desire. To adduce Kubrick's first feature, *Fear and Desire* (1953), George fears losing Sherry—"he looked over at Sherry and he was blinded to everything but . . . the realization that he was losing her"—as well as Sherry's desire to escape the "matrimonial travesty" that is her marriage: "My God, I get tired of this kind of life. I get tired of never having money, never going anywhere, doing anything."[45]

The crisscrossing of logic and desire is played out in the Olive Street meeting to review the heist plan that, domestic and loan-shark scenes aside, has driven *The Killing* up to this particular point. The camera cuts from Val's apartment, where he and Sherry stand next to a lamp lit from below like gangsters—"We gotta find out more about the overall plan"—to Marvin's apartment, where the gang's assembled around a table on which a map has been spread. Suddenly there's a noise in the hall. Randy and Johnny get up to investigate, after which the rest of the men follow—the camera tracking again from left to right—until there's the sound of a door opening, a woman gasping, a sharp blow, and, finally, a body slumping to the floor. When the camera begins to move again, it continues to track to a room where Johnny dumps an unconscious woman onto a bed, and George, seeing his wife, exclaims, "It's Sherry!" and Randy, outraged, slaps him.

In White's novel Sherry's bound and gagged, and after everyone else has been sent away, Johnny loosens the gag around her mouth and the necktie binding her wrists: "One God damn peep out of you and I'll knock your teeth down your pretty throat."[46] While Sherry's a "castrating vixen" in both *Clean Break* and *The Killing*,[47] she's even more of a "bad girl" in White's novel. Here, for example, is how the author records Sherry's reaction to the above threat: "As [Johnny] released her hands he . . . looked for the fear that he knew he would find there. She was looking right at him. She was laughing."[48]

In fact, Sherry tries to seduce Johnny, but in the film, perhaps because Fay has waited four years for him or because he has already pegged George's wife as completely avaricious—"You've got a great big dollar sign there where most women have a heart"—he never rises to the bait. In the novel Sherry's much more dangerous because sexually alluring. When Johnny begins to question her about what she knows about the caper, Sherry answers that she talks better with a drink; as he goes to make one, he tells her to stay where she is and she replies, "Why should I move? I like beds."

Despite Sherry's come-on, Johnny tries the rough stuff with her first, shaking her like a "rag doll" until she knees him in the groin. Johnny then tries to charm her, but after they kiss—"Her mouth was moist . . . he felt the fire of her tongue"—he realizes that it isn't "strictly business": "he knew that it was more than business; a lot more."[49] He's fumbling with the clasp of Sherry's bra when, "eel-like," she wriggles free and darts across the room, where she stands laughing. So much for the rough stuff *and* the charm. However, since he needs to be sure that she doesn't know anything, he agrees to see her again, though Johnny later asks Randy to handle her because, as he explains, he's the "wrong guy for the job."[50] In other words, once Johnny's lust has passed, he reverts to form. Which is to say that, as the word "job" suggests, sex for him is ultimately subject, like the heist, to an economic calculus.

The novel's twist is that after Randy and Sherry meet, they have sex and immediately fall for each other. Randy: "She was beautiful. She was a bum. He was nuts about her."[51] / Sherry: "My God, what was wrong with her that she never seemed able to resist falling for heels?"[52] The bad romance between Randy and Sherry is wonderfully perverse, not least as the femme fatale falls for a cop, albeit a rogue one. This said, the perversity is not without its dark side, as the last time we see Sherry in the novel, she's unconscious in the backseat of a car after having been worked over by Val. (In *Clean Break* Val's a stone-cold killer. There's also the suggestion that he has let one or more of his men "have fun with her."[53])

In the end we're not privy to exactly what Val does to break Sherry, though the effect of his handiwork is graphic: "She started to say something and at once her mouth filled with blood."[54] While it's extremely doubtful that the Production Code would have permitted either the graphic sex scene between Randy and Sherry or Val's brutal interrogation of her, in *The Killing* Sherry seduces George. The next morning over breakfast (a perverse scene in its own right as Sherry is the sort of women who wouldn't be caught dead cooking or, God forbid, washing dishes), she wheedles the truth out of her husband—that the heist will be going down that day—by insinuating that Johnny raped her.[55]

Still, Johnny's description of his rendezvous with Sherry as a "job" points to the fact that despite all the sexual byplay in Kubrick's film, the real climax is the heist itself. First, Maurice (Kola Kwariani), who, like Nikki Arcane (Timothy Carey), is being paid a flat fee to perform a certain task at a certain time, starts a rumble in the lobby by picking a fight with Mike, who's tending bar. Next, while Maurice is busy distracting security, Johnny slips inside a door marked "NO ADMITTANCE" that George has just opened. Johnny proceeds to the employees' locker room, where he removes a duffel bag from a briefcase and, from the flower box, the pump-action shotgun with a front-hand grip that Randy has previously left in one of the lockers.

One of the most inspired touches in *The Killing* is the clown mask that Johnny puts on to stick up the counting room. In the novel his disguise is "old school": a handkerchief that covers the lower part of his face. In the film the clown mask embellishes the blackly comic conceit that has already been introduced earlier in the film. (For example, after Randy slaps George, he brays, "C'mon, clown, sing a chorus from Pagliacci.") The clown mask that Johnny sports also references the January 1950 Brinks armored truck robbery, in which the members of the crew wore Halloween masks.

Target Practice: Johnny Clay (Sterling Hayden) and Nikki Arcane (Timothy Carey) discussing the shooting of Black Lightning in *The Killing* (1956).

Although the clown mask, combined with the shotgun, produces the appropriate note of terror when Johnny bursts into the main office of the racetrack, the heist in *The Killing* is not without its own absurd aspect, as the old man who empties the safe seems to spill almost as much money as he stuffs into the duffel bag. Johnny's escape is facilitated by an equally absurd event, one that he has scrupulously planned: the shooting of Black Lightning (Red Lightning in the novel), the favorite to win the one-hundred-thousand-dollar Lansdowne Stakes. In *Clean Break*, White, in addition to rendering the point of view of the various members of the gang as well as Sherry and Val, puts the reader inside the head of Maxie Flam, the jockey who's riding Red Lightning in the main race and who, before the horse is killed right out from under him, is dreaming of retiring at the end of the season to his farm in Maryland, "where the only thing he'd ever ride again would be the front seat of a Cadillac convertible."[56]

In the bedlam that ensues after Nikki has dropped Red Lightning with a "high-powered rifle with a telescopic sight," Johnny slips out the same door through which he previously entered—minus not only the mask, gloves, and rifle but the hat, shirt, and jacket that have just served as his disguise. Another brilliant bit in White's novel, especially from the retrospective standpoint of the film, is that after Johnny escapes the racetrack via a taxi and train, he ducks into a "newsreel theatre" at Grand Central. (He has a couple of hours to kill before he retrieves the money and meets up with the gang.) Johnny has in fact been able to make time march to his tune: with the exception of Nikki (who in the film is gunned down by a guard before he can make his escape from the parking lot in his MG convertible), the heist has gone just as he planned and virtually without a hitch. As Mike characterizes it in the novel, "It went off perfect."[57]

The core members of the crew are anxiously waiting for Johnny at Unger's apartment when Marvin hears the elevator. However, in an ironic echo of the scene where the gang discovers Sherry, it's not Johnny but Val and his associate Tiny (Joseph Turkel). (Note the vertical strips of shadow that wave like fronds on the door in front of which Val and Tiny stand.) When Val doesn't see George, who has just stepped out of the living room, he bellows, "Where's George? Where's the jerk?" at which point George comes out of the kitchen, gun blazing: "Here's the jerk!" By the time the dust settles, George is the only one left standing. In fact, the abrupt shift to his POV and to a shaky, handheld camera radically subjectivizes the post-shootout carnage in which the bodies, as in some Mannerist composition, are haphazardly stacked on top of one other or draped over the sofa like the mannequins in *Killer's Kiss* (1955). In what seems like the blink of an eye, design has devolved to disorder, concord to chaos.

As George staggers out of the apartment building, the lateral right-to-left tracking shot reverses the dominant movement of the camera in the film so far. It also rhymes with the earlier scene where Marvin "takes a powder" while Johnny grills Sherry. Now, after Marvin exits the building and lights a cigarette, he walks up a hill past a sedan—the cabin is unnaturally, if expressionistically lit—in which Val and Tiny are surveilling the action. Just as the "directional axis is flipped" when George crosses the street right in front of Johnny's car,[58] the point of view shifts from first to third person. Johnny has arrived belatedly at the scene of the crime ("Johnny arrived at the meeting place at 7:29, still fifteen minutes late") and the reverse camera movement, conjoined with his astonished gaze (the camera is situated in the backseat of his car), marks the violent return of the repressed.

In other words, if George wanted in on the heist in order to get enough money to keep Sherry happy, Sherry has squawked to Val because she's crazy about him. The problem, at least for Sherry, is that Val's not emotionally wedded to her. (For example, when they meet up for the first time in the film, Sherry asks him where's he's been, and he replies, "What I do is my own business. So I step out once in a while.") Accordingly, Val's in it not so much for the romance or sex—as George and Sherry arguably are—as for the loot. In this sense, Val's terminal position in the film's chain of causation offers yet another satiric twist on the film's donnée, as if the human, all-too-human desires of the other characters were a screen for a more fundamental root or drive: cold hard cash.

The conclusion to *The Killing* accents the role of luck and fate, chance and coincidence, in the film. First Johnny buys a suitcase from a pawnshop (two doors down from which there's a placard advertising "LENNY BRUCE"); then on the side of the road behind a hedge littered with garbage, he dumps the contents of the duffel bag into the suitcase. However, in his haste he doesn't even bother to get all the money into the suitcase, a scenario that, like the earlier safe scene, foreshadows the seriocomic dénouement of the film. Finally, Johnny snaps the clasp on the suitcase into place and turns the key only to discover that the lock's broken.

Cut to the airport, where, in a reprise of the post-heist scene at Marvin's apartment, Fay's anxiously waiting for Johnny. When he arrives, they quickly make their way to the ticket counter—in the process passing two plainclothesmen—where Johnny learns that he can't take his suitcase on board with him. While Johnny and Fay wait behind a fence to board their plane, the toy poodle of the elderly woman standing next to them starts barking. (In a quintessentially Kubrickian irony, the woman lavishes more affection on "Sebastian" than any person in the film lavishes on another human being.) As the plane taxis into position and the propellers begin to rotate, Johnny turns to see his suitcase precariously piled on top of a baggage cart that is swiftly crossing the tarmac. (Note the "FLAMINGO HOTEL" sticker on the side of the suitcase.[59]) When the poodle, noticing the cart, leaps out of the woman's arms, the cart swerves, the suitcase flies off, the lock gives way, and the money scatters in the prop wash like the snow in a crystal ball that has just been shaken.

Fay looks over at Johnny, and it's as if he's turned to stone. Taking his arm, she forcibly leads him back into the terminal, where, as they stride through the lobby, there's a whip pan from the plainclothesmen standing near the entrance to Johnny and Fay as they approach the exit. We watch from inside, through the glass doors, as Fay hails a taxi; before she can stop it, it drives past. Now we're outside as she hails another taxi, which zooms past, and then another, which whizzes past as well. Fay glances back at the terminal, where the desk clerk has run over to the plainclothesmen and is pointing at Fay and Johnny, who are standing all alone on the sidewalk:

FAY: Johnny, you've got to run.
JOHNNY: What's the difference?

In the final, deep-focus shot of the film, the brass-embellished score crescendos and the ticket clerk's standing stock-still in the rear of the frame between the two plainclothesmen, who, guns drawn, are advancing through separate doors.

In *The Heist Film* Daryl Lee remarks that the heist film is not simply about money but poetry—"the art of the crime."[60] In this light the salient passage in *The Killing* occurs when Johnny goes to a chess club to talk to Maurice about creating a distraction so that he can steal into the office where the cash is:

> You know, I often thought that the gangster and the artist are the same in the eyes of the masses. They are admired and hero-worshipped . . . but there is always present an underlying wish to see them destroyed at the peak of their glory.

It probably goes without saying that this self-consciously philosophical observation does not appear in White's novel. It is also worth noting that Kola Kwariani's speech is so garbled that it's virtually impossible to understand what he's saying. Consequently, the meaning of Maurice's utterance is effectively obscured, which is no doubt how Kubrick intended it.

Maurice's pronouncement nevertheless functions not unlike a mise-en-abîme of *The Killing*, reflecting in miniature the film's thematic concerns. One of these is the game of chess, which, along with movies and still photography, was one of Kubrick's lifelong passions: "Chess is an analogy. It is a series of steps that you take one at a time and it's balancing resources against the problem, which in chess is time and in movies time and money."[61] Kubrick's chess-informed analogy echoes Lee's observation that the heist "genre can be read as a locus . . . in which the business of film tries to work out its relation to art."[62] The notion that making a movie is, like a heist, about time and money has particular purchase with respect to *The Killing* since at this nascent point in Kubrick's career—he was only twenty-seven—the business of movies necessarily took precedence over the art. Though Kubrick and his producing partner, James Harris, had secured the services of Sterling Hayden for $40,000, United Artists agreed to advance them only $200,000 for the film and not a penny more. Therefore, in order to have a reasonable shooting schedule—say, twenty-four days—Harris had to put up $80,000 and his father another $50,000 for a final budget of $330,000. In the event, the film was shot with such economy that during the editing phase, Kubrick felt carefree enough to toss around a football on the set.[63]

However, Lee's claim that *The Killing* represents a "poetic act of bad faith" because all the members of the heist gang are ultimately killed or arrested, whereas Kubrick was able to triple the budget for his next project, *Paths of Glory* (1957), belies the complexity of the relation between Maurice's modernist pronouncement (art) and Kubrick's relation to motion pictures (business).[64] Which is to say that if, on one hand, Kubrick was an outsider in Hollywood (he was notorious for scorning the "show-business bible *Variety* and the other 'trades,'"[65] preferring instead to read *Film Quarterly*), he was nevertheless not above exploiting a B genre, albeit a prestigious one, to gamble on his future as a filmmaker. Indeed, if time +

money = movies, could there be a better formula for one's first Hollywood film than the heist picture, a subgenre that, entailing as it does assembling a crew and planning a time-sensitive operation, self-reflexively comments on filmmaking as a "left-handed form of human endeavor"?

PLUNDER ROAD: NEAR MINT

Plunder Road is a paradigmatic '50s heist film, but it also sheds light on the role of independent production in the aftermath of the 1948 divorcement. In 1955, after having produced *Rocketship X-M* (1950) as well as a trio of Samuel Fuller films, Robert Lippert contracted with Twentieth Century Fox to produce twenty-five "program-type" features.[66] The juvenile delinquent, horror, sci-fi, Western, and crime pictures that Lippert released in conjunction with Twentieth Century Fox under the banner of Regal Films were essential to the resurrection of the B film in the latter half of the 1950s.[67]

Hubert Cornfield, who directed *Plunder Road*, was part of this low-budget renascence. Cornfield spent the early, formative years of his career in Paris, where he developed friendships with such "modernist mavericks" of the French Nouvelle Vague as François Truffaut, Jean-Luc Godard, and Jean-Pierre Melville, "sharing their affection for American popular culture [and] especially the hard-boiled tradition of fiction and film."[68] Before helming *Plunder Road*, Cornfield directed *Sudden Danger* (1955), the second in a series of "five police procedurals starring Bill Elliott as a Los Angeles police detective," and *Lure of the Swamp* (1957), a lurid thriller adapted from Gil Brewer's equally lurid pulp novel *Hell's Own Destination* (1953).[69]

If Stephen Ritch's taut screenplay for *Plunder Road* is not anomalous in this B, not to say exploitation, context (one of his only other film script credits is for Irving Lerner's epidemiological noir, *City of Fear*),[70] the film's cinematography is A, directed by Ernest Haller, who lensed such film noirs as *Mildred Pierce* (1945) as well as other features from *Gone to the Wind* (1939) to *Rebel without a Cause*. One cannot emphasize enough Haller's impact on *Plunder Road*. With a limited budget ($125,000 or less), a short shooting schedule (one week), and a B cast (the "star" is Gene Raymond), what drives the film, in addition to the streamlined, dialogue-stripped screenplay, is its look, including and especially the B Cinemascope lenses and 2:35:1 widescreen ratio, Regalscope, a term that bespeaks both the film's bottom-drawer status and "regal"—that is, ostensibly elite—appeal.

The structure of *Plunder Road* is as straightforward as a drag race: three acts separated by driving sequences. The opening credit sequence, designed by Bob Gill, is illustrative: syncopated shots of the white divider stripes on an asphalt highway followed by arrows and intersecting white lines followed, in turn, by unbroken double lines. Since the "road markings appear to move faster as the credits progress" (a function in part of Irving Gertz's driving score),[71] the effect is of pure motion, an effect that's not unconnected with the spectatorial pleasures of motion pictures.

In the first post-credit sequence, the film cuts between a moving van and a crane truck traveling down a highway at night in the driving rain. In the cab of the moving van are Eddie Harris (Gene Raymond) and Frankie Chardo (Stephen Ritch); in the rear of the van, sitting on either side of a spring that's stabilizing a container of nitroglycerin, are Commando Munson (Wayne Morris) and Skeets Jonas (Elisha Cook Jr.). The crane truck is driven by Roly Adams (Stafford Repp), who, vigorously masticating gum, is dressed in a rain poncho and hat like a Gloucester fisherman. There's no dialogue, though the individual voice-overs punctuate the action like speech balloons in a comic strip:

EDDIE: Seven minutes late. Heavy on the foot, Frankie.
FRANKIE: Didn't figure on any rain.
ROLY: Six packages of gum. That oughta be enough.
COMMANDO: Maybe they forgot about this soup back here.
SKEETS: Frankie, slow it down.

The men in the heist gang appear to be a tight crew, but the one-shot voice-overs emphasize their monadic individuality, in which each man appears to be lost in his own thoughts.

Masked Men: Italian *fotobusta* of Eddie Harris (Gene Raymond) and Frankie Chardo (Stephen Ritch) en route to the train heist in *Plunder Road* (1957).

Reflection yields to action when the men arrive at their destination, an isolated railroad crossing outside Salt Lake City. While Eddie and Frankie manually switch the railroad tracks, Roly and Commando back up the crane truck to a trestle and raise an articulated crane ladder. The high-angle deep-focus shot of Commando, dressed in the same rain gear as Roly and with his back to the camera, looking down at the truck and silhouetted against the misting rain, conveys a sense of foreboding. What is he doing up there in the air, like a fireman without a fire?

It should be noted at the outset that one of the generic pleasures of *Plunder Road* (and they are both various and many) is that, at least in the first part, the film dispenses with the planning stage and pop psychology associated with the classic heist picture. Despite the voice-overs, we know virtually nothing about these men except that they act like pros and that the preparation must have been elaborate, as it involves a crew, timing, a crane truck, and the kind of "soup" that blows things into smithereens. Commando glances at his watch, and when a train whistles in the distance, he pulls a white stocking over his face. After the train sets off three successive explosions on the tracks, the conductor is forced to cut the speed, and as the train passes under the trestle, Commando leaps onto the roof of one of the cars. Crawling up to a vent, he sprays gas into the compartment below, the camera tilting down to a wide shot of two guards asleep there, one on a cot, the other in a chair with a rifle in his lap. A box with the words "U.S. MINT" stenciled on the side looms in the foreground of the frame. (Now we know what the object of the heist is: gold.) Though the guards wake up and try to escape, the crisscross shadows foretell their fate. A POV shot from the perspective of the locomotive as the train slows to a stop reveals a man standing in the middle of the tracks, swinging a lamp. The conductor climbs down from the engine and approaches him; when the man lifts his head, his face is covered by a ghostly white mask. Cut to the masked man knocking the conductor out like a light, then, when the engineer tries to phone for help, another masked man takes him out.

Skeets, head bowed, walks deliberately toward the train, carrying the nitro in his hands before him like a priest with a portable tabernacle. Once he sets the explosive and Roly unspools the electrical cable, they cautiously make their way back to the truck, where Commando hits the horn. Frankie responds, Skeets inserts the fuse into the truck's lighter, and the Treasury car explodes. The post-explosion shot of the ladder snaking into the now doorless car while the smoke disperses (the perspective is from inside the train) is surreal, like the earlier, high-angle trestle shot of Commando. Despite the fact that more boxes inscribed with "U.S. MINT" can be seen in the subsequent shot, the accent is on action. (This is no time, the film suggests, to dawdle.) The men use a winch at the end of the crane ladder to transfer the bullion-heavy boxes from the train to the moving van, and after the van and truck pull away, Roly hands a stick of gum to Skeets;

in the van, Frankie and Commando start laughing hysterically. Eddie cuts them off: "Before we start congratulating ourselves, let's remember that we have nine hundred miles to go. Nine hundred miles through every cop between here and the coast. You laugh it up like a couple of clowns." The reference to clowns recalls the mask that Johnny Clay dons during the racetrack heist in *The Killing*, a caper picture in which, not so incidentally, Johnny escapes with his life but not the loot.

The second act of *Plunder Road* can be said to begin as the truck and moving van enter a small town at dawn. As the camera pans to follow the passing van and truck, a church steeple is visible in the distance. The setting is significant: while everyone else is asleep, the men are hard at work. The close-up of a wheel turning in the hard light of day is the segue to a wide-angle shot of the van and truck turning onto a dirt road that leads straight to a warehouse. In the first, dissolve-linked montage, which is devoid of dialogue except for Eddie's order—"Let's go. We've got four hours"—the men transfer the boxes into the back of another van already crowded with boxes marked "COFFEE." In the second montage, the men, their shirts stained with sweat, move more boxes into the back of a truck partially loaded with what looks like the contents of a house: couch, mattress, chair, table, TV.

Once the men have lowered the remaining boxes into the hold of a chemical tanker, Eddie, a map spread out before him, rehearses the plan:

> Now, remember, stay on the main highway no matter what—no shortcuts, no back roads. Our best cover is to move right along with the rest of the traffic. Use that police wavelength only when you're absolutely in the clear. Otherwise, keep your radio set at sixteen hundred. We leave here at thirty-minute intervals. . . . Stop to eat every eight hours—only sandwiches. Change drivers every four hours and never go over ten miles beyond the speed limit. If a cop searches your truck, keep talkin' to him.

Eddie's instructions constitute the most extensive dialogue in the film up until this point. The fact no one else speaks—when the radio interrupts him, Eddie tells Roly to turn it off—indicates that he's in charge.

The rental van departs, and since there's no news on the police frequency, Skeets says, "Over a hundred miles out and not a whisper yet":

SKEETS: That Eddie's a genius, huh?
COMMANDO: That's a college education for you.
SKEETS: You know it's his first job. When Frankie told me, I thought he was nuts. I wasn't hooking up with an amateur. A job like that. He's no amateur.

If the medium two-shot and Commando's reply mark the above speech as dialogue, it retrospectively appears to be a prompt when the film cuts to a one-shot of Skeets as he begins to reminisce about his wife, who passed away two months ago—"She waited for me for twenty-three years while I'm in and out of stir like I was in a revolving door"—and his son, Harold: "I got a boy back East. Nothing but the best for him from now on. He's going to the biggest and best college in Rio." A woman's voice on the police frequency interrupts Skeets; he switches the radio off and, after turning the dial to a station that's playing contemporary instrumental music, continues:

> Let me tell you about Rio. In the first place there's over a million and a half people down there. Let's face it. You can get lost in a town that size, right? Me and the kid will take a boat. By the time we get there everything will have cooled off. . . . I'll get Harold one of those sports jobs. They've got a lot of beautiful streets down there. And get this—they don't use cement on the sidewalks. They got millions of different squares all painted different colors. They call them mosaics. Yeah, that's it. And they got a lot of hills where you can buy a house nobody knows anything about, and every day you can drive to the bay and the beach at Copacabana—they've got the whitest sands in the world there. White sand, blue sea. Plenty of room to move around. That's the place, I'm tellin' ya.
>
> COMMANDO: You been there, huh?
> SKEETS: No.

Cut on action to the van as it flashes down the highway. Like Doc Riedenschneider in *The Asphalt Jungle*, Skeets fantasizes about escaping to an exotic locale where he can settle down. Unlike Herr Professor's erotic fantasy, however, Skeets's dream wish is a domestic one: living with his son in a house in Copacabana. Just as Skeets's vision of moving to Rio contrasts with his current, constricted mode of transportation, his colorful description of the country vividly counterpoints the film's black-and-white film stock. Although Rio de Janeiro, as Skeets himself admits, has over a million people, it's not a city, it's a town; the sidewalks are made not of asphalt but mosaics; and every day is paradise: the whitest sand, the bluest sea. In this utopian scenario, Skeets's one-word answer to Commando's question—"You been there, huh?"—says everything: "No."

Back at the warehouse, thirty minutes have passed and Roly's about to depart when the music on the radio ends and an announcer comes on to report the "most daring robbery of all time." Cut to the rental van, where Skeets and Commando listen in as the announcer continues: "At approximately four a.m. this morning, an unknown number of men . . . stopped and looted a special train carrying over ten million dollars in gold." (Now we know how big the score was.) Suddenly Commando notices some police cars ahead and stops; then, when they ignore the van, he takes a fork in the road. In the rearview mirror, the police cars fan out to form a roadblock while, on the radio, the announcer reports that the "police, who have issued a ten-state alarm, describe it as the biggest train robbery in American history and, by the apparent speed with which it was executed, best planned."

Since we have witnessed just how well executed the heist was and, in the warehouse, how well planned, this is not news to the audience; the fact that it was the "biggest train robbery in American history," however, is. The historical association in the US between train robberies and the Old West is a resonant one, but it's significant that the heist in *Plunder Road* takes place during the 1950s, when railroads, with respect to travel and freight, had lost substantial ground to private automobiles and long-distance trailer trucks. The cinematic precedent is resonant as well: Edwin S. Porter's *Great Train Robbery* (1903), which, according to Stuart Kaminsky, is the "first Big Caper film," anticipating as it does the spatial logic and temporal dynamics of the classic heist film.[72]

At the warehouse, another thirty minutes have passed, Roly has departed, and the remaining members of the gang, Eddie and Frankie, are killing time. Frankie, whose nerves are so frayed that he previously turned up the radio to break the silence, paces. In order to distract him, Eddie asks him about auto racing, and Frankie reminisces about how he started out at sixteen—"The officials didn't know that, though"—and how three years ago he was barred for life from the Indianapolis Motor Speedway ("crummy officials") because, at least as Eddie puts it, he jumped a yellow light during the Indy 500. Frankie's still bitter, but as Eddie reminds him, if he hadn't been barred, he, Eddie, "wouldn't have the best wheelman in the business and [Frankie] wouldn't be a millionaire." The exchange between Eddie and Frankie, while abbreviated, marks the difference between the two men: while Frankie's hot, Eddie's cool. Moreover, Frankie's resentment against officials indexes, like Skeets's allusion to "stir," his prior adversarial relation to the law.

The first figurative red light in the film occurs when Roly's forced to stop at a roadblock and, as he steps down from the cab, a mess of gum wrappers flutters to the ground. He's momentarily able to discourage the police from searching the back of his truck by invoking an imaginary wife—"Would you kind of take it careful, fellas? If I get so much as a scratch on that stuff, my wife will kill me"—but when he turns on the radio (it's set to the police frequency), the cop's ears prick up. Though Roly takes off in the truck, a police cruiser cuts him off, and when he starts running, another policeman enters the frame from screen right—"Halt! Halt!"—stops, aims, and shoots: Roly, hit in the back, drops like a sack.

When Eddie and Frankie arrive on the scene, the police check the radio and the seal on the tanker, at which point Eddie pulls over to the side of the road, where, feigning engine trouble, he and Frankie watch as Roly's lifeless body, strapped to a stretcher, is wheeled to a waiting ambulance. (In the tight deep-focus shot, Eddie and Frankie are standing in the left foreground, imprisoned by the open hood of the tanker.) Meanwhile, in the rental van, Skeets is shaving and Commando, who's driving, is smoking a cigar when the radio announcer comes on with an update: "The first break in the fabulous gold robbery occurred about an hour and a half ago when . . . one of the bandits was shot and killed while attempting to run through a police roadblock." Hearing the news, Commando almost drives off the side of the road. Earlier, Frankie asked Eddie about the condition of the men who were gassed and taken out during the heist. Now, while Frankie drives and his partner sleeps, he learns that all the men "have been released from the hospital." In other words, Roly's dead and the police have recovered one-third of the gold, but no civilians have been killed—yet.

Later, Skeets is driving and Commando is asleep when the announcer relates that "in an effort to track the elusive gold bandits, police have tightened the web by calling in reserves, thus allowing them to establish an unprecedented number of roadblocks covering every highway and backroad as far east as Ohio." Here, *Plunder Road* enlists the rhetoric of the armed services ("reserves") to highlight the way law enforcement in the 1950s employed the new technologies of communication to map and master space. More specifically, if the new national network of roads facilitated unrestricted movement and regulated the flow of high-speed automotive traffic,[73] that same system was also subject to the most advanced, scientifically sophisticated surveillance that federal subsidies could buy.

This motif is reflected in the following sequence in which Skeets and Commando stop, as scheduled, for gas. While Skeets leaves for the men's room, Commando tells the attendant to fill up the truck, and the self-described "old codger" asks Commando "if they caught those robbers yet." Commando reflexively says no before catching himself and muttering, "I don't know." The attendant doesn't miss a beat, reflecting that the police "can't help but catch 'em": "Fellows like that hardly have a chance nowadays with radio and all that science against them. . . . Now, back a few years ago, it was different. Man had a real chance. Nowadays everything's got a system." If the attendant's sympathies lie with the robbers, it's clear that his remarks echo the radio announcer's account of the web tightening like a noose around the "elusive gold bandits." Moreover, if the announcer's recourse to words like "robbers" and, in particular, "bandits" mirrors the media's melodramatic narration of the unfolding events, it also reflects the old-fangled, frontier character of the heist. The gas station attendant's subsequent lament that he didn't decide to hitch onto "one single thing" and stick to it—"there's no telling where I would be today"—is therefore not without irony, since the members of the heist gang have chosen to commit to one single thing, illicit as that thing may be. That is to say, the gang does not so much contest as mimic the systemization of everyday life, in which the only way to beat the system is to game it.

Still, it's neither the law nor the system but, as in so many other heist films, human error that trips the crew up. When Commando, prompted by the attendant, checks the oil, he accidentally drops his gun and the attendant's so stunned—the gun lies between them for a long moment—he forgets to press the trigger on the nozzle and gas starts to spill out of the tank. Commando, snatching the gun, backs the attendant into the station (the camera is located inside as if it's aimed right at the viewer), where he shoots him at point-blank range. Once they're back in the cab, Skeets looks open-mouthed at Commando, as if to ask "Why?" Commando's curt response encapsulates his hard-boiled character: "Had to."

In the meantime, Eddie and Frankie have pulled over at a taco diner where an old jalopy is parked outside, and inside music's playing on the radio and two teenagers are discussing the robbery. A teenager with blond hair opines—"Look, the Canadian border is only five hundred miles from here. New York is two thousand"—to which the other, darker-haired one replies, "So the cops figure they head for the border. I say they're smarter than that. I say they're heading for New York." When Eddie and Frankie sit down at the counter, the waitress, Hazel (Nora Hayden), comments, not unlike the now dead gas station attendant, that she'd "like to see them get away with it." The blond teen, a cigarette dangling from his lips, quips, "You gotta watch her. She's got a criminal mind." (As Johnny Clay memorably puts it in *The Asphalt Jungle*, we've "all got a little larceny" in us.) The boys laugh, then the dark-haired one turns to Hazel and says, "What would you do with all that loot?"

Though Hazel answers the question in the same blithe spirit in which it was posed—"Go to London and Paris, the best of everything"—her smile quickly turns to a frown when she sees Eddie's grave demeanor. "Me, I'd build the fastest job on the road," the dark-haired teen interjects, "that would give the cops a lot of smoke."[74] Frankie's smiling at the hot-rod enthusiast's bravado when the music stops and the announcer comes on to report that the "grim shadow of murder may have fallen over the desperate plight of the gold thieves in the night. Less than an hour ago, a passing motorist discovered the body of an elderly gas station attendant shot to death." Hazel, shocked, wonders out loud, "What would make them do a thing like that?" Eddie: "Money."

Back on the road, Frankie, alarmed by the news of the shooting of the gas station attendant, says they should head straight for the Mexican border. Eddie, however, knows that Mexico is a no-go, "an idea couldn't get past the border right now." Crosscut to the van, where Commando, lighting another cigar, asks Skeets out of the blue how old his son is:

SKEETS: Seventeen.
COMMANDO: My son should be about eleven now.

SKEETS (confused): I thought you said you were never married.
COMMANDO: Never seen him.

Previously, commenting on Commando's stint as a stuntman in the movies, Skeets ventured that he "must have been married to a swell-looking girl." Commando's reaction—"I was never married"—not only stresses the differences between the two men (Commando, it's implied, is even more socially alienated than the ex-con Skeets) but also broaches the issue of women and family. Skeets aside, none of the members of the gang appears to be married, nor do any of them appear to be in touch with their families. While the men have rendezvoused for this job, they otherwise seem adrift, cut off like atoms from the socius and the nuclear ideal—wife, children, single-family detached home—that epitomized the American Dream in the 1950s.

It's no coincidence, then, that in the wake of the above exchange, Skeets and Commando notice a weighing station. As they pull over, a uniformed man in the booth waves to a police cruiser, which pulls up in front of the van, blocking it. Skeets tells the station man that their load is coffee, but when the guard weighs the van, it's forty-five hundred pounds overweight. Here, the very materiality of the gold that the gang has stolen gives Skeets and Commando away. In other words, if the ultimate success of the caper depends on the crew's ability to make ten million dollars' worth of gold "invisible in the new centrifugal space of highways and surveillance networks," it's virtually impossible to "render it undetectable."[75] From this perspective, the aftermath of the heist as opposed to the heist itself seems curiously anachronistic: "In an age of increasing immateriality, a world in which knowledge, wealth, and culture circulate at ever-greater speeds, stealing ten tons of gold is an obsolete criminal project."[76] As if to underline this paradox, the end of the road for Skeets and Commando, even more so than for Roly, is completely anticlimactic: instead of Skeets and Commando going out with guns blazing like folk heroes, the police simply arrest them.

Eddie's driving the tanker when the news breaks:

Astute police work tonight brought about the capture of two more members of the gang that held up the gold train. Less than an hour ago guards at a small weighing station . . . investigated the overweight load of a truck heading west and found one-third of the stolen gold hidden in a load of coffee. Authorities are certain that the remainder of the gang and the still missing third are in another truck still at large.

It's daytime, Eddie's asleep, and Frankie's driving when the announcer on the radio comes on again to report that the "authorities believe that the bandits may not be headed for the border as reported earlier but that they might have gone into hiding somewhere in Los Angeles." Subsequently, Frankie's asleep, Eddie's driving, and the announcer concludes that "three-and-one-half-million dollars seems to have vanished into thin air," a vanishing act that recollects Marx and Engels's celebrated pronouncement in *The Communist Manifesto* that in a capitalist economy, "everything solid melts into air."[77] In other words, Eddie and Frankie have somehow managed, for the time being at least, to render the gold undetectable as if, against all odds, an elephant had magically been made to disappear.

The third act of *Plunder Road* commences when Eddie and Frankie pull off the highway so that Eddie can make a phone call. Cut to a woman's hand picking up a receiver as the camera pans to a mirror in which an attractive, middle-age blonde in a black dress and pearls can be seen. Eddie says, "Okay, honey," and hangs up. In the mirror the woman—we later learn her name is Fran Werner (Jeanne Cooper)—bites her lip and returns the receiver to the cradle. Both the woman's anxious behavior and the wide-angle shot of the office—a clean, well-lighted place that's a model of mid-century corporate décor—foreshadow the early real-estate sequence in *Psycho* in which Marion Crane's (Janet Leigh) boss entrusts her with forty thousand dollars of his own money to deposit in the bank. In *Plunder Road* Fran gathers up her things and takes a taxi to a foundry, where she fires up the smelter. In the tanker Eddie and Frankie are passing a sign—"LOS ANGELES 14"—when a siren sounds in the distance. Though it turns out to be a false alarm (it's only an ambulance), the traffic as they approach Los Angles is already congested.

At the foundry Eddie and Fran embrace until Eddie interrupts them and they get down to work. First, Eddie bleeds the tanker, then he and Frankie use a winch to lift the boxes out of the hold. The three-shot of Eddie, Fran, and Frankie laboriously dragging a single box into the foundry—the back of Eddie's shirt is drenched in sweat—testifies to just how heavy the bullion is. Once Eddie and Frankie have secured the latch on the tanker, we finally get the "money shot," the screen dissolving to a pair of hands prying open one of the boxes stacked high with gold ingots. In the succeeding deep-focus shot, the two men, their faces partially masked by goggles, transport the molten gold to the molds, where the low-key lighting, combined with smoke and flames, imbues the foundry with an infernal cast. The dissolve from the men pouring the precious metal into the molds to Fran wiping her brow as she stacks the ingots in the backseat of a car reiterates the sheer physical nature of the labor involved. At the same time, in the wide chiaroscuro shot of Fran, which could come straight from a Caravaggio painting, the light glints off the buttons on the backseat of the car and, stacked below, the gold ingots symmetrically arranged like bars.

The ensuing exterior shot of the foundry, black smoke pouring out of a stack, seems superfluous until a police cruiser, "gumball" flashing, appears at the end of the alley and parks right across the street from the building. Fran and the men are inside taking a break, drinking coffee and eating sandwiches, when an alarm goes off. After Eddie cracks open the door, a uniformed man says he's from "air pollution control" and warns Eddie that he "better clean the oil out of that furnace": "Smoke is worse than a tar factory." The officer then gives Eddie a "smog ticket." If, on one hand, the scene is farcical—Eddie and his gang have stolen ten million dollars from the government and the cops are ticketing them for polluting the air—on the other hand, it's also prescient, throwing a spotlight on the deleterious effects of industrial and automobile pollution in Los Angeles circa 1957.[78]

Disaster averted, Eddie tells Fran and Frankie that it's time to get some rest. The constricted shot of Frankie fast asleep in the front seat of the car and Eddie in the back foregrounds, like the smog ticket, the prominence of automobiles in the film—here, the car as a home or coffin. The men are still asleep when Fran, poised in a shaft of light, gently wakes Eddie:

> FRAN: Let's forget the whole thing. Let's leave right now.
> EDDIE (sitting up): Are you crazy—after everything we've been through? Look, you're gonna get everything you want.
> FRAN: I've got everything I want. I didn't want you to steal, Eddie. A man's been killed.

Eddie, looking at his watch, doesn't even answer her—"It's one o'clock. We gotta be at the pier by ten"—and instead wakes Frankie: "C'mon, Frankie, wake up. C'mon, wake up." The camera stays on Eddie as, shaking his head and blinking his eyes, he struggles to wake from a dead sleep: there's more work to do.

Unlike the classic heist film, in which the actual heist is typically the most strenuous part of the process, in *Plunder Road* the aftermath depicts the sort of hard labor, elaborated at length and in exacting detail in the warehouse and foundry sequences, that the caper is presumably supposed to relieve the men of. In other words, the fantasy of the heist film is premised on the infinitely seductive notion of risking everything on one big job so you don't have to spend the rest of your life working. Hence the irony of the foundry part of *Plunder Road*, which explicitly references heavy industry and, specifically, the assembly line, an evocation that's consonant with the '50s heist film where the Fordist division of labor ("dividing tasks to minimize risks and to make the best use of resources") as well as Taylorist principles of scientific management (the separation of planning from execution[79]) are vividly dramatized. *Plunder Road* is unique, though, in that it reliteralizes the industrial-managerial tropes that underpin the classic heist film. This tropic twist is epitomized in the film when, in a high-angle shot, Eddie and Frankie remove the top of a mold—note, for instance, how the framing amputates their arms—to reveal a solid gold hubcap imprinted with the Cadillac insignia.

Cadillac: Eddie Harris (Gene Raymond) and Frankie Chardo (Stephen Ritch) prepare to transport a solid gold hubcap in *Plunder Road* (1957).

The Cadillac hubcap italicizes the extraordinary ingenuity of this particular heist, the poetry of which comes to the fore in the third act of the film. The Cadillac was not only the gold standard with respect to luxury automobility in the 1950s; it also possessed an illustrious history, having been named after Antoine de la Mothe Cadillac, the founder of Detroit, who, after arriving in the New World, invented a noble, blue-blooded title and a matching coat of arms. The latter, a multicolored crest encircled by a laurel wreath and capped by a royal crown, captures the entrepreneurial esprit and aspirational ethos of the Americas. The straight cut to Eddie, Frankie, and Fran outfitted in clean, sweat-free clothes—the men in sports jackets and open dress shirts, Fran in a button-down skirt with a striped cardigan over a white blouse—signals the magical, only-in-America transformation from labor to leisure. Where moments before Eddie, Frankie, and Fran appeared to be the embodiment of "blue collar" workers, now they're the very picture of mid-century "white collar" Americans setting out, complete with "Caddy," on a cruise to Europe.

As the Cadillac gradually enters traffic, a wide shot of the freeway reveals that all four lanes are already crowded with traffic. Cocktail music is playing on the radio, and Eddie, looking at his watch, remarks that "in another forty minutes we'll be in Pedro":

FRANKIE: How much is my half of this jalopy worth?
EDDIE: Where we're going—roughly a million.
FRANKIE: That's how I feel, like a million.

Fran, leaning her head against Eddie's shoulder, laughs, but the buoyant mood is broken when Frankie sees a roadblock ahead, the camera cutting to a POV shot of the traffic slowing down. Frankie immediately imagines the worst-case scenario—"It's gotta be a roadblock. Why else would it be piled up like this?"—but Eddie, as usual, remains coolheaded: "The morning rush—the people work for a living." In other words, while everyone else is driving to work and starting the daily grind, Eddie, Fran, and Frankie, having reaped the rewards of their labor, no longer have to work for a living.

While Frankie, still perturbed, continues to complain—"We haven't moved a mile in five minutes. I've never seen so many cars"—Eddie knows that the more cars there are, the better it is for the gang: "I love every one of them. The police don't know who we are or where we are or what we're driving." Suddenly the song on the radio ends and the announcer comes on with a traffic bulletin: "Police state that the Harbor Freeway outbound is heavily congested from the interchange to the Washington Boulevard exit due to a traffic accident." Frankie's about to lose it completely—"First they get you piled up like this and *then* they tell you there's a wreck!"—when Fran exclaims, "Hey, we must be getting near the accident." Cut to a POV shot of an overturned car and a motorcycle cop directing traffic, then on action to a wide shot of a woman in a big hat and white sunglasses in a two-toned Impala, whose eyes are fixed not on the road but on the accident. When her car smashes into the Cadillac, Eddie, Fran, and Frankie's bodies pitch forward like dummies.

The montage that follows—a low-angle shot of a policeman silhouetted against the smog-hazed sky; a high-angle shot of the locked bumpers; and, finally, a medium shot of a helmeted motorcycle cop rocking up and down on the bumpers—prefixes the dreaded and fateful line: "Hey, George, look at that bumper. It's gold!" Eddie, impulsive until the end, pulls a gun on the motorcycle cop and is shot, like Roly, in the back. Frankie takes off on foot, but the tracking shots of him fleeing with the police in pursuit (note the cars slowly passing in the background) possess, as in the earlier trestle shot of Commando and the tabernacle one of Skeets, a surreal character, as if we're watching the action in slow motion. Fran's fighting free of a policeman when Frankie climbs over the railing and hangs there until, timing his fall, he lets go. Although he lands safely on the roof of a passing trailer truck, he rolls right off and is run over by an oncoming car, the bumper flashing into view as the driver belatedly hits the brakes. Fran, fainting, collapses, and as a motorcycle cop whistles, the camera cranes past a row of spectators before rising on car after abandoned car stranded in the middle of the highway as if it were one big parking lot.

If the criminal trajectory in *Plunder Road* extends from Utah—via Los Angeles and San Pedro—to Lisbon, Portugal, there's no little irony that in this "trucking noir"—see, for example, *They Drive by Night* (1940), *Thieves' Highway*, and, most importantly, perhaps, *Wages of Fear* (1953)[80]—the rubber hits the proverbial road on the Harbor Freeway, once envisioned as the "Main Street" of Los Angeles.

"For what belongs more to everyday life . . . than the daily commute, the ritualized movement between the urban center and its environs that organized the schedules of so many who dwelled within it?"[81] In other words, the dénouement of *Plunder Road* portrays how the American Dream in the 1950s was predicated on the paradox of suburbanization: even as the suburbs represented an escape from the "asphalt jungle," the traffic signified the hidden costs of time, pollution, and accident-related fatalities.

Still, if the traffic jam in *Plunder Road* can itself be understood as the "return of the repressed of abstract space-time,"[82] it's worth reflecting on the fate of the individual members of the heist gang, three of whom die and the remainder of whom are arrested. With the exception of Fran, and to a lesser extent, Skeets and Frankie (who, like Fran, are not indifferent to the loss of human life), the audience is not encouraged to identify with the individual members of the gang: Roly is fatuous, Skeets is a two-time loser, Commando is a coldblooded killer, Frankie is neurotically impetuous, and Eddie, despite his obvious affection for Fran, is all business. Nor, it should be noted, are we encouraged to identify with the police, who are generally anodyne, if not faceless, instruments of the law, which, as in most '50s crime films, is inexorable. The spectator is aligned instead with the radio audience in the film, whose one wish, one imagines, is not so much to be a millionaire living the lush, expatriate life in Lisbon or lounging on the beach in Copacabana but to be distracted, however temporarily, from the vicissitudes of everyday life by the thrills and chills of a train robbery.

That a '50s heist film like *Plunder Road* is subversive, whether of assembly-line Fordism or the nuclear-familial American Dream, is a commonplace. Still, it may well be that the most subversive aspect of Cornfield's film is its quotidian address. Consider, in this context, Hazel or the gas station attendant, who are diegetic surrogates for the audience. From their perspective, the gang is not robbing a bank or an armored car, a racetrack or a jewelry store, but the US Treasury—which is to say, working stiffs like you and me, the same sort of people who, Eddie's contempt aside, commute to work every day, avidly listening to the news on the radio.

9

ODDS AGAINST TOMORROW

RACE, SPACE, AND SPUTNIK NOIR

> Far above him [Ingram] saw a single star shining
> in the sky. Everything was dark but the star. . . .
> Without one you couldn't have the other, he real-
> ized slowly. Without the darkness there wouldn't
> be any stars.
>
> —William P. McGivern, *Odds against Tomorrow*

The blacklisted screenwriter Abraham Polonsky's description of the cardinal scene in *Odds against Tomorrow* is both clipped and poetic: "EXT. INTERCHANGES AND BRIDGES. Burke's car in the beltline. The geometry of traffic."[1] The location is the Triboro Bridge in New York City. Burke is David Burke (Ed Begley), an ex-cop who was kicked off the force for refusing to testify to the State Crime Commission and who's the mastermind of the heist, and he's driving Earle Slater (Robert Ryan), an unemployed ex-serviceman, to the prospective scene of the crime. Because the shot is a high, extremely long one, Burke's car is lost, however, in the rapidly moving traffic on the bridges and interchanges. Robert Wise, the director, recalled that the camera was situated "on top on one of those apartment houses right by East River Drive" (the production was headquartered in Gold Metal Studios in the Bronx),[2] and the pattern, as the locution "geometry of traffic" points up, is abstract, not unlike a post-expressionist painting in which the individual *gestus* is subordinated to the grid of the super-metropolitan highway system.

The straight cut to a black sedan passing under a bridge and traveling north on a four-lane parkway, then to a medium interior shot of Burke and Earle, reestablishes the topographical coordinates, as do the dialogue—"It's about a hundred miles north up the Hudson"—and the zoom-in to a map with the name "Melton" roughly underlined in black. The subsequent montage features farmhouses on the outskirts of town; a factory and a water tower; a woman pushing a baby carriage, and schoolgirls, books in their arms, crossing a downtown street; another factory spewing smoke; a bus traveling down Main Street toward the camera; a kerchiefed woman crossing railroad tracks; and a church with a cross-tipped spire that tapers to the heavens. "In the atmospheric transition from New York to Melton," Alistair Phillips has remarked, "Joseph C. Brun's evocative cinematography captures a sense of unease as if the pastoral of the American small town seen in earlier generations of *film noir* to suggest a counterpoint to the city's inequities has now utterly vanished," replaced instead by an "industrial melancholy" that's reminiscent of Robert Frank's contemporaneous *The Americans* (1959).[3]

Despite the elegiac, late autumnal mood evoked by Brun's photography and John Lewis's "cool jazz" score, Melton in *Odds against Tomorrow* is in fact a booming "market town,"[4] and that means only one thing: money. It's therefore no surprise that the montage ends with a low-angle shot of the First National Bank, in front of which stands an old-fashioned street clock atop a cast-iron pole. (The date on the illuminated face reads "1836.") In a low-angle close-up, the clock reads 2:48 p.m. After a cutaway to a long high-angle shot of the Hudson River at dusk and downtown Melton as the streetlights are coming on, the clock reads 6:03 p.m. Cut to the Melton Hotel and a tight, extremely low-key shot of closed Venetian blinds that suddenly open onto a view of Main Street below. Burke: "Now watch the waiter." A man in a white hat, jacket, and chef's hat emerges from a drugstore, carrying a carton with coffee and sandwiches. As he walks down the street, the camera pans laterally to the left. The deliveryman pauses at the corner, then starts across the street. "Over here," Burke says, at which point he and Earle quickly move to a side window where they watch the waiter make his way to the bank, his shadow blown up like a giant's on the side of the building, and where, under a lamp that casts a cone of light, he knocks on a security window.

Burke breathlessly narrates the action in voice-over, the camera pushing in as the waiter hands the carton over the chain to the security guard inside:

Now, here's the setup. That side door is the key to the whole job. The bank stays open Thursdays till six. Most of the factories pay on Friday, so the bank is loaded with payroll cash and deposits from stores. Every Thursday night there's close to two hundred thousand dollars in untraceable cash sitting in there. A half dozen clerks stick around for an hour totaling up and straightening out the books. . . . That's it. That colored waiter from the drugstore brings them coffee and sandwiches just after six. The rest of the town's home at supper. You could take it with a water pistol!

Slatter: Burke (Ed Begley) and Earle Slater (Robert Ryan) track the delivery route of a black counterman in *Odds against Tomorrow* (1959).

As the waiter returns to the drugstore, Burke and Earl cross back to the first window:

> BURKE: Well, what do you think?
> SLATER: There's just one thing wrong with it.
> BURKE: What?

Earle, his face slashed with shadows from the "slatter" blinds, drawls, "You didn't say nothin' about the third man bein' a nigger."

The cut to Johnny Ingram (the editor is Dede Allen) is shocking in part because the object of the racial cut is played by Harry Belafonte, the "King of Calypso" and a black matinee idol in the 1950s who, with his trademark shades and turtleneck sweater, was the epitome of cool. Belafonte was also the film's producer, "the only African American [acting] in this capacity at the time" (his company was called HarBel Productions),[5] having previously acquired the rights to McGivern's novel. Belafonte was not, however, immune to racism. In a *60 Minutes* profile, he recounted an incident that occurred while getting off the bus to use the men's room during a 1955 tour of the South: "I heard a voice behind me, 'You let go a drop, you're a dead nigger.' I turned around . . . and there was a state trooper. . . . And I walked back on that bus, and I just sat there for the rest of the tour—devastated by the experience."[6]

Belafonte's experience echoes an incident that Johnny remembers in McGivern's novel. Ingram was returning to the North with his ill mother—she had been staying with his sister in Mobile, Alabama—when the train made an unscheduled stop in Anniston: "A woman claimed that she had been molested by her Pullman porter."[7] At one point someone switched on the lights in Johnny's

Pulp Fiction: cover of the 1958 Cardinal paperback edition of William P. McGivern's *Odds against Tomorrow*.

car, and a crowd of men who had gathered under the station shed suddenly noticed him in the window, "their eyes beginning to brighten with excitement."[8] A policeman told him, "Better get in one of the toilets, boy," and, as Johnny recounts, that's just what he did until the train began to move again.

It's different for Johnny in the North, though. In the "colored neighborhoods of large cities" where he's lived his whole life, he has adopted a manner that's both a pose—"a conciliatory politeness that usually protected him against slights and condescensions"—and a weapon, "a derisive burlesque of terrified humility."[9] In the film Ingram rejects both the "parody of shuffling conciliation" that characterizes Johnny in the novel and the pacific, assimilationist impulse associated with Martin Luther King Jr.[10] Not unlike the pre-Mecca Malcolm X, for whom the white man was the devil, Ingram as he's played by Belafonte in *Odds against Tomorrow* "bullets from the screen": he's "proud, belligerent, defiant, unyielding, and attractively hostile."[11] As Belafonte himself remarked about his character as written by Polonsky, "He walked in and he demanded his equality *just by his presence.*"[12]

None of this belies the fact that Johnny, like the classic gangster noir antihero, is trapped, and his entrapment has a specifically black dimension. Belafonte again: "In the way that Ingram was written, it became evident that the way he was 'heroic' is based upon the very way he was trapped in his skin and trapped in his environment."[13] Thus, in McGivern's novel Burke tells Johnny that he needs a "colored guy" for the heist, but when Ingram answers that he doesn't have the guts for the job, Burke replies, "Guts you don't need. . . . It's your skin I'm buying."[14] Moreover, in both the novel and the film, Johnny's trapped, as Belafonte points out, by circumstances. Like Randy Keenan in *The Killing*, he has a gambling problem and owes seventy-five hundred dollars to a loan shark named Bacco (Will Kuluva). The entrapping environment is a nightclub called Cannoy's where Ingram works—Johnny's not unlike an alcoholic who works as a bartender—and "where serious gambling is done upstairs by racketeers, . . . show people, or big-time spenders."[15] In fact, the only reason that Bacco "hasn't knocked [his] teeth in" is that Johnny has been paying him one hundred dollars a week in interest. While Johnny's driving downtown, he complains to Burke, who has bummed a ride, that his ex-wife is "worse than Bacco": "If that alimony isn't there on the first, the lawyer's there on the second." Still, as Johnny tells Burke just before he drops him off across the street from Central Park (and here he sounds like Dix Handley in *The Asphalt Jungle*), he's "praying for a miracle": "I've got five hundred on the nose of Lady Care today. Can't lose forever."

In the aforementioned shock cut from the Hotel Melton to Cannoy's Club, the lyrics of the song that Johnny's singing can be heard right before the cut:

At night I tell you people
When that cold, cold sun goes down. . . .
I cry, I sigh, I wanna die
'Cause my baby's not around.

Johnny's still singing the blues and playing the vibraphone when Bacco and his two henchmen, Coco (Richard Bright) and Moriarty (Lew Gallo), are shown to a table. Coco, who's flamboyantly gay (for the '50s), delivers Bacco's message: "Hey, baby, what's shakin'? Bacco wants to buy you a drink, and I wanna buy you a shiny new car." Coco's flirtatious behavior aside, Johnny doesn't realize that when he dropped Burke off at Central Park, the ex-cop went there to talk to Bacco about calling in Johnny's loan. (See the later carousel scene set in Central Park where the bobbing painted horses on the merry-go-round mock Johnny's "can't lose forever" credo.) When Burke approaches Bacco, the mobster is feeding cracked corn from a paper bag to a flock of pigeons, an ironically Franciscan image that recalls the street scene early in the film in which children are swooping in the wind off the river, "their coats open like wings."[16]

While Johnny's making his way to the office to ask Eddy Cannoy (Fred F. Scollay) to bail him out, a black security guard slips him a "juvenile delinquent." But when Johnny pulls the automatic on Bacco and his men, the loan shark, furious at Johnny for his impudence, threatens him: "Have the dough at my place tomorrow night or I collect it from you or that ex-wife of yours or your kid!" The word "tomorrow," alluding as it does to the film's title, suggests that the odds have abruptly turned, perhaps inexorably, against Johnny. Consequently, when we next see him, he has been drinking, Annie (Mae Barnes) is singing—"Well, it tells you in the good book / And they teach the same in school / Let a man get his hands on you / And he'll use you for a mule"—and Johnny's sticking his head into the frame, interrupting the chorus ("All men are evil") with "off-key, out-of-synch" interjections.[17]

The scene is shocking not simply because Johnny's vibraphone playing is so out-of-control—he bluntly wields the mallets as if they're hammers—but because he has so obviously lost his cool. Earlier, when Burke first broached the idea of the heist, Johnny scoffed, "Man, you're drifting. . . . That's for junkies and joy boys." Now, instead of a "headache," he's got "cancer." Burke, though, is pleased as punch: he's got his "nice shiny shoehorn,"[18] a turn of phrase that suggests that, for Burke, Johnny is merely a "shoeshine boy" or, in a word, "shine."

Later, at Burke's apartment, Earle and Johnny meet to go over the plans for the heist. While Slater takes stock of the weapons—"We got four police specials that have no history and a couple shotguns"—Johnny's busy thinking about how to solve the problem of the chain on the bank's door. However, as Slater sees it,

Johnny's role is completely perfunctory: all he has to do is be himself—which is to say, act the part of a stereotype—since the plan's founded on the "inability of whites to tell two dissimilar black men apart."[19]

> SLATER: Don't worry about it, boy, we'll be right there with you. All you have to do is carry the sandwiches. In a white monkey jacket. And give 'em a big smile. And say "yessir." You don't have to worry and you don't have to think. We'll take care of you.
> (Ingram's face is suffused with rage.)
> INGRAM: You'll have to start right now.
> BURKE: Don't beat out that Civil War jazz, Slater.[20]

"Civil War jazz" is an unusually resonant phrase, fusing the antiquated nature of Slater's racism (he's still fighting the lost cause of the South) and the film's progressive jazz score, which Belafonte commissioned Lewis to compose.

Here, Belafonte was following Polonsky's lead in his instructions for the film's music, as can be seen in the script's notations for the first sequence set in New York City on a "cross street in the Nineties": "It is in a modern, moody, sometimes progressive jazz vein, carrying an overture of premonition, of tragedy—of people in trouble and doomed."[21] In the late 1950s, Lewis was already an established figure in the world of jazz, having been present at the "Birth of the Cool," the memorable 1949 and 1950 recording sessions featuring him, Miles Davis, Gil Evans, and Gerry Mulligan. When Belafonte approached Lewis, he was also a "member of the famed Modern Jazz Quartet and the principal architect of the group's style and sound," which, post-bebop, appealed to both whites and blacks.[22] Lewis was therefore an inspired choice on Belafonte's part: just as the Modern Jazz Quartet sought to integrate jazz and classical music, so too Wise and Belafonte sought to mix "film noir and social commentary."[23]

Yet integration is not quite as harmonious in *Odds against Tomorrow* as it was in the MJQ, because the relationship between Johnny and Slater is a shotgun marriage that's a product of the characters' vexed relationships to women. Slater, for example, is economically dependent on Lorry (Shelley Winters) and feels totally emasculated. First, Lorry leaves him a note asking him to pick up a blue taffeta dress from the cleaner's and, when he gets home, to babysit the neighbor's child. Then, on the way home from the cleaner's, Earle stops at a bar where a young soldier is showing a girl some judo holds—"all this atom stuff"—and Earle, who's sitting at the bar, says without turning his head, "That stuff belongs to my war. Take her to Canaveral to launch her." Although the soldier baits him—"Come on, throw a punch"—Earle puts him off ("You better go back and play with the girls. Tell them all about Sputnik") until the soldier sarcastically refers to him as an "old veteran" and "Pop," taking the soldier up on his dare, knocks him down like a bowling pin.

Still, the ultimate indignity for Earle doesn't occur until Lorry comes home with good news—her boss is going to buy a new drugstore and, since she'll be managing it, she'll be making more money:

LORRY: You don't have to be the big man with me, Earle. . . .
SLATER: I know, but what happens when I get old?
LORRY: You are old now.

Lorry's retort recalls a previous exchange between the two when, packing for the trip to Melton to review the heist, Earle defiantly told her, "They're not gonna junk me like an old car."

It's therefore significant that while Earle doesn't appear to own a car (in the novel, it's Lorry's), Johnny's used to sporting around the city in a white Austin Healy and, when he parks outside Burke's apartment building, hands out money like Santa Claus to the children playing on the sidewalk: "All right, who'd like to make themselves a fortune?" In fact, Johnny's convertible and largesse speak to a certain class consciousness, an upwardly mobile one mirrored in the film's depiction of Johnny's ex-wife, Ruth (Kim Hamilton), whom we see interacting with a PTA steering committee. About this scene *Variety* wrote in 1959, "The home life of Belafonte's estranged wife is a unique view (for films) of a normal, middle-class Negro home—with an integrated Parent-Teachers Association meeting going on."[24] (The parenthetical qualification—"for films"—comments on the moribund state of Hollywood vis-à-vis the reality of the African American experience at the time.)

This scene, like the subsequent one of Johnny traveling by bus to Melton, is pregnant with meaning. In the South, Rosa Parks and the Montgomery bus boycott of 1955–1956 were potent symbols of the fight for civil rights. In the film Johnny's traveling by bus to Melton because Earle and Burke are driving the cars. (Johnny has left the keys to his Austin Healy with Ruth so that she can take their daughter, Eadie [Lois Thorne], out for a ride while he's "out of town.") As for the sort of integration represented by the PTA and its "mix of liberal whites and young black professionals,"[25] Johnny has nothing but scorn:

INGRAM: You're tough.
RUTH: Not tough enough to change you.
INGRAM: For what? To hold hands with those ofay friends of yours.
RUTH: I'm trying to make a world fit for Eadie to live in. It's a cinch you're not
    going to do it with a deck of cards and a racing form.
INGRAM: But you are, huh? You and your big white brothers. Drink enough tea
    with 'em and stay out of the watermelon patch, and maybe our little colored
    girl will grow up to be Miss America, is that it?

Johnny, unlike his wife, doesn't want to wait until "America" changes. He's making do the only way he knows how—by hustling the system, by gambling.

Despite the fact that Earle and Johnny are very different characters—Earle's a "hillbilly with temperament,"[26] and Johnny's a self-described "bone picker in a four-man graveyard"—their relationships with women suggest a certain consonance. Consider, for example, the racially charged scene at Burke's apartment, which represents a segue of sorts from the previous Hotel Melton scene and concludes with Burke's reprimand of Earle: "I don't want to hear what your grandpappy thought on the old farm down in Oklahoma." Later, Earle explains Burke's allusion to his "grandpappy" when he tells Lorry that the "wind blew us off the land in Oklahoma." In McGivern's novel Slater elaborates on his impoverished past: "I grew up in a shack on three dirt acres. . . . We lived like niggers. We lived right beside 'em, in the same kind of shack, eating the same stinking food, and wearing the same rotten clothes. And my old man tied me up and beat me like a dog for playing with them when I was a kid and didn't know better."[27]

In addition, in the critical scene where Earle and Johnny meet at Burke's apartment to review the heist, the author uses the masculine ritual of drinking to comment on the tense relation between the two men. Earle has just seen Johnny for the first time—"a little shock of confusion and hostility went through him; the man was colored"[28]—when Burke offers him a whiskey. Earle's response—"I got a kind of funny taste in my mouth"—prompts Johnny to say, signifying on him, "I'll bet you got a dark brown taste in your mouth, Mr. Slater."[29] Earle, who's angry and confused, wonders out loud whether Burke somehow got his and Johnny's glasses mixed up: "I'll work with Sambo if I have to, but I'm not about to drink out of the same glass."[30] Feeling as if he's been slapped, Johnny takes a sip of his whiskey and, smiling coolly, replies, "Pappy would say . . . don't use a dipper after the poor white trash."[31] Earle slaps Johnny across the face, but before Johnny can hit him back, Burke lashes out at Slater: "You fool, you crazy fool! . . . The only color I care about is green. You hear that? Green!"[32]

By contrast, in Wise's film Earle never lays a hand on Johnny and never calls him "Sambo"; instead, he employs the criminal lingua franca of dice that Burke uses earlier—"This is a one-time job, one roll of the dice"—to resolve the issue between the two men: "Like you say, it's just one roll of the dice. Doesn't matter what color they are, so's they come up seven." But human beings are not, needless to say, dice; what color they are—say, black—matters.

The film's dynamic contradictions are brilliantly realized in the driving sequence where Slater, testing the getaway car, opens it up en route to Melton:

EXT. HIGHWAY.
Car winding up and hurtling at CAMERA with a roar. The speedometer
    reads 112 mph.
INT. STATION WAGON.

Slater's face is almost exultant, enjoying the sense of power he gets from the
speed, the roar of the supercharged motor and the roar of the wind against
the car.[33]

To enhance this scene, in which Earle's momentarily inflated sense of masculinity
is fused with the car's supercharged performance, Lewis composed a "four-note
rhythmic ostinato" that becomes a pretext for Milt Jackson to "take an extended
vibes solo for almost sixty seconds."[34] The result is a "genuinely subversive moment in terms of crossing the racial divide," what David Butler calls "audiovisual
miscegenation": "Slater, a white racist, has his moment of emotional freedom
accompanied by an improvised jazz solo played on the instrument diegetically
associated with his colleague, Johnny, the black jazz musician."[35]

Once Johnny arrives in downtown Melton, tempers flare again when there's
a car accident and a policeman stops and questions him. Back at the riverfront,
where the men have agreed to rendezvous, Burke remains unruffled. Earle, however, is apoplectic: "You're just another black spot on Main Street." Burke turns
to Johnny:

BURKE: Listen to me, Johnny. That cop wouldn't recognize you in a hundred
years. We have to take some chances. You're a gambling man. Gamble.
INGRAM: Depends on the odds.
SLATER: The odds will never be right. I know how to handle him. I've been
handling them all my life. He's no different because he's got twenty-dollar
shoes.
INGRAM: All right, Slater, handle me!

When a train appears out of the blue, it momentarily silences the two men, after
which Burke's reply to Johnny's question—Johnny: "You're sure you wanna go
through with this?" / Burke: "It's gonna let us live again"—decides the matter.
Earle's still perturbed, though Johnny gets the last word: "You're just another
white spot to me."

The ensuing, meditative sequence, set on the waterfront as the men kill time
until it's "zero hour," is an exceptional one in the history of both crime and heist
films.[36] Johnny sits at the river's edge and watches the eddying current. Earle,
who's dressed like Burke in hunting clothes, drives to a field where he shoots at
and misses a rabbit, while on Parade Hill, beneath a war monument ("WHATSO-
EVER THY HAND / FINDETH TO DO, / DO IT / WITH THY MIGHT"),
Burke—in a match shot aslant with shadow—tosses pebbles at a beer can. The
sequence is completely devoid of dialogue, and Lewis's timpani-and-vibraphone
score invests the waning day with an anxious, pensive feeling.

Cut to a close-up of the bank clock—it's 6:00 p.m. on the dot—as a bell
tolls six times. While the men get into position—Burke walks briskly toward

the drugstore; Earle pulls up to a railroad crossing in the station wagon; and Johnny, smoking a cigarette, leans against a wall—the deliveryman declares to the teenagers gathered around the counter as he pours coffee into paper cups, "I don't know which is worse, the atom bomb or you kids and your do-it-yourself cars."[37]

Inside the station wagon, Johnny's checking the contents of the carton one last time when he asks Earle for the keys to the getaway car. Earle gets out of the car as if he hasn't even heard him. Outside the drugstore, a woman appears with two ten-year-old boys who are playing with water pistols: "There, I got you right in the mouth! I got you in the eyes. Right in the nose!" The scene is a rich one and recollects not only Burke's concluding boast at the Hotel Melton—"You could take it with a water pistol"—but also the exhilarating sequence near the end of Jules Dassin's *Rififi* (1955) where Tony le Stéphanois (Jean Servais) is driving back to Paris to return Tonio (Dominique Maurin) to his mother, and the boy, dressed in a cowboy outfit, is shooting a toy pistol into the air.

Despite the portentous references, the heist goes as planned. Even though Burke and Johnny take too long to bag the money and Earle has to sap the deliveryman when he shows up at the bank, it's Earle's insistence on giving the keys to Burke instead of Johnny that dooms the gang. Burke is the first to die. A policeman in a patrol car notices him exiting the bank, and when an alarm goes off, Burke is as good as dead. In the ensuing exchange of fire, he's hit and ends up facedown on the sidewalk. Earle pleads with him: "The key . . . the key!" Burke, blood trickling from his mouth, is crawling toward Earle and Johnny when he's hit again. The close-up of his outstretched hand and, just beyond his reach, the keys shimmering in the light (the original title of the film was "Reach for Tomorrow") reflects the impossible distance between fantasy and reality.

Earle's first impulse is to clear out, but Johnny, the good soldier, violently disagrees: "We can't leave Burke here." Burke's last words are addressed, not surprisingly, to him—"Run, Johnny!"—after which Burke puts the gun to his head and pulls the trigger. Earle's epitaph—"He sure ain't goin' to talk now"—is, however, the last straw for Ingram, who grabs Slater by the throat and slams him up against the side of the building: "You bastard! . . . You killed him!" Earle takes off across the street, and after Johnny fires, winging him in the shoulder, Earle turns a corner and Johnny tears after him. Now it's Johnny who's the hunter and Earle the hunted.

The climax of *Odds against Tomorrow* is spectacular in every sense of the word. Set in a gas-tank complex, the concluding chase sequence, like the riverfront one, is devoid of dialogue and reduced to the essence of the medium: sound and image. The percussive underscore—cymbals, timpani, and snare drum rolls—combined with the camerawork—canted angles, high-contrast lighting, and constricted shots of enormous gas tanks and horizon-receding pipes—prefigures Earle's and Johnny's fate. In a key sequence, the camera angle is low, and Earle, caught behind a chain link fence in the blinding glare of a searchlight, starts up a vertiginously steep staircase, his shadow doubled on an adjacent tank, his footsteps reverberating off the steel steps. Cut to a high-angle shot of Johnny at the base of another tank, the camera zooming in to his face as he begins to climb. Cut again, this time to a high wide-angle shot of the gas tanks arranged in a semicircle as Earle crosses a ramp from the first to the second landing. Earle and Johnny—alone, at last, on the top of the tanks "like figures on the moon"[38]—face off against each other as if it's the finale of a classic Western, then fire away. There's a fireball and a "Niagara of gorgeous sparks cascade into the night."[39]

CODA

In the appendix to *In a Lonely Street*, Frank Krutnik categorizes the "social problem crime film" as one in a number of 1950s crime film cycles. (His first example is *Crossfire*, in which Robert Ryan, as in *Odds against Tomorrow*, plays a bigoted character—in *Crossfire*, a violently anti-Semitic one.) While *The Killing* is not a social-problem crime film, it's not without interest in this context. I'm referring to the scene where Nikki Arcane arrives at the Lansdowne racetrack to take down Black Lightning, and an African American attendant (James Edwards) with a lame leg tells him that he can't park in the lot. (Edwards appeared not only in *The Phenix City Story* but also as Peter Moss in *Home of the Brave* [1949].)

Nikki, thinking fast, as it were, on his feet, explains even as he's stuffing money into the attendant's pocket that he needs to park there because he lost the use of his legs in the Battle of the Bulge. The parking attendant is sympathetic and later brings Nikki a race program. However, when he subsequently reappears with a horseshoe for good luck just as the race is about to begin, Nikki can no longer restrain himself:

NIKKI: Oh, now look, keep your junk and leave me alone, will ya?
PARKING ATTENDANT: Somethin'. . . somethin' wrong?
NIKKI: You're wrong, nigger.

Any number of commentators have, I think, misread this scene, attributing a racist intent to Arcane's character. James Howard, though, persuasively argues that while it's a "minor incident," it "appears to be a recurring feature in several of Kubrick's movies": "a man forced to act in a way . . . in order to complete a predetermined course of duty."[40] The interest of this minor but prototypical moment in *The Killing* is the way it juxtaposes an offensive speech act ("nigger") with the force of necessity (the shooting of Black Lighting or, more generally, the commission of the heist). Simply put, in Kubrick's film, genre or form trumps content or social message.

Odds against Tomorrow, it's safe to say, is an entirely different sort of picture, since the social-problem aspect is inseparable from the heist or crime film format. As opposed to *The Killing*, in which Nikki's racial slur signifies a moment of excrescence in an otherwise rhetorically modulated film, the relation between crime thriller and social commentary in Wise's film can be said to turn the generic glove inside out so that the heist picture becomes a *vehicle* for social protest. (Transportation—in the largest sense of the word—is, as I note below, the dominant conceit of the film.) The coda to *Odds against Tomorrow* reflects this inversion. The film cuts from the gas tank explosion to a charred, smoking landscape where police and Red Cross workers survey two blanketed bodies laid out on stretchers.

An ambulance attendant lifts up one of the blankets, then the other one:

ATTENDANT: Which is which?
CHIEF: Take your pick.

As the attendants carry out the two bodies, they pass a sign on a chain link fence— "STOP DEAD END"—a didactic ending that differs substantially from the cool, philosophical dénouement of Kubrick's *Killing* and that constitutes, as well, a radical revision of the optimistic conclusion to McGivern's novel.

In the novel, as in the film, Burke is killed, although both Earle and Johnny escape by car to a farmhouse. Although Slater has been seriously wounded in the shootout, he convinces Johnny to catch a bus to Philadelphia to contact Lorry, who agrees to return with him to the farmhouse. (When Johnny enters the drugstore where Lorry's working, he thinks to himself, "Rob a bank, okay. But don't go ordering a cup of coffee."[41]) Because he also goes for a doctor to treat Earle,

"Take Your Pick": blanketed remains of Johnny Ingram (Harry Belafonte) and Earle Slater (Robert Ryan) in *Odds against Tomorrow* (1959).

in the end Johnny, not Earle, holds the keys to the kingdom. "'Give it here,' Earle said, 'Give it here, Sambo.'"[42] Later, despite the fact that Earle and Lorry plan to make their escape without him, Johnny hands the keys to Slater.

Not unlike a remarkably similar scenario in *The Defiant Ones* (1958), Earle, delirious from the gunshot wound and remembering a fellow soldier he dragged to safety from a Nazi-occupied farmhouse in Germany, abandons Lorry at a gas station in order to return for Johnny.[43] In the final scene, Earle's gunned down by the police outside the farmhouse, and as he lies dying—"I shouldn't have left. ... We're in the same outfit"—Johnny squeezes his hand. This moment of rap-prochement rhymes with the concluding sequence of *The Defiant Ones*, in which Noah Cullen (Sidney Poitier) and John "Joker" Jackson (Tony Curtis) are racing to catch a train while being pursued by a Doberman-led posse. Cullen manages to climb aboard, but Joker, who's weak from a gunshot wound, is falling behind when Cullen puts out his hand. Cullen can't pull him aboard, yet rather than let Joker go (and this is the happy ending), he leaps off the train to be with his fellow convict.

When *The Defiant Ones* was released in 1958, this happy ending must have seemed particularly topical and forward-looking. In retrospect, *Odds against To-morrow* is the more dialectical and symptomatic picture. Part of the reason is generic. Unlike *The Defiant Ones*, in which the positive social message is com-promised by its ultimately regressive take on the prison picture, the apocalyptic, seemingly nihilistic conclusion to *Odds against Tomorrow* represents a negative critique of both the heist and social-problem picture. In other words, Wise's film can be said to be a "civil rights noir,"[44] an oxymoron that foregrounds the limits of the classic social-problem film at the same time that it italicizes the utopian promise of the heist picture.

The key to the latter, futuristic impulse is the film's literal and figurative ac-cent on transportation. I've already referenced Johnny's white Austin Healy, but the allusions to Sputnik and Cape Canaveral are equally, if not more, pointed. The Civil Rights Act was passed in 1957; 1957 was also the year that the Soviet Union launched Sputnik. In his acceptance speech at the 1960 Democratic Na-tional Convention, John F. Kennedy, responding to the impact that this satellite, which could be seen with the naked eye, had on the psyche of the United States, famously evoked a New Frontier of "uncharted areas of science and space" as well as "unconquered problems of ignorance and prejudice."[45] The connection in Kennedy's speech between civil rights and space exploration is manifest. Just as Kennedy's position on civil rights prepared the ground for the 1964 Civil Rights Act, the Cape Canaveral launch of *Friendship 7* in 1962 put the first American in orbit and represented a dramatic leap forward in realizing Kennedy's dream of landing a man on the moon and returning him safely to earth.

Compared, then, to *The Asphalt Jungle*, which in the person of Dix Handley can be said to look backward to the nation's agrarian past, *Odds against Tomorrow* looks to the future. If the fiery, sci-fi-inflected conclusion of *White Heat* and the explosive, apocalyptic ending of *Kiss Me Deadly* mark the death of the classic gangster picture and film noir, respectively, *Odds against Tomorrow* evokes the lunar landscape of the moon and, by implication, science, space travel, and civil rights in the oppressive face of "ignorance and prejudice."

CODA

POST-'50S SYNDICATE, ROGUE COP, AND "BIG CAPER" FILMS

Show me a man without a dream
And I'll show you a man that's dead

—"Eee-O-Eleven," Sammy Cahn/Jimmy Van
Heusen (1960)

NEO–GANGSTER NOIR SYNDICATE PICTURE: *UNDERWORLD, U.S.A.*

In his book *Underworld U.S.A.* Colin McArthur remarks that "in relation to the syndicate cycle of gangster films," Samuel Fuller's *Underworld, U.S.A.* (1961) exhibits a "classical purity."[1] Fuller's picture is about recently released convict Tolly Devlin (Cliff Robertson), who, as a child, witnessed four men—Vic Farrar (Peter Brocco), Gela (Paul Dubov), Gunther (Gerald Milton), and Smith (Allan Gruener)—beating his father to death in an alley. After a dying Farrar gives up the names of the other three men, who have since risen to the top of their respective rackets—narcotics, labor, and prostitution—Devlin vows to exact revenge.

Fuller's *Underworld, U.S.A.* owes something to his earlier film noirs and gangster pictures. For example, the beating of Devlin's father, obliquely conveyed via dynamic silhouettes, revels in the expressionist effects of classic noir. At the same time, *Underworld, U.S.A.* echoes earlier '50s "big combo" pictures such as *The Phenix City Story* and *The Brothers Rico*. For instance, the shocking, constructively edited sequence in which Earl Connors's (Robert Emhardt) hit man, Gus, runs over the daughter of a potential witness while she's riding her bike appears to be a direct quote of the scene in *The Phenix City Story* where syndicate henchman Clem Wilson swerves his car in order to hit and kill a bicycling newspaper boy.[2] More generally, *Underworld, U.S.A.* appears to mime the final act of *The Phenix*

"The Facts . . . The Faces . . .": title card for *Underworld, U.S.A.* (1961) with a silhouette shot of the beating death of Tolly Devlin's (Cliff Robertson) father at the hands of the syndicate.

City Story, where Eddie Rico is determined to avenge the death of his two younger brothers at the hands of the syndicate.

In this sense, *Underworld, U.S.A.* reads like a late, not to say belated, instance of the syndicate picture. Yet despite, or perhaps because of, its titular allusion to Josef von Sternberg's *Underworld* (1927),[3] Fuller sought to differentiate his film from the flood of "retro," Prohibition- and Depression-era gangster movies made in the aftermath of Don Siegel's *Baby Face Nelson*, which appeared the same year as *The Brothers Rico*. In promotional interviews, Fuller revealed that *Underworld, U.S.A.* would be "set in the contemporary world of organized crime" rather than in the 1920s and the 1930s, the period of the first cycle of gangster pictures, and would "work against the cliché—gangster idiom or noir."[4] Fuller: "These mob guys are businessmen, part of society, members of the Rotary Club . . . [who] sit around the pool on sunny afternoons and cold bloodedly plan who they're going to bribe."[5] Connors, the syndicate "chief of staff" in *Underworld, U.S.A.*, embodies this crooked "Rotary Club" ethos, telling his "department" heads that they'll prosper as long as they "run National Projects with legitimate business operations and pay [their] taxes on legitimate income and donate to charities and church bazaars."

In the ten years between *The Enforcer* and *Underworld, U.S.A.*, the "acquisition of a businesslike façade was," as Carlos Clarens concludes in "The Syndicate," "the most disturbing aspect of the syndicate."[6] *Underworld, U.S.A.* signifies a "cut-off point in the genre"—just beyond is *Point Blank*, which "pulverizes the classical style."[7] Unlike the "private eye" cycle epitomized by Jack Smight's *Harper* (1966), the protagonist of which derives from Hammett and Chandler, John Boorman's *Point Blank* represents a brash synthesis of gangster noir tropes (flashback and voice-over narration) and European art-house film (jump cuts and color-coded sets) as if, to paraphrase David Thompson, Boorman's picture were a Michelangelo Antonioni film remade by Sam Fuller.[8] If the Antonioni film is *L'Eclisse* (1962) or *Blow Up* (1966), the Fuller film is *Underworld, U.S.A.*, since Walker's (Lee Marvin) sole raison d'être in *Point Blank* is to get back at his former partners in crime, his wife, Lynne (Sharon Acker), and Mal Reese (John Vernon), and recover his share of the ninety-three thousand dollars that he's owed.

Though syndicate executive Fairfax (Keenan Wynn), like Carl Stephans in *711 Ocean Drive*, walks away at the end of *Point Blank*, the circularity of Walker's revenge quest departs from the rise-and-fall narrative that characterizes the classic gangster picture. Moreover, unlike *711 Ocean Drive*, *The Captive City*, and *The Big Combo*, neither law enforcement nor the federal government in the form of a congressional committee intrudes upon the hermetic world of Boorman's film. In *Underworld, U.S.A.* Tolly Devlin may die, but he manages to take down the syndicate with him; in *Point Blank* Walker may not even be alive and appears to have been a mere pawn in Fairfax's scheme to streamline the Organization.

THE POST-'50S ROGUE COP FILM: *CAPE FEAR*

The first postclassic successor to the rogue cop film, *Cape Fear* (1962) is a crime movie in which the protagonist is not an officer of the law but a lawyer. In J. Lee Thompson's Hitchcockian thriller, attorney Sam Bowden (Gregory Peck) is busy going about his happy, well-ordered life complete with home and family when the past returns with a vengeance in the form of ex-convict Max Cady (Robert Mitchum). Cady blames Bowden for testifying against him in court on sexual abuse and battery charges and, as he informs the counselor after accosting him in his car, he's now out having just served "eight years, four months, and thirteen days" in prison. Cady's campaign of terror, one that will involve threats, stalking, harassment, and trespassing, is about to commence.

First, Cady shows up at a bowling alley where, sporting a Panama hat and a big stogie, he checks out Bowden's wife, Peggy (Polly Bergen), and their daughter, Nancy (Lori Martin). Bowden wastes no time contacting Chief of Police Dutton (Martin Balsam), who orders Cady to be picked up on vagrancy and public drunkenness. However, Cady, who has studied law in prison, gives the name of a doctor to test whether he's drunk and produces a bank statement to prove that he's not a vagrant. Next, after the Bowden's dog is mysteriously poisoned, Cady hires a lawyer who claims that his client is constantly being persecuted by the police and cites Cady's detention in jail, his interrogation on suspicion of armed robbery, his forced appearance in a lineup on suspicion of purse snatching, and his arrest on suspicion of murder and grand theft auto.

The chief of police, legally stymied, advises Bowden to hire a private detective, Charles Sievers (Telly Savalas), who, after watching Cady hook up with a "drifter," Diane Taylor (Barrie Chase), calls the police to bring Cady in on charges of "lewd vagrancy." Despite the fact that Cady has subjected Taylor to a severe beating, she refuses to testify against him, and he shows up at a marina where he openly leers at Nancy, taunting Bowden: "She's getting to be almost as juicy as your wife, ain't she?" An incensed Bowden takes a couple of swings at his nemesis, but Cady refuses to fight back, telling the bystanders who have suddenly materialized around them, "Guess you saw that, didn't you? Never laid a hand on him."

Later, Nancy's waiting for her mother after school when Cady appears, and she runs terrified into the street, where she's hit by a car. While Bowden momentarily considers shooting Cady, Peggy convinces her husband to pay him off. Cady, however, refuses the offer, and after Bowden takes Sievers's advice and pays some hired hands to rough him up, a bloodied but unbroken Cady calls Bowden at home and tells him that he doesn't "know what the bar association thinks of its members compounding a felony," but "you just put the law in my hands and I'm gonna break your heart with it."

With the express assent of the chief of police and the assistance of a deputy, Bowden decides to lure Cady to a houseboat on the Cape Fear River where Peggy and Nancy will be the bait. Cady strangles the deputy and terrorizes Peggy, but Bowden finally intervenes and, first in the water, then on land, battles and finally wounds him. Like Bannion in *The Big Heat*, Bowden does not succumb to his desire for bloodlust—he does not kill Cady. "No, no, that would be letting you off too easy, too fast," Bowden tells him, repeating Cady's own earlier threat: "We're gonna take good care of you. We're gonna nurse you back to health. You're gonna live a long time—in a cage." If in the end Bowden is able to use the law to sentence Cady to a fate that, at least for Cady, is worse than death, the fact that his closing speech occurs not in a courtroom but in the mangrove swamp suggests they've both been reduced to their antediluvian selves and that the representative of the law, Bowden, is a double of the outlaw—in other words, that the law itself is not without a perverse, sadistic aspect.

This sadism is explicit in *Dirty Harry* (1972), the trailer for which boasts, "This is a movie about a couple of killers. Harry Callahan and a homicidal maniac. The one with the badge is Harry." Callahan's vigilante defense of law and order in Don Siegel's film is reminiscent of Jim Wilson's sadomasochistic brutalization of criminals in *On Dangerous Ground*—see the scene where Scorpio (Andy Robinson) says about Harry's .44 Magnum, "My, that's a big one"—with the proviso that Callahan's vigilantism is inflected with a certain sardonicism. Since Harry has lost his wife (she died when a drunk driver "crossed the center line"), he's also reminiscent of Dave Bannion in *The Big Heat*. But whereas Bannion's animus is directed at the syndicate, Harry's is squarely aimed at the late '60s, post-Manson counterculture, of which Scorpio, costumed in bell bottoms and a peace sign belt buckle, is a paranoid, fantasmatic projection.

POSTCLASSIC HEIST MOVIE: *OCEAN'S 11*

In *The Heist Film* Daryl Lee isolates three subgenres of the heist picture in the postclassic era: "cosmopolitan" capers such as *Seven Thieves* (1960) and *Topkapi* (1964), "Las Vegas" heist movies such as *Ocean's 11* (1960) and *They Came to Rob Las Vegas* (1968), and heist films from the civil rights era such as *The Split* (1968), *Cool Breeze* (1972), and *Across 110th Street* (1972).[9]

Ocean's 11, shot in widescreen like *Seven Thieves* and in color like '50s heist pictures such as *Violent Saturday* (1955) and *I Died a Thousand Times* (1955), can be seen as a hybrid of the above three subgenres, crossing as it does the faux-cosmopolitan caper film—a key location is the Riviera resort in Las Vegas—with the post-'50s black heist film and, not so incidentally, the "combat mission" picture. (The director is Lewis Milestone, who in 1930 made *All Quiet on the Western Front*.) The heist gang in Milestone's movie is composed of ex-servicemen—in this case, paratroopers from the 82nd Airborne Division—who scheme to rob five Las Vegas casinos, the Sands, the Sahara, the Flamingo, the Desert Inn, and the Riviera. At the house of Spyros Acebos (Akim Tamiroff), the "brains" of the caper, former sergeant Danny Ocean (Frank Sinatra), places a handkerchief imprinted with the names of the five casinos on a pool table. Jimmy Foster (Peter Lawford) announces—"Mission: to liberate millions"—then explains to the assembled "Army cronies," "H hour is New Year's Eve. Units involved: special combat teams made up of former members of the 82nd Airborne."

The "confederates" in *Ocean's 11*, with the exception of Tony Bergdorf (Richard Conte), are not ex-cons or pros—what Sam Harmon (Dean Martin) calls "regular heisters"—but amateurs. Though Bergdorf was previously nabbed for helping a jewelry store owner rob his own store and has just been released from San Quentin, Danny tells him, "You're no hoodlum. You got no connection to the underworld." In fact, Bergdorf agrees to join the crew only because he's been diagnosed with a terminal illness and wants to leave enough money to send his son to college. It's therefore no surprise that he's the only casualty of the caper when he drops dead of a heart attack in the middle of a street after having blacked out the "whole town" by rigging the casinos' switchboxes.

The interest of *Ocean's 11* vis-à-vis the classic heist film is a function of its comic or, more precisely, seriocomic tone, its celebrity-studded cast—the picture is in part a cinematic version of the "Summit" shows the Rat Pack was performing in the Copa Room at the Sands at the same time that they were shooting the movie—and its provocative representation of race. While *Odds against Tomorrow* may well be, with respect to the issue of civil rights, didactic, *Ocean's 11* is, at best, satirical.

Consider, for example, the scene right before the gang reviews the heist in which Danny, Sam, Jimmy Foster, and Josh Howard (Sammy Davis Jr.) are bantering about politics. In an overt allusion to Lawford's offscreen relationship with the Kennedy family (Peter had married Pat Kennedy, and Jack, Pat's brother, was already campaigning for president), Jimmy muses about "turning money into power" and buying a government appointment. Sam counters with his platform:

> SAM: Repeal the Fourteenth and the Twentieth Amendment. Take the vote
>   away from the women and make slaves out of them.
> JOSH: Hey, now, that's something that's real constructive.
> DANNY: Hey, will it cost much?
> SAM: Oh, no, we've got price controls. No inflation on slaves.

Sam, Josh, and Danny then discuss what country Jimmy should be an ambassador to, and after Danny suggests "Andorra" and Sam "Pomona," Josh, a big grin on his face, chimes in "Little Rock." Josh's reference to Little Rock, Arkansas—in 1957 Governor Orval Faubus had called up the National Guard to prevent nine African American students from enrolling at Central High School—caps the exchange on a satirically progressive note. However, Josh's occupation as a garbage collector effectively negates whatever force the satire may be said to possess.

The ring-a-ding-ding racial pranking of *Ocean 11* is reprised near the end of the film when Sam, Josh, Danny, and Jimmy are driving in Josh's garbage truck to the mortuary to hide the stolen money in Bergdorf's casket. As Sam and Danny are rubbing black shoe polish on their faces, Josh laughingly remarks, "I knew this color would come in handy one day." When Jimmy queries, "Hey, Josh, how do you get the stuff off?" Josh starts to respond "I usually . . ." when he realizes the joke's on him (not unlike the rib-and-watermelon joshing that Sammy pretended to get a kick out of during the 1960 Summit shows[10]). Consequently, if the scene points to Sam, Danny, and Jimmy's white privilege, it also stages, given Sam's earlier, anti-abolitionist sentiment, a minstrel-like denigration of performers like

Song and Dance Man: German lobby card of Josh Howard (Sammy Davis Jr.) dancing as he sings "Eee-O-Eleven" in *Ocean's Eleven* (1960).

Sammy Davis Jr., who, as Josh, we've previously seen singing "Eee-O-Eleven" on a raised platform that looks like a shoe box.

In this musical-historical context, it's telling that the "Moulin Rouge Agreement," in which the hotels and casinos in Vegas were finally integrated, was not signed until March 1960—after the principal photography on the Vegas part of *Ocean's 11* had been completed.[11] The reprise of "Eee-O-Eleven" under the closing credits not only duplicates Josh's earlier, "shoe box" rendition but also glosses both Davis and his character's double bind: at once a presiding member of the fabled Rat Pack and the butt of racist jokes, an integral member of Danny Ocean's ring of thieves and a lowly garbageman. From the servile perspectives, Martin Luther King Jr.'s "I Have a Dream" speech could only have seemed impossibly aspirational:

> Once I had a dream
> But that dream got kicked in the head
> Dream dead.

Notes

PREFACE

1. On the demise of the classic gangster picture, see, for example, Colin McArthur, *Underworld U.S.A.* (London: Secker & Warburg, 1972), 51–52; Eugene Rosow, *Born to Lose: The Gangster Film in America* (New York: Oxford University Press, 1978), 212–27; Carlos Clarens, *Crime Movies* (New York: Norton, 1980), 152–70, 172–90; Jonathan Munby, *Public Enemies, Public Heroes: Screening the Gangster from* Little Caesar *to* Touch of Evil (Chicago: University of Chicago Press, 1999), 110–14; and Ronald Wilson, *The Gangster Film* (London: Wallflower, 2015), 51–58.

2. Fran Mason, *American Gangster Cinema* (London: Palgrave Macmillan, 2002), 78.

3. Ibid.

4. For a synopsis of the differing critical takes on the heist film as a genre or subgenre, see Daryl Lee, *The Heist Film* (London: Wallflower, 2014), 11.

5. On "atomic noir," see Robert Miklitsch, *The Red and the Black: American Film Noir in the 1950s* (Urbana: University of Illinois Press, 2014), 19–91.

6. For the recent wave of work on HUAC and the blacklist, anti-Communism, and the Cold War, see, for example, J. Hoberman, *An Army of Phantoms: Movies and the Making of the Cold War* (New York: New Press, 2011); John Sbardellati, *J. Edgar Hoover Goes to the Movies: The FBI and the Origins of Hollywood's Cold War* (Ithaca, NY: Cornell University Press, 2012); Rebecca Prime, *Hollywood Exiles in Europe: The Blacklist and Cold War Film Culture* (New Brunswick, NJ: Rutgers University Press, 2014); Jeff Smith, *Film Criticism, the Cold War, and the Blacklist: Reading the Hollywood Reds* (Berkeley: University of California Press, 2014); Bernard F. Dick, *The Screen Is Red: Hollywood, Communism, and the Cold War* (Jackson: University of Mississippi Press, 2016); and Thomas Doherty, *Show Trial: Hollywood, HUAC, and the Birth of the Blacklist* (New York: Columbia University Press, 2018).

7. On the '50s "red menace" film, see Miklitsch, *Red and the Black*, 95–159.

8. Ronald Wilson, "Gang Busters: The Kefauver Crime Committee and the Syndicate Films of the 1950s," in *Mob Culture: Hidden Histories of the American Gangster Film*, ed. Lee Grieveson, Esther Sonnet, and Peter Stanfield (Oxford, UK: Berg, 2005), 68.

9. See Peter Stanfield, "Punks!: Topicality and the 1950s Gangster Bio-Pic," in *Media, Popular Culture, and the American Century*, ed. Kingsley Bolton and Jan Olsson (Bloomington: Indiana University Press, 2010), 185–215.

10. Jack Shadoian, *Dreams and Dead Ends: The American Gangster Film* (New York: Oxford University Press, 2003), 177.

11. On this trope, see Lee Bernstein, *The Greatest Menace: Organized Crime in Cold War America* (Amherst: University of Massachusetts Press, 2002), 67. The *Time* cover image referred to is from the March 12, 1951, issue.

12. Mason, *American Gangster Cinema*, 78.

13. Shadoian, *Dreams and Dead Ends*, 122; italics mine. Polonsky and producer Bob Roberts wanted to title the film "The Numbers Racket," but the Production Code Administration objected to the word "racket." See Munby, *Public Enemies*, 127.

14. Munby, *Public Enemies*, 142.

15. Ibid.

16. Joseph Losey, *Conversations with Losey*, ed. Michel Ciment (London: Methuen, 1985), 100.

17. Kim Newman, "The Caper Film," *The BFI Companion to the Crime Film*, ed. Phil Hardy (Berkeley: University of California Press, 1997), 70.

18. Stuart Kaminsky, *American Film Genres: Approaches to a Critical Theory of Popular Film* (Dayton, OH: Pflaum, 1974), 199.

19. Munby, *Public Enemies*, 138; Lee, *Heist Film*, 33.

20. James Naremore, *More Than Night: Film Noir in Its Contexts* (Berkeley: University of California Press, 1998), 128.

21. Mason, *American Gangster Cinema*, 78.

22. See J. P. Telotte, "Fatal Capers: Enigma and Strategy in Film Noir," *Journal of Popular Film and Television* 23 (1996): 163–70.

23. Munby, *Public Enemies*, 210.

INTRODUCTION

1. Jack Anderson and Fred Blumenthal, *The Kefauver Story* (New York: Dial Press, 1956), 144.

2. Ibid., 145.

3. Ibid.

4. Ibid., 140.

5. Joseph Bruce Gorman, *Kefauver: A Political Biography* (New York: Oxford University Press, 1971), 77–78.

6. Charles L. Fontenay, *Estes Kefauver: A Biography* (Knoxville: University of Tennessee Press, 1980), 168.

7. Ibid., 180.

8. Gorman, *Kefauver*, 91.

9. Anderson and Blumenthal, *Kefauver Story*, 179.

10. William Howard Moore, *The Kefauver Committee and the Politics of Crime, 1950–1952* (Columbia: University of Missouri Press, 1974), 204.

11. Fontenay, *Estes Kefauver*, 182, 183.

12. Lee Bernstein, *The Greatest Menace* (Amherst: University of Massachusetts Press, 2002), 77.

13. Gorman, *Kefauver*, 89.

14. Estes Kefauver, *Crime in America* (New York: Greenwood, 1968), 13.

15. Ibid.

16. Moore, *Kefauver Committee*, 33.

17. McArthur, *Underworld U.S.A.*, 198.

18. Burton B. Turkus and Sid Feder, *Murder, Inc.: The Story of the "Syndicate"* (New York: Farrar, Straus, and Young, 1951), 3.

19. Ibid., 424.

20. Ibid., 425.

21. Clarens, *Crime Movies*, 234–36.

22. See Martin Short, *Crime, Inc.: The Story of Organized Crime* (London: Methuen, 1984), 235.

23. Clarens, *Crime Movies*, 236.

24. See Mike Davis, *City of Quartz* (London: Verso, 1990), 17–97.

25. Ibid., 41.

26. Geoff Mayer, *Encyclopedia of Film Noir*, ed. Brian McDonnell and Geoff Mayer (Westport, CT: Greenwood, 2007), 124.

27. On *The Glass Web*, see Miklitsch, *Red and the Black*, 212–28.

28. Mayer, *Encyclopedia of Film Noir*, 124.

29. Shadoian, *Dreams and Dead Ends*, 216.

30. Ibid.

31. Robert Porfirio, "*The Captive City*," in *Film Noir: The Encyclopedia*, ed. Alain Silver et al. (New York: Overlook Duckworth, 2010), 65.

32. Robert Wise, in Sergio Leemann, *Robert Wise on His Films: From Editing Room to Director's Chair* (Los Angeles: Silman-James Press, 1995), 109; Richard C. Keenan, *The Films of Robert Wise* (Lanham, MD: Scarecrow Press, 2007), 77.

33. Moore, *Kefauver Committee*, 50.

34. Will Straw, "Urban Confidential: The Lurid City of the 1950s," in *The Cinematic City*, ed. David B. Clarke (London: Routledge, 1997), 116.

35. For the "true crime" story, see Robert C. Donnelly, *Dark Rose: Organized Crime and Corruption in Portland* (Seattle: University of Washington Press, 2011).

36. Shadoian, *Dreams and Dead Ends*, 203.

37. R. Barton Palmer, "Cold War Thrillers," in *The Wiley-Blackwell History of American Cinema*, ed. Cynthia Lucia, Roy Grundmann, and Art Simon (Malden, MA: Wiley-Blackwell, 2012), 255.

38. Straw, "Urban Confidential," 120.

39. Ibid.

40. Wheeler Winston Dixon, "*The Racket* (1951)," *Film Noir of the Week* (May 22, 2015). http://blog.unl.edu/dixon/2015/05/22/robert-ryan-and-robert-mitchum-in-the-racket-1951.

41. Dennis L. White, "*The Racket*," in *Film Noir: An Encyclopedic Reference to the American Style*, ed. Alain Silver and Elizabeth Ward (Woodstock, NY: Overlook, 1992), 237.

42. Mason, *American Gangster Cinema*, 111.

43. Ibid., 112.

44. On this aspect of the "rogue cop" film, see Frank Krutnik, *In a Lonely Street: Film Noir, Genre, Masculinity* (London: Routledge, 1991), 193.

45. Pierre Kast, "An Essay on Optimism," trans. R. Barton Palmer, in *Perspectives on Film Noir*, ed. R. Barton Palmer (New York: G. K. Hall, 1996), 48.

46. Raymond Borde and Étienne Chaumeton, *A Panorama of American Film Noir, 1941–1953*, trans. Paul Hammond (1955; San Francisco: City Lights, 2002), 83.

47. Ibid., 158.

48. Dennis Broe, *Film Noir, American Workers, and Postwar Hollywood* (Gainesville: University Press of Florida, 2009), 93, 89; italics mine.

49. Borde and Chaumeton, *Panorama of American Film Noir*, 9.

50. On the contemporary reception of *The Naked City* and the impact of Albert Maltz's and Jules Dassin's politics on the final cut of the film, see Miklitsch, "Introduction: Back to Black," in *Kiss the Blood Off My Hands: On Classic Noir* (Urbana: University of Illinois Press, 2014), 5–7.

51. Will Straw, "Documentary Realism and the Postwar Left," in *"Un-American" Hollywood: Politics and Film in the Blacklist Era*, ed. Peter Stanfield et al. (New Brunswick, NJ: Rutgers University Press, 2007), 141.

52. Borde and Chaumeton, *Panorama of American Film Noir*, 7.

53. Broe, *Film Noir*, 89.

54. Krutnik, *In a Lonely Street*, 205.

55. Broe, *Film Noir*, 60.

56. Ibid., 57.

57. Ibid., 96.

58. John Buntin, *L.A. Noir* (New York: Harmony, 2009), 183.

59. Ibid., 185.

60. Ibid., 188.

61. Joe Domanick, *To Protect and to Serve: The LAPD's Century of War in the City of Dreams* (New York: Pocket, 1994), 124.

62. Buntin, *L.A. Noir*, 185.

63. Ibid., 189.

64. Geoff Andrew, *The Films of Nicholas Ray: The Poet of Nightfall* (London: BFI, 2004), 55.

65. Imogen Sara Smith, *In Lonely Places: Film Noir beyond the City* (Jefferson, NC: McFarland, 2011), 39.

66. Ibid., 37.

67. A. I. Bezzerides, "The Thieves' Market: A. I. Bezzerides in Hollywood," in *The Big Book of Noir*, ed. Ed Gorman, Lee Server, Martin H. Greenberg (New York: Carroll & Graf, 1998), 120.

68. Ibid.

69. Orson Welles, "Interview with Orson Welles," in *Touch of Evil: Orson Welles, Director*, ed. Terry Comito (New Brunswick, NJ: Rutgers University Press, 1991), 204.

70. On Masterson's novel and *Touch of Evil*, see John Stubbs, "The Evolution of Orson Welles' *Touch of Evil* from Novel to Film," in Comito, *Touch of Evil*, 175–93.

71. Ibid.

72. Jerry Clark and Ed Palattella, *A History of Heists: Bank Robbery in America* (London: Rowman & Littlefield, 2015), 75.

73. Ibid.

74. Ibid., 208.

75. Daniel J. Wakin, "The Heist, the Getaway, and the Sawed-Off Leg," *New York Times*, August 26, 2007, http://www.nytimes.com/2007/08/26/nyregion/thecity/26heis.html.

76. Leonard J. Leff and Jerold L. Simmons, *The Dame in the Kimono: Hollywood, Censorship, and the Production Code from the 1920s to the 1960s* (New York: Anchor Books, 1990), 167.

77. John McCarty, *Hollywood Gangland: The Movies' Love Affair with the Mob* (New York: St. Martin's, 1993), 154.

78. Ibid., 155.

79. The Paramount Consent Decree of 1948, in addition to outlawing various distribution practices such as block booking, mandated a separation between film distribution and exhibition.

80. PCA staff member Albert Schmus commented that with the sudden erosion of the mass audience for movies as a result of the rise of television, "the creative people weren't going to be stopped. They had had to go into areas that would offer something that was *not* on television" (quoted in Leff and Simmons, *Dame in the Kimono*, 144).

81. Munby, *Public Enemies*, 122.

82. Ibid., 125.

83. Quoted in Naremore, *More Than Night*, 129.

84. Kaminsky, *American Film Genres*, 87.

85. Lee, *Heist Film*, 87.

86. Louis B. Mayer, quoted in Lawrence Grobel, *The Hustons* (New York: Avon, 1989), 336.

87. Naremore, *More Than Night*, 130.

88. Shadoian, *Dreams and Dead Ends*, 65.

89. W. R. Burnett, *High Sierra* (New York: Knopf, 1940), 200.

90. Lee, *Heist Film*, 23.

91. Shadoian, *Dreams and Dead Ends*, 341; Clarens, *Crime Movies*, 200.

92. Shadoian, *Dreams and Dead Ends*, 341n2.

93. Ibid.

94. Lee, *Heist Film*, 22.

95. See Shadoian, who argues with respect to *High Sierra*, "Here it is no rise and all fall, but by falling the hero rises." *Dreams and Dead Ends*, 79.

CHAPTER 1. THE COMBINATION

1. Moore, *Kefauver Committee*, 112.

2. Fontenay, *Estes Kefauver*, 173.

3. Moore, *Kefauver Committee*, 108.

4. Fontenay, *Estes Kefauver*, 172.

5. Kefauver, *Crime in America*, 36, 52.

6. See the entry for *711 Ocean Drive* in the online catalog of the American Film Institute: http://www.afi.com/members/catalog/images/background_v4.jpg.

7. Brian McDonnell, "*711 Ocean Drive*," in McDonnell and Mayer, *Encyclopedia of Film Noir*, 372.

8. Robert Porfirio, "*711 Ocean Drive*," in Silver et al., *Film Noir: The Encyclopedia*, 262.

9. McDonnell, "*711 Ocean Drive*," 373.

10. Porfirio, "*The Captive City*," 65.

11. Keenan, *Films of Robert Wise*, 76.

12. Porfirio, "*The Captive City*," 65.

13. Ibid.

14. Clarens, *Crime Movies*, 237.

15. See J. Hoberman, *An Army of Phantoms: American Movies and the Making of the Cold War* (New York: Free Press, 2012), 191; and Wes D. Gehring, *Robert Wise: Shadowlands* (Indianapolis: Indiana Historical Society, 2013), 151.

16. Justin E. A. Busch, *Self and Society in the Films of Robert Wise* (Jefferson, NC: McFarland, 2010), 23.

17. Keenan, *Films of Robert Wise*, 76.

18. Ibid., 78. See also my discussion of this shot in *Siren City: Sound and Source Music in Classic American Noir* (New Brunswick, NJ: Rutgers University Press, 2011), 130–31.

19. Nicholas Christopher, *Somewhere in the Night: Film Noir and the American City* (New York: Free Press, 1997), 162.

20. Busch, *Self and Society*, 23.

21. Christopher, *Somewhere in the Night*, 162.

22. Ibid., 161.

23. Mason, *American Gangster Cinema*, 105.

24. Ibid.

25. Ibid., 106.

26. Chris Hugo, "*The Big Combo*: Production Conditions in the Film Text," in *The Book of Film Noir*, ed. Ian Cameron (New York: Continuum, 1993), 249.

27. Ibid., 248.

28. Ibid.

29. Ibid.

30. Ibid.

31. Howard Hughes, *Crime Wave: The Filmgoer's Guide to the Great Movies* (London: I. B. Tauris, 2006), 56.

32. Ibid., 58.

33. Ibid.

34. Todd McCarthy, introduction to John Alton's *Painting with Light* (Berkeley: University of California Press, 1995), xxix.

35. David Butler, *Jazz Noir* (Westport, CT: Praeger, 2002), 99.

36. Tom Flinn, "*The Big Heat* and *The Big Combo*: Rogue Cops and Mink-Coated Girls," *Velvet Light Trap* 11 (Winter 1974): 27.

37. On the use of subjective sound and camera, see ibid.

38. Ibid., 26.

39. Butler, *Jazz Noir*, 100.

40. Ibid., 101.

41. Flinn, "*The Big Heat* and *The Big Combo*," 26; Robert Singer, "The 'How Big Is It'? Combo: Noir's Dirty Spectacles," in *The Films of Joseph H. Lewis*, ed. Gary Rhodes (Detroit: Wayne State University Press, 2011), 194.

42. Ibid., 192.

43. Joseph Lewis, in Peter Bogdanovich, *Who the Devil Made It: Conversations with Legendary Film Directors* (New York: Ballantine, 1998), 685.

44. Naremore, *More Than Night*, 156.

45. See Richard Dyer's "Queer Noir," where he argues that because *The Big Combo* is a B picture, it "can allow itself pretty well unequivocally queer characters in minor roles." Dyer, *Queer Cinema*, ed. Harry Benshoff and Sean Griffin (New York: Routledge, 2004), 97.

46. Flinn, "*The Big Heat* and *The Big Combo*," 27.

47. Singer, "'How Big Is It?' Combo," 188.

48. I'm thinking here of Lucie Arbuthnot and Gail Seneca's reading of *Gentlemen Prefer Blondes* (1953) in which the heterosexual romance narrative is a "pre-text" for "another, more central text." Arbuthnot and Seneca, "Pre-Text and Text in *Gentlemen Prefer Blondes*," in *Hollywood Musicals: The Film Reader*, ed. Steven Cohan (New York: Routledge, 2001), 77.

49. David Hogan, *Film Noir FAQ* (Milwaukee, WI: Applause, 2013), 149.

50. "In any erotic rivalry, the bond that links the two rivals is as intense and potent as the bond that links either of the rivals for the beloved." Eve Kosofsky Sedgwick, *Between Men: English Literature and Homosexual Desire* (New York: Columbia University Press, 1985), 21.

51. Eddie Muller, *Dark City* (New York: St. Martin's Griffin, 1998), 31.

52. As David Butler demonstrates via a comparison with Raksin's score for *Laura* (1944), "Raksin opposed the simple and obvious equation of jazz with a 'woman like Laura.' . . . By scoring Susan's theme as a jazz-inflected piece, Raksin draws on the film's crude coding of jazz as the seedy music of a stripper (Rita) and turns it on the film's privileged female character," Susan Lowell. Butler, *Jazz Noir*, 102.

53. Flinn, "*The Big Heat* and *The Big Combo*," 26.

54. Ibid., 27.

55. Mason, *American Gangster Cinema*, 78.

CHAPTER 2. *THE PHENIX CITY STORY*

1. Edwin Strickland and Gene Wortsman, *Phenix City: The Wickedest City in America* (Birmingham, AL: Vulcan Press, 1955), 11.

2. Jonathan Rosenbaum, "Reality and History as the Apotheosis of Southern Sleaze: Phil Karlson's *The Phenix City Story*," in *Essential Cinema: On the Necessity of Film Canons* (Baltimore: Johns Hopkins University Press, 2004), 138.

3. Ibid.

4. Ibid., 142.

5. Ibid.

6. Ibid.

7. On "gangster noir," see Mason, *American Gangster Cinema*, 77–97.

8. Ibid.

9. Phil Karlson, "Phil Karlson," interviewed by Todd McCarthy and Richard Thompson, *Kings of the Bs: Working within the Hollywood System*, ed. McCarthy and Charles Flynn (New York: Dutton, 1975), 330.

10. Ibid.

11. See Hugo, "*Big Combo*," 249.

12. Brent Wilson, "Crane Wilbur: Pondering the Potentate of Prison Pictures, from *The Perils of Pauline* to Police Procedurals," *Noir City* 51 (Spring 2011), www.filmnoirfoundation. org.

13. Daniel Mainwaring, "Daniel Mainwaring," interviewed by Robert Porfirio, in *Film Noir Reader 3: Interviews with Filmmakers of the Classic Noir Period*, ed. Robert Porfirio, Alain Silver, and James Ursini (New York: Limelight, 2002), 151.

14. Ibid.

15. Ibid.

16. Mark Bergman, "*The Phenix City Story*: 'This Will Happen to Your Kids, Too,'" in McCarthy and Flynn, *Kings of the Bs*, 197.

17. Karlson, "Phil Karlson," 335.

18. Clarens, *Crime Movies*, 245.

19. Karlson, "Phil Karlson," 234.

20. Bergman, "*Phenix City Story*," 202.

21. Ibid.

22. John Seydl, "Decadence, Apocalypse, Resurrection," in *The Last Days of Pompeii: Decadence, Apocalypse, Resurrection*, ed. Victoria C. Gardner Coates, Kenneth Lapatin, and John Seydl (Los Angeles: Getty Productions, 2012), 21.

23. Ibid.

24. Ibid., 22.

25. See Adrian Stahli, "Screening Pompeii: The Last Days of Pompeii in Cinema," in Coates et al., *Last Days of Pompeii*, 78–87.

26. Howard S. Berger and Kevin Marr, "*The Phenix City Story* (Karlson, 1955)," *Destructible Man*, February 18, 2011, http://www.destructibleman.com/2011/02/phenix-city-story-phil-karlson-1955.html.

27. "*The Phenix City Story*," American Film Institute: Catalog of Feature Films, http://www.afi.com/members/catalog/DetailView.aspx?s=&Movie=51617.

28. On the postwar history of reform in Phenix City, see Alan Gray, *When Good Men Do Nothing: The Assassination of Albert Patterson* (Tuscaloosa: University of Alabama Press, 2003), 15–19.

29. Rosenbaum, "Reality and History," 140.

30. Shadoian, *Dreams and Dead Ends*, 203.

31. Bergman, "*Phenix City Story*," 202.

32. On Orson Welles's *The Stranger*, see my "Split Screen: Sound/Music in *The Stranger/Criss Cross*," in *Film Noir*, ed. Homer B. Pettey and R. Barton Palmer (Edinburgh: Edinburgh University Press, 2014), 122–42.

33. Rosenbaum, "Reality and the Apotheosis of Southern Sleaze," 140.

34. On the burning of Albert Patterson's office, see ibid., 16.

35. On the bombing of Hugh Bentley's house in early 1952, see ibid., 16.

36. On vote fraud in Alabama politics and, in particular, Russell County, see Grady, *When Good Men Do Nothing*, 7, 17. For example: "In 1952, vote fraud in Phenix City was widespread and expected. Trading one's vote for a bottle of whiskey or a few dollars was neither unusual nor unacceptable. . . . At one polling place, an RBA member saw taxi after taxi unloading prostitutes, a rare sight before dark. As they got out, she overheard such questions as 'What name is mine?' and 'How do I vote?' At another polling place, seven goons beat poll watchers Hugh Britton, Hugh Bentley, and Bentley's 16-year-old son, Hughbo, along with Columbus newsreporters Tom Sellers and Ray Jenkins." Ibid., 18.

37. Berger and Marr, "*Phenix City Story*."

38. Shadoian, *Dreams and Dead Ends*, 203.

39. Gene Howard, *Patterson for Alabama* (Tuscaloosa: University of Alabama Press, 2008), 23.

40. Ibid.

41. "*Phenix City Story*," American Film Institute: Catalog.

42. Rosenbaum, "Reality and History," 143.

43. Ibid.

44. "*Phenix City Story*," American Film Institute: Catalog.

CHAPTER 3. *THE BROTHERS RICO*

1. Macek, "*The Brothers Rico*," in Silver and Ward, *Film Noir: An Encyclopedic Reference*, 44.

2. Ibid.

3. Andrew Spicer, *Film Noir* (Harlow, England: Longman/Pearson, 2002), 60.

4. Martin Scorsese, DVD commentary, *The Brothers Rico*, Columbia Pictures, Film Noir Classics II (2010).

5. Although there are a number of reasons why Simenon expatriated to the United States, one was the rumor that he had collaborated with the Germans during the occupation of France (e.g., his association with the jury of the Prix de la Nouvelle France; adaptations of his books were made by Continental, a German production company; etc.).

6. Georges Simenon, *The Brothers Rico*, trans. Ernst Pawel (London: Hamish Hamilton, 1954), 154.

7. Ibid., 162.

8. Ibid., 151.

9. See, in general, Kent Minturn, "Peinture Noir: Abstract Expressionism and Film Noir," in *Film Noir Reader 2*, ed. Alain Silver and James Ursini (New York: Limelight, 1999), 270–309.

10. Ibid., 155.

11. Shadoian, *Dreams and Dead Ends*, 211–12.

12. Simenon, *Brothers Rico*, 278.

13. Ibid., 282.

14. Ibid., 285.

15. Ibid.

16. Ibid., 180.

17. Shadoian, *Dreams and Dead Ends*, 209.

18. Ibid.

19. Simenon, *Brothers Rico*, 243.

20. Blake Lucas and Alain Silver, "*The Brothers Rico*," in Silver et al., *Film Noir: The Encyclopedia*, 140.

21. Jack Lait and Lee Mortimer, *New York Confidential* (New York: Crown, 1948), 221.

22. Ibid.

23. Straw, "Urban Confidential," 115.

24. J. R. R. Tolkien, cited by Greg Olson, in *David Lynch: Beautiful Dark* (Lanham, MD: Scarecrow, 2008), 134.

25. Tom Gunning, *The Films of Fritz Lang: Allegories of Vision and Modernity* (London: BFI, 2000), 409.

CHAPTER 4. *WHERE THE SIDEWALK ENDS*

1. Krutnik, *In a Lonely Street*, 193.

2. McDonnell, *Encyclopedia of Film Noir*, 226; Meredith Brody and Alain Silver, "*I Wake Up Screaming*," in Silver and Ward, *Film Noir: An Encyclopedic Reference*, 142.

3. On Dashiell Hammett's novels and the various film adaptations, see my "Dashiell Hammett and the Classical Hollywood Cinema," *Literature/Film Quarterly* 43, no. 3 (2015): 236–40.

4. For my reading of *The Bribe*, see *Siren City: Sound and Source Music in Classic American Noir* (New Brunswick, NJ: Rutgers University Press, 2014), 211, 214–16.

5. Chris Fujiwara, *The World and Its Double: The Life and Work of Otto Preminger* (New York: Faber and Faber, 2008), 120.

6. Ibid., 123; italics mine.

7. Sidney Kingsley, *Detective Story* (New York: Random House, 1949), 15, 17.

8. Ibid., 63.

9. Ibid., 110.

10. Ibid., 8.

11. Joan Cohen and Elizabeth Ward, "*Detective Story*," in Silver and Ward, *Film Noir: An Encyclopedic Reference*, 89.

12. Broe, *Film Noir*, 98.

13. McDonnell, *Encyclopedia of Film Noir*, 438.

14. Fujiwara, *World and Its Double*, 121.

15. Spicer, *Film Noir*, 86.

16. William Stuart, *Night Cry* (New York: Dial Press, 1948), 33.

17. Foster Hirsch, *Otto Preminger: The Man Who Would Be King* (New York: Knopf, 2007), 169.

18. Gaylyn Studlar, "'The Corpse on Reprieve': Film Noir's Cautionary Tales of 'Tough Guy' Masculinity," in *A Companion to Film Noir*, ed. Helen Hanson and Andrew Spicer (Waltham, MA: Wiley-Blackwell, 2013), 376–78.

19. Fujiwara, *World and Its Double*, 121.

20. McDonnell, *Encyclopedia of Film Noir*, 438.

21. Krutnik, *In a Lonely Street*, 133.

22. Carl Macek, "*Where the Sidewalk Ends*," in Silver and Ward, *Film Noir: An Encyclopedic Reference*, 310.

23. Fujiwara, *World and Its Double*, 123.

24. Ibid., 125.

25. McDonnell, *Encyclopedia of Film Noir*, 438.

26. Stuart, *Night Cry*, 14.

27. Ibid., 17.

28. Ibid., 33.

29. Ibid., 84.

30. Ibid., 72.

31. Ibid., 183.

32. Ibid.

33. Ibid., 198.

34. Ibid., 208.

35. Ibid., 198.

36. Ibid., 192.

37. McDonnell, *Encyclopedia of Film Noir*, 257.

38. Alastair Phillips, "*Where the Sidewalk Ends*, Otto Preminger, 1950," in Jim Hillier and Alastair Phillips, *100 Film Noirs* (London: BFI, 2009), 257.

39. James McKay, *Dana Andrews: The Face of Noir* (Jefferson, NC: McFarland, 2010), 112.

CHAPTER 5. THE THIN BLUE LINE

1. Broe, *Film Noir*, 81.

2. Andrew Hurley, *Diners, Bowling Alleys and Trailer Parks: Chasing the American Dream in the Postwar Consumer Culture* (New York: Basic, 2001), 2.

3. Kenneth T. Jackson, *Crabgrass Frontier: The Suburbanization of the United States* (New York: Oxford University Press, 1985), 233. See also Lizabeth Cohen, *A Consumer's Republic: The Politics of Consumption in the Postwar Era* (New York: Vintage, 2003).

4. Ibid., 238.

5. Sumiko Higashi, *Stars, Fans, and Consumption in the 1950s* (Basingstoke, Hampshire, UK: Palgrave Macmillan, 2014), 8.

6. Thomas A. Bonsall, *Cadillac: The Postwar Years* (Stanford, CA: Stanford University Press, 2004), 1.

7. Robert G. Ackerson, *Cadillac: America's Luxury Car* (Blue Ridge Summit, PA: Tab Books, 1988), 24.

8. Ibid.

9. On the commodity-body-sign, see my *From Hegel to Madonna: Towards a General Economy of "Commodity Fetishism"* (Albany: SUNY Press, 1998), 61–95.

10. Joseph Losey, in *Losey on Losey*, ed. Tom Milne (Garden City, NJ: Doubleday, 1968), 106, 82.

11. Joseph Losey, in Michel Ciment, *Conversations with Losey* (London: Methuen, 1985), 104–5.

12. Losey, in *Losey on Losey*, 108.

13. Ibid.

14. Ibid., 82.

15. Foster Hirsch, *Joseph Losey* (Boston, MA: Twayne, 1980), 49.

16. Mark Osteen, *Nightmare Alley* (Baltimore: Johns Hopkins University Press, 2013), 258.

17. Reynold Humphries, "The Politics of Crime and the Crime of Politics," in *Film Noir Reader: The Crucial Films and Themes*, ed. Alan Silver and James Ursini (Pompton Plains, NJ: Limelight, 2004), 241.

18. This may also be an allusion, as Humphries notes, to the "role of certain members of the [Hollywood] Ten in the Screen Writers Guild and the struggles for union recognition." Ibid., 240.

19. Hirsch, *Joseph Losey*, 49.

20. Frank Krutnik, "'A Living Part of the Class Struggle': Diego Rivera's *The Flower Carrier* and the Hollywood Left," in *"Un-American" Hollywood: Politics and Film in the Blacklist Era*, ed. Frank Krutnik, Steve Neale, Brian Neve, and Peter Stanfield (New Brunswick, NJ: Rutgers University Press, 2007), 67.

21. Pierre Rissient, quoted in David Caute, *Joseph Losey: A Revenge on Life* (New York: Oxford University Press, 1994), 391.

22. Hirsch, *Joseph Losey*, 50.

23. Losey, in Ciment, *Conversations with Losey*, 105.

24. Raymond Lefevre, quoted in Caute, *Joseph Losey*, 391.

25. Caute, *Joseph Losey*, 91.

26. Osteen, *Nightmare Alley*, 256; Hirsch, *Joseph Losey*, 50.

27. See Osteen, who notes that Calico embodies the "history of American exploitation": "of plundering the earth of its riches, and then abandoning it once it is used up." *Nightmare Alley*, 260.

28. Krutnik, "'Living Part of the Class Struggle,'" 63.

29. Osteen, *Nightmare Alley*, 258.

30. Krutnik, "'Living Part of the Class Struggle,'" 63.

31. Paul Mayersberg, quoted in Caute, *Joseph Losey*, 92.

32. Edith de Rham, *Joseph Losey* (London: Andre Deutsch, 1991), 58.

33. On Losey's own take on the screenplay, see Ciment, *Losey on Losey*, 103. See also Caute, *Joseph Losey*, 91–92. On *film gris*, see Thom Andersen, "Red Hollywood," in Krutnik et al., "*Un-American Hollywood*, 225–63.

34. William McGivern, *The Big Heat* (New York: Dodd, Mead, 1952), 9.

35. Ibid.

36. Ibid., 12.

37. Ibid., 30.

38. Ibid.

39. Ibid., 87.

40. Ibid., 126.

41. Ibid., 127.

42. Ibid., 98.

43. Ibid.

44. Ibid., 14.

45. Ibid., 16.

46. Ibid., 34.

47. Gunning, *Films of Fritz Lang,* 413. Since I have taught Gunning's chapter on *The Big Heat* numerous times in conjunction with Lang's film, my reading should be read in dialogue with it.

48. McGivern, *Big Heat*, 45.

49. See Colin McArthur, *The Big Heat* (London: BFI, 1992), 5.

50. Gunning, *Films of Fritz Lang,* 100.

51. McGivern, *Big Heat*, 101.

52. Gunning. *Films of Fritz Lang,* 413.

53. See Mason, *American Gangster Cinema*, 115.

54. Gunning, *Films of Fritz Lang,* 413.

55. McGivern, *Big Heat*, 25.

56. Ibid., 67.

57. Gunning, *Films of Fritz Lang,* 414.

58. Jans Wager, *Women and Representation in the Weimar Street Film and Film Noir* (Athens: Ohio University Press, 1999), 104.

59. On the atomic "structure of feeling" in Lang's *The Big Heat*, see Walter Metz, "'Keep the Coffee Hot, Hugo': Nuclear Trauma in Fritz Lang's *The Big Heat*," *Film Criticism* 21, no. 3 (1997): 43–65.

60. Gunning, *Films of Fritz Lang,* 421–22.

61. McGivern, *Big Heat*, 77.

62. Ibid., 91.

63. Ibid., 173.

64. Ibid.

65. Gunning, *Films of Fritz Lang,* 431.

66. McArthur, *Big Heat*, 18.

67. McGivern, *Big Heat*, 185.

68. William P. McGivern, *Shield for Murder* (New York: Dodd, Mead, 1951), 70–71.

69. Ibid., 71.
70. Ibid., 72.
71. Ibid.
72. Ibid., 30.
73. Ibid.
74. Ibid., 72–73.
75. Ibid., 5.
76. Ibid., 35.
77. Ibid., 26.
78. Ibid.
79. Ibid., 27.
80. On the "canary" in classic American noir, see Miklitsch, *Siren City*, 164–250.
81. McGivern, *Shield for Murder*, 33–34.
82. Ibid., 31.
83. Ibid., 50.
84. Ibid., 50–51
85. Ibid, 51.
86. Ibid.
87. Ibid., 52.
88. Ibid., 44.
89. Ibid., 216.
90. Ibid., 212.
91. Ibid., 173.
92. Ibid., 13.
93. Ibid., 148.
94. Ibid., 235.
95. Ibid., 232.
96. Ibid., 247–48.
97. Ibid., 248.
98. Ibid., 128.
99. Ibid.
100. Ibid., 63.
101. Ibid., 127.
102. Ibid.
103. Ibid., 128.
104. Ibid.

CHAPTER 6. *TOUCH OF EVIL*

1. Albert Zugsmith, "Albert Zugsmith," in McCarthy and Flynn, *Kings of the Bs*, 420. Whit Masterton was the pen name of Robert Alison Wade and Bill Miller.

2. As Stephen Heath remarks, "The opening of *Touch of Evil* with its 'extraordinary' tracking shot has become a famous point of reference in 'film culture' and . . . is one element among many others which can be systematized in reading [as] the [sign] 'Orson Welles,'

the style of the author." Heath, "Film and System: Terms of Analysis, Part One" *Screen* 16, no. 1 (1975): 36.

3. Quinlan's entrance, like the "extraordinary" opening tracking shot, not only features his cane and cigar—the latter of which visually allies him with Grandi, the former of which will henceforth be associated with the possession of Susan's body—but also is marked as a "star" and auteur turn. Ibid., 40.

4. Comito, *Touch of Evil*, 20, 56.

5. Kelly Oliver and Benigno Trigo, *Noir Anxiety* (Minneapolis: University of Minnesota Press, 2003), 116.

6. Carl Richardson, *Autopsy: An Element of Realism in Film Noir* (Metuchen, NJ: Scarecrow, 1992), 131.

7. Simon Callow, *Orson Welles*, vol. 3: *One-Man Band* (New York: Viking, 2015), 256.

8. Ibid.

9. James Naremore, *The Magic World of Orson Welles* (Dallas: Southern Methodist University Press, 1989), 160.

10. William Anthony Nericcio, *Tex(t)-Mex: Seductive Hallucinations of the "Mexican" in America* (Austin: University of Texas Press, 2007), 44–45.

11. Ibid., 71.

12. Naremore, *Magic World*, 155.

13. Heath, "Film and System," 72.

14. Paul Arthur, "The Gun in the Briefcase; or, The Inscription of Class in Film Noir," in *The Hidden Foundation: Cinema and the Question of Class*, ed. David E. James and Rick Berg (Minneapolis: University of Minnesota Press, 1996), 105–9; Orson Welles, "Interview with Orson Welles," in Comito, *Touch of Evil*, 204.

15. Arthur, "Gun in the Briefcase," 106.

16. Orson Welles, "Interview with Orson Welles," 206.

CHAPTER 7. *THE ASPHALT JUNGLE*

1. Munby, *Public Enemies*, 45.

2. Ibid., 135.

3. W. R. Burnett, *The Asphalt Jungle* (Carbondale: Southern Illinois University Press, 1980), 67.

4. Ibid.

5. W. R. Burnett, *The Asphalt Jungle* (New York: Knopf, 1949).

6. Ibid., 10.

7. Ibid., 112.

8. Ibid., 113.

9. Ibid., 114.

10. Ibid., 113.

11. Ibid.

12. W. R. Burnett, "Afterword," *The Asphalt Jungle*, 146.

13. Ibid., 145.

14. Ibid.

15. Ibid.

16. Ibid.

17. Burnett, *Asphalt Jungle* (1949), 5.

18. Munby, *Public Enemies*, 45.

19. Burnett, *Asphalt Jungle* (1949), 20.

20. Munby, *Public Enemies*, 134.

21. Burnett, *Asphalt Jungle* (1949), 4.

22. Madeline Vives, "On Man: *The Asphalt Jungle*," *Positif* (1952), trans. R. Barton Palmer, *Perspectives on Film Noir*, 53.

23. See Clarens, *Crime Movies*, 205.

24. Ibid.

25. Burnett, *Asphalt Jungle* (1949), 43.

26. Ibid., 41

27. Mason, *American Gangster Cinema*, 122.

28. Burnett, *Asphalt Jungle* (1949), 46.

29. Mason, *American Gangster Cinema*, 99

30. Ibid.

31. Burnett, *Asphalt Jungle* (1949), 42.

32. Ibid., 59.

33. On the casting of Marilyn Monroe, see Lawrence Grobel, *The Hustons* (New York: Avon, 1989), 334–35.

34. Burnett, *Asphalt Jungle* (1949), 55.

35. Ibid.

36. Martin Rubin, *Thrillers* (Cambridge: Cambridge University Press, 1999), 122.

37. Telotte, "Fatal Capers," 165.

38. Ibid., 169.

39. Ibid., 165.

40. Burnett, *Asphalt Jungle* (1949), 27.

41. Ibid., 140.

42. Vives, "On Man," 58.

43. On what Vives calls "The Dance," see ibid., 57–58.

44. Ibid., 262.

45. Ibid., 267.

46. Lee, *Heist Film*, 34.

47. Ibid., 31.

48. Carl Macek, "*The Asphalt Jungle*," in Silver and Ward, *Film Noir: An Encyclopedic Reference*, 15; Munby, *Public Enemies*, 136.

49. *The Hollywood Reporter* (April 27, 1949), quoted in Grobel, *The Hustons*, 330.

50. Sterling Hayden, as James Naremore notes, "became one of the first 'friendly' witnesses" during the second round of HUAC hearings that occurred in the aftermath of *The Asphalt Jungle* but remained "tormented by guilt for naming names." *More Than Night*, 290n43. However, the real, extra-diegetic irony is Marc Lawrence, who plays the "snitch" Cobby in

the film and who became a friendly witness during the second round of HUAC hearings. Ibid., 295n44.

51. Munby, *Public Enemies*, 136.

CHAPTER 8. THE BIG CAPER

1. Jack Alexander and Carroll Moore, "Robbery in Brooklyn," *New Yorker*, May 13, 1939, www.newyorker.com/magazine/1939/05/13/robbery-in-brooklyn-i. Jack Alexander and Charles Bender, "Robbery in Brooklyn–II," *New Yorker*, May 20, 1939, www.newyorker.com/magazine/1939/05/20/robbery-in-brooklyn-ii.

2. Alexander and Moore, "Robbery in Brooklyn."

3. Ibid.

4. Hogan, *Film Noir FAQ*, 198.

5. Ibid.

6. Ibid.

7. Osteen, *Nightmare Alley*, 178.

8. Mason, *American Gangster Cinema*, 99–100.

9. On *The Thief* and *The Atomic City*, see Miklitsch, *Red and the Black*, 110–20, 120–30.

10. Kaminsky, *American Film Genres*, 80.

11. For my reading of *Criss Cross*, see "Split/Screen," in *Film Noir: The Classic Tradition*, 122–42.

12. Osteen, *Nightmare Alley*, 178.

13. Ibid.

14. Eddie Muller, *Dark City: The Lost World of Film Noir* (New York: St. Martin's/Griffin, 1998), 154.

15. Hogan, *Film Noir FAQ*, 198.

16. Wheeler Winston Dixon, "*Hoodlum* (1951)," *Film Noir of the Week*, August 30, 2011, www.noiroftheweek.com/2011/08/hoodlum-1951.html.

17. Lionel White, *Clean Break* (1955; Berkeley, CA: Black Lizard, 1988), 1.

18. Ibid., 4.

19. Ibid.

20. Ibid., 3.

21. Ibid., 4, 6.

22. In his biography of Jim Thompson, Robert Polito concludes: "All circumstantial evidence around the screenplay—Kubrick's amateurish writing for *Killer's Kiss*, the embellishments from Thompson's novels, the account of the New York work sessions—indicates that *The Killing* issues from an intense collaboration. Thompson merited, at least, a solid co-writing line." *Savage Art: A Biography of Jim Thompson* (New York: Knopf, 1998), 399.

23. James Naremore, *On Kubrick* (London: BFI, 2007), 73. After receiving a "derisory offer" from Time, Inc. (who owned the *March of Time* series), Kubrick eventually sold *Day of the Fight* to RKO, which screened it as part of its *This Is America* series. David Hughes, *The Complete Kubrick* (London: Virgin, 2000), 10.

24. Ibid., 38.

25. See Mario Falsetto, *Stanley Kubrick: A Narrative and Stylistic Analysis* (Westport, CT: Praeger, 1994), 10.

26. Krutnik, *In a Lonely Street*, 138.

27. White, *Clean Break*, 7.

28. Ibid., 99.

29. Ibid., 10.

30. Ibid., 13.

31. Ibid., 14, 17, 18.

32. Ibid., 21.

33. Ibid., 44.

34. On Marvin's "homosexual attachment to Johnny in *The Killing*," see Gaylyn Studlar, "Men, Women, and the Heist Film," in *Best Laid Plans: Interrogating the Heist Film,* ed. Jeannette Sloniowski and Jim Leach (Detroit: Wayne State University Press, 2017), 94.

35. Ibid., 23.

36. Mark Osteen, "A Little Larceny: Labor, Leisure, and Loyalty in the '50s Heist Film," in *Kiss the Blood Off My Hands*, ed. Robert Miklitsch (Urbana: University of Illinois Press, 2014), 172. See also Andrew Pepper, "Post-War American Noir: Confronting Fordism," in *Crime Culture: Figuring Criminality in Fiction and Film*, ed. Brian Nichol, Eugene McNulty, and Patricia Pulham (London: Continuum, 2011), 90–106.

37. Homer B. Pettey, "Economic Sentiments in Kubrick's *The Killing* and Furukawa's *Cruel Gun Story*," in Sloniowski and Leach, *Best Laid Plans*, 164.

38. Thomas Allen Nelson, *Kubrick: Inside a Film Artist's Maze* (Bloomington: Indiana University Press, 2000), 36.

39. Hugh Manon, "'One Watches Cells': Kubrick's Film Noirs in Context," in *Stanley Kubrick: Essays on His Films and Legacy*, ed. Gary D. Rhodes (Jefferson, NC: McFarland, 2008), 57.

40. Naremore, *On Kubrick*, 71; Hughes, *Complete Kubrick*, 46; White, *Clean Break*, 23.

41. Naremore, *On Kubrick*, 71.

42. Hughes, *Complete Kubrick*, 42.

43. On the trope of the "woman in bed" in heist films, see Studlar, "Men, Women, and the Heist Film," 94–96.

44. Naremore, *On Kubrick*, 76–77.

45. White, *Clean Break*, 27, 26.

46. Ibid., 51.

47. Naremore, *On Kubrick*, 77.

48. White, *Clean Break*, 51.

49. Ibid., 54.

50. Ibid., 85.

51. Ibid., 93.

52. Ibid., 94.

53. Ibid., 148.

54. Ibid., 126.

55. While it's understandable why critics might not want to discuss the discourse of rape in White's novel, it's inseparable from the novel's sexual politics. For example, after George

has sex with Sherry, the narrator relates: "Later, he was completely convinced that he had raped her." *Clean Break*, 66. In addition, when Johnny talks to Randy about how to handle Sherry when he meets up with her, he tells him: "She may be an oversexed little lush, but . . . she wants to be romanced, not raped" (86).

56. White, *Clean Break*, 136.

57. Ibid., 142.

58. Manon, "One Watches Cells," 63.

59. As Lee notes, Flamingo Films was the name of the "production company Kubrick started with his partner, James Harris, in 1955, and [*The Killing*] was their first film." *Heist Film*, 54.

60. Ibid., 10.

61. Vincent LoBrutto, *Stanley Kubrick* (New York: Donald I. Fine Books, 1997), 19.

62. Lee, *Heist Film*, 10.

63. However, the completed film opened in only one theater in New York City before being released as the second feature on a double bill with *Bandido!* (1956) and, after two years, had earned—at least according to United Artists—only thirty thousand dollars.

64. Lee, *Heist Film*, 10.

65. Ibid., 82.

66. Blair Davis, *The Battle of the Bs: 1950s Hollywood and the Rebirth of Low-Budget Cinema* (New Brunswick, NJ: Rutgers University Press, 2012), 88.

67. Ibid., 92–93.

68. Gary Deane, "Gil Brewer, Hubert Cornfield, and the Irresistible Lure of the Swamp," *Noirworthwatching*, August 6, 2015, http://noirworthwatching.blogspot.com/2015/08/gil-brewer-hubert-cornfield-and.html.

69. Ibid.

70. For my reading of *City of Fear*, see *Red and the Black*, 137–43.

71. Edward Dimendberg, *Film Noir and the Spaces of Modernity* (Cambridge, MA: Harvard University Press, 2004), 198.

72. Kaminsky, *American Film Genres*, 75. See also Lee, *Heist Film*, 16.

73. John B. Rae, *The American Automobile: A Brief History* (Chicago: University of Chicago Press, 1965), 179.

74. The teen's fantasy of building a "hot rod" and leaving the cops in the dust references the emerging sports car culture of the 1950s inspired by Robert Peterson's *Hot Rod Magazine*, which first appeared in 1948, and Henry George Felsen's *Hot Rod Gang* (1950), both of which inspired a rash of B, "hot rod"/JD movies in the 1950s. See, for example, Peter Stanfield, *Pop Fifties Cinema: The Cool and the Crazy* (New Brunswick, NJ: Rutgers University Press, 2015), 112–34.

75. Dimendberg, *Film Noir and the Spaces of Modernity*, 201.

76. Ibid.

77. Karl Marx and Friedrich Engels, *The Communist Manifesto* (London: Verso, 1998), 38.

78. With its unique "geographical and meteorological conditions," the region "witnessed the growth of automobile use from over 1.1 million cars in 1940 to 2.3 million vehicles in 1954." The ecological consequence: "Incomplete combustion caused some 850 tons of hydrocarbons to enter the atmosphere every day in Los Angeles County in 1954." John Heitmann, *The Automobile and American Life* (Jefferson, NC: McFarland, 2009), 145.

79. Osteen, "A Little Larceny," 186.

80. Andrew Nette, "The Big Nowhere #3—*Plunder Road*," *The Big Nowhere*, November 12, 2015, http://fourthreefilm.com/2015/11/the-big-nowhere-3-plunder-road-dir-hubert-cornfield-1957.

81. Dimendberg, *Film Noir and the Spaces of Modernity*, 202.

82. Ibid., 202.

CHAPTER 9. *ODDS AGAINST TOMORROW*

1. *Odds against Tomorrow: The Critical Edition*, ed. John Schultheiss (Northridge: Center for Telecommunication Studies, California State University, 1999), 42. Since Polonsky was blacklisted at the time, he was "fronted" by the black writer John Oliver Killens. One of the ironies of this collective "subterfuge" was that precisely because of Killens's "indictment of Hollywood's traditional portrayal of blacks," he was the "perfect front." Schultheiss, "*Odds against Tomorrow*: Film Noir without Linguistic Irony," in *Odds against Tomorrow: Critical Edition*, 241.

2. Schultheiss, "Annotations to the Screenplay," in *Odds against Tomorrow: Critical Edition*, 145.

3. Hillier and Phillips, *100 Film Noirs*, 197.

4. Schultheiss, *Odds against Tomorrow: Critical Edition*, 43.

5. Schultheiss, "*Odds against Tomorrow*," 165. Keith Gilyard argues that Killens "reportedly acknowledged he contributed little to *Odds against Tomorrow*, but that he contributed any less than Nelson Giddings, who still has co-script credit, is doubtful." Gilyard, *John Oliver Killens: A Life of Literary Activism* (Athens: University of Georgia Press, 2010), 144.

6. Schultheiss, "*Odds against Tomorrow*," 280n113.

7. William McGivern, *Odds against Tomorrow* (New York: Carroll & Graf, 1996), 49.

8. Ibid., 48.

9. Ibid., 37.

10. Ibid., 36.

11. Arnold Shaw, *Belafonte: An Unauthorized Biography* (Philadelphia: Chilton, 1960), 316.

12. Harry Belafonte, quoted in Schultheiss, "*Odds against Tomorrow*," 252.

13. Ibid., 251.

14. McGivern, *Odds against Tomorrow*, 40.

15. Schultheiss, *Odds against Tomorrow: Critical Edition*, 46.

16. Ibid., 15.

17. Morris Holbrook, *Movies, Meanings, and Markets: Cinemajazzamattazz* (New York: Routledge, 2011), 259.

18. McGivern, *Odds against Tomorrow*, 40.

19. Mark Osteen, *Nightmare Alley*, 172.

20. Schultheiss, *Odds against Tomorrow: Critical Edition*, 93.

21. Ibid., 14.

22. Martin Myrick, "John Lewis and the Film Score for *Odds against Tomorrow*," in Schultheiss, *Odds against Tomorrow: Critical Edition*, 299.

23. Busch, *Self and Society*, 101.

24. Belafonte, quoted by Schultheiss, "*Odds against Tomorrow*," 243.

25. Schultheiss, "*Odds against Tomorrow*," 200.

26. McGivern, *Odds against Tomorrow*, 30.

27. Ibid., 46.

28. Ibid., 43.

29. Ibid.

30. Ibid.

31. Ibid., 51.

32. Ibid., 43.

33. Schultheiss, *Odds against Tomorrow: Critical Edition*, 98.

34. David Butler, "'No Brotherly Love': Hollywood Jazz, Racial Prejudice, and John Lewis' Score for *Odds against Tomorrow*," in *Thriving on a Riff: Jazz and Blues Influences in African American Literature and Film*, ed. Graham Lock and David Murray (New York: Oxford University Press, 2009), 230.

35. Ibid., 231, 230. On this scene as an example of the turn to "broad daylight" rather than "darkness" in the "second cycle" of film noir, see Henrik Gustafsson, "A Wet Emptiness," in Hanson and Spicer, *Companion to Film Noir*, 61.

36. Schultheiss, *Odds against Tomorrow: Critical Edition*, 111.

37. Charlie's comment recalls the diner scene in *Plunder Road* and effects a provocative equation, not unlike *Kiss Me Deadly*, between atomic energy and hot-rod youth culture. For my reading of *Kiss Me Deadly*, see "Periodizing Classic Noir," in *Kiss the Blood Off My Hands*, 193–218, and *Red and the Black*, 144–59.

38. Schultheiss, *Odds against Tomorrow: Critical Edition*, 133.

39. Ibid.

40. James Howard, *A Companion to Stanley Kubrick* (London: B. T. Batsford, 1999), 49.

41. McGivern, *Odds against Tomorrow*, 122.

42. Ibid., 194.

43. On *Odds against Tomorrow* and *The Defiant Ones*, see Jonathan Munby, "Hollywood and the Black Stickup: Race and the Meaning of the Heist on the Big White Screen," in Sloniowski and Leach, *Best Laid Plans*, 122–24.

44. John F. Kennedy, "1960 Democratic National Convention, 15 July 1960," John F. Kennedy Presidential Library and Museum, https://www.jfklibrary.org/learn/about-jfk/historic-speeches/acceptance-of-democratic-nomination-for-president.

45. Douglas Field, "JFK and the Civil Rights Movement," in *The Cambridge Companion to John F. Kennedy*, ed. Andrew Hoberek (New York: Cambridge University Press, 2015), 76–77. As Field argues, the debate between those critics who point to JFK's "civil rights achievements" and those who contend that he did not act swiftly enough to hasten what Martin Luther King Jr. calls the "snail-like pace of desegregation" remains unresolved (75).

CODA

1. McArthur, *Underworld U.S.A.*, 145.

2. Lisa Dombrowski, *The Films of Samuel Fuller: If You Die, I'll Kill You!* (Middletown, CT: Wesleyan University Press, 2008), 21.

3. Fuller himself has referenced Sternberg's *Underworld* in the context of *Underworld U.S.A.* See Samuel Fuller, *A Third Face* (New York: Knopf, 2002), 383.

4. Samuel Fuller, "Samuel Fuller," in Silver and Ursini, *Film Noir Reader*, 46.

5. Ibid.

6. Clarens, *Crime Movies*, 257–58.

7. Ibid.; Shadoian, *Dreams and Dead Ends*, 254.

8. In an interview, Boorman remarked that the first draft of David and Rafe Newhouse's screenplay for *Point Blank* turned Richard Stark's, aka Donald E. Westlake's, novel *The Hunter* (1962) into a "dated and slightly nostalgic gangster story in the style of Raymond Chandler—another *Harper.*" John Boorman, in Michel Ciment, *John Boorman*, trans. Gilbert Adair (Faber and Faber, 1986), 16; David Thompson, "As I Lay Dying," *Sight and Sound* 8, no. 6 (1998): 16.

9. Lee, *Heist Film*, 74.

10. Frank: "Hurry up, Sam, the watermelon's getting' warm" and "Why don't you be yourself and eat some ribs?" Cited in Shawn Levy, *Rat Pack Confidential* (New York: Doubleday, 1998), 113.

11. In the end, as Wil Haygood records, "The old civil rights organization [NAACP]—and not the Rat Pack—had the last laugh. An integration decree was signed on the west side of Las Vegas, at the Negro-populated Moulin Rouge nightclub." Haygood, *The Black and the White: The Life of Sammy Davis, Jr.* (New York: Knopf, 2003), 307.

Index

ROBERT MIKLITSCH is a professor in the Department of English Language and Literature at Ohio University. He is the editor of *Kiss the Blood Off My Hands: On Classic Film Noir* and the author of *The Red and the Black: American Film Noir in the 1950s.*

The University of Illinois Press
is a founding member of the
Association of University Presses.

University of Illinois Press
1325 South Oak Street
Champaign, IL 61820-6903
www.press.uillinois.edu